RESEARCH IN
ECONOMIC HISTORY

Volume 11 • 1988

RESEARCH IN ECONOMIC HISTORY

A Research Annual

Editor: PAUL J. USELDING
School of Business
University of Northern Iowa

VOLUME 11 • 1988

 JAI PRESS INC.

Greenwich, Connecticut   London, England

CONTENTS

LIST OF CONTRIBUTORS

Ben Baack

Department of Economics
Ohio State University
Columbus

Rolf H. Dumke

West Falische Wilhelms
    Universtat
Institut fur Wirtschafts
    und Sozialgeschichte
Federal Republic of Germany

Peter J. George

Dean of Social Sciences
McMaster University
Hamilton, Ontario
Canada

Charles M. Kahn

Hoover Institution
Stanford University

John Komlos

Department of History and
    Economics
University of Pittsburgh

Dennis M. P. McCarthy

Department of History
Iowa State University
Ames

Clark Nardinelli

Department of Economics
Clemson University

Thomas C. Owen

Department of History
Louisiana State University
Baton Rouge

Edward John Ray   Department of Economics
                                       Ohio State University
                                       Columbus

Thomas M. Renaghan   Public Utilities Commission
                                       California State Building
                                       San Francisco

Philip J. Sworden   Department of Social Sciences
                                       McMaster University
                                       Hamilton, Ontario
                                       Canada

Paul B. Trescott   Department of Economics
                                       Southern Illinois University
                                       Carbondale

PREFACE

In over a decade since its inception, *Research in Economic History* has enjoyed the intellectual support and patronage of the international scholarly community. The current collection of original research articles reflects a continuum of methodologies and extraordinary variety in cultural and substantive focus.

The flexibility of format allows for the publication, where appropriate, of articles well beyond the usual journal-imposed limits and the full explication of fact and underlying theory. As a result of this feature, a number of articles appearing in REH in the past decade have become standard reference pieces. The traditions established in earlier volumes continue in the present one, and I believe they have served our profession well.

Roger Ransom of the University of California, Riverside will take over the editorship of REH commencing with volume 12. He is a first-class scholar with universal tastes in economic history, and I am sure his own editorial tradition for REH will enrich both the series and our community of scholars.

Paul J. Uselding
Series Editor

INCOME INEQUALITY AND INDUSTRIALIZATION IN GERMANY, 1850–1913:

IMAGES, TRENDS AND CAUSES OF HISTORICAL INEQUALITY

Rolf H. Dumke

Income distribution cannot be blamed on the engineers and the birth rate. Edward J. Nell (1972)

I.

In the last decade important new empirical studies in the fields of economic history and economic development have helped clarify a question raised by Simon

Research in Economic History, Volume 11, pages 1–47.
Copyright © 1988 by JAI Press Inc.
All rights of reproduction in any form reserved.
ISBN: 0-89232-677-8

1

Kuznets (1955), whether the process of modern economic growth and changes in the size distribution of income are in some way systematically related. On the basis of his interpretation of fragmentary historical data of a few presently industrialized countries and some evidence from underdeveloped countries in the 1950s Kuznets had suggested that the early phase of economic development or industrialization was characterized by an increasing income inequality, a state which he thought would only be slowly eroded by subsequent economic growth. This pattern of first rising, then falling income inequality over time and development has become well-known as the inverse-U or Kuznets curve of inequality. Since this change in income distribution is one of the sociopolitically most sensitive of all those important structural changes which are thought to occur in the process of economic development, there is good reason for the widespread interest in the Kuznets curve.

At present there are a large number of empirical cross-section studies of development levels and income inequality available.[1] They suggest that the relationship between inequality and per capita GNP tends to have an inverted-U shape: among groups of countries in the cross section, inequality rises in the early stages of economic development and falls in the middle and later stages. However, as Gary S. Fields (1980) points out, "In all cases, the proportion of variation in inequality explained by income level is small, which suggests that the initial stage of rising inequality is avoidable." When it comes to *changes* in the distribution of income in less developed countries, "the evidence is similarly mixed" (p. 123). Fields' conclusion of an overview of the LDC growth and inequality data is quite interesting: "Growth itself does not determine a country's inequality course. Rather, the decisive factor is the *type* of economic growth as determined by the environment in which growth occurs and the political decisions taken" (p. 94).

It may be of some interest to point out that the search for an empirical "law" of development or for identifying an important structural change during modern societal development was a concern typical of the German Historical School of economics before World War I. Indeed, H. Chenery's and M. Syrquin's celebrated study of patterns of development (1975) can be thought of as the culmination of the Historical School approach, but now using the computer to identify the laws. Chenery's and Syrquin's notion of economic development as a multidimensional transition from one relatively constant structure to another (p. 8) seems entirely congenial to the inductive approach of the Historical School. Moreover, a significant part of their list of 10 crucial structural changes during economic development (Table 1, p. 9) seems to derive from questions first asked by members of the Historical School. This is true of the rise in government's share, better known as Wagner's Law,[2] changes in the trade ratio, known as Sombart's Law,[3] changes in the structure of domestic demand, based upon Engel's well-known Law, and, perhaps, of urbanization and of changes in the size distribution of income during economic development.

Thus, it should not surprise that the question of long-term trends in income distribution, an eminently Historical School type of question, was in fact first raised by Gustav Schmoller[4] and answered more or less in the manner of Kuznets. Because Schmoller was interested in a very long-run view, he compared Gregory King's social tables of England in 1688 with those of R. Dudley Baxter in 1867. He concluded, as would Lee Soltow[5] almost three-quarters of a century later, that there was a very long-run constancy of income inequality; however, Schmoller also surmised that inequality may have been higher at the beginning of the nineteenth century with the advent of capitalist British growth. Strangely, Schmoller's argument is not cited by Soltow nor in Jeffrey Williamson's (1985) recent important study of British inequality history. Neither, I am sure, are the previously cited development economists aware of which methodology they are really following.[6]

It will become clear later in this paper that other almost forgotten or unusual "old" data sources, inequality measures and theories of income inequality can be surprisingly useful. However, the main point I wish to make here is that Kuznets' question was not only an eminently German historical question of the turn of the century, the only available historical data which supported his idea of increasing inequality during the early phase of economic development was also German. Kuznets' analysis, then, can be seen as a continuation and extension of the German inequality debate of the turn of the century.[7] There are, for instance, strong parallels to his concern about the relative size of the middle class in developed versus underdeveloped economies in pre-1914 Germany.[8]

Since then there have been several attempts to reinvestigate German historical income inequality.[9] One main purpose of this paper is to integrate promising elements of these and older[10] studies to see if Kuznets' interpretation of the German data—the statistical heart of the first phase of his inverse-U curve of income inequality—can still be supported. Moreover, by reconnecting the Kuznets analysis with the German inequality debate before World War I the present analysis of historical inequality can be informed by the nature of the historical concern about inequality.

A second main purpose of the paper is to provide a view of historical inequality, the German case, as a possible contrast to the stimulating, but problematic, new interpretations of the history of income inequality in the United States and in Britain as offered by Peter Lindert and J. Williamson.[11] The addition of the German case to existent historical studies can begin a debate about the nature and sources of historical income inequality in presently advanced Atlantic countries. The following basic questions must be addressed by any historical inequality analysis: (i) Which data sources should be used? (ii) Which measures of income inequality are to be calculated? (iii) Which theory of income inequality is to be entertained? The German case study to be presented below differs from the new U.S. and U.K. inequality histories on almost all these accounts.

These differences derive from a fundamentally different assessment of the usefulness of certain modern or "new stylized facts of distribution" in history.[12]

According to Williamson (1982, pp. 1–2),

"(R)ecent analyses of the twentieth-century evidence has shown that conventional property income distribution and its share in total income explains very little of the variance of incomes in today's industrialized societies. . . . *What is true of the sources of cross-sectional variance in income inequality also seems to hold for time series.* Trends in the distribution of wage and salary income by occupation and skill have been shown to be far better correlates of trends in the size distribution than are conventional property income shares. (Emphases added.)

For these reasons—which unfortunately are not sufficiently documented—Lindert and Williamson largely ignore the major distributional question since the time of the classical economists, that of changes in the functional distribution of income among the social classes of wage earners, land owners, and capitalists, in favor of an analysis of occupational wage and salary dispersion and of earnings differentials by skills. This "is to ignore nonlabor incomes entirely as atavistic residuals," a "major error" of today's distributional analysis, according to Martin Bronfenbrenner.[13] How much more mischief will it generate by applying this assumption to the past?

Edward Nell (1972, p. 445) quite rightly pointed out that the "systematic analysis of the (economic) power structure in society *as a whole* . . . is what the *functional* distribution [of income]. . . . is all about." By neglecting the returns to property owners in analyzing inequality history one emasculates it of an important political dimension which is obviously also an important historical dimension.[14] Standard neoclassical economic analysis of income distribution is in any case already inured against the use of political or economic power arguments. The story of the functional distribution of income it tells has a "striking and ideologically significant implication: distribution depends solely on technology and factor proportions. (In the Cobb-Douglas case even factor proportions do not matter.) This is what the critics cannot stomach" (Nell, p. 449). But Nell rightly objects, "Income distribution cannot be blamed on the engineers and the birth rate" (p. 452).

That, however, is precisely the story which Lindert and Williamson seem to be telling in their study, *American Inequality* (1980). Changes in labor supply—fertility and immigration—but especially in unbalanced technological progress between sectors—a type of biased technical change) are held accountable for first the surge in wage and income inequality before the Civil War and the income leveling after 1929 (see pp. 286-89). Williamson's recent model for explaining British inequality trends in the nineteenth century—a rise of earnings inequality and in pay differentials by skill between 1821 and 1861 and a subsequent decline between 1861 and 1911[15]—is more complete; it includes, for example, the effects of terms of trade changes on inequality. Nevertheless, he argues that "one component part stands out as the key driving force: unbalanced productivity advance appears to have driven both industrialization and inequality experience across the nineteenth century" (1985, p. 159).

Another potent criticism is touched upon by Williamson himself (1985, p. 204): "It seems a bit unsettling to conclude. . . . that unbalanced productivity advance across sectors and the rate of skill-deepening economy-wide are the most critical factors driving British inequality across the nineteenth century, when these are variables about which the least is known." Yet more disturbing to the historian may be the fact that the theoretical tools with which Williamson operates, the concepts of human capital and of aggregate technological change, are by no means undisputed. In an assessment of the work on human capital Sherwin Rosen (1977, p. 750) concluded, "(W)hen all is said and done, however, a theory based entirely on unobservables is bound to have limitations." Aggregate technological change, defined as "total factor productivity," has been called one of economics' empty boxes.[16] An explanation of historical inequality changes in which these empirically empty boxes play the leading causal roles and in which returns to property ownership and political power relations are largely ignored will appear to many as extraordinarily bizarre. "Where's the beef?" the historian will rightly ask.

Tendencies towards "plutocratic development" are certainly in evidence in Germany. S.N. Procopovitch (1926)

II.

A.

I have argued that a historical interpretation of historical inequality must concern itself, nay begin, with how contemporaries themselves viewed inequality. What, then, were the images of and concerns about inequality in late nineteenth-century Germany? In contrast to a thesis advanced by Albert O. Hirschman concerning the tolerance of inequality during initial industrialization in less developed countries today,[17] the beginning of industrialization and attendant changes in income inequality were not looked upon in a hopeful or benign fashion in Germany. The example of British modern growth, especially the negative view transmitted by Friedrich Engels of the impact of this growth on the laboring class in Manchester, provided pessimistic expectations about inequality developments during capitalist economic growth. This severely reduced the tolerance for inequality in Germany already at the outset of such modern growth around mid-century. German society's adaptation to industrialization and its unequal developments was thus more difficult and called forth demands for greater political controls.

One prominent voice was Gustav Schmoller's. In his introductory address in Eisenach, October 1872, to the first assembly of academic economists and social reformers (the so-called "Kathedersozialisten," the academic socialists) who subsequently formed the Verein fuer Socialpolitik (Germany's first economics association), Schmoller warned of the social consequences of a growing chasm between property owners and educated elites on the one side and the workers on the other. His image of a healthy society was one of a ladder of ascending existences with no missing spokes or spokes spaced too for apart.[18] This picture suggests that Schmoller viewed income and social mobility up the income ladder as a necessary condition for social integration and political stability. However, the Germany of those times, Schmoller believed, was threatened by the breaking out of the middle spokes of the income ladder. He and the "Kathedersozialisten" thought state reforms were necessary to elevate the status of the worker (factory laws and inspections), to bridge the gap to other social classes (education), and to outlaw the excesses of an unfettered Manchester-style of capitalism (banking and insurance laws, for example).

The threat of growing class antagonisms between bourgeoisie and labor, the threat to the middle classes, especially to handicrafts and tradesmen, from modern industrial, mass retail, and banking developments, as summarized by the image of the income ladder with the torn-out spokes in the middle, dominated German distributional debates for the next 25 years.[19] Indeed, the famous Erfurt Program (1891) of the Social Democratic Party,[20] the last socialist party program in Germany to enunciate a clear, unmitigated Marxist prognosis of increasing class conflicts, proletarianization and exploitation, entertained essentially the same view of the threat to the middle classes as did Schmoller in Eisenach. However, by the turn of the century Schmoller had changed his mind about the fate of the middle classes, arguing that although some traditional trades were declining there was a new recruitment from a new middle class of white-collar workers, the "Angestellten" (Schmoller, 1897). The social ladder had, somehow, been repaired and a requisite amount of social mobility was seen as definitely possible. As well, E. Bernstein, who began the famous Revisionist Debate among the Social Democrats about the reformist possibilities of capitalism, had moved away from the theses of the declining middle classes[21] and of the increasing proletarianization of the workers.

Although the thesis of an absolute decline of the members of the middle classes and that of the decline in the standard of living of the workers were now beginning to be rejected, the spectre of an evolving two-class society was not yet theoretically eliminated and continued to haunt contemporary observers. As Schmoller observed in his influential *Grundriss der Allgemeinen Volkswirtschaftslehre* (1904, p. 174),

> The general antagonism between capital and labor will always remain, and it is perhaps the most important of the modern economy; the whole process of production and distribution is dominated by the same; the great social battles of the present spring from this fount; their reconciliation and the creation of a proper bond between them must be the precondition of all great economic reforms of the present.

The distribution debate at the turn of the century was dominated by Adolph

Wagner's continued pessimism. In 1907 Wagner charged that "a new large economic (money-) aristocracy has arisen which far supersedes the old one in numbers, income and wealth, next to an elevated laboring class and a depressed middle class."[22] Wagner subscribed to another of Rodbertus' views of an emerging and alarming two-class society, top-heavy with wealth. This critical image of inequality as a misshapen bottle with a hydrocephalic money-bags head resting on a too slender neck became very popular. It was often contrasted with a supposedly "healthy" pyramidal income hierarchy.[23] However, the most widely spread concept of inequality, which was evidently related to the money-bags hydrocephalus, was a reformulation of the term "money-aristocracy" into the more political term "plutocracy," society's domination or rule by money.[24] Wagner (1893, pp. 679, 723) had warned of the "plutocratic danger" since 1893 and this term gained wide currency in the decades before 1914. The subsequent debate about the inequality tendencies of German capitalism was largely framed with this more political concept in mind; some like Helfferich (1913, pp. 133–37), for example, sought to refute the charge of plutocratic tendencies, others, like Procopovitch (1926) supported the notion.[25] Kuznets, who relied so much upon Procopovitch's German data, however, ignored this political dimension of inequality.

In the German political context, where severe property, residence, and income restrictions were placed on voting rights for the state and local elections, a tendency towards income concentration automatically implied a greater degree of political inequality. This was particularly true of the Prussian three-class electoral system employed in the Prussian state and local elections. There were three classes of voters in these indirect elections. The top third comprised the total number of well-to-do persons contributing one-third of the local tax revenues; the second class of voters were those contributing the second third of revenues, etc. Each class of voters elected the same number of electors, who, in turn, chose the representatives. In this system, therefore, the vote of a rich industrialist like Friedrich Krupp was weighed by his contribution to local taxes. In the 1880s, before some of the following electoral reforms, the weight of his and his factory's vote (legal persons had the right to vote, also weighed by their contribution to local taxation!) in local elections was as great as that of all of the workers in the city of Essen combined.[26] Given the electoral system, income concentration and income taxation, therefore, amounted to the plutocratic control of the cities of Germany.

The rise of plutocracy, Wagner believed, also went hand in hand with a rising share of national income for the "class of property owners, who govern production, exploit business booms and pocket speculative gains," while the relative shares of the lower classes or workers declined. The property owners, moreover, are seen to gain a disproportionate quota of the rising output of national labor which is due to increasing productivity.[27] Julius Wolf (1898, p. 412) appropriately characterized this view of the "Kathedersozialisten" as one of technology pessimism; in this view "technical progress . . . left to itself, develops along antisocial and plutocratic lines." In contrast, Wolf was one of a minority of technological optimists of the times, who believed in an automatic connection between technical progress and social progress, or in the elevation of the living standards of the masses particularly by the decline in the costs of production of commodities important in the laborer's budget.[28] I shall come back to Wolf's interesting argument later in the paper.

Thus, the images of inequality held by informed and concerned German observers before World War I stressed the cleavages between the class of property owners and that of the workers; that is, the historical emphasis was evidently upon the functional distribution of income. An important force, besides monopoly gains, which was thought to drive this distribution towards greater inequality was the perceived biased nature of technological progress. Because many capitalists were seen to be making extraordinary gains, the change in the functional distribution of income was also seen to be reflected in the personal distribution of income, with a dramatic increase in the number of persons with very high incomes. Given that income taxes played an important role in peacetime Germany before World War I, the nature of the franchise, particularly in Prussia, magnified the effect of economic inequality into an even greater political inequality. If there was a tendency towards income concentration, this automatically carried a plutocratic threat.

B.

This interesting story about historical German income inequality has never been systematically supported and told. Nevertheless, as Frank Taussig pointed out, some of the requisite data have been around for a long time: "The best tax statistics, of a kind to show the distribution of income among individuals of a large country, were those of Prussia in the days before the war of 1914–1918."[29] These statistics which go back into the early nineteenth century are an important source for inequality history. Franz Grumbach (1957) has used these data, along with the income tax data of other German states, to calculate the Pareto alpha coefficient of income inequality.[30]

This measure is particularly sensitive to changes in the distribution of income affecting the top income receivers. For example, in the U.S. case Pareto's alpha is strongly correlated with Kuznets' estimates of the income share of the top 1 percent of income receivers in the years 1913 to 1952; but alpha's correlation with the shares of the top 5 and top 10 percent of the income receivers becomes increasingly loose.[31] Similarly, in Prussia the correlation between Mueller's and Geisenberger's estimates of the share of income flowing to the top .1 percent of income receivers and Pareto's alpha is very high between 1874 and 1913, $R^2 = .92$. The correlation of alpha with the share of income flowing to the top income receivers also decreases in the Prussian case as the income receivers become less exclusive: with the top 1 percent share, R^2 = .93 (excluding the outliers 1874 and 1891), with the top 5 percent share, R^2 = .66 (excluding the outliers 1874, 1875, and 1891).[32]

The insensitivity of the Pareto alpha coefficient to changes in the income shares of income recipients in the bottom and middle of the distribution is one reason why it is rarely used in distribution analysis today, when the Gini coefficient has become the usual measure of personal income inequality. However, the alpha coefficient used to be an important analytical tool at the turn of the century for Pareto, Bresciani-Turroni and others.[33] It may be that the change in the preferred measure of inequality between then and now may also reflect changing concerns about the nature of inequality.[34] At a time of "robber barons" and a rising new "money aristocracy" the possible usurpation of political power implicit in wealth concentration worried contemporaries everywhere. Precisely this sensitivity towards changes in the top of the income distribution would recommend this measure for German distribution history; a better measure of plutocracy, defined as both economic control and political dominance of society, can hardly be found.

The nature of the Pareto alpha coefficient as an elasticity, measuring the decrease in the number of income recipients when passing to higher income classes, is also of interest. The alpha, thus, can also be understood as a kind of aggregate income *mobility* indicator and it may be one of the few inequality indicators with this dual interpretation as inequality measure *and* income mobility measure. Because the contemporary German debate about inequality emphasized the income mobility dimension, this characteristic of the alpha provides another reason for its use in the German historical case.

Anthony Atkinson (1970) has stressed that the use of *any* measure of income inequality implicitly entails the use of value judgments about distribution. This continues a line of argumentation starting with Dalton's classic (1920) article and the work of Champernowne (1937, published 1973). Champernowne's study of merits of various inequality measures comes to the conclusion that there can be no single "best" measure and that the choice of a measure should depend on the particular aspect of inequality in which one is interested, because some measures are more suited to reflect particular aspects of distribution than others.[35] In particular, different measures have a different sensitivity to the kinds of possible redistributions—for example, between rich and less rich, between poor and rich, between middle income recipients and slightly less high income receivers, etc. It turns out that the Gini measure is highly sensitive towards redistribution in the middle of the income range,[36] which is not necessarily a useful historical inequality criterion. Thus, a relative toleration of inequality within the middle of the distribution may go in hand with a historical intolerance of inequality generated by a rising share of income going to the top few income recipients. In the German case I have argued that an important contemporary concern about inequality focused upon that between the very wealthy and the middle income groups, in particular also because of the implications about political inequality.

Moreover, it is not impossible that trends of an inequality measure which is highly correlated with the income shares of the top income recipients also provide signals about general inequality trends. Williamson and Lindert, for example, point out that the income leveling which occurred in the United States after 1929 is also indicated by a decline in the shares of the top income and wealth recipients. Interestingly, this hypothesis of a great twentieth-century American income revolution is supported by a simultaneous change in a number of inequality measures and indicators ranging from occupational skill premia, the unskilled labor share of income, to wealth inequality, and, apparently to the Pareto alpha, as well.[37] The reason for this intriguing simultaneous movement, however, deserves further debate.

C.

In Figure 1 estimates of Pareto's alpha for Prussia, the largest of the German states and the one generally thought to be representative of Germany as a whole in economic and income analysis, and Walther G. Hoffmann's estimates of labor's share of income in Germany are compared over a long historical time span, 1850–1950.[38] As well, a rough measure of skill differentials in the industrial sector, the ratio of the average annual earnings of textile workers to that of workers in the metals trades, is plotted on the graph.[39] The former are acknowledged to have been relatively unskilled while the latter included highly skilled members of the labor aristocracy.[40] The paucity of wage data for the German economy before 1914 prevents the calculation of a reliable long run of relative wages of skilled to unskilled workers in any major branch of industry besides the building trades, which, however, appeared to be dominated by custom. Thus, this imperfect substitute.[41]

Nevertheless, the information contained on this graph—when supported by further bits of wage, income, and wealth distribution data—provides a surprisingly useful overview of all the major distribution changes in Germany between 1850 and 1950. The long-run time path of personal income inequality suggested by the values of the Pareto alpha of the Prussian tax statistics in the nineteenth and twentieth centuries and the German tax statistics in the twentieth century conforms to Kuznets' inverse-U hypothesis. The sharp distributional changes in the twentieth century (due to war, inflation, Great Depression, and Nazi economic policy) between 1914 and the late 1930s can be understood as relatively short-term distributional shocks overlying the long-term trend. It is of interest to compare these distribution trends to distribution history indicated by the use of more conventional distribution measures, the share of income of the top 5 percent (or of the top 10 percent) of income receivers. The century-long trend indicated in Franz Kraus' graph[42]—see Figure 2—is similar to the trend indicated by the Pareto alpha. However, the twentieth-century shocks to distribution may be somewhat exaggerated by the Pareto measure. Nevertheless, the inequal-

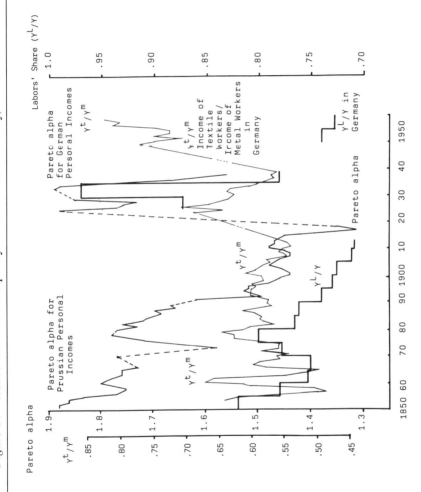

Figure 1. Trends in Income Inequality in Prussia and Germany, 1850–1950

ity rise in the course of the Great Depression and Nazi economic policy, the dramatic wealth and income leveling during the German Inflation and the initial phase of the Great Depression, the inequality engendered by war profiteering, in all these major episodes of distribution history, the Pareto alpha moves in the expected direction and is thus a good indicator for these developments. Thus, there is some reason for expecting the alpha also to indicate changes in the personal income distribution over the industrialization experience before World War I, as well.

We see that over most of the century, 1850–1950, the Pareto alpha measure of personal income inequality and labor's share of income move in parallel fashion, suggesting that changes in the functional distribution of income are driving this measure of the personal distribution of income. Because the Prussian income tax was administered in a manner which, in effect, took three-year moving averages of incomes centered on the last, i.e., the assessment, year,[43] I transformed the Hoffman data on labor's share of income accordingly to make the variables comparable in the period 1850–1913. In this exercise, the details of which are not reported here, the lead-lag relationships between the two magnitudes became more evident; changes in capital's share of income led and thus "caused" the changes in Pareto alpha, our measure of the inequality of the personal income distribution. Because capital incomes are very much more unequally distributed than labor incomes in Germany of those times,[44] the change in capital's share is thus accorded the prime place in the search for causes of the historical changes in the personal income distribution.

The essence of this argument was developed some time ago by Pigou (1920). In contrast to Pareto, he noted that changes in the form of the "income-curve," i.e., of the coefficient alpha, need not await dramatic events like revolutions.[45]

According to Pigou,

> (It is not) necessary to imagine so large a change as the destruction of inheritance laws, in order that the form of the income-curve may be largely affected. There is ground for believing that a like result would come about in consequence of anything that affected, in a marked way, the proportion between "earned" income and income derived from investments. The reason for this opinion is twofold. First, it is found by experience that incomes from property are distributed much more unevenly than incomes from either head-work or hand-work. . . . Secondly, the distribution of earned income itself is likely to be more uneven, the greater the importance of the unevenly distributed income from investments. This result comes about because differences in income from investments make possible different degrees of educational training and afford different opportunities for entering lucrative professions (pp. 697–98).[46]

Grumbach (1957, p. 90), in contrast, stressed the effect of changes in the composition of capital on the personal distribution of income. In this more complicated and to my mind subsidiary, possibly complementary, argument the rise of industrial capital and the large differential returns to this new type of capital are held accountable for the rise of inequality in capital incomes and thus of income inequality, in general, as indicated by the fall of Pareto's alpha.

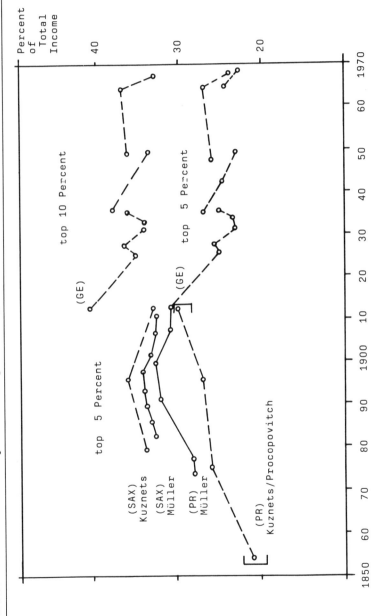

Figure 2. Income Shares of Top Income Recipients, Long-Term Trends in Prussia (PR), Saxony (SA), and Germany (GE)

Source: F. Kraus (1981) p. 17)

13

The parallel movement between the functional and the personal distribution of income, however, breaks down after World War II. In 1950 the estimated alpha for West German tax statistics is at the level of 2.0, signifying a shift towards greater equality (this is also indicated by the ratio of textile incomes to those of metal workers) but labor's share declines in comparison with the period between the wars. In accordance with "modern stylized facts of distribution" the functional income distribution and the personal income distribution go their separate ways. In the inter-war period, however, all the measures move in a roughly parallel fashion–a result which is in accordance with the findings by Williamson and Lindert for the United States.

The reasons for the parallel movement of all three indicators in Weimar Germany and in comparison to the *status quo ante* World War I are not difficult to sort out. Franz Grumbach's argument that changes in the distribution of wealth drive the distribution of income is applicable here, as Carl-Ludwig Holtfrerich[47] has recently shown. The destruction of liquid assets by the German inflation eliminated a whole class of rentier persons in Germany by the end of the inflation in 1924. Not only does the distribution of wealth change, the functional distribution changes, as well, because of the decline of investment incomes. Further, compared to 1913, the personal distribution becomes more equal not only because of the elimination of high investment incomes but also due to the historic narrowing of skill differentials resulting from the cost of living adjustments during inflation. The parallel movement of all these indicators is, thus, due to a common cause, hyperinflation.

When further information on skill differentials in the building industry, by G. Bry and Ch. Boschan (1965),[48] is considered (see Figure 3), a major difference in trends between the Pareto alpha and skill differentials is noteworthy during World War I. During the war unusual changes shape the personal income distribution: top incomes become more concentrated due to war profiteering—a phenomenon also noticed in the Dutch case by Jan de Meere (1983)—but wage incomes are leveled between skills. The operation of more or less equal cost of living adjustments to the whole wage hierarchy narrows the differentials dramatically; unskilled wages rise more than skilled wages.[49] Thus the strong movement of Pareto's alpha towards greater inequality runs counter to the equalizing of wage incomes. Neither of the two indicators of personal income inequality can alone provide an unambiguous answer to the question, Did income inequality rise during World War I? However, *both* pieces of information are useful to support the argument that there was a relative decline of the middle-income groups because the income shares going to the rich and to the unskilled both rose. Juergen Kocka's argument that German society during the First World War became much more of a two-class Marxist-type society than peacetime ever knew, would be substantially strengthened by the use of the Pareto alpha.[50] At the end of the war alpha had sunk to historic low levels in both Prussia and Saxony, indicating the most extreme income inequality in German history since

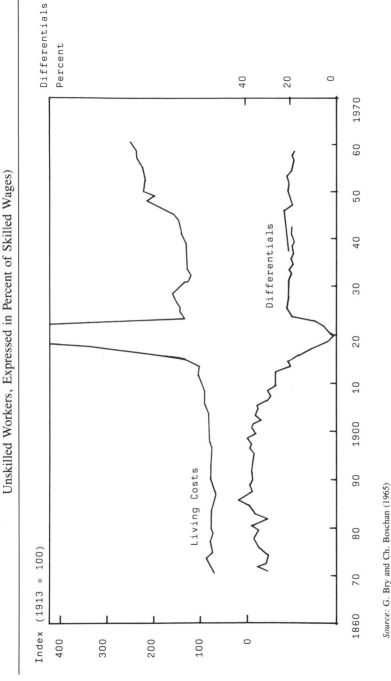

Figure 3. Skill Differentials in the Building Industry and the Cost of Living, Germany 1870–1961 (Skill Differentials Computed as Differences between Wages of Skilled and Unskilled Workers, Expressed in Percent of Skilled Wages)

Source: G. Bry and Ch. Boschan (1965)

15

1850. Had we chosen to rely upon the information on skill differentials, the approach taken by Williamson and Lindert in their argument of an income leveling during the First World War in the United States, the story of wartime distribution in Germany, so told, would be seriously defective.

Before 1914 most of the evidence on skill differentials or industrial wage or earnings differentials at our disposal points towards a long-run stability in these ratios. Our indicator of skill differentials, the ratio of earnings of textile workers to metal workers, also remains constant at a level around .57 between 1850 and 1913, although there are significant short-run swings, possibly due to the typical lead-lag relationships between capital goods and consumer goods industries over the business cycle. In contrast, both the functional and the personal distribution of income experience major long-run shifts towards a larger capital's share of income and a concomitant increase in personal income inequality. The correlation between a three-year moving average of labor's share in the German economy and Pareto's alpha for Prussia is high, R^2 between these two variables in the period 1852 and 1913 is 67.29. When a dummy variable is added, giving all years after 1891 (when a major change in the tax laws occurred) the value of one and previous years the value of zero, a yet larger degree of the variance of Pareto's alpha can be explained by changes in labor's share of income and the dummy shift variable: R^2 now is 88.43. The estimated equation and coefficients are as follows:

$$\text{(1)}$$

$$\text{Pareto Alpha} = \underset{(3.1791)}{.7605} + \underset{(4.1083)}{1.2676} \text{ LabShare} - \underset{(-10.0333)}{.2053} \text{ After1891Dummy}$$

$$n = 55, \qquad \text{t ratios in parentheses}$$

This is a fairly strong evidence that the personal income distribution is largely driven by changes in the functional distribution of income.

Because of the major but short-run disributional changes in the 1870s it makes sense for the history of distribution (as it is the case in productivity history) to consider breaking up the more than half a century span between 1850 and 1913 into two subperiods of rising inequality, 1850–1870 or 1873, and 1880 (or 1878)–1913. During the second phase of inequality widening alpha declines from a level of 1.78 in 1878 to a level of about 1.46 after 1900, when a phase of inequality stability is reached at highest historic peacetime levels of income inequality. This inequality increase can generally be corroborated by the movement of the Mueller/Geisenberger (1972, pp. 44–45) estimates of the top 0.1 percent, 1 percent, and 5 percent of income receivers' share of income between 1876–1880 and 1911–13: the top 1 percent (5 percent) share rises from 15.2 percent (28.4 percent) to 18.9 percent (32.6 percent) in 1896–1900 and then falls slightly to 18.0 percent (30.6 percent) in 1911–13.

The fall in alpha between 1891 and 1892 from a level of 1.62 to 1.5, however, is due to a major change in the Prussian income tax law. For the first time self-declaration of income was required for the higher income recipients. The income tax administration inspected a great number of returns, around 25 percent were audited, and took a number of fraudulent returners to court in a number of spectacular trials. This stiffer assessment led to more honest reporting particularly by the higher income receivers and thus to a once-and-for-all decrease in alpha. We have made adjustments for this change by introducing a time dummy variable in the regression above. With this technical correction made, it is still evident that inequality rises during the 1880s and 1890s.

Undoubtedly, one of the most discussed periods in German distribution history has been the decade or two before World War I which was characterized by an unusual stability of the personal income distribution. The discussion goes back to Nitschke (1902), K. Perls (1911), and K. Helfferich (1913). But the best analysis and data presented to argue the case for distributional stability was provided by Arthur Friedmann (1914). He was one of the first German analysts to use a Lorenz curve-type measure in the analysis of nominal and real income inequality.[51] This period of distributional stability coincides with a major new-growth phase of the German economy, the "Aufschwungsspanne" 1895–1913, as Arthur Spiethoff termed it.[52] Helfferich was impressed by the fact that this dramatic growth phase during Wilhelmine Germany—part of the Second Industrial Revolution (Landes)—was not accompanied by a rise of inequality or by "plutocratic developments." Our Figures 1 and 2 both suggest that in the period immediately before World War I a historic high plateau of inequality in peacetime had been reached, after which the long-run decline in income inequality began. "The places and points in time when a transition from one form of relationship to another occurs are identified as critical junctures in the history of nations," R. A. Hanneman suggests; and these should be "singled out for further study."[53] This is one reason why the period before World War I has been so intensively investigated.

One reason for the relatively innocuous results of some of the research on German income distribution in the decades before World War I is, therefore, the low variance of the dependent variable, inequality. Thus, it should not surprise that the statistical "full-press" which Geisenberger puts upon the Prussian data between 1891 and 1910 results in no clear-cut breakthroughs in our understanding of historical inequality. Among other statistically interesting approaches, Geisenberger formulated a discriminant function on the basis of which he tests if the two groups of years, 1891–1900 and 1901–1910, which show different inequality trends, are also characterized by other developments. In particular, he looks at the rising influence of unions, the business cycle, wage developments, different investment behavior, and changes in rough estimates of the share of income accruing to capital, land, labor, and profits. Geisenberger was able to significantly differentiate the two groups of years by using the indicated variables. The two most important distinguishing variables were (a) the rough indicator of labor's share of income and (b) the level of investments. The unionization and wage variable, however, were disappointing in this respect.

More convincing and interesting is Geisenberger's attempt to explain the movements of the top 1 percent and top 5 percent income receivers' share of income in Prussia as a whole and in several of its western industrial, eastern agrarian, and middle mixed counties between 1891 and 1913 on the basis of rough indicators of income categories. These are the shares of income arising from profits, labor income, rental income, and investment income. This information is known for the group of higher income receivers, i.e., those with an income more than 3000 Marks, a group of persons roughly equal to 4 percent of all households. Given this rough indicator it is astonishing how well the shares of profit (PShare) in the total income of upper-income taxpayers and the share of labor incomes (LShare) of those same taxpayers do in explaining movements of the top 5 percent share of income. For Prussia as a whole Top 5 percent is correlated with PShare, $R^2 = 0.63$; in Duesseldorf R^2 between these two variables is an astonishing 0.96! in Aachen R^2 is 0.49 while the R^2 between Top 5 percent and LShare is 0.37; in Gumbinnen R^2 between Top 5 percent and PShare is 0.89; in Marienwerder R^2 is 0.77; in Koeslin it is 0.72; in Erfurt and Magdeburg it is around 0.66.[54] These are very impressive results for the effects of an improperly measured profits share of income (of the top income receivers' income only). These results stimulated my work in finding yet better connections between the functional and the personal distribution of income. Geisenberger points out, correctly, that explaining the personal income distribution with the categorial or the functional distribution is but one step towards a final explanation, because the latter, in turn, need to be explained. Precisely this shall be the point of the following Section III.

Before concluding this section a note on the political history of the Kaiserreich as presented by Hans-Ulrich Wehler's much debated text (1973) is in order. Wehler argues that in German imperial times an "organized capitalism," a symbiosis of state and capitalistic orders, was created, wherein the state took over some of the stabilizing functions for the new industrial capitalism which was endangered by increasing class tensions due to rising inequality and by increasingly hard battles for market shares. V. Hentschel (1978) directly confronted the thesis of a rising income inequality by underlining the distributional stability in the Wilhelmine decades before World War I. However, this critique will not suffice to refute the Wehler hypothesis. If we ignore the abnormally low values of alpha in 1873 at the end of the boom of the founding years of the empire and the subsequent rebound of alpha to higher levels in 1878, the *long-run* trends of income distribution during the Kaiserreich were towards significantly greater inequality. This is particularly so during the 1880s and the early 1890s. By focusing on the relative stability of distribution immediately preceding the First World War, a foreshortening occurs which is biased against Wehler's thesis. Lengthening the time frame of analysis, however, restores substantial support.

Moreover, it is possible that social and political tensions can also characterize the stable but high inequality plateau after 1900.

Because of the intractability and complexity of the income and differentiated head tax system in Prussia before 1873 few students have felt competent to estimate inequality based on measures of the shares of income accruing to the top income receivers. Actually, only Procopovitch's estimates are available for this earlier important period. He uses very rough estimates of the per capita income of persons exempt from the income tax. Thus the Pareto alpha measure is a useful independent and supplementary measure of inequality during the phase of inequality widening between 1850 and 1873, the time of Germany's economic take-off.[55]

The idea that German industrialization and a rise in income inequality characterize nineteenth-century development, however, is not new. C. Bresciani-Turroni (1915) had calculated Pareto alpha coefficients using the Prussian income tax and the "Klassensteuer," a graduated head tax on occupations, for selected years throughout the nineteenth century. On the basis of his calculations, he argued, "It appears without doubt that . . . a rise in the inequality of the distribution of income (occurred throughout the nineteenth century in Prussia)" (p. 16). The significant rise in inequality (i.e., decline in the value of alpha), however, occurred after 1850.

The early insights gained by application of Pareto's useful formula to the Prussian income tax statistics, however, have not been kept alive. The rise of inequality during industrialization, the stability before World War I, the subsequent wartime rise—these important historical distribution episodes are all documented by the alpha coefficient and are all noted upon by Bresciani in 1915. Yet none of the recent historical treatises by Wehler (1973), Hentschel (1978), and Kocka (1973) covering these different epochs take cognizance of this empirical support of their arguments.

D.

In discussing the Pareto measure I have noted that it is particularly sensitive to distributional change in the top of the distribution. Is it entirely irrelevant or insensitive to what happens at the bottom of the distribution? One useful measure of inequality which is sensitive to distributional change at the bottom has been developed and extensively utilized by Williamson and Lindert (1976). This is the income share of the working poor (p. 95ff.) According to the author's "This index is highly correlated with our pay ratio series . . . It follows that the proxy correlates well with the extant twentieth century income distribution data [in the United States] from 1913 onwards. The proxy suggests that there was a surge in American inequality from 1839 to the early 1880s" (p. 96). In fact, this proxy is an interesting and new inequality measure in the Williamson/Lindert study. I have calculated this inequality index for Germany as the ratio of unskilled day laborers' wages to net domestic product per man per day. To obtain this measure an index of unskilled daily laborers' wages had to be estimated from various sources. Our index is bounded above by the excellent historical wage series of the unskilled day laborers in the Krupp Steel Casting Works in Essen and at the bottom by agricultural day laborers in western German regions. In general the index of unskilled wages moves in line with some evidence on the wage of day laborers in the Prussian railways and of unskilled laborers in the building industry. The index of unskilled labor's share of income is plotted on Figure 4 in comparison with Hoffmann's (1965) data on labor's share of income. We note a strong parallel movement of these two series over time; R^2 between them, 1850 to 1913, is 0.78. If one excluded two outliers, the values for 1850 and 1851, the correlation would be improved yet further. Since I used a constant number for the working days per year (300) for the whole time period, when in fact there was a decline, this biases the index of unskilled labor's share of income to indicate a stronger falling than actually took place. Possibly much of the vertical difference in 1850 between the index of the unskilled labor's share and that of labor's share is due to this assumption about the number of working days per year. That is, there may be an even greater similarity between these two variables.

If this is so, an interesting conclusion appears. Williamson and Lindert rejected the usual measure of labor's share as irrelevant to modern stylized facts of distribution. In its stead they created a new and apparently more useful analytic concept, the unskilled labor's share of income, which they find correlated with movements in pay ratios and therefore a good proxy for the latter. For this substitution to make analytic sense the new unskilled labor's share should itself not correlate well with the usual measure of labor's share. However, this is precisely the case in Germany. Thus, the index of the German unskilled labor's share provides little new information beyond that which is already contained in the usual measure of labor's share. This result *also* implies that changes in human capital's (or labor skill's) share of income do not move contrary to changes in the unskilled labor's share; i.e., skilled labor and unskilled labor can be added up without causing the analytical havoc Williamson and Lindert fear. Their focus upon unskilled labor's share was also justified by the argument that human capital and physical captial are complements in production and that both are substitutes for unskilled labor; thus it would make theoretic sense to split up labor. However, the correlation of the two labor shares in Germany before World War I cast doubt upon the aptness of the Williamson/Lindert assumptions of substitution or complementarity of factors in production for the German historical case. This carries us into some of the concluding arguments in the following section on the causes of inequality in Germany.

However, what needs to be emphasized here is that movements of the Pareto alpha coefficient do in fact indicate distributional shifts in the bottom of the distribution of income. For if the unskilled labor's share of income is highly correlated with labor's share—and that, as we have already seen, is correlated

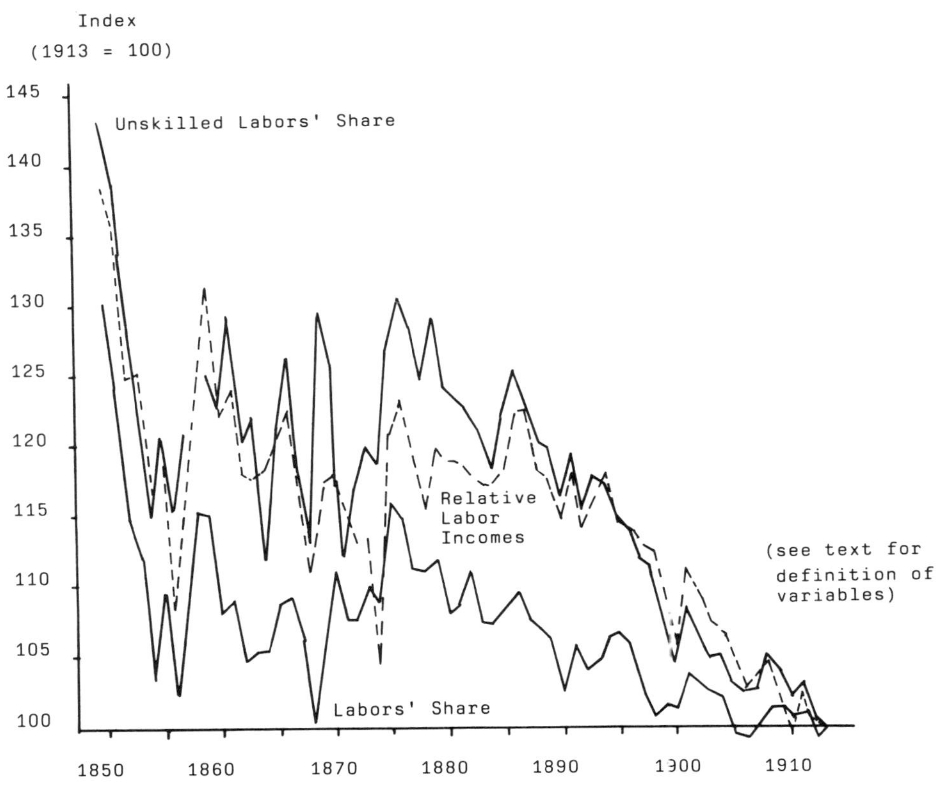

Figure 4. Labors' Share of Income, Unskilled Labors' Share and Relative Labor Incomes, Germany, 1850–1913

with alpha, as well—then alpha will also indicate distributional changes in the bottom. The difference to the U.S. case is quite remarkable. Williamson/Lindert argue that the unskilled share is a good proxy for pay ratios in the United States; in contrast, in Germany we could say (exaggeratedly, to be sure) that it is a proxy for the Pareto alpha.

The previous description of long-run trends in Prussian income inequality between 1850 and 1913 rests upon the published income tax data. However, this is a meaningful exercise only if the possibility of a particular systematic bias in the assessment of taxable income can be ruled out. The crucial question is, did the local assessment boards learn to assess incomes—in particular the top incomes—more correctly, thereby subjecting ever higher proportions of income to the income tax over time? If so, such administrative learning behavior would lead to a progressive decline in underassessments and introduce a bias into the reported taxable income figures, causing them to show a misleading rise in inequality as well as a faster increase in incomes than took place in fact. Another way of putting the question is: Who was becoming cleverer, the tax subjects, in disguising sources, types and levels of income, or the tax administration, in ferreting out that information?

A reporting bias of the sort considered here, which is due to an ascendency of tax administration over tax payers, seems not to have happened. Although there was a decline in underassessments—see Table 37 in Hoffmann/Mueller (1959) pp. 76–77 for estimates—they occurred in a number of steps after tax law changes, the most notable of which was Finance Minister Miquel's income tax reform of 24 June 1891.[56] That is, changing tax regimes did in fact result in artificial shifts in the alpha coefficient of inequality, but these are limited to particular dates and can, therefore, be identified. However, *within* the time of a particular tax law a tendency towards underreporting of incomes must have taken place. In this leapfrogging, the tax administration evidently lost ground to the tax payers over the period 1850–1913 as a whole, as the following comparison between different estimates of national income indicates. Besides the Hoffmann/Mueller (1959) estimate of German national income which is based on the taxable income data of the German states—corrected for changes in underreporting between successive tax laws—there are two more recent and preferred estimates in Hoffmann *et.al.* (1965) based upon expenditures (p. 825) and factor inputs (p. 507) in current prices. A comparison of the trends of these three estimates of national income between 1850 and 1913[57] points to the substantially slower rise of national income estimated on the basis of the income tax data in the period before 1891. Hoffmann (1965, p. 169) suggests that this is evidently due to deficiencies in the assessment techniques which only captured part of the rise in incomes. Even after 1891, when significantly stricter assessment procedures were introduced, *Der Deutsche Oekonomist*, a liberal weekly, continued to criticize lax assessments which permitted a large degree of underreporting especially of top incomes.[58] In other words, if there is a bias in the reported taxable income data between 1850 and 1913, it is most probably towards underreporting and thus understating the rise in income inequality during this period.

There is law and relative regularity everywhere else—why not in production and distribution?
P.H. Douglas

III.

The functional and the personal distribution of income in Germany change in a systematic way during her classic industrialization phase, 1850–1913: capital's share of income and personal income inequality both rise. Moreover, the changes in capital's share correlate well with changes in the net investment ratio.[59] These findings are consistent with a view of growth which sees it as fueled by the savings and investments made possible by the propertied rich. A growth-equity conflict during German industrialization must, therefore, be seen as a historic possibility   at least until the time when more complex modeling might rule it out.[60]

How can the rise of inequality, or the first part of the Kuznets-U, be explained in the German histocial case? Different kinds of "explanations" are possible and in this section we shall see what can be learned from them for understanding German inequality history. Because personal income inequality was seen to depend upon the functional distribution of income, a good explanation of the latter will suffice. We shall assess three attempts to explain historic changes in labor's share of income. The first two, (i) the estimation of a bias parameter in the CES aggregate production function and (ii) the search for sectoral productivity growth gaps, are concerned with ways of identifying a bias in aggregate technological change, which can help explain movements in labor's share in a neoclassical setting. The third moves away from the neoclassic world view and seeks to find an explanation of the functional distribution akin to Kalecki's, in which the monopoly power of producers (the power to mark-up prices) play a role. None of these explanations, however, provides an acceptable "parable"[61] for German distribution history, largely because (a) the level of aggregation employed seems inappropriate, disguises the structural changes characteristic of German industrialization, and (b) the assumptions behind the neoclassical theoretic view of the world (particularly those of well-functioning factor markets and fully employed and mobile factors) do not seem to apply in the historic case at hand.

Before continuing it should be recalled here that the definition of labor's share of income employed in this study comes from Hoffmann (1965). An essential aspect of that definition is the splitting up of the incomes of unincorporated businesses, proprietary income, or that of the self-employeds and their helping family members into capital and labor incomes by assigning the self-employeds and their working family members a mark-up or a percentage of the average wage of the economic sector in which they are active. Their capital incomes are thus a residual after labor incomes have been subtracted from their total incomes.

In contrast, Albert Jeck has provided an analysis of what could be called the *categorial* income distribution: income is distributed to certain categories of income recipients; to dependent workers (wage and salary share), to self-employeds and working family members (unincoporated business or proprietory and entrepreneurial incomes), incorporated business (capital incomes), etc. According to Jeck, the share of wage and salary income increased in Germany between 1875 and 1913 from about 30 to 50 percent of total incomes, mostly because of "structural changes, such as the contraction of agriculture, the increase in the proportion of wage- and salary-earners in the gainfully employed and the rise of the joint-stock companies."[62] However, it should be noted that "this trend is not so much a question of a change in income distribution as of a shift in the distribution of income receivers."[63] Dr. Jungenfeld pointed out in his perceptive comments on Jeck's paper that despite "an increasing share of wages and salaries . . . due . . . to the declining importance of non-incorporated businesses. . . . it was not obvious whether the changes had meant any redistribution between capital and labour in the functional sense" (p. 107). But this latter information is necessary together with data on capital per employee for "analysing the effects of technological change [upon the distribution of income] along the lines of the neoclassical theory," a test which Jungenfeld urged should be attempted in the German case (Marchal/Ducros 1968, p. 108).

Ironically, the first test of this kind on German historical material had been made a year before Jungenfeld's remarks by Walther Hoffmann (1967). In this study Hoffmann attempted to apply the neoclassical theory of income distribution[64] and its concepts of an aggregrate production function, an aggregate elasticity of substitution between capital and labor, and of biases in technical change to explain long-term changes in labor's share in Germany. After much wrestling with those concepts, Hoffmann comes to the conclusion that the historical changes in the capital-output ratio (first a decline until 1873, thence a rise until 1913) and in labor's share (a rise between the 1850s and the 1870s, thence a decline until 1913) in the *industrial sector* can only be explained by an appeal to shifts in the type of Harrod-non-neutral technical change over time. The first phase must have been dominated by capital-saving technical change, the latter by labor saving.[65] Hoffmann's discussion is based upon mere assumptions about the nature and the size of the parameters of the aggregate production function. However, both the elasticity of substitution and the technological bias parameters can be estimated simultaneously, as P. David and Th. van de Klundert (1965) have argued. They provided an often-copied econometric technique for estimating the parameters of a constant elasticity of substitution (CES) production function which uses factor inputs in constant efficiency units. In this approach technical change is factor augmenting, i.e., it improves the efficiency of either or both capital and labor. If labor efficiency is raised more than that of capital, one can speak of a Hicksian labor augmenting bias in technical change, which is the same as a labor saving innovation if the elasticity of substitution is less than unity. In other words, this technological bias introduces a reason for changes in the relative scarcity of factor inputs beyond the usual changes in the capital-labor ratio measured in conventional units.

Bernhard Gahlen (1972) has utilized the David/van de Klundert method in his investigation of German historic data and provided a host of estimates of both the elasticity of substitution and of the type of technological bias. Some of his results for the economy as a whole between 1850 and 1913 seem to bear out the usefulness of this approach: the elasticity of substitution is below unity and technical change is strongly labor augmenting. (pp. 240, 265) Although the capital-labor ratio, measured in conventional units, rises during this time period and labor becomes more scarce, the labor augmenting technical change is so strong as to overturn this trend in relative scarcity and now makes capital, measured in constant efficiency units, more scarce than labor. In the face of limited substitution possibilities, the rise of the rate of return to capital relative to that of labor reflects relatively rising marginal productivities and helps explain the rise in capital's share. "Everything seems to fit well into the neoclassic theoretic view of the world," Gahlen states, before he demolishes this view (p. 265). If shorter time periods are taken, if the regressions are run on sectoral data, or if slightly different but theoretically sensible specifications of the variables are used, a bewildering array of senseless parameter estimates (e.g., negative elasticities of substitution) raise their head. Moreover, even if one uses the parameter estimates which conform best to the neoclassical parable (p. 265)—and which well describe the historic movement of output, labor productivity, and capital-labor ratio—this does not guarantee that the estimated production function is a useful distribution function. The estimated marginal products of capital and labor and the estimated labor's share move in wildly divergent trends compared to the historic wage rates, rates of return to capital and the share of labor (p. 266). After providing similar demonstrations of the failure of the parameters of an estimated CES production function to provide sensible distribution estimates in the more homogeneous historical period 1880–1913 (no wars, reparations, founding booms and busts), for the agricultural sector, and for post-World War II West Germany, 1950–1966 Gahlen argues that the theoretical assumptions which are required for the neoclassical theory to hold and the econometric estimates to produce sensible results do not apply in history. In particular the smooth functioning of competitive factor markets which should equate marginal rates of return to factor prices is being questioned, among other assumptions (e.g., constant returns to scale). Of course, there are also data problems and biases in econometric estimation which could also play an important role in bedeviling the outcome. Nevertheless, this gauntlet thrown before the feet of the neoclassical theorists in Germany has not really been picked up. Whether aggregate production functions have useful distributional attributes in the German historic case must remain a moot question.

However, there is another way to identify a technological bias in the economy as a whole under the assumption that it functions like the neoclassic model. This test focuses upon sectoral productivity growth gaps as a source of aggregate technological bias and was initially introduced by Williamson and Lindert in their analysis of U.S. distribution history (1980). The argument is that if total factor productivity rises faster in the industrial sector, this is an exogenous causal force for higher industrial growth and industrial sector expansion relative to the other sectors of the economy. If the industrial sector is characterized by a range of unique, technologically determined factor intensities, for example, higher capital-labor ratios than obtain elsewhere in the economy, then the industrial sector expansion will usher in a rising scarcity of capital (in this particular example), higher relative returns to capital economy-wide, and a rise in capital's share of income. That is, the productivity growth gap just described functions exactly like an economy-wide labor saving bias in technical change. Indeed, it can be an important "cause" for a technological bias on the level of the whole economy. Nevertheless, it should be clear that the line of reasoning employed in this argument already presupposes an economy functioning like the neoclassical model. Without this assumption the bias cannot be identified; this same problem exists in interpreting the estimated bias parameter in the CES aggregate production function exercise, which was discussed above. In other words, technological bias at the aggregate level can *only* be identified when the world is neoclassical. If that assumption isn't appropriate, no such bias can be identified. But without the "information" about the technological bias no consistent neoclassical story (the parable) of distribution can be told. This is the reason why Gahlen criticizes the scarcity of genuine information about the real economy in neoclassic stories of aggregate production and distribution. Everything lies in the assumptions. Moreover, there is a further source of aggregate technology bias, one which functions *within* the individual sectors of an economy; this possible source is ignored here.

Thus we have here a second problematic way to tell a neoclassical tale of distribution. Tables 1–4 and Figure 5 are relevant to test this explanation. Noteworthy are the following historical facts of German output growth, industrialization, and sectoral differences between 1850 and 1913:

1. The capital-labor ratio grows at a steady rate.
2. The capital-output ratio remains fairly constant.
3. Sectoral differences in growth rates are largely dictated by agricultural output growth.
4. If capital's share is held constant in the economy's sectors, industrialization and the attending shift in sectoral size would have resulted in a *lowering* of capital's share of income, because the industrial sector is the least capital intensive sector in the economy and capital's share of income is lower than in agriculture or in the rest of the economy.

Table 1. Unbalanced Rates of Output Growth and Changes in the Capital-Output and Capital-Labor Ratios

| | Rates of Output Growth in[a] | | | Unbalanced Growth | Growth Rates of Inputs[b] | | | Trends in the Ratios of Capital to | | |
| | Agricult. | Gewerbe | Total Output | | Labor Force | Hours | Capital | Output | Labor | Hours |
	(1)	(2)	(3)	(2)-(1)	(4)	(5)	(6)	(6)-(3)	(6)-(4)	(6)-(5)
1850–1860	1.76	3.05	2.05	1.29	.63	.57	1.77	-.28	1.14	1.20
1860–1870	.92	3.70	2.04	2.78	.72	.55	2.48	.44	1.76	1.93
1870–1880	1.14	3.40	2.24	2.26	1.42	1.13	2.49	.25	1.07	1.36
1880–1890	1.86	4.14	2.92	2.28	1.31	1.03	2.07	-.22	1.39	1.67
1890–1900	2.53	4.35	3.47	1.82	1.34	.93	3.27	-.20	1.93	2.34
1900–1910	.68	3.43	2.62	2.75	1.42	.99	3.16	.54	1.74	2.17
1910–1913	1.98	5.26	4.10	3.28	1.72	1.23	3.37	-.73	1.65	2.14
1850–1870	1.34	3.36	2.05	2.02	.67	.56	2.12	.07	1.45	1.56
1880–1913	1.71	4.10	3.10	2.39	1.39	1.01	3.08	-.02	1.69	2.07
1850–1913	1.50	3.75	2.63	2.25	1.17	.88	2.73	.10	1.56	1.85

(a) Data Source: D. Andre, p. 78, Table 2
(b) ibid.; Hours on p. 127.

Table 2.   Changing Sectoral Output Mix and Its Effects
on Capital's Share

	Sectoral Output Shares[a]			Capital's Share	
	Agriculture	Gewerbe[b]	Rest[c]	Estimated[d]	Actual[e]
1850	.47	.28	.25	.262	
					.199 (1850–1860)
1860	.45	.31	.24	.259	
					.248 (1860–1870)
1870	.40	.36	.24	.256	
					.215 (1870–1880)
1880	.36	.41	.23	.251	
					.236 (1880–1890)
1890	.33	.46	.21	.246	
					.264 (1890–1900)
1900	.30	.50	.20	.243	
					.282 (1900–1910)
1910	.25	.54	.21	.241	
					.292 (1910–1913)
1913	.23	.56	.21	.239	

(a) taken from Doris Andre, *Indikatoren des technischen Fortschritts, Eine Analyse der Wirstschaftsentwicklung in Deutschland von 1850 bis 1913*, Göttingen, 1971: Vandenhoeck & Ruprecht, Tabelle 4, p. 80. Her calculations are based on the data in W.G. Hoffmann, et. al., *Wachstum* (1965).
(b) Mining, Industry and Crafts, Trade, Banks, Insurance, Transport excluding Railroads and the Post.
(c) A rather heterogeneous sector including Non-Agricultural Housing, Government, Railroads and the Post, Domestic Service, Defense.
(d) Using constant (average of the years 1850–1913) capital shares in Agriculture (.261), Gewerbe (.192), and Rest (.342) as weights; see Andre, Table 33, p. 122.
(e) Average of the years indicated; see Andre, p. 122.

Table 3.   Changing Sectoral Capital Shares and Their Impact on
the Total Capital Share of Output

	Sectoral Capital Shares[a]			Total Capital's Share	
	Agriculture	Gewerbe	Rest	Estimated[b]	Actual[c]
1850–1860	.158	.212	.248	.201	.199
1860–1870	.278	.183	.313	.247	.248
1870–1880	.196	.174	.330	.218	.215
1880–1890	.243	.162	.366	.238	.236
1890–1900	.312	.183	.377	.274	.264
1900–1910	.321	.222	.386	.295	.282
1910–1913	.355	.228	.375	.308	.291
1850–1870	.220	.198	.281	.225	.224
1880–1913	.301	.194	.376	.274	.264
1850–1913	.261	.192	.341	.251	.244

(a) Taken from D. Andre, p. 122. Averages for the years indicated.
(b) Using constant (1880) sectoral output shares: Agriculture (.36), Gewerbe (.41), Rest (.23) as weights.
(c) Andre, p. 122.

Table 4.   Total Factor Productivity Growth and Productivity Growth Gaps

	Total Factor Productivity Growth[a]			Productivity Growth Gap
	Agriculture (1)	Gewerbe (2)	Total Economy (3)	(2)-(1)
1850–1860	1.49	1.33	1.14	−.16
1860–1870	.36	1.98	.90	1.62
1870–1880	.00	1.35	.56	1.35
1880–1890	1.59	.72	1.27	−.87
1890–1900	2.09	1.33	1.67	−.76
1900–1910	−.28	1.14	.78	1.42
1910–1913	1.00	2.51	1.98	1.51
1850–1870	.92	1.64	1.02	.72
1880–1913	1.12	1.21	1.30	.02
1850–1913	.89	1.36	1.08	.47

(a) D. Andre, p. 124; average annual growth rates for the years indicated.

5.   If no change had occurred in the relative size of the industrial and other sectors, capital's share of income would have increased just as much as it actually did, because capital's share was rising in all the major sectors of the economy.

This suggests that industrialization, as measured by the increase in the size of the industrial sector, does not provide a reason for increasing the scarcity of capital, its relative returns and its share of income.

6.   Contrary to the Williamson/Lindert (1980) argument for the United States, sectoral productivity growth gaps (their new way of "identifying" biased technological change in the aggregate economy) seem not to be responsible for inequality changes in Germany. In precisely those decades when inequality is rising strongly (the 1850s, 1880s, and 1890s) the productivity growth gap disappears in Germany and balanced growth rules.

With the failure of both attempts to find a technological bias at the aggregate level, we should not rule out the reason for a third: a possible bias existing within the major sectors of the economy. Thus we should search for changes in sectoral capital intensities and attempt to characterize the spread of new technologies within sectors to explain changes of the functional distribution within sectors. However, we shall see that a closer look at the major economic sectors, agriculture and industry, does at this date result in no more than puzzles.

It is of interest to note that there exists a strong correlation between the economy-wide capital's share and that in agriuclutre between 1850 and 1913. Thus the functional distribution of the economy seems to have been dominated by the functional distribution in its major sector. The rising capital's share of income within agriculture could be accounted for by the rise of agrarian capitalism. Here the argument is that German agriculture was industrializing, i.e., became

Figure 5.   Factor Inputs and Productivity in Germany, 1850–1913

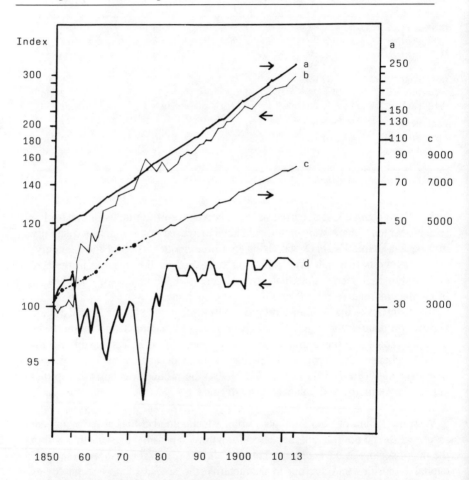

(a) Capital Stock in Constant 1913 Prices (Billion Marks)
(b) Labor Productivity
(c) Capital Intensity (Marks/Labor Force)
(d) Capital—Output Ratio

Source: K. Borchardt (1976)

more capital intensive and technologically progressive. This would fit well with the new interpretation of the agrarian revolution based on root crops recently formulated by J.A. Perkins (1981). Moreover, it should be noted that the effects of policy are not negligible in this field. The production of sugar beets, the basis of new German agrarian capitalism, was initially stimulated by the prohibitive sugar tariffs imposed at the start of the Zollverein in 1834. While there is a certain plausibility to the sugar beet theory of income distribution in Germany, we need to know much more about the nature of agricultural technology to explain distributional trends in German agriculture. Nevertheless, it is clear that at the sectoral level of aggregation it becomes possible to utilize or find real facts (as opposed to mere assumptions) about the nature of technical change and on economic policy measures which have implications for the functional distribution. Indeed, the task of explaining the functional distribution of income may become easier at a yet more disaggregated level.

The idea that it is necessary to disaggregate in order to understand distributional trends is particularly applicable to the industrial sector in Germany. A sizable part of that sector consisted of numerous traditional artisans and handicrafts with a high level of skills. J. J. Lee (1978) suggests that the growth of modern industry in Germany was bolstered by the availability of these labor skills in traditional industry. Thus, industrialization in Germany, with an old and large artisanal sector, was different than in the United Sates. Modern industrial growth meant competition for resources and markets with the traditional industry, which being skill intensive eliminated possible skill bottlenecks. Moreover, the German, especially the Prussian, compulsory elementary school system and the introduction of higher technical schools meant that in the realm of formal education, human capital formation achieved relatively high rates in the nineteenth century.[66] With agriculture shedding its excess unskilled labor force, and a part of the traditional artisanal sector shedding both unskilled and skilled workers to the modern industrial sector, labor (both skilled and unskilled) bottlenecks should not have been a problem for German industrialization. It is difficult to know what these relative factor supply trends imply for the functional distribution of the whole of the amorphous industrial sector. What we really are interested in is the income distribution in the new, modern, and essentially *urban* part of industry, settling into the massively growing cities.

The nice thing about fables or parables is that they are simple stories—and with a treacherously simple point? The argument advanced here, that the neoclassical story when enhanced by some real technological facts at a smaller level of aggregation has a chance to provide a real argument, becomes more complicated the more disaggregated is the level of analysis. The price of including ever more real technological facts is incomprehensibility of the resulting distributional argument.

The third method of "explaining" labor's share of income utilizes a definition or tautology developed by Phelps-Brown and Browne (1968). Here the real wage is identically equal to labor productivity times the share of the wage earner in the product times the number of units of consumables obtained per unit of product. In the rates of change formulation, the growth of labor's share can be defined as equal to the growth of real wages less the growth of the terms of trade between the workers' consumption and national output less the growth of labor productivity. This measure has a family resemblance to Kalecki's (1938)[67] degree of monopoly argument of income inequality, where a high degree of monopoly is indicated by higher mark-up of prices over costs, and to Juergen Kuczynski's (1931)[68] concept of a relative immizeration of the workers due to the terms of trade effect. Thus, this investigation of the effect of prices on inequality is of wider interest. Our estimates of the terms of trade effect on labor's share utilizes Rainer Goemmel's (1979) cost of living index, which is superior to the widely used index of Kuczynski. The data on average labor incomes, net national product, and the price index of NNP come from Hoffmann (1965); an index of labor hours is taken from Hesse/Gahlen (1965); and the resulting estimates of labor's share, termed relative labor incomes to differentiate these numbers from Hoffmann's (1965) historical estimates, are plotted on Figure 4. The time trend follows that of our previously estimated unskilled labor's share of income very closely, except for some major differences in the 1870s. As well, this estimate of labor's share is also highly correlated with Hoffmann's labor share data.

The contribution of different economic forces to changes in the relative labor incomes is indicated in Table 5. If the development of labor productivity is thought to be determined by exogenous technological trends and real labor incomes by labor force growth and emigration, then the exercise of monopoly pricing power (which would be reflected in changes in the terms of trade) would result in a lowering of the so estimated labor's share of income (the relative labor income). However, the distributional effect of the terms of trade is smaller than that of the other two forces over the period as a whole; but, more importantly, in the subperiods where its impact is important, in the 1850s and 1870s, the terms of trade effect *increases* labor's share. Consequently, this exercise can show no systematic dominating influence of monopolists on profit shares by way of monopoly power in pricing. Possibly, the level of aggregation is again too high to test for the effects of monopoly.[69]

The table can be read to provide other kinds of interpretations of the decline of labor's share which may be of interest. We can now comment on J. Wolf's critique of the Historical School interpretation of the pessimistic effects of productivity advances on the distribution of income. In the long run, declines in labor's share are mainly the result of wages falling behind labor productivity advances; moreover, the beneficial effects of changing terms of trade due to a decline in the price of goods in the laborer's budget are not so large as to counteract this lag. The effect is positive, as Wolf opined, but very small. Thus, Table 5 would strengthen the Historical School position against technology optimists, such as Wolf.

Table 5.   Sources of Changes in the Relative Labor Incomes (Labor's Share)
Average Annual Percentage Rates of Change

	real avg.[a] labor incomes (deflated by[b] cost of living)	labor[c] productivity per[d] man hour	NNP deflator[e] divided by cost of living[b]	est. labor's share (1-2-3 = 4)[f]
	(1)	(2)	(3)	(4)
1850–60	−0.95	1.45	−1.13	−1.27
1860–70	1.04	1.60	−0.22	−0.35
1870–80	−0.46	1.01	−1.54	0.08
1880–90	2.07	1.87	0.55	−0.35
1890–1900	1.91	2.42	0.31	−0.82
1900–10	0.64	1.72	−0.48	−0.60
1910–13	2.97	2.70	0.23	0.38
1850–70	0.04	1.53	−0.68	−0.82
1870–1913	1.67	2.07	0.14	−0.54
1850–1913	0.81	1.73	−0.39	−0.53

Sources:

(a) W.G. Hoffmann (1965), p. 495.
(b) R. Goemmel (1979), pp. 27–29.
(c) Hoffmann (1965), p. 454.
(d) H. Hesse, B. Gahlen (1965), p. 496.
(e) Hoffmann (1965), p. 599.
(f) see, e.g. E.H. Phelps-Brown, M.H. Browne, *A Century of Pay*, London 1968, pp. 167ff.

growth rates are estimated by the formula $Y = Ab^t$
where Y is the value at the end of the period,
     A is the value at the beginning
     b = (1 + the average annual growth rate)
     t is the number of years.

To the degree to which one moves to larger cities and to major urban centers (''Groszstaedte''), which are the so-called exponents of modern industrial civilization and the seats of new wealth, the divergence [of income] between given parts of the population rises quickly.

C. Bresciani-Turroni (1915)

IV.

In the previous section it was suggested that an appropriate level of aggregation needs to be specified to understand modern German industrial growth and income inequality. It is clear that contemporary critics viewed *urban* social and income cleavages in particular alarm. When Schmoller stated in his authoritative *Foundations of Economic Analysis* (*Grundriss* II, 1904 p. 532) that ''the ruling social antagonism of our times is that between entrepreneurs and the industrial workers'' he had in mind an urban setting. The large towns, whose numbers and size were growing dramatically in the half-century before 1913, were the "exponents of modern industrial civilization." Industrialization was the prime cause of urbanization in Germany[70]; and German history during that period is characterized by unusually high rates of economic growth and urbanization. What, therefore, can be more natural than to focus upon the rise of the cities and the divergences between town and countryside as the appropriate backdrop to analyze the history of income in Germany?

Sherman Robinson (1976) has provided a mathematical demonstration that the Kuznets-U hypothesis can be derived from a simple model which divides the economy into two sectors with different sectoral income distributions and finds the cause of income inequality changes in the monotonic population migration between the two, an idea first suggested by Kuznets (1955). Rather than using sectors, we can apply this model to the urban versus rural regions in Germany. It has been demonstrated for some time—Bresciani (1915), Grumbach (1957), Mueller/Geisenberger (1972)—that urban income inequality exceeded that in rural areas. Thus the historic migration and urbanization movements found in Germany between 1850 and 1913 would *alone* suffice to cause the historic rise in income inequality. This simple relationship, however, needs to be modified by the fact that the income distributions within the regions did not remain stable. Grumbach (1957) pointed out that while inequality in Prussian cities began to diminish after 1900, this did not occur in rural areas. Mueller/Geisenberger (1972) also identified an interesting difference in inequality trends for different Prussian regions between 1874 and 1913. In the more industrial and urbanized counties ("Regierungsbezirke") of Duesseldorf (the most industrialized county in Prussia), Aachen, and Arnsberg there is a clear decline of inequality since before 1900. In contrast, the mainly agrarian eastern counties of Koeslin, Marienwerder, and Gumbinnen show a steady rise of income inequality. These regional trends, in particular the reason why the rise of inequality was first checked in the cities and industrial regions, need to be explained as well. A test for the effect of *both* the change in the regional population weights and of within-region trends in income inequality would recommend itself as a useful historical exericse in the case of Germany.

This approach to analyzing distribution as the result of regional changes is congenial to dual economy models of development such as the Lewis-Fei-Ranis models of surplus labor.[71] The stable historic long-run wage differential between rural and urban regions and a massive emigration from backward rural areas which lasts until the 1890s are historic facts which fit these models. Irma Adelman and C.T. Morris (1973) have argued that their empirical analysis of income distribution in less developed countries today is consistent with the distributional implications of dual economy models. These models suggest that the initial spurt of growth in the modern sector in a low-income country worsens the relative income distribution, and that this situation continues until the marginal product of labor in the agricultural sector rises to the level of the institutional wage in the industrial sector. The rising scarcity of agricultural labor in Germany since the 1890s and the peaking of aggregate inequality around 1900 could possibly be fruitfully analyzed by recourse to the dual economy model.

A further advantage of the application of the dual economy models and of the Kuznets-Robinson migration approach to German industrialization, urbanization, and income inequality is that they help clarify the distributive impact of most of the important government policies of the times. Government policy which encouraged migration (the poor laws), urbanization (unprecedented urban public investment, the basis of Wagner's law of state expenditures), industrialization of a particular type (tariffs on iron and steel), and capital-intensive rather than labor-intensive agriculture (tariffs on sugar and grains) had an inegalitarian impact. Thus, the pace if not the type of economic growth which the country experienced was affected by public policy. By speeding up the process of industrialization, urbanization, and migration, public policy in Germany also promoted the rise of income inequality. This suggests, that a part of the growth-equity conflict which German society experienced during the industrialization period, 1850–1913, was self-imposed and could have been avoided with a different set of policies. Thus the position on the growth-equity trade-off reveals something about society's preferences, or the preferences of society's ruling groups. Given this policy preference for greater growth and greater inequality, the early German introduction of social security legislation becomes understandable as a form of social control, as a way of calming the relatively disadvantaged masses.

V. SUMMARY

In this paper I have attempted to show that the inequality debate ushered in by Kuznets is but the continuation of a discussion raised by the German Historical School before World War I. Historical concerns and perceptions of inequality at those times focused upon the possible political disruptions in an industrial order ruled by "plutocrats." A useful historic measure of personal income inequality which is attuned to those perceptions is the Pareto alpha coefficient, which can be easily calculated from the income tax data of those times. Moreover, the alpha is also correlated with the income share of the working poor and the functional distribution of income (capital's share of income). All these indicators, as well as more conventional measures of personal income inequality (e.g., the share of income of the top 5 percent of income receivers) point to a rise of inequality in Germany between 1850 and 1913, her classic industrialization phase. Since capital incomes were more unequally distributed than labor incomes, a rise in capital's share can be seen as causing a rise in the personal income inequality. This story of inequality is more attuned to the arguments formed by classical economists, Marx, and those of the Historical School pessimists, and it confronts in many ways the history of income inequality in the United States and in Great

Britain as told by Williamson and Lindert. Several neoclassical explanations of the functional income distribution in German history were discussed and rejected. The paper concludes with the suggestion that the application of dual economy models to investigate the German case of distribution looks fruitful because they help focus the analysis upon migration and the distributional implications of Germany's unusual rate of urbanization.

ACKNOWLEDGMENTS

This paper is part of a larger research project on the history of economic inequality and German industrialization which has been supported by the Minister fuer Wissenschaft und Forschung des Landes Nordrhein-Westfalen. It was presented to the international Conference on Income and Wealth Distribution in Utrecht, August, 20–22, 1986 and before the Workshop on Income and Wealth Distribution of the 9th International Congress of Economic History in Bern, August, 24–30, 1986. Earlier versions have been presented to economic history workshops at Oxford University, Northwestern University, University of Chicago, University of Toronto, Emory University, and the Research Triangle Workshop in Raleigh, N.C., whose participants provided useful critical commentary. In particular, I have benefited from discussion with N.F.R. Crafts, Charles Calomiris, Robert Fogel, Robert Gallman, and Peter Lindert. Their suggestions have substantially improved the paper.

NOTES

1.   Among the many available studies the following are notable: Paukert (1973), Chenery *et. al.* (1974), and Chenery and Syrquin (1975).

2.   On Wagner's Law, see Timm (1961) and Pryor (1968, p. 50).

3.   See Sombart (1921, pp. 168–69, 369–70).

4.   Schmoller (1895, pp. 1067ff). A short discussion, in English, is provided by Bresciani-Turroni (1939, pp. 116ff).

5.   Soltow (1968). See also, P. Lindert and J. G. Williamson (1983, pp. 94–109): "Reinterpreting Britain's social tables, 1688–1913''; and Williamson (1985, pp. 65–72): "How did the 'social arithmeticians' see (inequality)?'' Lindert and Williamson's revisions result in a *rise* of inequality between 1688 and 1867, with a reduction thereafter.

6.   This would be a nice topic of investigation for historians of economic thought. The Chenery/Syrquin method has recently been fruitfully applied in economic history by N.F.R. Crafts (1984) who tested for the existence of Gerschenkronian patterns of development in nineteenth-century Europe.

7.   It is unclear if Kuznets knew about Schmoller's (1895) article. His primary source for German data was S. N. Procopovitch (1926).

8.   Kuznets proposed the thesis that the share of the middle income groups was smaller in the developing than in the developed countries in his (1955) paper as well as in his larger study (1963, pp. 1–80). N. C. Kakwani (1980, p. 382) has argued that this Kuznets argument "implies that in the course of economic development, the Lorenz curve changes its shape with respect to its skewness.'' An analysis of the Lorenz curve in 50 developed and developing countries indicates that the skewness of the curves differs systematically between the two country groups. Kakwani accordingly states, "This observation supports Kuznets' hypothesis that the income share of the middle income group is higher in the developed than in the developing countries'' (p. 385). Moreover, he finds that "the

income share of the intermediate groups, that is, from the 40th to the 80th percentile, is appreciably larger in the developed than in the developing countries'' (p. 389). For a discussion of the German concern about the decline of the middle class see the important article by Gustav Schmoller (1897).

9.   Franz Grumbach (1957). See also, the publication of Grumbach's data in W. G. Hoffmann, *et. al.* (1965, p. 515ff). J. H. Mueller and S. Geisenberger (1972); V. Hentschel (1979) and (1978, p. 62ff). A recent useful overview is provided by Hartmut Kaelble (1983); see also, H. Kaelble and H. Volkmann (1986).

10.   S. Procopovitch (1926); Constantino Bresciani-Turroni (1914, 1915); A. Friedmann (1914).

11.   P. H. Lindert (1978); J. G. Williamson and P. H. Lindert (1980); J. G. Williamson (1985).

12.   See Williamson (1982, pp. 1–3); Lindert and Williamson (1976, p. 105).

13.   Bronfenbrenner (1981, p. 613) was in fact criticizing Jan Tinbergern's 1975 distribution monograph in his review of Harold Lyall, *A Theory of Income Distribution* (1975); but the critique applies to Williamson as well.

14.   And in so doing, a large part of the historical concern for economic inequality is sidestepped. The jacket cover of Williamson's book, *Did British Capitalism Breed Inequality?* reproduces a revealing illustration from *Punch* bearing the caption ''Capital and Labour.'' This is a pictoral allegory in which a concerned Britannia, positioned at the lower left side of the picture on the same level as Labour, views a British society cleaved into two very evidently unequal classes. The capitalists are depicted on top, in plush interiors surrounded by servants. Emaciated labourers and their miserable families are shown toiling and living antlike in the mines below in a scene which is separated from Capital above by chains. Contemporary observers quite evidently thought about inequality in class terms. Because, for the previously discussed reasons, Williamson does not analyze distribution in class terms in this book at all, one is baffled by the choice of this illustration. Unfortunately, he did not follow his sound historical intuition in the book's analysis. We draw the conclusion that if inequality history is to be history, it cannot ignore historical perceptions of inequality.

15.   See Ch. 10 ''Accounting for the Kuznets Curve, 1821–1911,'' (1985).

16.   According to Z. Griliches (1965, p. 344), ''The fact that standard economics had no theory of technical change explains, I think, why when we got around to trying to measure it, we had to measure it as the 'residual.' Because it was an *empty box*, we proceeded to define it as everything that cannot be explained by standard theory.'' (Emphasis added.)

17.   A. O. Hirschman and M. Rothschild (1973). Hirschman's basic proposition (p. 545) is: ''In the early stages of rapid economic development, when inequalities in the distribution of income among different classes, sectors, and regions are apt to increase sharply, it can happen that society's *tolerance* for such disparities will be substantial.'' The reason for this initial tolerance of inequality is seen to lie in the generation of expectations that the income and social mobility which some members of society come to enjoy with the advent of growth will spread to the rest. When, or if that does not happen (soon enough?), this tolerance can turn into a great intolerance and political opposition.

18.   Schmoller (1873, p. 4). For an enlightening discussion of the social influences upon the curriculum of the Verein see Irmela Gorges (1980).

19.   Fr. J. Neumann (1892, p. 367) suggested that the ladder image, which was formulated by Karl Rodbertus around mid-century, dominated German, especially the Prussian, distributional debates for most of the second half of the century.

20.   See Karl Kautsky and Bruno Schoenlank (1892).

21.   E. Bernstein (1898). A good flavor of this and other distributional views and disputes is given by Julius Wolf (1898), especially on pp. 249–61.

22.   Wagner (1907, p. 467).

23.   According to Wagner (1907, p. 466), Rodbertus had introduced this powerful metaphor for an increasing income inequality into the contemporary debate. K. Nitschke (1902) attempted to disprove this view of distribution trends. The glowing review of Nitschke by v. Zedlitz-Neukirch (1902) also critically discusses this pessimistic view of distribution trends.

24.   For a contemporary definition of this new term see the article *"Geldherrschaft* (Geldoli-garchie, Argyrokratie, Plutokratie)" in *Meyers Grosses Conversations-Lexikon* (1905, p. 517): "The rule of state and society by capitalist," particularly in the case where there are important limitations to the franchise.

25.   Procopovitch (1926, p. 73) challenges Helfferich's argument.

Helfferich, when analysing the distribution of incomes in Prussia in 1896–1912, expressed the view that "the equality with which the shares of various classes of society in the great increase in national income since 1896 are distributed is simply striking." Accordingly, he emphatically rejects the proposition that there was in Germany any tendency to "plutocratic development" in the sense that the wealth of the richest few increased at a much faster rate than that of the people in general. Our figures, however, would appear to suggest that this conclusion is in contradiction with facts. Tendencies towards "plutocratic development" are certainly in evidence in Germany, in common . . . with other capitalist countries.

26.   See W. Hofmann (1964) for a discussion of the limitations of the Prussian franchise. For the Krupp case in Essen see the classic study by Helmut Croon (1960).

27.   See Wagner's argument in (1893, p. 718).

28.   See Wolf for his contrasting view to the "Kathedersozialisten" (1898, p. 412).

29.   See Taussig, "Inequality and its Causes," Ch. 55 in his *Principles* (1924, p. 254).

30.   The coefficient alpha refers to the value of "a" in the formula

$$N = A \, / \, Y^a, \text{ or in logarithmic transformation}$$
$$\log N = \log A - a \log Y, \text{ where}$$

N = the number of income receivers with an income of at least Y
A = a constant
Y = the level of income
a = the Pareto alpha.

It turns out in practice that in plotting the number of income receivers versus the income Y on double-log paper, most personal income distributions take on a negatively sloped linear shape, whose slope is alpha. The nature of alpha is thus one of a convenient descriptive device for inequality analysis. According to N. Kakwani (1980), the Pareto distribution describes most personal income distributions only at some point above the mode (p. 16). When the value of alpha is high, income is more equally distributed than when it is low. The equation with the variables in log form implies that the elasticity of N with respect to Y is "-a." In other words, if income Y increases by 1 percent, the proportion of income receivers having an income greater than or equal to Y declines by "a" percent. "The parameter 'a' can, therefore, be interpreted as the elasticity of decrease in the number of [income receivers] when passing to a higher income class" (Kakwani, p. 15).

31.   See the graphs in Grumbach (1957, p. 23).

32.   Results of own correlations between the income shares data in Mueller, Geisenberger (1972) with values of alpha in Grumbach (1957).

33.   See V. Pareto (1897, Vol. 2, pt. I, Ch. 1). On the basis of a few empirical tests, Pareto believed that alpha was a constant with an approximate value of 1.5, invariant in space and time. Thus, the distribution of income depended more upon the individual characteristics and the nature of persons than on the economic organization of society. (p. 363) The point of Pareto's argument of a natural constancy of alpha was, in effect, to prove that a growth-equity conflict does not exist: "We may say generally that the increase of wealth relatively to population will produce either an increase in the minimum income, or a diminution of the inequality of income, or both these effects in combination." (p. 234; the translation is from A. C. Pigou 1920, p. 694). This hypothesis is nicely criticized by Pigou in Ch. 11, "Pareto's Law," p. 693ff. C. Bresciani-Turroni (1915); see particularly,

pp. 10–19, "Ueber das Paretosche Gesetz." In contrast to Pareto, Bresciani-Turroni stressed that alpha was variable and showed it to be systematically related to the type of economic organization of societies. Rufus S. Tucker, (1938, p. 551ff).

34. The point here is that over time societies have changed in their tolerance for particular types of inequalities.

35. N. C. Kakwani (1980) provides a good discussion in Ch. 5 "Measures of Income Inequality," p. 63ff.

36. See N. C. Kakwani's (1980) proof of the lemma, "The Gini index attaches more weight to transfers of income near the mode of the distribution than at the tails" (p. 72).

37. See Williamson and Lindert (1976), Figure 1, pp. 74–75; Figure 2, pp. 78–79, and; Figure 3, p. 81. The last provides information about the share of U.S. wealth held by the top 1 percent of free males between 1780 and 1960.

38. Grumbach's (1957) estimates of Pareto's alpha (p. 29) are also reproduced in W. G. Hoffmann (1965, pp. 512–15; for Hoffmann's estimates of labor's share of net domestic product at factor cost see Table 132, pp. 506–509. For the definition of Prussian taxable income and tax units (households and single-person households) see Mueller/Geisenberger (1972) as well as W. G. Hoffmann and J. H. Mueller (1959, pp. 6–11 and pp. 59–85). The latter work is an attempt to utilize the published income tax data of the German states to generate appropriate national income accounting estimates of income. Numerous ingenious adjustments to the taxable income of private households needed to be made, for example, adjustments for underreporting income, the assessment of the income of persons not subject to the income tax because of low income or exemption, contributions to social security and life insurance premia, undistributed profits of corporations, profits of public enterprises, are the main adjustments. These adjustments make it clear that taxable income and income in the national accounting sense differed substantially. The following figures (taken from Tables 37 and 43, pp. 76–77 and 86–87) indicate the degree of divergence in 1851 and in 1913 for Prussia. In the first of these years taxable income was 1.296 billion Marks, the income of households 4.113 billion, and national income amounted to 4.128 billion Marks. In 1913 the respective figures are 19.018, 28.173, and 30.184 billion Marks. Thus, the most important reason for divergence between the two income concepts was due to the exemption of low incomes. Nevertheless, the legal, taxable income definition included a substantial proportion (from one-third to two-thirds) of all incomes throughout the period 1851–1913.

39. The data source is Hoffmann (1965, Table 108, pp. 468–71, columns 3 and 5.

40. According to J. J. Lee (1978, p. 448),

It seems probable that the overall level of skill was influenced more by changes in the industrial structure than by changes in skill quotients within individual industries. The increase between 1846 and 1939 in the relative importance of metals, dominated by skilled labour, and the decline in the relative importance of textiles, with its lower proportion of skilled workers, exerted particular influence in this respect.

See also, p. 447 for a table on the skill distribution of the German male labor force, 1933, which still supports the argument of large skill differences between these two branches.

41. The authoritative treatment of this subject is by Gerhard Bry, "Skill Differentials," in his *Wages in Germany 1871–1945* (1960), especially, pp. 81–88. His Chart 10 (p. 82) provides estimates of skill differentials in the building industry and of cotton spinners, both between 1871 and 1913, of miners in Dortmund since 1879 and of miners in ten mining centers since 1890. The trends of the skill differentials in the building industry and of cotton spinners are roughly parallel, first widening for about a decade and a half after 1871, then falling in the two or three decades before World War I. However, differentials in the ten coal mining centers remain without trend between 1890 and 1913. Bry states somewhat obliquely, "Evaluation of the actual size of skill differentials and comparison of their variation between industries is, at best, complex. And, in view of the meager factual informa-

tion available for the period before 1913, meaningful interpretation is impossible'' (p. 83). Nevertheless, he does in practice take the differentials of the building industry as representative of the German economy-wide differentials. In light of his qualifications about the meaning of industrial differences and the near impossibility of weighing them, this choice can be questioned. Moreover, because skill differentials in the building industry seem to be rather stable in history (see Graph III), the argument that in this industry differentials may be largely governed by custom is not easily dismissed. Thus, I question the propriety of using the skill differentials from this very probably custom-bound trade for an analysis of historical long-run development. See also, Note 48.

My use of long-run industrial wage ratios as an indicator of the relative scarcity of skills can be supported by similar arguments in Melvin W. Reder (1962, esp. p. 276ff): ''Interindustry Differentials. Long Run.'' Reder states that ''in the long-run, real wage differentials among industries will reflect differences in the skill mix'' (p. 276). Unfortunately, it is not clear how long the long run should be for this argument to hold. This is one reason why it is difficult to interpret Franz Grumbach's and Heinz Koenig's (1957 II) findings of a significant decline in interindustry wage differentials between 1888 and World War I. The period may be too short. A second, more important cause for doubt is their use of a problematic indicator of interindustry spread, the non-weighed standard deviation of annual earnings in 14 industry groups of substantially different size. It turns out that earnings in only two industries, printing and railways, revert significantly to the mean industrial earnings in this period. Most of the decline of the earnings dispersion is thus due to the unrepresentative printing trades' total loss of skill differentials, when compared to the industrial average. When the Grumbach and Koenig figures are re-calculated, using 1890 and 1913 employment weights in the different industries, the standard deviation of earnings in the different industries remains *constant* before World War I.

42.   F. Kraus (1981, p. 197 Figure 6.2).

43.   See the discussion in Mueller and Geisenberger (1972) as well as in Grumbach (1957, p. 31).

44.   See, for example, the different Lorenz curves in Wuerttemberg 1909, where the concentration of income of rentier-capitalists, entrepreneurs, and owners of rental housing is substantially greater than that for workers, in Albert Jeck (1970, p. 242). See p. 244 for a similar picture in Saxony in the year 1900.

45.   In his later *Manuale* Pareto conceded that a change in alpha was possible: ''We cannot assert that the form of the curve would not change if the social constitution were to change radically; if, for example, collectivism were to take the place of the system of private property.'' I cite from Pigou (1920, p. 597).

46.   This latter interesting argument connects the functional distribution of income to investment in human capital and thus could help to explain why skill premia and the functional distribution of income might move in a parallel fashion over time. However, there are other, possibly more powerful arguments to consider, as well. Pigou (1920, p. 699) continues to provide one of the first clear statements of the effect of human capital on earnings distributions:

> Moreover, there is yet another way in which the form of the income curve might be modified. A change in the distribution of training and so forth, that is, *of investment of capital in people*, may take place apart from variations in income from investments. When this happens, the change must tend directly to alter the distribution of earned income, even though original capacities are distributed in accordance with some . . . law of error. (Emphasis added.)

47.   Holtfrerich (1980, pp. 273–74). See also, Grumbach (1957, p. 92). The argument is also developed in Paul Jostock and Albert Ander (1960, pp. 221–22). Thus, the distribution of *types* of assets between wealth classes determined the distribution of losses from hyperinflation. Nevertheless, there were winners in this game as well. If the owners of real assets (purchased with debts which the hyperinflation eliminated) were wealthy persons, too, then the *net* effect of inflationary redistribution of assets could be zero! This is a possibility which has not been sufficiently discussed in the

literature. Moreover, it could be the case that the income data reported by the income tax system is severely biased in periods of inflation. The gainers of real asset transfers during an inflation can be regarded as obtaining important capital gains, a type of income which would not be well reported by those lucky enough to gain and would therefore not be recorded by the income tax officials. Again, if those winners were in the top of the income ladder, only the losses of other top income receivers would be reported but not the gains by others in the top group. Thus the combination of biased income reporting and real asset redistribution to other top income groups could make much of the previously discussed income and wealth distribution during and after the hyperinflation a statistical mirage. Certainly, more work needs to be done to establish the distribution of asset *types* and to assess the importance of the bias due to nonreported capital gains.

48.   Bry and Boschan (1965, see Graph V. Before World War I skill differentials in the building industry in all three countries (Great Britian, the United States, and Germany), but especially in Great Britain, seem to be dominated by custom, as indicated by a more or less long-run constancy of the extent of the differential. Moreover, the twentieth-century decline in the differentials since the beginning of World War I is largely dictated by the influence of the index of the cost of living.

49.   For further documentation see Holtfrerich (1980) and Kocka (1973).

50.   Juergen Kocka, *Klassengesellschaft im Krieg* (1973, p. 96ff).

51.   Apparently independently of M. O. Lorenz's now famous paper (1904/1905). It may be of interest to note that Lorenz was moved to provide his new measure of inequality in criticism of the weaknesses of several contemporary German measurements by J. Wolf and Soetbeer. However, the German confusion concerning which measure of inequality to use was not thereby affected. Lorenz's curve diffuses there a long time after World War I and has no effect at all on the contemporary German debate. It is not even noted in the usual handbooks of policital economy.

52.   Spiethoff (1955). Spiethoff's long waves of economic growth have had an important impact on major historical interpretations of the era of Bismarck, which largely coincides with Spiethoff's "Stockungsspanne" of 1874–1894, the so-called "Grosse Depression" of nineteenth-century Germany.

53.   Hanneman (1980, p. 182). Hanneman reports Gini coefficients of income inequality in Germany for selective years since 1850 and compares them with three measures of economic development, real GNP per capita, energy consumption per capita and the share of labor in mining and industry. In all three cases only Germany indicates elements of the U-shaped development; the high point of inequality being at the turn of the century. Unfortunately, Hanneman reports no details of his sources and methods of calculations of his Gini coefficients, which must, therefore, remain doubtful.

54.   See Mueller/Geisenberger (1972, pp. 142–55). The reader should be cautioned against some of the regressions reported there (esp. p. 142, Eq. 1) because they are good examples of a version of the dummy variable trap in econometrics. Because all the income category shares add up to one, it is not permissible to use all categories, because only n-1 are really independent variables.

55.   See R. H. Tilly (1981).

56.   For a discussion of the introduction of the income tax by German states and the changing tax legislation see Johannes Popitz (1926, pp. 437–91). See also the valuable overview of the different stages of the Prussian income tax system in the nineteenth century and of the significant reforms in 1891 by Adolph Wagner (1891, p. 103ff) who also discusses the problem of underassessment of high incomes. Paul Jostock (1943 I) compared the income tax systems and the probable degree of under-reporting of incomes before World War I in a number of European countries and the United States. This article uses and cites most of the important literature on the subject of tax evasion and fraud in western European countries before World War I.

57.   See Hoffmann *et. al.* (1965, Schaubild 25, p. 170). The graph, it should be noted, is mis-labeled as depicting variables in constant prices, when in fact, they are in current prices.

58.   See the articles "Widersprueche in der preussischen Einkommensteuer-Veranlagung," Vol. XIII, No. 634, 9 Feb. 1895; "Interessantes und Unbegreifliches aus der preussischen Einkommenbe-steuerung," Vol. XXIII, No. 1157, 25 Feb. 1905; "Einkommen und Einkommensteuer in Preussen,"

Vol. XXV, No. 1282, 20 July 1907; ditto, Vol. XXVI, No. 1338, 15 August 1908.

See also Franz Meisel's discussion (1911) of the tax morality and assessment techniques. Like the *Deutsche Oekonomist* Meisel entertained exceeding pessimism concerning the high level of underreporting of incomes after 1891. The *trend* in underreporting in the decades before World War I, however, must have been minimal. At least, this is what the comparison of the previously discussed estimate of national income imply after 1891: the tax-based estimate moves more or less in line with the others.

59. R^2 = .52 between five-year averages of capital's share of income and the ratio of net investment to net national product in current prices, R^2 = .67 between capital's share and the net investment ratio in *constant* (1913) prices. The different results are occasioned by the dramatic rise in the price of investment goods during the founding boom of the empire in the early 1870s. This raises the investment ratio in nominal terms but not in real terms. The data source is Hoffmann (1965, Table 23, p. 87 [as corrected by Jeck, 1970—see Note 76—pp. 123–24] and Table 36, pp. 104–105). A more precise way to test the relationship, but adjusting for a common time trend and for the effect of changes in wholesale prices on the price of investment goods is possible. Changes in capital's share of income can be said to proxy shifts in the savings function, for a rise in capital's share increases savings disproportionately if high income receivers and property owners have high propensities to save. These considerations motivated the following regression of the Net Investment Ratio (taken from Hoffmann 1965, p. 825) on changes in Capital's Share, Time and the Wholesale Price Index (Jacobs/Richter Index as reported in Reinhard Spree 1978, p. 188) for the years 1851 to 1913. The regression results, t-ratios in parentheses below the coefficients, are:

Net InvRatio = −1.28 + .536 deltaCapShare + .138 Time + .097 WS Price
                       (−.62)   (5.00)   (8.67)   (4.93)

R^2 adjusted for degrees of freedom = 57.59

R^2 = 59.64   n = 63

The impact of changes in CapShare on the Investment Ratio is statistically highly significant and when the results are compared to an alternative specification which excludes the role of CapShare, the proportion of the variance of the Investment Ratio which is explained by the model (the R^2) drops considerably, by about 17 percent.

60.   J. G. Williamson (1979) rules it out in the case of the United States.

61.   Following Voltaire's view that "history is a fable agreed upon," Paul A. David and Moses Abramovitz (1973, p. 428) suggest that "Surely any history of an economy's growth will today be no more, and no less than a *parable* agreed upon."

62.   A. Jeck (1968, p. 86). Jeck's subsequent study (1970) focuses upon the ratio of the average incomes of workers to that of the self-employeds, which is not the usual definition of labor's share of income. By his very choice of definitions Jeck side-steps the historically and theoretically important issue of the distribution of income between capital and labor.

63.   Jeck (1968, p. 81).

64.   The classic paper of this topic is by C. E. Ferguson (1968). A more recent textbook treatment can be found in Paul Stoneman (1983; see Ch. 14, "Technical Change and the Distribution of Income").

For initial work in Germany which estimates various aggregate production functions for the period 1850–1913 see Helmut Hesse and Bernhard Gahlen (1965).

On estimating the elasticity of substitution in Germany see Gahlen (1972).

65.   See Stoneman (1983, pp. 4–6, 298–99) for a discussion of the different concepts of technological bias.

66.   The pathbreaking quantitative article in this field is by Peter Lundgreen (1976).

67.   A good exposition of this argument and an application to the Federal Republic of Germany

can be found in Ernst Helmstaedter (1966).

68. Kuczynski also used this index in 1933 as well as in later publications (see 1963, where, however, the index was redefined as the relationship of real wages per industrial worker to the ratio of the index of industrial production per head of population. Here the terms of trade effect is eliminated.

69. In a separate manuscript, ''Urban Inequality in Wilhelmine Germany,'' I investigate possible causes of urban inequality (measured as the share of income of the top 5 percent of income recipients) in 45 cities. The proxy for monopoly gains, city size, provided a statistically significant positive effect on inequality in a multivariate analysis. Thus, the urban level of aggregation seems promising for inequality investigations.

70. See H. Matzerath (1981).

71. W. A. Lewis (1954), and J. C. H. Fei, and G. Ranis (1964).

REFERENCES

Adelman, I., and C. T. Morris (1973), *Economic Growth and Social Equity in Developing Countries.* Stanford.

André, D. (1971), Indikatoren des Technischen Fortschritts, Eine Analyse der Wirtschaftsentwicklung in Deutschland von 1850 bis 1913. Goettingen.

Atkinson, A. B. (1970), ''On the Measurement of Inequality.'' *Journal of Economic Theory*, 2: 244–63.

Bernstein, E. (1898), ''Der Kampf der Socialdemokratie und die Revolution der Gesellschaft.'' *Neue Zeit*, 16/4, (29 Jan.): 548ff.

Bresciani-Turroni, C. (1914), ''Un Des Aspects de L' 'Urbanisme' L'Agglomeration des Richesses.'' *Revue economique internationale.* (March): 480–501.

Bresciani-Turroni, C. (1915), ''Kritische Betrachtungen ueber einige Methoden der Einkommenstatistik.'' *Statistische Monatschrift*, pp. 1–30.

Bresciani-Turroni, C. (1939), ''Annual Survey of Statistical Data: Pareto's Law and the Index of Inequality of Incomes.'' *Econometrica*, 7: 107–133

Bronfenbrenner, M. (1981), Review of Harold Lyall's A Theory of Income Distribution (1975). *Journal of Political Economy*, 89: 611–13.

Bry, G. (1960), *Wages in Germany 1871–1945.* Princeton.

Bry, G., and C. Boschan (1965), ''Secular Trends and Recent Changes in Real Wages and Wage Differentials in Three Western Industrial Countries: The United States, Great Britain and Germany.'' *Second International Conference of Economic History. Aix-en-Provence. 1962.* Paris: Mouton & Co.

Champernowne, D. G. (1973), *Distribution of Income between Persons.* Cambridge: Cambridge University Press.

Chenery, H. B. *et. al.* (1974), *Redistribution with Growth.* London.

Chenery, H. B., and M. Syrquin (1975), *Patterns of Development, 1950–1970.* London: Oxford University Press

Crafts, N. F. R. (1984), ''Patterns of Development in Nineteenth Century Europe.'' *Oxford Economic Papers*, New Series 36: 438–58.

Croon, H. (1968), *Die gesellschaftlichen Auswirkungen des Gemeindewahlrechts in den Gemeinden und Kreisen des Rheinlandes und Westfalens im 19. Jahrhundert.* Koeln.

Dalton, H. (1920), ''The Measurement of the Inequality of Incomes.'' *Economic Journal*, 30: 348–61.

David. P. A., and Th. van de Klundert (1965), ''Biased Efficiency Growth and Capital-Labor Substitution in the U.S., 1899–1960.'' *American Economic Review*, 55: 357–394.

David, P. A., and M. Abramovitz (1973), ''Reinterpreting Economic Growth: Parables and Realities.'' *American Economic Review*, 63: 428–439.

de Meere, J. M. M. (1983), "Long-Term Trends in Income and Wealth Inequality in the Netherlands 1808–1940." *Historical Social Research*, 17: 8–37.

Der Deutsche Oekonomist, (1895–1908).

Fei, J. C. H., and G. Ranis (1964), *Development of the Labor Surplus Economy: Theory and Policy*. Homewood, Ill.

Ferguson, C. E. (1968), "Neoclassical Theory of Technical Progress and Relative Factor Shares." *Southern Economic Journal*, 34: 490–504.

Ferguson, C. E., and Edward J. Nell (1972), "Two Books on the Theory of Income Distribution: A Review Article." *Journal of Economic Literature*, X/2: 437–453.

Fields, G. S. (1980), *Poverty, Inequality, and Development*. Cambridge: Cambridge University Press

Friedmann, A. (1914), "Die Wohlstandsentwicklung in Preussen von 1891–1911." *Jahrbuecher fuer Nationaloekonomie und Statistik*, 103: 1–51.

Gahlen, B. (1965), "Das Wachstum des Nettoinlandprodukts in Deustschland, 1850–1913. Berechnung von makroekonomischen Produktionsfunktionen." *Zeitschrift fuer die gesamte Staatswirtschaft*, 121/3: 352–497.

Goemmel, R. (1979), *Realeinkommen in Deutschland. Ein internationaler Vergleich (1810–1913)*. Nuernberg.

Gorges, I. (1980), *Sozialforschung in Deutschland 1872–1914. Gesellschaftliche Einfluesse auf Themen- und Methodenwahl des Vereins fuer Socialpolitik*. Koenigstein/Ts.: Anton Hain.

Griliches, Z. (1965), Commentary on J. Schmookler, "Technological Change and Economic Theory." *American Economic Review. Papers and Proceedings*, LV: 344.

Grumbach, F. (1957), "Statistische Untersuchungen ueber die Entwicklung der Einkommensverteilung in Deutschland." Unpublished doctoral dissertation, University of Muenster.

Grumbach, F., and H. Koenig (1957 II), "Beschaeftigung und Loehne der deutschen Industriewirtschaft 1888–1954." *Weltwirtschaftliches Archiv*, 79: 125–155.

Hanneman, R. A. (1980), "Income Inequality and Economic Development in Great Britain, Germany, and France; 1850 to 1970." *Comparative Social Research*, 3: 175–184.

Helfferich, C. (1913), *Deutschlands Volkswohlstand 1888–1913*. Berlin: Georg Stilke.

Helmstaedter, E. (1966), "Die Entwicklung der Einkommensverteilung in der Bundesrepublik Deutschland unter Verteilungstheoretischem Aspekt 1950–1965." *Jahrbuecher fuer National-oekonomie und Statistik*, 179: 389–417.

Hentschel, V. (1978), *Wirtschaft und Wirtschaftspolitik im wilhelminischen Deutschland*. Stuttgart.

Hentschel, V. (1979), "Erwerbs- und Einkommensverhaeltnisse in Sachsen, Baden und Wuerttemberg vor dem ersten Weltkrieg (1890–1914)." *Vierteljahrschrift fuer Sozial- und Wirtschaftsgeschichte*, 66: 26–73.

Hesse, H., and B. Gahlen. (1972), *Der Informationsgehalt der Neoklassischen Wachstumstheorie fuer die Wirtschaftspolitik*. Tuebingen.

Hirschman, A. O., and Michael Rothschild (1973), "The Changing Tolerance for Income Inequality in the Course of Economic Development." *Quarterly Journal of Economics*, LXXXVII: 544–566.

Hoffmann, W. G., and J. H. Mueller (1959), *Das Deutsche Volkseinkommen 1851–1957*. Tuebingen: J. C. B. Mohr (Paul Siebeck).

Hoffmann, W. G. et. al. (1965), *Das Wachstum der Deutschen Wirtschaft seit der Mitte des 19. Jahrhunderts*. Heidelberg: Springer.

Hoffmann, W. G. (1967), "Die Entwicklung von Kapitalkoeffizient und Lohnquote." *Jahrbuecher fuer Nationaloekonomie und Statistik*, 180: 179–210.

Hoffmann, W. (1964), *Die Bielefelder Stadtverordneten*. Luebeck.

Holtfrerich, C.-L. (1980), *Die deutsche Inflation 1914–1924*. Berlin.

Jeck, A. (1968), "The Trends of Income Distribution in West Germany." In J. Marchal and B. Ducros (eds.), *The Distribution of National Income*. London.

Jeck, A. (1970), *Wachstum und Verteilung des Volkseinkommens*. Tuebingen: J. C. B. Mohr (Paul Siebeck).

Jostock, P. (1943), "Ueber den Umfang des der Besteuerung entgehenden Einkommens. Ein Beitrag zur Volkseinkommenstatistik." *Weltwirtschaftliches Archiv*, 57: 27–80.

Jostock, P., and A. Ander (1960), "Konzentration der Einkommen und Vermoegen." In H. Arndt (ed.), *Die Konzentration in der Wirtschaft. Erster Band*. Berlin.

Kaelble, H. (1983), *Industrialisierung und soziale Ungleichheit. Europa im 19. Jahrhundert-Eine Bilanz*. Goettingen.

Kaeble, H., and H. Volkmann (1986), "Streiks und Einkommensverteilung im spaeten Kaiserreich." In J. Bergmann *et. al., Arbeit, Mobiltaet, Partizipation, Protest*. Opladen.

Kakwani, N. C. (1980), *Income Inequality and Poverty. Methods of Estimation and Policy Analysis*. New York: Oxford University Press.

Kalecki, M. (1938), "The Determinants of Distribution of the National Income." *Econometrica*, 6: 97ff.

Kautsky, K., and Bruno Schoenlank (1892), *Grundsaetze und Forderungen der Sozialdemokratie. Erlaeuterungen zum Erfurter Programm*. Berlin.

Kocka, J. (1973), *Klassengesellschaft im Krieg. Deutsche Sozialgeschichte 1914-1918*. Goettingen: Vandenhoeck & Ruprecht.

Kraus, F. (1981), "The Historical Development of Income Inequality in Western Europe and the United States." In P. Flora and A. J. Heidenheimer (eds.), *The Development of Welfare States in Europe and America*. New Brunswick.

Kuczynski, J. (1931), "Der Anteil des deutschen Industriearbeiters am Sozialprodukt—zum Problem der relativen Verelendung." *Koelner Sozialpolitische Vierteljahresschrift*, X/1: 85–95.

Kuczynski, J. (1933), *Loehne und Konjunktur in Deutschland 1887-1932*. Berlin.

Kuczynski, J. (1963), *Geschichte der Lage der Arbeiter in Deutschland* Vol. 13. Berlin-East.

Kuznets, S. (1955), "Economic Growth and Income Inequality." *American Economic Review*, 45: 1–28.

Kuznets, S. (1963), "Quantitative Aspects of the Economic Growth of Nations, III: Distribution of Income by Size." *Economic Development and Cultural Change*, 11: 1–80.

Lee, J. J. (1978), "Labour in German Industrialization." In Peter Mathias and M. M. Postan (eds.) *The Cambridge Economic History of Europe. Volume VII. The Industrial Economies. Capital, Labour, and Enterprise. Part I*. Cambridge: Cambridge University Press.

Lewis, W. A. (1954), "Economic Development with Unlimited Supplies of Labour." *Manchester Sch. Econ. Soc. Stud.*, 22: 139–91.

Lindert, P. H., and J. G. Williamson (1976), "Three Centuries of American Inequality." *Research in Economic History*, 1: 69–123.

Lindert, P. H. (1978), *Fertility and Scarcity in America*. Princeton: Princeton University Press.

Lindert, P. H., and J. G. Williamson (1983), "Reinterpreting Britain's Social Tables, 1688-1913." *Explorations in Economic History*, 20: 94–109.

Lorenz, M. O. (1904/1905), "Methods of Measuring the Concentration of Wealth." *Publications of the American Statistical Association*, IX, (1904-1905): 209–219.

Lundgreen, P. (1976), "Educational Expansion and Economic Growth in Nineteenth-Century Germany: A Quantitative Study." In L. Stone (ed.), *Schooling and Society. Studies in the History of Education*. Baltimore.

Matzerath, H. (1981), "The Influence of Industrialization on Urban Growth in Prussia (1815-1914)." In H. Schmal (ed.), *Patterns of European Urbanisation since 1500*. London.

Meisel, F. (1911), "Moral und Technik bei der Veranlagung der preussischen Einkommensteuer." In G. Schmoller (ed.), *Jahrbuch fuer Gesetzgebung, Verwaltung und Volkswirtschaft im Deutschen Reich*. 35: 285–373.

Meyers Grosses Konversations-Lexikon (1905) 7: 517. Leipzig a. Vienna. Article "Geldherrschaft."

Mueller, J. H., and S. Geisenberger (1972), *Die Einkommenstruktur in verschiedenen deutschen Laendern, 1874-1814*. Berlin.

Nell, E. (1972); see Ferguson and Nell.

Neumann, F. J. (1892), "Zur Lehre von den Lohngesetzen. VII. 3. Die Steigerung des Gegensatzes von Arm und Reich in Preussen bis 1848." *Jahrbuecher fuer Nationaloekonomie und Statistik*, 3rd. Ser., Vol. 4: 366–397.

Nitschke, K. (1902), *Einkommen und Vermoegen in Preussen und ihre Entwicklung seit Einfuehrung der neuen Steuern mit Nutzanwendung auf die Theorie der Einkommensverteilung.* Jena: G. Fischer.

Pareto, V. (1897), *Cours d'economique politique*, Vol. 2. Lausanne.

Paukert, F. (1973), "Income Distribution at Different Levels of Development: A Survey of the Evidence." *International Labour Review*, 108: 97–125.

Perkins, J. A. (1981), "The Agricultural Revolution in Germany, 1850–1913." *Journal of European Economic History*, 10/1: 71–118.

Perls, K. (1911), *Die Einkommen-Entwicklung in Preussen seit 1896 nebst Kritik an Material und Methoden.* Berlin.

Phelps Brown, E. H., and M. H. Browne (1968), *A Century of Pay. The Course of Pay and Production in France, Germany, Sweden, the United Kingdom, and the United States of America, 1860-1960.* London.

Pigou, A. C. (1920), *The Economics of Welfare.* London: Macmillan.

Popitz, J. (1926), "Einkommensteuer. B. Geschichte und geltendes Recht." In L. Elster, *et. al., Handwoerterbuch der Staatswissenschaften*, Vol. 3. Jena (4th ed.), pp. 437–91.

Procopovitch. S. N. (1926), "The Distribution of National Income." *Economic Journal*, 36: 69–82.

Pryor, F. L. (1968), *Public Expenditures in Communist and Capitalist Countries.* Homewood, Ill.

Reder, M. W. (1962), "Wage Structure Theory and Measurement." In National Bureau of Economic Research, *Aspects of Labor Economics. A Conference of the Universities-National Bureau Committee for Economic Research* (NBER Special Conference Series 14). Princeton: Princeton University Press.

Robinson, S. (1976), "A Note on the U Hypothesis Relating Income Inequality and Economic Development." *American Economic Review*, 66: 437–40.

Rosen, S. (1977), "Human Capital: Relations Between Education and Earnings." In Michael D. Intriligator (ed.), *Frontiers of Quantitative Economics*, IIIB. Amsterdam: North Holland, pp. 731–53.

Schmoller, G. (1873), Address to the First Meeting of the Verein fuer Socialpolitik. *Schriften des Vereins fuer Socialpolitik*, Vol. I, Leipzig.

Schmoller, G. (1895), "Die Einkommensverteilung in alter und neuer Zeit." *Jahrbuch fuer Gesetzgebung, Verwaltung und Volkswirtschaft*, 19: 1067ff.

Schmoller, G. (1897), "Was verstehen wir unter dem Mittelstande?" *Verhandlungen des 8. Evangelisch-sozialen Kongress abgehalten am 10. und 11. Juni 1897 in Goettingen.* Goettingen.

Schmoller, G. (1904), *Grundriss der allgemeinen Volkswirtschaftslehre. Zweiter Teil.* Leipzig: Duncker & Humblot.

Soltow, L. (1868), "Long-Run Changes in British Income Inequality." *Economic History Review*, 21: 17–29.

Sombart, W. (1921), *Die Deutsche Volkswirtschaft im Neunzehnten Jahrhundert.* Berlin (5 ed.).

Spiethoff, A. (1955), *Die wirschaftlichen Wechsellagen. Aufschwung. Krise, Stockung. Bd. 1: Beschreibende Erklaerung.* Tuebingen. Reprint of the article "Krisen." In *Handwoerterbuch der Staatswissenschaften*, Vol. 4 (1923).

Spree, R. (1978), *Wachstumstrends und Konjunkturzklen in der deutschen Wirtschaft von 1820 bis 1913.* Goettingen.

Stoneman, P. (1983), *The Economic Analysis of Technological Change.* Oxford.

Taussig, F. (1924), *Principles of Economics*, II. (3rd ed. revised). New York.

Tilly, R. H. (1981), "The Take-Off in Germany." In E. Angermann (ed.), *Oceans Apart. Comparing Germany and the United States.* Stuttgart.

Timm, H. (1961), "Das Gesetz der wachsenden Staatsausgaben." *Finanzarchiv* N. F. 21: 201–47.

Tucker, R. S. (1938), "The Distribution of Income among Income Taxpayers in the United States, 1863-1935," *Quarterly Journal of Economics*, 52: 547–87.

von Zedlitz-Neukirch (1902), "Review of Nitschke." *Zeitschrift fuer Socialwissenschaft*, V/10: 835–36.

Wagner, A. (1891), "Die Reform der direkten Staatsbesteuerung in Preussen im Jahre 1891." *Finanz-Archiv*, 8: 71–330.

Wagner, A. (1893), *Grundlagen der Volkswirtschaft*, I/1, 3rd ed.

Wagner, A. (1907), *Theoretische Sozialoekonomik oder Allgemeine und Theoretische Volkswirtschaftslehre*. Leipzig: C. F. Winter.

Wehler, H.-U. (1973), *Das Deutsche Kaiserreich 1871-1918*. Goettingen.

Williamson, J. G. (1979), "Inequality, Accumulation and Technological Imbalance: A Growth-Equity Conflict in American History?" *Economic Development and Cultural Change*, 27(2): 231–54.

Williamson, J. G., and P. H. Lindert (1980), *American Inequality. A Macroeconomic History*. New York: Academic Press.

Williamson, J. G. (1982), "The Structure of Pay in Britain, 1710–1911." *Research in Economic History*, 7: 1–54.

Williamson, J. G. (1985), *Did British Capitalism Breed Inequality?* London: Allen a. Unwin.

Wolf, J. (1898), "Illusionisten und Realisten in der Nationaloekonomie, I, II, III, IV, V, VI." *Zeitschrift fuer Socialwissenschaft*, I: 4ff, 89ff, 249ff, 352ff, 407ff.

BANK FAILURES, INTEREST RATES, AND THE GREAT CURRENCY OUTFLOW IN THE UNITED STATES, 1929–1933

Paul B. Trescott

ABSTRACT

The large withdrawal of currency from the U.S. banking system in 1930–1933 exerted a strong deflationary effect on the economy. In this study, regressions are estimated for individual Federal Reserve districts and selected combinations to evaluate the relative influence of bank failures and interest rates. Bank failures are shown to be the predominant cause of the currency outflow, while interest rates had no statistically significant effect. The study also stresses that Federal Reserve note withdrawal was concentrated in the urban northeast portion of the country.

Research in Economic History, Volume 11, pages 49–80.
Copyright © 1988 by JAI Press Inc.
All rights of reproduction in any form reserved.
ISBN: 0-89232-677-8

I.

One of the central elements in the banking panic of 1930–1933 in the United States was the great drain of currency out of the banking system. Currency in circulation increased from about $3.6 billion in October 1930, to about $5.6 billion in February 1933.[1] From 1929 to 1933, nominal GNP fell by about half of its 1929 value, so average currency in circulation rose from about 3.75 percent of GNP in 1929 to 9.04 percent in 1933.

This currency drain exerted strong downward pressure on bank reserves and thus contributed to the decline in the supply of money and bank credit. The net effect of the currency outflow depended, of course, on the extent to which it was counteracted by Federal Reserve defensive open-market operations. These actions, which were relatively complete in 1924–1929, continued to be substantial in 1930, but from 1931 on became increasingly inadequate to prevent bank reserves from declining.[2]

Since falling prices and declining real incomes would have reduced desired holdings of currency, explanations of the increase in currency have stressed two other factors. The one which received the most attention from contemporary observers was the great volume of bank failures which occurred in 1930–1933. Deposits of suspended banks, 1930–1933, were estimated to total $6.8 billions, reflecting the distress closing of about 9,000 banks.[3] More recent studies, however, have suggested that some rise in currency demand resulted from the drastic decline in interest rates, particularly those on bank deposits.

The relative roles of these two variables are quite crucial to one's interpretation of the role of money supply as a cause of the great contraction of income. If the currency outflow reflected primarily a response to bank failures, the way is open for stressing money supply reduction as a relatively exogenous force in the decline. Contrariwise, if interest rates were a large factor in the currency outflow, this would support a view in which monetary contraction was a relatively endogenous response to relatively exogenous decline in spending. Temin, for instance, stresses the notion that spending decreases led to the decline in interest rates, and that with an interest-elastic money supply function, the actual stock of money declined as a passive adjustment.[4]

The present study attempts to clarify the relative roles of interest rates and bank failures by examining monthly data for 1929–1933 on the volume of Federal Reserve notes outstanding from each of the 12 Reserve banks. Our results show that detailed response differed in different regions of the county to such an extent that national aggregation is questionable. In the disaggregated estimates, despite such differences, the role of interest rates is shown to be at best rather minor and, in a number of areas, practically nonexistent.

While local bank failures had a significant positive effect on currency withdrawals in most regions, the proportional size of the response differed substantially between regions. As a result, while bank failures were widely dispersed around the country, the bulk of currency drain was concentrated in the urban, industrial Northeast. This regional pattern is important in interpreting the relative importance of various well-publicized bank failures, such as those associated with Caldwell and Company in 1930.

II. PREVIOUS STUDIES

A number of studies have explored these matters quantitatively. Cagan estimated a single regression equation which estimated the ratio of currency to total commercial bank deposits for the period 1919–1955 (annual data) as a function of the rate of return on deposits, real permanent income per capita, and the ratio of personal taxes to income.[5] In estimating the deposit rate, Cagan included interest paid on demand and time deposits, and deducted service changes and an allowance for expected deposit loss through bank failure. The last element was calculated by applying the permanent income formula to current and recent ratios of depositor loss to total deposits.

Using Cagan's data, the present author reestimated his regression for the time periods 1919–1955, 1919–1933, and 1934–1955. One set of estimates retained Cagan's deposit rate adjusted for expected loss. Another set used the deposit rate with no allowance for expected loss. In either form, the regressions displayed significant instability, according to a simple Chow test. And for the crucial 1919–1933 period, the estimate which incorporated deposit loss fit *less* well than the estimate which ignored deposit loss. We must conclude that Cagan's specification does not capture the impact of bank failures on currency.

In a simultaneous equations study, Anderson and Butkiewicz (AB) estimated the currency ratio as an element entering the supply functions for both M1 and M2.[6] Using a Koyck formulation on quarterly data for 1921 III through 1933 I, they estimated the ratio of currency to M1 and M2 as a function of nominal income, interest rates, and bank failures. Aside from the lagged dependent variable, only the bank failure variable was significant for M1 and M2. The percentage of banks failing was more significant in explaining Cu/M1, and the percentage of failed deposits to total deposits was more significant in explaining Cu/M2.

Boughton and Wicker (BW) provided separate estimates for currency and for demand deposits, in addition to estimates explaining their ratio.[7] BW used a Koyck formulation with monthly data for the period January 1921 through June 1936. They explained the level of the log of the real (domestic) currency stock (CU/P) by the log of department store sales (also deflated by prices), by the number of bank failures, and by the interest rate on demand deposits, the latter measured by a new series compiled by the authors from data of the New York Clearing House. The authors tested measures of the dollar volume of bank failures, but found them inferior to the number of failures. Of the three determinants, the demand-deposit interest rate had the largest significance (t = 3.21) with the expected negative sign. The bank failure variable was marginally significant but quite small, and the transactions variable positive but of quite marginal significance (t = 1.54). By simulation over the panic period, the authors concluded that the fall in interest rates contributed more to the rise in the currency ratio 1930–1933 than did bank failures.

The BW results imply a relatively large elasticity of demand (about –0.5) for currency with respect to the rate of return on demand deposits. Noting this contrasts with postwar studies finding small interest elasticities, BW concluded "This conflict appears to be explained by the fact that prior to June 1933 banks made explicit interest payments on medium and large demand deposit accounts."[8]

However, as I have shown elsewhere, the BW results, like Cagan's, are marred by instability. A series of Chow tests isolated the period July 1924–February 1933 as a relatively stable core, differing significantly from both previous and subsequent periods. For the 1924–1933 period, regressions using the BW data and specification showed that interest rates had no significant effect on currency, while the impact of bank failures was much larger and more significant than the original BW estimates indicated.[9]

A related study, though it does not deal explicitly with currency, is that of Gandolfi.[10] He estimated cross-section regressions to explain the state-by-state holdings of (real) commercial bank deposits for each year 1929–1933. He concluded that the significant determinants were real permanent income per capita, the rate of return on deposits, and deposits involved in bank failures. Explicit stability tests were consistent with the hypothesis of a single uniform demand function explaining all of the five years.

These studies leave many issues unsettled, to which the present study is directed. They may be summarized as follows:

1.   The studies here reviewed do not explicitly explain the nominal level of currency held. Cagan and AB deal only with currency ratios, while BW deal only with "real" currency. Restricting estimates to the ratio assumes both currency and deposits adjust with the same speed to their determinants. In fact, currency in circulation always reflects the quantity demanded. But demand deposits are subject to significant disturbances arising from the supply side. These may be resolved in a period of less than a year, as Gandolfi's results imply, but in a period as disturbed as 1930–1933, one can hardly assume they were resolved in a month or a quarter.

The present study directly estimates the volume of nominal currency. The price level is included as one of the exogenous variables.

2.   The studies mentioned, with the exception of Gandolfi, do not apply explicit stability tests. Both the Cagan and BW results prove unacceptable because of instability. AB did use the consideration of stability as their reason for terminating their study with 1933, but did not test whether the estimates

for 1931–1933 were stable.

Considering the violent upheaval in the monetary system in 1930–1933, explicit test of stability seems essential. Further, it can be asserted that the relation of currency outflow to bank failures was quite different in 1933 than in 1930–1932. Figure 1a provides the basis for this assertion. In 1930–1932, currency drain came after bank failure, and when the rate of bank failure slackened off in 1932, currency was actually flowing back into the banks. The currency avalanche of February–March 1933, however, was all out of proportion to the bank failures experienced up to March 4. In large degree, currency withdrawals in early 1933 were a response to the widespread declaration of bank "holidays" by individual state governments, a process not reflected in the bank failure data. The closing of the banks by presidential decree in March 1933 was a totally different process from the closing of individual banks by banking regulatory agencies over the previous years.[11] Instead of precipitating a currency outflow, the presidential bank holiday put an end to the currency panic. Thus the response of currency to

Figure 1a.   Total currency in circulation, Federal Reserve notes outstanding, and cumulative deposits of failed banks, monthly, 1929–1933.

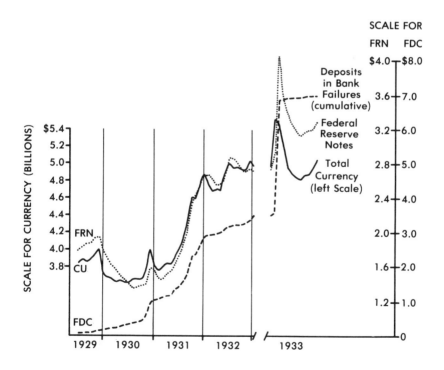

current and lagged bank closings was dramatically different in 1933 from the preceding years.

The present study is confined to the emergency period and the months immediately preceding it. Emphasis is on estimates of change in currency outstanding for 12-month periods beginning with the 12 months ending in July 1930 and ending with the 12 months ending January 1933.[12] All of the variant forms of the estimating equations are also estimated for shorter periods and those are used for explicit stability tests.

3.   The existing studies all make rather strong prior assumptions about the form of lagged relations. Cagan and Gandolfi rely on the specific lag form implied in the calculation of "permanent income," and Cagan imposes that same form on his estimate of the "expected loss" on deposits. Both BW and AB use the Koyck form of estimation. This presupposes that all the independent variables operate with the same lag, and restricts the form of the lag to involve geometrically declining weights.

The first difference specification used here is itself a method of incorporating lagged information. In addition, we use polynomial distributed lags to estimate the influence of bank failures, scale variables, and in some cases, interest rates. The lag pattern for bank failures emerges as remarkably uniform for all areas, and is not consistent with a Koyck approach.

4.   The existing studies are all on a nationally aggregated basis. The present study proceeds on a decentralized basis, with estimates for individual Federal Reserve districts and, in some cases, aggregations of a few contiguous districts. These capture a number of important regional variations in currency behavior. A number of the basic regression equations were used to generate pooled regressions for the entire country. In every case, the pooled estimates raised estimating error so much that the validity of pooling was decisively rejected.

5.   The empirical studies cited misspecify the form of the relationship between bank failures and currency. They treat the level of currency (or its ratio with deposits, which also involves levels) as a function of the current number of dollar value of bank failures. However, a much better relation appears if we relate the level of currency to the cumulative bank failures in the crisis, and relate the change in currency to the change in this cumulative amount. Figure 1 shows the visual evidence for this specification. Figure 1a compares the levels of total currency and Federal Reserve notes outstanding each month with the cumulative dollar volume of bank failures, beginning with July 1929. Figure 1b shows the 12-month first differences of these series. The conformity is particularly striking or the first differences, and this is the basis for the specification used in this study.

What is the economic logic of this approach? Most of the previous studies have stressed the precautionary response: currency was withdrawn because the level of past bank failures acted on depositors' expectations of further failures to come.[13] Clearly this outlook would not explain why currency remained so high

Figure 1b.   Twelve-month first differences of currency in circulation, Federal Reserve notes outstanding, and cumulative deposits in failed banks, 1929–1933.

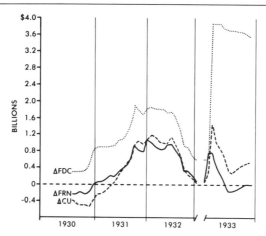

after 1933, when the risk of further deposit loss was reduced effectively to zero. We need also to take account of the enormous reduction in the number of bank offices in the country. The decline was very extreme—from 28,323 offices in 1929 to 17,236 in 1933. Reopenings brought the total up to a near-constant level of roughly 18,400 in 1934–1936.[14]

It seems plausible that the currency drain in 1930–1932 reflected a shifting combination of precautionary response and facility loss. The lag pattern in the influence of bank failures supports the existence of a two-part process. The forced bank closings of early 1933 added greatly to the facility loss, but the circumstances of bank reopenings, including the coming of deposit insurance, removed the precautionary motive for further withdrawals.

6.   Most of the empirical studies cited follow the widespread econometric practice of concentrating on the "one best equation." This concentration often involves treating the regression coefficients of the "best equation" as relatively accurate measures of the underlying function. Yet the "best equation" has often been generated by an extensive search process in which the investigator has run a great many other regressions, results of which are referred to only incidentally, if at all. What is often missing is a sense of how sensitive the results are to changes in specification.[15]

One purpose of the present study is to estimate regressions in the same form for a variety of geographic areas. However, we have also estimated the regressions for each area using a large number of alternative specifications. While we can't resist the lure of the "best equation" (see Table 4), generalizations about the size, signs, and significance of regression coefficients are based on a large number of regressions.

III. BEHAVIOR OF FEDERAL RESERVE NOTES
IN TIME AND SPACE

The current study relies on regression estimates of the demand for Federal Reserve notes (FRN), using monthly data for individual Federal Reserve districts (and selected combinations). For the national economy, there is a very high correlation between levels of total currency and Federal Reserve notes, (shown in Figure 1a) and between first differences of the two (shown in Figure 1b).[16] Almost all the dollar change in currency outstanding was concentrated on Federal Reserve notes. As a result, the share of FRN in total currency increased substantially. Consequently, *proportional* changes in total currency are not accurately reflected in Federal Reserve notes, and it would be inappropriate to use a logarithmic form for FRN.[17]

Our original regressions were estimated using each of the 12 Federal Reserve districts as a separate unit. However, there is no reason why banks in one district could not draw currency from another district. Therefore, we experimented with a large number of possible combinations of contiguous districts. On the basis of statistical considerations, we decided to combine districts 1, 2, and 3 into one unit, and to combine districts 8, 10, and 12 into another unit. The first aggregation is easy to defend a priori, as it combines Boston, New York, and Philadelphia districts. The resulting combination is still geographically compact and logically focuses on the New York financial center. The other combination involves St. Louis, Kansas City, and San Francisco. These form a continuum stretching from St. Louis to the Pacific (see map). Detailed statistical justification for these aggregations is presented in the appendix.

Figure 2 shows the time pattern of the rates of change of Federal Reserve notes in the eight regions for which our regressions are presented. The four smaller districts in the upper panel show substantial diversity, but the larger districts in the lower panel are much more nearly uniform. Table A3 in the Appendix shows the correlation matrix for these rates of change. The unweighted average correlation coefficient over the 28 pairs is only .739.

Some of the difference in currency expansion among districts reflects difference in the regional incidence of bank failure. The Chicago District (#7) had by far the largest dollar volume of failed deposits between July 1929, and January 1933, and witnessed also the largest increase in Federal Reserve notes. However, as our regression results demonstrate, the volume of Federal Reserve notes withdrawn per dollar of bank failure also showed wide diversity from district to district.

The data in Table 1 illustrate disparities between the incidence of bank failure and the local increase in Federal Reserve notes. The percentage data on the right show the ratio of deposits in failed banks to the 1929 volume of total commercial bank deposits. In most districts, failed deposits exceeded 1 percent of the 1929 total in each year 1930, 1931, and 1932.

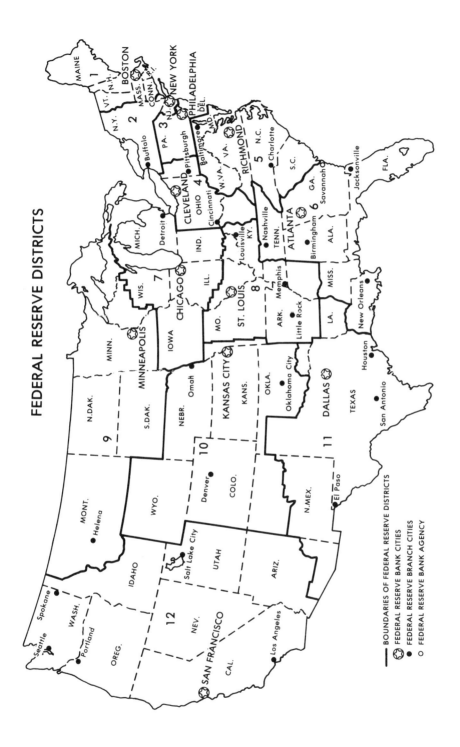

FEDERAL RESERVE DISTRICTS

BOUNDARIES OF FEDERAL RESERVE DISTRICTS

⊛ FEDERAL RESERVE BANK CITIES

● FEDERAL RESERVE BRANCH CITIES

○ FEDERAL RESERVE BANK AGENCY

Table 1. Bank Deposits, Bank Failures, and Change in Federal Reserve Notes By Federal Reserve District, 1929–1932 (dollar figures in millions)

District	Commercial Bank Deposits, June 1929 (BD)	Deposits of Banks Failing in 12 mo. ending Dec. (FD)				Change in Federal Reserve Notes, 12 mo. ending Dec. (Δ FRN)				FD as percent of BD			
		1930	1931	1932	Total	1930	1931	1932	Total	1930	1931	1932	Total
1. Boston	$ 3,327	$ 39	$ 121	$ 72	$ 232	$ -77	$ 42	$ 23	$ -12	1.2%	3.6%	2.2%	7.0%
2. New York	13,720	190	152	10	352	14	202	45	261	1.4	1.1	0.1	2.0
3. Phila.	3,561	61	193	25	279	-30	138	-34	74	1.7	5.4	0.7	7.8
4. Cleveland	4,397	42	497	-25	514	4	125	-35	94	1.0	11.3	-0.6	11.7
5. Richmond	2,175	86	122	41	249	-1	5	1	5	4.0	5.6	1.9	11.5
6. Atlanta	1,699	95	51	22	168	-19	-7	-24	-50	5.6	3.0	1.3	9.9
7. Chicago	8,035	113	450	230	793	-172	371	168	367	1.4	5.6	2.9	9.9
8. St. Louis	2,044	202	46	46	294	-9	2	16	9	9.9	2.3	2.3	14.5
9. Minn.	1,636	29	68	27	124	-15	17	13	15	1.8	4.2	1.7	7.7
10. K.C.	2,142	35	59	37	131	-20	14	9	3	1.6	2.8	1.7	6.1
11. Dallas	1,278	18	50	7	75	-16	16	-10	-10	1.5	3.9	0.5	5.9
12. S.F.	4,587	16	62	107	185	-17	53	2	38	0.3	1.4	2.3	4.0
Total	48,601	926	1,871	599	3,396	-358	978	174	794	1.9	3.8	1.2	6.9
1+2+3	20,608	290	466	107	863	-93	382	34	323	1.4	2.3	0.5	4.2
8+10+12	8,773	253	167	190	610	-46	69	27	50	2.9	1.9	2.2	7.0
2+7	21,755	303	602	240	1,145	-158	573	213	628	1.4	2.8	1.1	5.3

Sources:
Current issues of *Federal Reserve Bulletin*. Deposit data (BD) combine member-bank totals from *Banking and Monetary Statistics* (Washington: Board of Governers, Federal Reserve System, 1943) with non-member bank data from the *Bulletin*. Since the latter include mutual savings banks, estimates of MSB, derived from the state-by-state totals in *Banking and Monetary Statistics*, were deducted. Deposit data include interbank and government deposits.

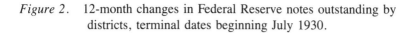

Figure 2.   12-month changes in Federal Reserve notes outstanding by
districts, terminal dates beginning July 1930.

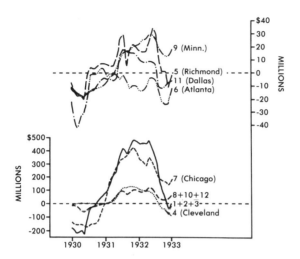

The three western districts (Kansas City, Dallas, and San Francisco) ranked
below average in the proportional incidence of bank failures, and also contributed
little to the currency drain. But Richmond, Atlanta, and St. Louis, each of which
was relatively hard hit by bank failures, sustained as a group a *decrease* in note
circulation. The three northeast districts focusing on New York, plus Cleveland
and Chicago, essentially accounted for all the increase in Federal Reserve notes
over the period 1930–1932 combined.

IV. SPECIFICATION OF REGRESSION ESTIMATES

We have estimated regression equations for each Federal Reserve district or
combination using many permutations and combinations of a small number of
variables. The dependent variable is the 12-month change in Federal Reserve
notes (FRN) outstanding in the district. For each district, this variable is scaled
by the level of commercial bank deposits for June 1929 (first column in Table 1.)
The purpose of this scaling was to make the regression coefficients relatively
comparable from district to district (particularly for experimenting with pooled
estimates) and to give us a dependent variable which is a pure number. Since the
scaling is done by a constant, it does not affect the goodness of fit of the
regressions nor the standard errors of individual coefficients. Using monthly data,
principal regressions were estimated for dependent-variable values July 1930–
January 1933. Estimates for subperiods July 1930–March 1932 and April 1931–
January 1933 were used to test for stability.

The independent variables used were as follows:

1.   The dollar volume of bank failures (FDC) for the particular district.[18] These were cumulated from July 1929, and then the cumulative total was differenced to obtain 12-month rates of change. These differences were scaled by the same district deposit total used for the dependent variable. Thus the regression coefficients on the bank failure variable can be interpreted as dollar-for-dollar impacts. The bank failures variable was incorporated using a second degree polynomial applied to current and 11 lagged monthly observations.

2.   Two series on interest rates, both treated as uniform across district lines. We used the data on the commercial paper rate and the estimated rate on demand deposits used by BW and kindly supplied by Professor Wicker. We experimented with a number of ways of incorporating interest rates, including polynomial distributed lags and simpler unconstrained forms.

3.   Two alternative scale variables were used. One was the dollar value of department store sales, which BW also used. (Our study uses the non-seasonally adjusted data).[19] This is a national aggregate, the same for all districts. The other was bank debits, for which monthly data were available by districts. Whichever scale variable was used, we based the estimates on the 12-month first difference in the logarithm, used to derive a second degree polynomial distributed lag with current and 14 lagged monthly observations.

4.   We included the same price index used by BW, taking the 12-month first difference of its logarithm. Since our regressions typically included two other current-dollar variables (the scale variable and dollar volume of failed deposits), this way of entering the price level tested whether price changes were already adequately accounted for by those other two variables.

5.   A set of regressions were estimated including a term (FRNO) for Federal Reserve notes of other districts. We used the 12-month first difference in dollar value, with no lag allowed for. This variable tested the degree to which currency withdrawal responded to national, rather than regional influences.

Regressions using Almon-lag specifications for interest rates fit very well but were otherwise poorly specified. The interest rate coefficients were overwhelmingly positive and many of the estimates were unstable. These estimates will receive relatively little attention.

The remaining equations either included a simple 12-month first difference (lagged one month) of one or both interest rates, or omitted both. A general formula for these regressions is as follows:

$$\frac{FRN_t^g - FRN_{t-12}^g}{BD^g} = \frac{\sum_{t-12}^{t} \alpha_t^g (FDC_t^g - FDC_{t-12}^g)}{BD^g} \tag{1}$$

$$+ \sum_{t-15}^{t} \beta_t^g (\ln SCALE_t^g - \ln SCALE_{t-12}^g)$$

$$+ \gamma^g (\ln P - \ln P_{t-12})$$

$$+ \delta^g \quad (FRNO_{gt} - FRNO^g_{t-12})$$

$$+ \Theta^g_1 \quad (CPR_{t-1} - CPR_{t-13})$$

$$+ \Theta^g_2 \quad (DDR_{t-1} - DDR_{t-13})$$

$$+ \quad constant$$

In this formula, SCALE is represented in the regressions by either bank debits or department store sales. The superscript g refers to the region being estimated. Table 3a shows which variables are included in each specification.

Before examining results for individual districts, we present estimates for Eq. 1–7 estimated for the national economy as a whole, using total currency (not seasonally adjusted) as the dependent variable, and of course, excluding the FRNO variable. Results are shown in Table 2. The estimates fit well, with $\bar{R}^2$ values approximating 0.97 for Eq. 1–6. All equations are stable when

Table 2. Regressions Explaining Change in Total Currency, U.S., 1930–1933[a]

Equation:	1	2	3	4	5	6	7
Regressor:							
CPR	−.0018	−.0010	x	x	x	x	x
	(2.01)	(0.89)					
DDR	−.0016	−.0031	−.0034	−.0042	x	x	x
	(.85)	(1.54)	(1.87)	(2.52)			
ΣFailed							
Deposits	1.024	1.106	.769	.888	.508	.528	.699
	(5.00)	(3.40)	(4.47)	(4.19)	(4.79)	(3.03)	(13.19)
ΣScale	.008D	.005S	−.007D	−.014S	−.024D	−.051S	x
	(0.35)	(0.10)	(0.30)	(0.33)	(1.09)	(1.13)	
Price							
Level	.104	.118	.074	.089	.031	.025	.005
	(2.40)	(2.33)	(1.71)	(2.32)	(0.80)	(0.78)	(0.21)
Constant	−.0055	−.0067	−.0055	−.0068	−.0054	−.0066	−.0079
	(3.41)	(4.29)	(3.21)	(4.41)	(2.99)	(3.84)	(4.95)
$\bar{R}^2$	.9736	.9739	.9699	.9742	.9666	.9682	.9479
DW	1.64	1.83	1.75	1.90	1.76	1.70	1.07

The 12 individual regression coefficients for failed deposits for equation 4 are shown in Table 7.
Notes:
CPR: Commercial paper rate
DDR: Demand deposit rate
  x: variable omitted
  a: t-ratios in parentheses
  D: bank debits
  S: department store sales

compared with the sub-periods. From Eq. 1–4, one can infer a modest but significant negative influence for interest rates. The best fitting equation, #4, implies an interest elasticity of about −0.33. However, there is little loss of fit if interest rates are excluded. When we examine the district and regional estimates we find less apparent interest rate influence. The disparity may arise because of aggregation bias, or because of discrepancies between behavior of Federal Reserve notes and other currency.

In the nationwide estimates, bank failures have a strong positive influence on balance. When we examine the 12 lag coefficients for the seven equations, we find that all for the first five months are positive and all but one have t-ratios above 1.75. By the seventh month most coefficients are negative. However, of 29 negative coefficients, only four are significant. The lag pattern for Eq. 4 is compared with the district and region estimates in Table 7 below. Although the general shape is similar, it appears that the nationwide estimates distort somewhat the timing pattern shown in the disaggregated estimates. For the nationwide estimates, about half of the individual lag coefficients are significant, while for the disaggregated estimates the proportion is substantially higher.

Table 3 summarizes the adjusted coefficients of determination ($\bar{R}^2$) for the 15 alternative regression specifications used for this study. Since each regression was estimated for eight regions, there are a total of 120 entries. However, the table also reports significant results for each equation's stability, reflecting two additional estimates for shorter time periods. In addition, F-statistics are reported for seven pooled regressions testing for nationwide aggregation (and decisively rejected in each case). Table 2 thus represents the distillation of 367 different regression estimates.

A number of important conclusions emerge from these data, as follows:

1.   The regressions fit very well, considering they are being applied to first differences in the data. Of the 86 equations reported (excluding the Almon-lag versions) 43 have $\bar{R}^2$ values of .9742 or over, while only 14 are below 0.9.

Scanning the $\bar{R}^2$ values across each line enables us to judge the relative significance of several of the variables. Comparing Eq. 1–4 with 5 and 6 illustrates that inclusion or exclusion of interest rates does not affect goodness of fit very much. In no case does the interest-free $\bar{R}^2$ fall short of the overall maximum by as much as .01.

Eq. 7 and 1a–2b indicate the results of omitting the scale variables, FRNO, or the price level. Omitting FRNO and the price level do not lower $\bar{R}^2$ very much, whereas the loss of fit from the scale variable is greater. However, omitting any one of these variables causes deterioration of statistical quality showing up in such forms as autocorrelated residuals and increased instability. (An exception is district 11, where including FRNO aggravated instability; thus we have omitted FRNO for this district only.)

Table 3. Adjusted Coefficient of Determination ($\bar{R}^2$) for Regressions Explaining Change in Federal Reserve Notes 1930–1933

	Almon-Lag For Interest				Interest Lagged One Month				No Interest			Interest Lagged One Month			
	CPR		DDR		CPR-1 and DDR-1		DDR-1 only					Ex FRNO		Ex FRNO and Price	
District	Debits	Sales	Debits	Sales	Debits	Sales	Debits	Sales	Debits	Sales	No Scale				
Eq. #	I	II	III	IV	1	2	3	4	5	6	7	1a	2a	1b	2b
1+2+3	.9939 /**	.9940 */	.9928	.9943 */*	.9927 /**	.9946	.9922 /**	.9947	.9925 /*	.9948	.9893	.9863 */	.9883 **/**	.9856 */	.9880 */*
4	.9975	.9949 /**	.9972	.9951 /*	.9932 /*	.9963	.9885 /**	.9962	.9858[a] /**	.9953	.9837[a] */	.9891	.9900 **/***	.9895 /*	.9900 */*
5	.9436	.8410	.9346	.8862	.8937	.8489	.8936	.8250	.8863	.7999[a]	.7472[a] */**	.8979	.8186	.8911 /*	.7620 */**
6	.9553	.9591 **/	.9622 **/*	.9584 **/	.9639 **/	.9613 **/	.9565 **/	.9563 **/	.9536 **/*	.9565 **/	.8576[a] **/	.9223 **/	.9207 **/*	.8870 **/*	.8960 **/*
7	.9934	.9858	.9859	.9881	.9799	.9808 /*	.9808	.9830	.9791[a]	.9828	.9721[a]	.9790	.9750	.9792	.9740
9	.9965 */**	.9968 **/*	.9972 /*	.9966	.9962 /*	.9955 */*	.9959	.9943	.9961	.9945 /*	.9945 /*	.9959	.9950	.9953	.9950
11 (ex FRNO)	.9489	.9366 /*	.9504 /*	.9094 **/	.9511 /*	.8843 */*	.9532	.8885 /*	.9549	.8933 /*	.8526[a] /*	at left		.9514 */	.8890 /**
8+10+12	.9796	.9724	.9739	.9709	.9715	.9537	.9708	.9556	.9708	.9536	.9509[a]	.9384[a]	.9246[a]	.9411[a]	.9190
Degrees of Freedom	19	19	19	19	20	20	21	21	22	22	25	21	21	22	22
F for pooling					34.32	37.06	40.87	47.53	46.76	54.96	57.45				

Symbols:

*Designate unstable regressions. One asterisk indicates stability is rejected at the 95 percent level of probability, and two asterisks indicate rejection at the 99 percent level. Asterisks to the left of the slash designate instability in comparison with the regression for 1930–1932, and to the right, in comparison with the regression for 1931–1933.

[a]Durbin-Watson statistic is less than 1.25. (No equation shown had a D-W larger than 2.75.)

63

Table 3a.   Variables Included in Each Equation

Equation Number	CPR Almon	t-1	DDR Almon	t-1	Debits	Sales	Price	Failed Deposits	FRNO
I	x				x		x	x	x
II	x					x	x	x	x
III			x		x		x	x	x
IV			x			x	x	x	x
1		x		x	x		x	x	x
2		x		x		x	x	x	x
3				x	x		x	x	x
4				x		x	x	x	x
5					x		x	x	x
6						x	x	x	x
7							x	x	x
1a		x		x	x		x	x	
2a		x		x		x	x	x	
1b		x		x	x			x	
2b		x		x		x		x	

Notes:

CPR: Commercial paper rate. Almon-lag is 2nd degree polynomial applied to 12-month differences using 15 lags. Nationwide variable.

DDR: Demand deposit interest rate. Almon lag same as CPR. Nationwide variable.

Debits: 2nd degree polynomial applied to 12-month first difference in logarithms using 15 lags. This variable is specific to each district.

Sales: Department-store sales (nationwide aggregate, same for each district), entered in same manner as debits.

Price: 12-month first difference in logarithm of price level. No lag. Nationwide.

Failed Deposits: The dollar volume of deposits in failed banks was cumulated beginning with July 1929. Dollar 12-month first differences in this total were entered into a 2nd degree polynomial using 12 lags. Entered as percent of base deposits in district. This variable is specific to each district.

FRNO: Federal Reserve notes of other districts. 12-month first difference in dollar amount. This variable is specific to each district.

Dependent variable is 12-month first difference in dollar volume of Federal Reserve notes outstanding in each district, scaled by base deposits for each district.

2.   Instability is encountered in many of the equations. By altering the input mix and by aggregation, we were able to identify good-fitting regressions with otherwise good quality which were not unstable for every district or combination except #7 (Chicago).[20] By comparing longer and shorter period regressions in Table 4 below, we infer that, for Chicago, the impact of a dollar of bank failures was apparently much larger in 1929–1932 than in months from March 1932 through January 1933.

Our view is that Eq. 1–6 represent the best-specified regressions for this study. One basis for this view is that instability is relatively less of a problem in this group than in I–IV or 7–2b.

3.   Regressions are estimated using two alternative scale variables. Of these, bank debits is specific to each district, while department store sales is a national aggregate and thus uniform for all districts. In three areas (5, 11, and $8 + 10 + 12$), debits produces significantly better fit than sales. In the other areas, there is not much difference in $\overline{R}^2$. However, the choice of scale produces significant differences in stability and also affects the regression coefficients substantially.

To assess the relative role of interest rates and bank failures, we need to find plausible measures of their regression coefficients. We approach this problem in two ways. The first is to indulge in the "one best equation" approach, while the second approach involves looking for consensus in the estimates covered in Table 3. The "one best equation" approach is based on maximizing goodness of fit subject to the following constraints:

1.   Since there is no economic theory which predicts a positive influence from interest rates on demand for currency, we require our regression have negative interest rate effects (on balance) or none.

2.   Since there is likewise no economic theory which would give a negative influence from real income and the price level on demand for currency, we require the combined influence of scale variable and price level be non-negative, (measured by the sum of the two regression coefficients).

3.   Acceptable regressions should be free from instability (95 percent level) and from autocorrelated residuals (Durbin-Watson statistic must lie between 1.25 and 2.75).

The "one best equation" for each district or combination is displayed in Table 4. Since District 7 is unstable, we also display its regression for 1930–1932, chosen by the same optimization process. In five of the eight areas, the regression with the highest $\overline{R}^2$ (of Eq. 1–7) also fulfills the constraints. In three cases (districts 6, 7, and 9) the best-fit regressions were rejected because they displayed net positive interest rates effects. Only in district 6 did this lower $\overline{R}^2$ appreciably.

Table 4. "One Best Equation" for Each Federal Reserve District (or Combination) Explaining Change in Federal Reserve Notes, 1930–1933

| | | Regression Coefficients and t-Values | | | | | | | | | |
District	Equation Number	CPR	DDR	Failed Deposits[a] Σ	Scale Σ	Price Level	FRNO (.0000) (omitted)	Const.	$\bar{R}^2$	DW	F for Stability[b]
1+2+3	6	x		.449 (2.20)	-.032S (1.44)	.035 (2.05)	.180 (5.14)	-.0065 (4.82)	.9948	2.46	0.91 / 0.72
4	2	-.0010 (1.91)	-.0013 (1.27)	.147 (3.42)	-.019S (1.23)	.061 (2.48)	.094 (6.03)	-.0020 (1.69)	.9963	1.81	1.71 / 1.68
5	1	-.0010 (1.02)	-.0028 (1.00)	1.205 (3.54)	2.54D (2.89)	.099 (1.51)	.019 (.41)	-.0043 (1.43)	.8937	1.66	2.85 / 0.36
6	6	x	x	.239 (1.59)	-.026S (1.78)	.207 (5.28)	.243 (5.34)	-.0081 (2.81)	.9565	2.29	0.35 / 1.22
7 (1930–33: unstable)	6	x	x	1.437 (4.58)	.102S (.99)	-.043 (.53)	.258 (3.38)	-.0111 (2.28)	.9828	1.40	9.03** / 2.23
7 (1930–32)	7	x	x	2.371 (9.15)	x	.020 (.61)	.226 (3.39)	-.0173 (4.44)	.9918	1.84	1.81 / 0.40
9	5	x	x	.911 (7.21)	.028D (3.23)	.040 (2.52)	.030 (1.56)	-.0079 (7.40)	.9961	1.82	0.51 / 2.27
11	5a	x	-.0004 (.23)	.751 (7.14)	.020D (1.00)	.040 (.88)	x	-.0072 (3.42)	.9549	1.71	1.03 / 0.96
8+10+12	1	-.0006 (1.22)		-.325 (1.07)	-.020D (.91)	.041 (1.22)	.157 (5.03)	.0071 (3.94)	.9715	1.81	1.04 / 0.38
Nationwide: all currency	4	x	-.0042 (2.52)	.888 (4.19)	-.014S (0.33)	.089 (2.32)	x	-.0068 (4.41)	.9742	1.90	

Notes:

[a]: regression coefficients and t-statistics for individual lag terms are shown in Table 7.

[b]: First value uses estimate for July 1930–March 1932; second uses April 1931–January 1933.

x: variable omitted.

D: bank debits.

S: department store sales.

V. THE ROLE OF INTEREST RATES

The regressions cited in Table 4 give a very low mark to interest rates as an influence on currency demand in 1929–1932. In districts 6, 7, and 9, the interest rate coefficients were, on balance, positive. In two others they were inconsequential. In the remaining three, the interest coefficients were uniformly negative, but only one displayed a significant t-ratio. In the important $8 + 10 + 12$ area, the interest-rate coefficients were very small.

Even if the true interest-rate effects were on the order of those indicated for districts 4 and 5, a commercial-paper-rate coefficient of $-.001$ implies an elasticity of -0.13, and a demand-deposit-rate coefficient of $-.002$ implies an elasticity of -0.18. These combine to substantially less than the BW estimate of -0.5 for DDR.

In Table 5 we tabulate the interest rate results from all the regressions summarized in Table 2, plus Eq. 3a, 3b, 4a, and 4b, which contain DDR only.

We also include separate regression results for the New York district. Presumably the demand deposit rate for New York Clearing House banks should have its best fit in the New York district. However, the New York regressions show no case of a significant negative coefficient.

These results do not indicate that interest rates had a negative influence on currency withdrawal of any significance. When the Almon-lag is used for each interest rate, the majority of the terms have positive coefficients and their sum is positive; of the negative coefficients, most are not significant. In the other specifications, there are roughly equal numbers of positive and negative coefficients, but most negative coefficients are insignificant and the average coefficients do not generally differ significantly from zero.[21]

Table 5. Distribution of Regression Coefficients on Interest Rates
for Various Regression Specifications, 1930–1933

Equation	Commercial Paper Rate					Demand Deposit Rate				
	Positive		Negative			Positive		Negative		
	Sig.	Not sig.	Sig.	Not sig.	Average size	Sig.	Not sig.	Sig.	Not sig.	Average size
I–IV	66	103	22	49	+ .0062	63	97	15	65	+ .0057
1–4	3	1	3	9	− .0007	1	13	23	16	+ .0004
1a–4a	3	7	2	4	+ .0005	2	13	3	14	+ .0002
1b–4b	4	8	1	3	+ .0007	6	17	2	10	+ .0013
New York	0	0	0	6	− .0008	2	10	0	0	+ .0043

Notes: Equations I–II contain 15 Almon-lag terms for CPR, and equations III–IV contain 15 terms for DDR. With 8 areas, this yields 240 terms.

Significance is determined by $t \geqslant 1.75$.

Average size for equations I–IV uses sum of lagged regression coefficients.

Average in each case is unweighted across 8 areas.

New York data include equations 1–4, 1a–4a, and 1b–4b.

VI. ROLE OF BANK FAILURES

The "best equations" summarized in Table 4 show the sum of the current and lagged influence of bank failures on currency outflow. In seven of eight areas the total impact of bank failures was substantially positive and in six of eight the sum of the coefficients was more than twice the standard error.

However, the size of the bank failure coefficients is somewhat sensitive to changes in specifications. To judge the reliability of the orders of magnitude suggested in Table 4, we calculated the average total impact of bank failures from Eq. 1–6, as well as the standard deviation around that average. (In districts 5 and 11, where the regressions using sales as the scale variable fit substantially less well, only the three equations using debits were averaged.) These are shown in Table 6.

Table 6 indicates that the general orders of magnitude of bank failure impact shown in Table 4 are representative of those obtained for various other specifications. In only one area (districts $8 + 10 + 12$) is the standard error of the six coefficients as large as half the average of the coefficients.

Thus we can safely conclude that the proportional impact of bank failures differed substantially from one area to another. The total impact was largest in districts 5 (Richmond) and 7 (Chicago), where a dollar of bank failures generated currency outflow of a dollar or more, slightly smaller but still substantial in districts 9 (Minneapolis) and 11 (Dallas), where currency outflow averaged around $.75 for each dollar of failed deposits, and smaller still in the important

Table 6.   Sums of Regression Coefficients for Bank Failures, Equations 1–6

District	Average coefficient sum	Standard deviation	Ratio	Coefficient Sum Shown in Table 4
$1 + 2 + 3$	.590	.177	3.33	.449
4	.189	.088	2.15	.147
5	1.227	.054	22.72	1.205
6	.186	.044	4.23	.239
7a	.983	.331	2.97	1.437
7b	1.807	.210	8.60	2.371
9	.774	.169	4.58	.911
11	.779	.020	38.95	.751
$8 + 10 + 12$	−.198	.117	1.69	−.325
Nationwide	.804	.228	3.53	.888

Notes: For districts 5 and 11 only the three equations using debits were averaged.

For other districts, average coefficient sum is calculated from equations 1–6.

$1+2+3$ northeast combination, where the impact was about $.50. In districts 4 (Cleveland) and 6 (Atlanta) the total impact was only about $.20, and in the $8+10+12$ combination, the total impact was negative. The negative impact is not consistent with any economic theory, and we can infer that it reflects bank failures acting as a proxy for the declining scale variable. (If we drop FRNO from the regression, the bank-failure coefficient sum becomes strongly positive.)

Some very important additional results emerge when we look at the detailed lag distribution of the regression coefficients for the impact of bank failures. These are shown in Table 7 and in Figure 3. Figure 3 shows the remarkable

Table 7. Regression Coefficients for Bank Failures for Equations Cited in Table 4[a]

					District					
	Nation-wide	1+2+3 N.E.	4 Cleve.	5 Rich.	6 Atlanta	7a Chicago	7b Chicago	9 Minn	11 Dallas	8+10+12 West
Equation	6	2	1	6	6	7		5	5a	1
Month										
0	.229	.265	.120	.134	.189	.437	.496	.126	.327	.083
	(5.70)	(7.19)	(10.92)	(3.49)	(6.54)	(3.41)	(7.23)	(3.03)	(10.07)	(2.04)
−1	.190	.206	.078	.112	.140	.280	.221	.094	.219	.039
	(8.11)	(6.99)	(9.93)	(3.90)	(8.64)	(3.83)	(4.81)	(3.27)	(11.06)	(1.25)
−2	.154	.153	.042	.095	.097	.154	.013	.070	.129	.002
	(10.67)	(6.12)	(7.43)	(3.98)	(12.04)	(3.86)	(0.04)	(3.74)	(11.84)	(0.10)
−3	.122	.105	.013	.082	.059	.056	−.130	.052	.057	−.027
	(7.61)	(4.60)	(2.89)	(3.54)	(7.56)	(1.35)	(5.20)	(4.57)	(7.31)	(1.19)
−4	.093	.062	−.008	.074	.027	−.011	−.206	.040	.003	−.050
	(4.38)	(2.82)	(1.92)	(2.99)	(2.38)	(0.19)	(8.05)	(5.40)	(0.32)	(2.25)
−5	.067	.024	−.023	.072	−.0004	−.049	−.217	.036	−.033	−.065
	(2.66)	(1.12)	(5.29)	(2.65)	(0.03)	(0.72)	(7.66)	(5.28)	(3.05)	(2.95)
−6	.044	−.009	−.032	.073	−.022	−.057	−.161	.038	−.051	−.073
	(1.62)	(0.41)	(7.33)	(2.55)	(1.55)	(0.82)	(5.15)	(5.67)	(4.96)	(3.26)
−7	.024	−.036	−.033	.080	−.039	−.036	−.038	.047	−.051	−.074
	(.87)	(1.72)	(8.35)	(2.63)	(2.63)	(0.57)	(1.08)	(8.56)	(6.60)	(3.07)
−8	.008	−.059	−.027	.092	−.050	.015	.150	.062	−.036	−.068
	(.27)	(2.67)	(7.64)	(2.80)	(2.95)	(0.28)	(3.39)	(19.55)	(6.41)	(2.39)
−9	−.005	−.077	−.015	.108	−.056	.096	.405	.084	.002	−.054
	(.14)	(3.03)	(3.78)	(2.93)	(2.40)	(1.63)	(6.82)	(16.53)	(0.21)	(1.50)
−10	−.015	−.089	.004	.129	−.056	.206	.725	.113	.056	−.034
	(.32)	(2.84)	(0.70)	(2.95)	(1.66)	(2.28)	(8.95)	(9.27)	(2.73)	(0.70)
−11	−.022	−.097	.030	.155	−.051	.346	1.112	.149	.127	−.006
	(.34)	(2.38)	(3.45)	(2.87)	(1.06)	(2.42)	(10.18)	(6.77)	(3.74)	(0.09)
Total	.888	.449	.147	1.205	.239	1.437	2.371	.911	.751	−.325

[a] t-ratios in parentheses.

Figure 3. Lag structure, impact of failed deposits on Federal Reserve
notes by district, regressions cited in Table 4.

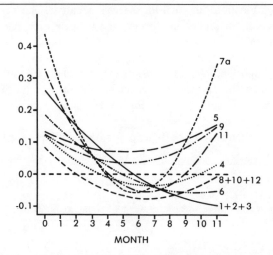

degree of conformity of the lag patterns for the eight areas. Table 7 indicates that
most of the individual lag terms carry significant t-ratios, so that the common pattern can be regarded as highly reliable. Of the 96 regression coefficients listed in
Table 7 (excluding the nationwide estimate and Eq. 7b), 72 have t-ratios above 1.75.

The general lag pattern is U-shaped or parabolic. In all eight regions, the first
three regression coefficients on bank failures are positive. The immediate impact
of bank failure increase is a substantial currency outflow, which then tapers off.
In most districts the coefficients turn negative after 4–6 months, indicating a
tendency for some of the withdrawn currency to flow back into the banking
system. Then the curves begin to turn upward again and in several cases become
significantly and substantially positive, indicating renewed currency outflow
after 7–12 months. Only for districts 1 + 2 + 3 does the curve continue to decline,
and for district 6 it becomes essentially flat. The other six curves turn up, and
five of them end up in the positive domain by the final month. The shapes
reflected in Figure 4 are not sensitive to specification; we find them replicated
through virtually all of the regressions estimated. This type of lag distribution is
not consistent with the Koyck approach to estimating lags.

Additional thoughts concerning the lagged impact of bank failures on currency
are reflected in Figure 4. Figures 4a and 4b show the cumulative response of
Federal Reserve notes to bank failures, derived by summing the successive
coefficients shown in Table 7. We conjecture that these can result from combinations of two effects previously identified as the precautionary effect and the
facility effect. The precautionary effect is expected to be hump shaped, though
not necessarily symmetrical and not necessarily returning entirely to zero. The
facility effect shows the influence of the permanent closing of bank offices. We

Figure 4. Cumulative currency response to bank failures and a possible interpretation.

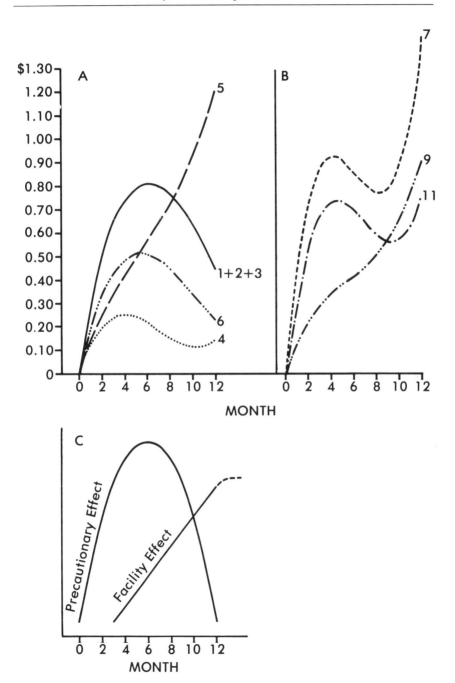

believe it to be related to the timing of payoffs to the holders of deposits in closed banks. These payoffs did not generally begin until at least three months after the closing, and tended to be spread out over several subsequent years.[22] We would expect the steepness and timing of the curve to vary from one region to another. And presumably the curve would level off beyond some point.[23] By varying the timing and magnitude of the two curves shown in 4c, most of the patterns shown in 4a and 4b could be reproduced.

With the exception of district 11 (Dallas), our regressions contain a term for Federal Reserve notes of other districts (FRNO). The equations cited in Table 3 show a very consistent pattern of influence. All seven FRNO coefficients are positive and five are highly significant. This term captures the influence on currency demanded in one region exerted by developments elsewhere in the country. Such influence was clearly significant. Since change in Federal Reserve notes in most regions was dominated by the impact of bank failures in that district, FRNO reflects the transmission to other regions of that bank-failure impact. In interpreting the pattern shown for districts $8 + 10 + 12$, this means that the apparent negative impact of local bank failures needs to be compensated by the sizeable positive impact of failures outside the region acting through the FRNO term. When FRNO is omitted for this region, the impact of local bank failure turns sharply positive.

VII. SCALE AND PRICE TERMS

The scale variables and price level perform quite erratically in Table 4, with rather weak statistical showing in a number of districts. One associates the influence of scale and price level principally with demand for transactions money. And there is evidence that transactions demand for currency did conform only rather poorly to changes in income and prices.[24] Table 8 presents two types of evidence indicating such poor conformity. One series is taken from an innovative doctoral dissertation by Robert Laurent, in which he used data on the physical issue and redemption of paper currency of each denomination to estimate the dollar volume of currency transfers each year. His estimates for 1929–1933 are shown. (The entire table is dated for fiscal years ending June 30.) His data show an estimated volume of currency transfers in 1932 equal to the peak volume of fiscal 1930, with 1933 only 13 percent below that same peak. We also show data on the value of coins (other than gold coins) and of silver certificates (the total of which is almost exactly equal to the sum of $1 and $2 bills when those were reported separately beginning in October 1930). Both coin and silver certificates show an almost horizontal path, with totals declining only by 10 percent for coin and 8 percent for certificates.

Thus both stock of transactions currency and flow of currency transactions show very little decline during the downswing. These may be contrasted with Barger's estimates of total outlay for goods and services and with the volume of

Table 8.   Some Measures of Transactions Currency, 1929–1933

Year ending June 30	Currency Transfers	Outstanding Stock of Non-gold Coin	Silver Certificates	Bank Debits Outside NYC (268 centers)	Total Outlay
1929	$431 bil.	$442 mil.	$392	$360.8 bil.	$83.3 bil.
1930	443	443	400	362.9	82.0
1931	380	429	384	285.4	66.0
1932	442	413	371	213.1	52.7
1933	374	397	360	164.0*	41.9

*Total for 11 months multiplied by 12/11.
Sources: Currency transfers: Robert D. Laurent, "Currency Transfer by Denomination," Ph.D. dissertation, University of Chicago (1970, pp. 20–48). Total Outlay: Harold Barger, *Outlay and Income in the United States, 1921–1938,* (New York, National Bureau of Economic Research, 1942) pp. 114–7 (quarterly data). Other series: *Banking and Monetary Statistics* (1943, pp. 411–15, 236–7).

bank debits outside New York, both of which illustrate the magnitude of the decline in aggregate spending and income.

VIII. SOME IMPLICATIONS

Our investigation has indicated that the currency drain from the banking system during the downswing of 1929–1933 was chiefly a response to bank failures, but that the timing and magnitude of that response differed substantially from one region to another. Now we examine more closely the relative importance of bank failures in different areas during the early stages of the panic in 1930.

Narratives of the onset of the currency panic have tended to stress two focal points. One is the failure in November and December, 1930, of a large number of banks associated with Caldwell and Company.[25] While the organization's headquarters were in Nashville and thus affected the Atlanta district, the largest dollar volume of Caldwell failures were in the St. Louis district, centering on large banks in Louisville and in Little Rock. There were also some associated failures in Asheville, N.C., in the Richmond district. As Table 1 illustrates, these three districts sustained the largest proportion of 1930 bank failures among the 12 districts.

Yet, as Figure 2 somewhat illustrates, none of these three districts contributed significantly to the drain of Federal Reserve notes. In Figure 2, to be sure, both the Richmond and Atlanta curves for Δ FRN turn sharply upward in late 1930, but they are moving from a large decrease to a much smaller decrease. Both districts have somewhat special circumstances. Richmond, according to Table 4, was the one district with a strong scale effect. Presumably, therefore, the bank failures in that district prevented a large income-generated decrease in currency. In the Atlanta district, Florida had been experiencing a heavy incidence of bank failures ever since the collapse of the land boom in 1926. As early as mid-1929 the Atlanta district had a much larger proportional circulation of Federal Reserve notes than any other district. So the currency panic had begun earlier in that area.

No such special circumstances seem to apply to the St. Louis district itself. Since we have not shown it separately in Figure 2, we note that in December 1930 Federal Reserve note circulation in the district was still $9 million below that of a year previous, remained about $7 million below a year previous in the first quarter of 1931, and rose to equal its year-before level only in June 1931.[26]

It may well be that, without the Caldwell failures, currency circulation in these districts would have decreased substantially. But the record indicates that these districts did not contribute significantly to the massive outflow of currency which got underway in late 1930.

The second episode which is celebrated in the narratives is the failure of New York's Bank of United States with about $161 million of deposits on December 11, 1930. Our regressions for the New York district alone and for districts $1 + 2 + 3$ combined give this failure a heavy impact. According to Table 7, failures in the three northeastern districts generated currency outflows in the first six months equal to about 80 percent of the dollar volume of the failures. Thus the short run impact of the Bank of United States failure could have been a currency drain of $135 million or more. A similar high proportional impact presumably resulted from the failure of Philadelphia's misnamed Bankers Trust with about $40 million of deposits, closed December 22, 1930.

Narratives of the period do not usually dwell on Chicago bank failures. There were no large and spectacular failures, thanks in part to some emergency mergers. Chicago city experienced no failures during the last quarter of 1930. But the city had already sustained 12 in the preceding 12 months, with deposits of $22 million. And over the 18 months beginning January 1931, the city experienced no less than 106 failures, with about $200 million of deposits.[27] Since the regression coefficients for failed deposits were consistently greater than unity for the Chicago district, the impact of the Chicago failures, even in 1930, far eclipsed that of the Caldwell banks.

Of course, bank failures had direct adverse effects on income and expenditure, in addition to the effects through currency drain, bank reserves, and the money multiplier.[28] With regard to the currency drain, our findings support the emphasis which Friedman and Schwartz gave to the Bank of United States failure, as against Temin's claim that its macroeconomic effects were negligible.[29]

Considering the geographic dispersal of bank failures, why was the currency drain so heavily concentrated in the Northeast? One possibility is that the currency drain was an urban, perhaps metropolitan phenomenon.[30] New York City had experienced two widely publicized bank failures in 1929. New York residents were also constantly being reminded of the bank failures going on elsewhere.[31] The importance of urbanization is also suggested by the fact that the proportion of currency to bank deposits in the country as a whole continued to decline until late 1930, despite the high incidence of rural bank failures over the previous decade.

IX. CONCLUSION

Using monthly data for individual Federal Reserve districts or combinations, we estimated regressions explaining the change in Federal Reserve notes as a function of bank failures, interest rates, the price level, and alternative measures of transactions. Results consistently showed a strong influence from bank failures and negligible influence from interest rates. The size and timing of influence of bank failures on currency demand differed widely from one region to another. As a result, despite wide dispersal of bank failures across the country, the currency drain was heavily concentrated in the urban northeast. Despite the variations in size of impact, however, the shape of lag distribution on bank failures was very similar from one region to another. We interpreted the lag distribution to reflect a strong precautionary effect in the first months, followed by some currency inflow, followed by renewed outflow due to the loss of banking facilities because of the failures.

APPENDIX

The F statistic for evaluating stability over time is calculated in the following manner:

$$F = \frac{(SSE - SSE_1)/n_2}{SSE_1/(n_1\text{-}k\text{-}l)},$$ with the terms identified as follows:

SSE: Sum of squares of error for the entire period July 1930–January 1933 (31 months).

SSE_1: Sum of squares of error for a subperiod, either July 1930 through March 1932 (21 months), or April 1931, through January 1933 (22 months).

n_1: Number of observations for the relevant subperiod generating SSE_1 (21 or 22).

n_2: Number of observations not directly covered by the subperiod regression (10 or 9).

k: Number of independent variables in the model (allowing three terms for each 2nd degree polynomial).

Critical values of the F statistic are obtained for n_2 and n_1-k-1 degrees of freedom.

Aggregation

Since there is no logical reason why currency demand in one district could not be met by banks drawing currency from another district, we tested a large number of possible combinations of adjoining districts to see if the combination displayed superior fit and other elements of quality. We only considered those aggregations for which the sum of squares of error for the aggregation was lower than for the individual districts taken separately.

For districts $1 + 2 + 3$ the decision to aggregate was based on overwhelming statistical evidence coming on top of the high plausibility of combining the three northeasterly districts, with their high population density and small area. Table A1 compares the $\bar{R}^2$ values obtained when we ran our basic seven regressions for the three districts individually and for the three combined. The $\bar{R}^2$ for the combination is consistently higher than any of the three taken individually. There is also some improvement in stability and autocorrelation.

Considering the relatively poor fit of district 5 (Richmond) we tested adding it in to its northern neighbors $1 + 2 + 3$, but this did not yield further improvement. Nor did combining it with 6 (Atlanta). We also tested a number of possible aggregations involving district 7 (Chicago), hoping to reduce instability. Again, none of these brought improved fit. It is noteworthy that two of Chicago's neighbors, Cleveland and Minneapolis, have exceptionally good fit when estimated separately.

Table A2 provides the statistical basis for aggregating districts 8, 10, and 12. As the map indicates, these districts form an east-west continuum. The chief statistical evidence favoring aggregation is that the best $\bar{R}^2$ values for the aggregation, those using debits, are higher than any of the $\bar{R}^2$ values for the individual districts, while those using sales are not significantly below those of the better fitting districts and are above their adjusted average. Further, all the aggregated estimates are stable, and 1–6 are free from autocorrelation. In contrast, all the

Table A1. Adjusted Coefficient of Determination, Districts 1, 2, 3 Separate and Combined

District	Equation Number						
	1	2	3	4	5	6	7
1. Boston	*/ .9709	*/ .9780	*/ .9550	.9637	*/ .9513	.9613[a]	/** .9117[a]
2. New York	**/** .9253	.9781	*/** .9287	.9786[a]	*/** .9280	.9763	.9416[a]
3. Philadelphia	/* .9644	.9653	*/** .9629	.9661	*/** .9620	*/ .9667	**/ .9504
1 + 2 + 3 Combined	/** .9927	.9946	/** .9922	.9947	/* .9925	.9948	.9893[a]

Symbols: *Indicates instability. One asterisk is at 95% level, two asterisks at 99% level. Asterisk to left of slash indicates instability with respect to regression run for 1930–1932, and to right, for 1931–1933.
[a]Durbin Watson statistic is less than 1.25. In no case did DW > 2.75.

observations for district 10 taken in isolation displayed instability and auto-correlation. District 8 taken in isolation displayed relatively poor fit compared with all other districts.

Table A2. Adjusted Coefficient of Determination, Districts 8, 10, 12 Separate and Combined

District	Equation Number						
	1	2	3	4	5	6	7
							*/
8. St. Louis	.9162	.8073	.8695	.8072	.8721	.8115	.5045[a]
	/**	/**	/*	/**	/**	/*	/**
10. Kansas City	.9544[a]	.9670[a]	.9525[a]	.9576[a]	.9527[a]	.9585[a]	.9379[a]
					*/		
12. San Francisco	.9709	.9656	.9677	.9659	.9518	.9586	.9530[a]
8 + 10 + 12 Combined	.9715	.9537	.9708	.9556	.9708	.9536	.9509[a]

Symbols are the same as in Table A1.

Table A3. Correlation Matrix for 12-Month Change in Federal Reserve Notes, Compared Over Eight Regions

District	District							Average of 7 Correlation Coefficients
	1 + 2 + 3	4	5	6	7	9	11	
1 + 2 + 3								.851
4	.844							.701
5	.896	.692						.782
6	.543	.323	.682					.427
7	.933	.754	.770	.367				.793
9	.871	.612	.754	.239	.906			.727
11	.925	.909	.831	.440	.878	.782		.811
8 + 10 + 12	.944	.772	.851	.396	.945	.925	.910	.820
All								.739

ACKNOWLEDGMENT

The author wishes to thank David Sivan for extraordinary research assistance.

NOTES

1. Milton Friedman and Anna J. Schwartz, *A Monetary History of the United States, 1867–1960* Princeton University Press for National Bureau of Economic Research, (1963, pp. 712–4).

2. The extent of Federal Reserve defensive open-market operations is shown in my paper, "Federal Reserve Policy in the Great Contraction: A Counterfactual Assessment." *Explorations in Economic History* 19:211–20 (1982).

3. *Banking and Monetary Statistics* Board of Governers, Federal Reserve System, (1943, p. 283).

4. Peter Temin, *Did Monetary Forces Cause the Great Depression*? New York: National Bureau of Economic Research (1975).

5. Phillip Cagan, "The Demand for Currency Relative to Total Money Supply," New York: W. W. Norton, 1958.

6. Barry L. Anderson and James L. Butkiewicz, "Money, Spending, and the Great Depression." *Southern Economic Journal* (Oct. 1980):388–403.

7. James Boughton and Elmus R. Wicker, "The Behavior of the Currency-Deposit Ratio during the Great Depression." *Journal of Money, Credit, and Banking* (Nov. 1979):405–18.

8. Ibid., p. 416. Compare the relatively low elasticities estimated by Stephen Goldfeld for the postwar period, in "The Demand for Money Revisited." *Brookings Papers* 3:577–638 (1973).

9. "The Behavior of the Currency-Deposit Ratio during the Great Depression: Comment." *Journal of Money, Credit and Banking* XVI, 3 (August 1984):362–5.

10. Arthur Gandolfi, "Stability of the Demand for Money During the Great Contraction, 1929–1933." *Journal of Political Economy* (Sept.–Oct. 1974):969–83.

11. Carl M. Gambs, "Bank Failures—An Historical Perspective." *Monthly Review*, Federal Reserve Bank of Kansas City (June 1977):16.

12. To extend our estimates backward to data prior to 1929 would add no useful information for most regions. In re-estimating the BW regression for the period 1924–1929, we found that currency showed no significant correlation with transactions, the demand-deposit rate, or bank failures. The demand deposit rate changed only once between February 1925, and March 1930. The total variance of currency was 77 times as large in 1929–1933 as in 1924–1929.

13. Cagan, op. cit.; Elmus Wicker, "A Reconsideration of the Causes of the Banking Panic of 1930." *Journal of Economic History* XL, 3 (Sept. 1980):571–83.

14. *Historical Statistics of the United States, from Colonial Times to 1970*. (pp. 631–5).

15. See Thomas F. Cooley and Stephen F. Leroy, "Identification and Estimation of Money Demand." *American Economic Review* 71,5 (Dec. 1981):825–44; Edward E. Leamer, "Let's Take the Con Out of the Econometrics." *American Economic Review* 73,1 (March 1983):31–43; and, "Sensitivity Analysis Would Help." ibid., 75,3 (June 1985):308–13.

16. A simple regression relating 12-month first differences of Federal Reserve notes and total currency was estimated for terminal dates July 1930–January 1933, with this result:

$$\Delta CU = .740\,\Delta FRN + \$161\,mil.\,R^2 = .971 \quad DW = 1.38$$
$$(31.28) \qquad (10.21)$$

The date on FRN include bank holdings, while estimates of total currency exclude bank holdings. The FRN data are monthly averages of daily figures, while the total currency data are for the end of the month. Data on Federal Reserve notes by district are from current issues of *Federal Reserve Bulletin*. Total currency data used in comparison are the seasonally adjusted estimates of Friedman and Schwartz (pp. 712–4), adjusted in reverse by using the seasonal adjustment given in *Federal Reserve Bulletin* (December 1932):742.

17. In June 1929, Federal Reserve notes constituted only 38 percent of total currency held by the public and the commercial banks. By January 1933, the proportion of FRN had risen to 50.5 perent. *Banking and Monetary Statistics* (1943, pp. 411–12). It would be inappropriate to deflate FRN by the

price level, since a 10 percent decline in prices, while reducing demand for total currency by 10 percent, would probably cause a larger (but not constant) proportional decline in FRN.

18.   The data we used for bank failures were those published in current issues of the *Federal Reserve Bulletin*. In 1937 the Federal Reserve published more refined monthly estimates for the entire country covering 1921–1936. (*Bulletin*, Sept., 1937, p. 909). We regressed the 1937 series (denoted FD) against the monthly national total of the district-by-district data we used (denoted FDD) with the following results (July 1929–February 1933):

$$FD = .845 \; FDD + \$9 \text{ mil.} \qquad R^2 = .985 \qquad DW = 1.64$$
$$(52.25) \qquad (4.02)$$

19.   *Federal Reserve Bulletin* (October 1936):631.

20.   Equation I was not unstable for Chicago but was badly specified, with strongly positive interest rate and negative values for price level, scale and bank failures.

21.   A negligible role for interest rates seems implied by data for the United Kingdom. According to David Sheppard, the ratio of deposits to currency increased there from 5.89 in 1929 to 6.30 in 1933, during which time the interest rate on Treasury bills fell from 5.26 percent to 0.59 percent, and "bankers allowance on deposits" fell from 2.5–4.5 percent in 1929 to 0.5 percent in 1933. See David K. Sheppard, *The Growth and Role of UK Financial Institutions 1880–1962* (London, Methuen, 1971, pp. 41, 190); *Banking and Monetary Statistics* (1943, pp. 657–8).

22.   A detailed analysis of the timing of deposit payoffs is contained in my unpublished paper "The Role of Bank Failures in the Economic Downswing of 1929–33 in the U.S.," presented to Southern Economics Association meetings, Washington, D.C. 1980.

23.   The absence of any apparent facility effect in the northeast region might reflect the fact that most of the mutual savings banks were concentrated in that region. Mutual savings banks experienced virtually no failures during the downswing. Their deposits increased from $8.9 billion in July 1929, to $10 billion in November 1931, after which time they leveled off (Friedman and Schwartz, *Monetary History*, op. cit. pp. 712–3).

24.   Our re-estimates of the BW regressions for 1924–1933 and two subperiods showed uniformly insignificant coefficients for the transactions variable, department-store sales. Recall they incorporated the price level as a deflator for currency and sales.

25.   John B. McFerrin, *Caldwell and Company* (Chapel Hill: University of North Carolina, 1939); Wicker, "Reconsideration." op. cit.

26.   Our regressions for the St. Louis district taken by itself consistently show that the impact of bank failures was statistically very significant but small. Eq. 1, which shows the best $\bar{R}^2$ (.916), implies a total impact in the first five months of only .09; thereafter coefficients turn negative and the total effect is slightly negative. This implies that the $174 million of failed deposits in November and December 1930, generated only about $16 million of currency withdrawal at maximum.

An obvious possibility, comparing the very low impact of failed deposits in the St. Louis district with the very large impact in the neighboring Chicago district, is that that the banks in the St. Louis district were drawing currency from the Chicago district. We tested whether combining districts 7 and 8 reduced total estimating error. Since the Chicago regressions showed instability, the aggregation was tested for the two shorter subperiods. In each case, aggregation raised total estimating error significantly. Similar results were obtained when we combined the St. Louis district with its two Caldwell neighbors, Richmond and Atlanta. In our final choice, which aggregates the St. Louis district with Kansas City and San Francisco, the bank-failure impact is also relatively small.

27.   Estimated deposits of failed banks in Chicago city were tabulated from mimeographed worksheets compiled by the staff of the Federal Reserve board and dispersed through the materials of the Committee on Branch, Group, and Chain Banking in Record Group 82, National Archives. For narrative, see F. Cyril James, *The Growth of Chicago Banks* New York, Harper, v.2.

28.   Trescott, "The Role of Bank Failures . . ." op. cit.; Ben S. Bernanke, "Nonmonetary Effects of the Financial Crisis in the Propagation of the Great Depression." *American Economic Review* 73,3 (June 1983):257–76.

29.   Friedman and Schwartz, *Monetary History.* op. cit. pp. 309–12; Temin, *Monetary Factors,* op. cit. pp. 90–94.

30.   According to Aaron Hardy Ulm, "Large-scale hoarding evidently was provoked in the main by fears aroused by collapsing of city banks rather than by more widespread and numerically great collapsing of small country banks." "When Large City Banks Close." *Barrons*, June 6, 1932, p. 20. Table 1 shows that the five northeast districts (1, 2, 3, 4, 7) effectively accounted for all the increase in FRN over 1930–1932. Population estimates by district show that these five had almost exactly half of the country's population. In these five districts, the proportion of population living in urban areas (50,000 and over) was 46.9 percent. By contrast, in the other seven districts, the urban proportion was only 22.2 percent. *Annual Report of Federal Reserve Board for 1931*, p. 286; U.S. *Statistical Abstract, 1931*, pp. 22–26.

31.   The suspensions of City Trust (February 1929) and Clarke Brothers (private bankers, closed June 1929) were heavily publicized because of political involvement and violations of law. *New York Times Index* (Jan.–March, 1929):98; (April–June 1929):111–2; (July–Sept. 1929):115–8; (Oct.– Dec. 1929): 118–9; 1930, pp. 585–6.

Over the 10 months January through October 1930, the *New York Times* ran stories on bank failures (not including City and Clarke) on 54 separate dates, with references to 86 different banks. *New York Times Index 1930* (1931):268–71.

BUREAUCRACY, BUSINESS,
AND AFRICA DURING
THE COLONIAL PERIOD:
WHO DID WHAT TO WHOM AND
WITH WHAT CONSEQUENCES?

Dennis M. P. McCarthy

ABSTRACT

Government bureaucracies and businesses that were sometimes bureaucratized have
not received the kind of analytical attention they deserve during the colonial period
in Africa. There are compelling needs to differentiate state action more rigorously,
to refine the portrait of business, and to distinguish more sharply government-
business relations. Towards those ends a pioneering comparative profile of state

Research in Economic History, Volume 11, pages 81–152.
Copyright © 1988 by JAI Press Inc.
All rights of reproduction in any form reserved.
ISBN: 0-89232-677-8

action, based largely on primary sources, is first presented. As the empirical centerpiece of the essay, this profile serves as prelude to a more theoretical consideration of the concepts involved in research on government-business relations. Both empirical profile and conceptual discussion put the final section, which spotlights some of the more valuable case studies from the secondary literature, into a provocative perspective.

The full story of bureaucracy and business in Africa from the 1880s into the 1960s and beyond has not yet been written. Much current writing and discussion here in the United States as well as overseas treats colonial governments too superficially and businesses too stereotypically. One can imagine, then, the degree of refinement that characterizes analysis of relations between government bureaucracies and businesses that were sometimes bureaucratized. Some portray government as abettor or acquiescor in business endeavors to use Africa and its residents in ways vividly captured in the acronym that comes from the title of one of the more vigorous journals in its field, *Review of African Political Economy*. Others, decidedly outnumbered by those with an almost Manichean view of business as inherently evil, emphasize the positive contributions which they attribute to certain business activities in Africa. Too much discussion of bureaucracies, businesses, their relations and impacts in both Africa and elsewhere in the so-called "Third World" is dichotomized, limited in assumptions and approaches, and marked by conclusions more polemical than substantive.

The time has come not to promise "revolutionary new departures" nor to hype "radical revisions," but to seek a "middle ground" in current argument, one that does history "the old-fashioned way"—with evidence presented in the "new sacks" of a wide-ranging comparative approach. Some basic assumptions of this approach are elementary. If you have seen one colonial bureaucracy in action, you have not seen them all. Business must be defined as comprehensively as possible, to include "foreign" corporations as well as single-member "local" trading operations and individual farmers. And no single ideology or method monopolizes the powers of illumination.

The tasks which this approach confronts are not as straightforward as its assumptions. The formal European partition of Africa in the 1880s, a consequence of centuries of more variegated continental involvement, brought the establishment of official colonial administration in many locations. This was the seeming transfer in a widespread way of what some call "western-style" bureaucracy to Africa, which resulted in the creation of numerous territorial administrations. Each enacted over time its own economic regulations. Of course, these exhibited strong similarities and in some instances were identical. But important differences do characterize territorial regulatory profiles. These come from the obvious fact that local conditions were not the same everywhere in Africa and from the less appreciated facts that not all territorial bureaucracies at all times pursued identical objectives nor faced similar external and internal constraints and pressures. So one major task is to present as detailed an analysis as possible of comparative economic regulation. This will show the reader some aspects of what bureaucracy did to both business and Africa.

What business did to both bureaucracy and Africa constitutes another important set of issues. Consider first business-government relationships. Just as one must disaggregate the category "government," so also must one specify what the rubric "business" means in particular cases. With specific agents and agencies of both business and government identified, one can begin to investigate particular relationships and assess their impact on all relevant parties. It is especially important that our approach remain open to the applicability of various concepts. Some have used the notions of cooperation and conflict in their analyses of particular relations. Others have suggested that the interests of a bureaucracy and a business both converge and diverge, depending on what is at stake, and that thinking in terms of zones of convergence and divergence might prove illuminating. Nor should one forget the images of government as collaborator or spectator in a business "exploitation" of Africa. These are possible outcomes in some situations, but they should no longer dictate the domain of inquiry.

There are yet other tasks, even an adequate definition of which may prove elusive. Analyzing impact in all its dimensions is perhaps the most major. Bureaucracy and business affected Africa separately and jointly, but asserting the gross is easier than assessing the roles of each in situations of "joint product." So far "Africa" has appeared in this introduction as a continent acted upon or as home for some residents manipulated by bureaucracy and/or business. But anyone with experience of any part of that continent, whether through reading or actually living there, knows that it has many guises, plays many roles, and affects people, especially those who try to control it, in sometimes imperceptible ways. One can observe aspects of this phenomenon in the local transformations of colonial bureaucracies as they entrenched themselves on the continent. Business people of all kinds must also have encountered the psychological power of the continent.

To the completion of tasks that may focus a volume or volumes the present essay attempts a contribution. Comparative economic regulation, the first task mentioned above, is its initial concern. Bureaucracy affected business in numerous ways. From its many endeavors to manipulate the general economic environment to a host of more immediate measures government impinged on business activity with a degree of constraint that varied according to one's position in the economic process and perspective on the type of regulation at issue. To illustrate the range of government action we shall examine several instances of that more general manipulation as well as multiple examples of those more immediate measures. This investigation will start us towards our first goal—the construction of a detailed, systematic comparative profile that will demonstrate decisively just how important inter- and intra-territorial differences in economic regulation were.

This inquiry comes first for a number of reasons, It is the empirical centerpiece of the essay, based largely on primary sources. It does introduce some of the terms, such as "world-economy," "territorial economy," and "role of the state," that receive more detailed semantic consideration in a section that opens Part II. But the author prefers that readers have before them the material in Part I—the comparative regulatory profile—before considering more extended theoretical observations concerning the concepts that pervade current discussion of bureaucracy and business in Africa. Then, with both empirical foundation and conceptual analysis in mind, readers can better appreciate the selected case studies of government-business relations, drawn from secondary sources, that complete the essay. Let us begin forging our comparative regulatory profile by first studying some bureaucratic attempts to manipulate the general economic environment.

I. WHAT BUREAUCRACY DID TO BUSINESS AND AFRICA: A COMPARATIVE REGULATORY PROFILE

A. Manipulating the General Economic Environment

Colonial bureaucracies usually sought a legally enforceable redefinition of key aspects of the general economic environment for various sometimes linked reasons of stability, security, or revenue. The nature, forms, and location of the act of exchange itself received particular attention. Let us focus first on the nature and forms of exchange.

1. Remaking the Exchange Arena: Moneys and Barter

All bureaucracies introduced some version of their money into their respective territories. British territories in both East and West Africa promoted acceptance of money with regional status as well: East African shillings and cents; British West African shillings and cents. French administrative units endeavored to popularize a version of the franc linked to, but not identical with, the French franc. This was the advent and diffusion of a "money economy" defined in official terms, which subsumed existing indigenous media of exchange under the undifferentiated rubrics of "barter," "near money," "pre-money," "inferior money," or "native currencies." There was also "illegal money"—trading coins (such as the Maria Theresa dollar) widely used or the coins and paper of other European countries than the one administering the territory in question. Equating "money economy" with government-defined legal tender must rank as one of the major alien intrusions into the African environment, with consequences for business people and indeed entire populations that to this day have not been probed in a sufficiently comprehensive framework.

The increasing presence of European-orchestrated monetary systems on the African landscape elicited some reactions from that continent's residents that most observers, including a number of colonial officials, noticed. One major set of reactions rested on an ever keener appreciation of the basic distinction between extrinsic and intrinsic value insofar as money is concerned. In simplest terms extrinsic value is what a governing body says something is worth. Contrasting with government-mandated value is that which inheres in money regardless of political vagaries; as most paper money is virtually worthless in itself, intrinsic value applies to the precious metallic content of coinage. In a 1921 statement that represents the spirit though not the exact conceptual framework of other witnesses, H. W. Leigh, the acting chief secretary for the Northern Territories of the Gold Coast, commented, in the best "accentuate-the-positive" style of colonial reportage, that "in spite of the joy with which alloy coinage was accepted last year, the natives have a very good idea of the intrinsic value of silver and other metals" (1921 *AR*, Northern Territories of Gold Coast, p. 3). The universal concept of intrinsic value, given heightened immediacy in Africa at this time by the additional risks and uncertainties associated with colonial administration, infused every local reaction to alien monetary systems and affected as well decisions that Africans made with respect to the components of their *de facto* investment portfolios of coins, livestock, land, produce-bearing plants and trees, and indigenous media.

The precise make-up of those European-inspired systems changed over time (as did indigenous ones) in several ways: new types of coins and paper were introduced; some were phased out officially in response to internal bureaucratic needs or because of African treatment; the volume of particular components actually in circulation fluctuated; the interpenetration of alien and indigenous systems increased. The official version of the Nigerian money supply in 1927 indicates the types of money supposedly available in that territory. And since the West African Currency Board, started in 1912, controlled Nigeria's official money supply along with those of the other British West African territories, the Nigerian profile, with some alterations, also illustrates the meaning of legal tender elsewhere in BWA.

Let us consider the official British money supply component by component (Table 1), mainly in West Africa but with reference to other locations, and use

Table 1. Nigeria's Official Money Supply (Coins and Notes), 1927

Coins
U.K. gold, silver, and bronze
West African silver and alloy coins of two (2/-) and one (1/-) shillings; six (6d.) and three (3d.) pence
Nigerian nickel-bronze coins of 1 penny, ½ penny, and 1/10 penny
Paper
U.K. notes
West African notes of one pound (1£), and ten shillings (10/-)

Source: 1927 *AR*, Nigeria (p. 5). U.K. coins in 1927 were "being superseded by W.A. and Nigerian coinage."

the Nigerian listing as our organizing principle. As far as gold coins went, a Gold Coast report in 1913 summed up the situation in most African locations. There were "practically no gold coins in circulation; those that are introduced being hoarded and buried by the natives" (1913 *AR*, Gold Coast, p. 7).

Gold did not meet with the same reception everywhere nor does it appear that Gresham's law is for everybody. In 1905 a reporting officer in the Somaliland Protectorate, in northeastern Africa, noted that the British sovereign (a British gold coin minted only for use abroad) was also used on the coast: ". . . but the native from the interior is conservative and will only accept the rupee [a silver coin from India] in exchange for his produce. Consequently, a comparatively large reserve of gold is accumulating in the local Treasury" (1905–1906 *AR*, Somaliland Protectorate, p. 6). The same point was made in the next annual report, although shorn of its ethnocentric economic language ("conservative" and "will only accept"): "Interior natives prefer silver coinage for trading purposes" (1906–1907 *AR*, Somaliland Protectorate, p. 5). Translated into more contemporary economic lingo, commercial requirements fueled a high transactions demand for silver among upcountry residents. In this specific case of sovereign versus rupee there was a huge denominational imbalance, as the rupee, in terms of British-denoted extrinsic value, was worth a small fraction of the sovereign. This fact in itself made the rupee far more business apt for the majority of commercial transactions and negated the utility of the sovereign for the same exchange zone. Speculative and precautionary demands for gold, so strongly in evidence most everywhere else in Africa as typified in the Gold Coast example, may have increased among upcountry Somaliland Africans, as yet a later report contains the observation that the reserve of gold noted in 1905 "gradually diminishes" (1907–1908 *AR*, Somaliland Protectorate, p. 6). Demand mix remains ambiguous here, and such factors as a greater coastal transactions requirement for gold and/or a governmental decision to repatriate some of that metal may have played a part.

The evidence strongly suggests, therefore, the appropriateness of a framework that integrates the distinction between intrinsic and extrinsic value with the tripartite demand for money. Most Africans did not always operate on the principal of intrinsic value for its own sake, although enough examples abound to demonstrate the existence if not of a Gresham's "law" at least its underlying insight that inferior money in terms of intrinsic value usually drives the superior out of circulation. Rather, most Africans applied intrinsic value within a construct of their own particular transactions, precautionary, and speculative demands for money, which included both alien systems and local media. Examine next the fate of several silver-based coins in light of our framework.

As to U.K. and West African silver coins, their common fate was to diminish in circulation. In part, this outcome resulted from the operation of indigenous precautionary and speculative demands for such coins, which some British officers continued to report in language exemplified in a 1921 Gold Coast report. From

1883 to 1921 "it is probable that as much as £3,000,000 to £3,500,000 [in coins] during this period, has been melted down for ornaments or buried and the whereabouts lost to the present generations or" (and this acknowledges the unquantifiable reality of cross-border seepage) "has been exported over the land frontiers" (1921 *AR*, Gold Coast, p. 11). Accelerating silver diminution was a British government policy of withdrawing over the years a substantial amount of silver coin from circulation in West Africa and repatriating that sum to London, where it was also melted down. Apparently, a British melt down, in their eyes, was done for reasons of "high policy"; an African melt down must have been done "for ornaments." As the British withdrew silver, they increased the amount of silver alloy coinage in circulation in West Africa, although the rise was not linear. The raw numbers available for Nigeria during the 1920s demonstrate the shifting components of that country's official money supply under the impact of governmentally sponsored debasement (Table 2, p. 88).

During 1930 the mode of reporting money supply figures changed. It was no longer possible to ascertain specifically Nigerian figures, "owing to the intercolonial movement of coins and notes." So the numbers, also the products of official "estimates," cover all of British West Africa, presumably including the Gold Coast, Sierra Leone, the Gambia, the British mandate in Cameroon, and so forth. The results of this up-aggregation are intriguing (Table 3, p. 89).

Taken together the two tables illustrate in detail the mechanics of official monetary debasement for Nigeria/British West Africa. The process was not constant in every respect on an annual basis. Estimates of circulating silver do decrease every year on both territory and regional tables. Shifting the reporting mode from Nigeria to all of British West Africa did produce a striking and, frankly, suspicious result for silver. As of 31 March 1929 on Table 2, silver estimated at £285,750 was circulating in Nigeria, about 67.5 percent of the £423,000 sum reported one period earlier and not quite double the amount of £148,638 to be filed one year later. As of 30 June 1929 on Table 3, about three months later than Table 2's estimate, British West African silver circulation, which supposedly included a number in the neighborhood of £285,750 for Nigeria, had peaked at £2,228,482, leaving £1,942,732 in silver allegedly circulating elsewhere in British West Africa. This state of affairs was highly improbable, given the strength of indigenous precautionary and speculative demands for silver and a climate affecting that metal intensified by British silver withdrawal.

Estimates of alloy circulation zigzag: Nigerian increases throughout the late 1920s until a diminution reported for FY ending 31 March 1929; a West African slide through 30 June 1932, two periods of ups and downs, then from 1935 through 1937 accelerating increases that produced the highest reported sum for circulating alloy, £14,748,387, followed by a decline that still kept the amount well above all years prior to 1937. Nickel bronzes, with the single exception on both tables of 1931–1932, increase steadily. Paper currency in circulation bounces up and down over the reporting period, but does surge over 2½ times from 30

Table 2.   Nigeria's Official Money Supply (Coins and Notes),
1921–1930 (partial)
(amounts in £s for 31 March of respective year)

	1921	1922	1923	1924	1925
Silver coin withdrawn	1,763,700	1,174,500	1,349,064	746,510	426,000
Silver coin shipped to U.K. to be melted down	same	same	1,548,408	780,085	379,631
Alloy in circulation				3,698,000	5,359,000
Total coinage in circulation				5,827,700	7,076,000
Silver					
Nickel coin					
W.A. currency notes (Throughout W.A. colonies)					

	1926	1927	1928	1929	1930
Silver coin withdrawn	331,000	241,339	149,513	173,458	144,325
Silver coin shipped to U.K. to be melted down	352,000	283,484	153,413	118,023	150,000
Alloy in circulation	5,517,000	5,713,000	5,972,000	6,168,803	5,443,904
Total coinage in circulation	6,929,000	6,724,000			
Silver			423,000	285,750	148,638
Nickel coin			416,000	443,128	446,585
W.A. currency notes		728,835	764,672	753,588	
(30th June)		(1,098,152 notes)	(1,143,409 notes)	(1,131,186 notes)	
(Throughout W.A. colonies)					

Sources: 1921 *AR*, Nigeria (p. 10); 1922 *AR*, Nigeria (p. 10); 1923 *AR*, Nigeria (p. 14); 1924 *AR*, Nigeria (p. 13); 1925 *AR*, Nigeria (p. 14); 1926 *AR*, Nigeria (p. 14); 1927 *AR*, Nigeria (p. 10); 1928 *AR*, Nigeria (p. 11); 1929 *AR*, Nigeria (p. 11); 1930 *AR*, Nigeria (p. 12).
The 1928 report estimates total value of West African currency notes throughout the West African colonies on 31 March 1928 at £791,313. Other reports cite the lower figure noted above for 30 June 1928.

Table 3. Official Money Supply of British West Africa
(Coins and Notes), 1929–1938 (amounts in £s)

	30 June 1929	30 June 1930	30 June 1931	30 June 1932
W.A. silver coin	2,228,482	2,081,038	1,860,590	1,677,891
W.A. alloy coin	10,042,542	9,075,991	6,327,436	6,168,317*
W.A. nickel bronze coin	587,524	595,461	599,464	597,706
W.A. currency notes	753,588	759,370	668,964	628,122
	30 June 1933	30 June 1934	30 June 1935	30 June 1936
W.A. silver coin	1,543,736	1,432,650	1,348,318	1,290,300
W.A. alloy coin	6,716,944	5,374,078	7,276,567	9,541,138
W.A. nickel bronze coin	606,193	624,628	653,065	732,474
W.A. currency notes	705,140	697,024	747,295	976,247
	30 June 1937	30 June 1938		
W.A. silver coin	1,257,241	1,208,067		
W.A. alloy coin	14,748,387	11,710,310		
W.A. nickel bronze coin	888,574	949,096		
W.A. currency notes	2,374,909	2,500,324		
	1930–1931	1931–1932	1932–1933	1933–1934
Silver withdrawn	136,307	106,918	96,593	78,041
Silver shipped to U.K.	143,086	131,768	same	same
	1934–1935	1935–1936	1936–1937	1937–1938
Silver withdrawn	83,300	54,000	26,000	50,555
Silver shipped	same	same	same	same

Note: *For 30 June 1932 6,168,317 might be 6,168,347.
Sources: 1931 *AR*, Nigeria (p. 47); 1932 *AR*, Nigeria (pp. 60–61); 1933 *AR*, Nigeria (p. 71); 1934 *AR*, Nigeria (pp. 74–75); 1935 *AR*, Nigeria (p. 74); 1936 *AR*, Nigeria (p. 78); 1937 *AR*, Nigeria (pp. 86–87); 1938 *AR*, Nigeria (p. 82).

June 1936 through 30 June 1938, reaching its high-water mark of £2,500,324. So by 1938 England had reduced the proportion within the total official money supply (coins and paper currency) of the coins with the greatest intrinsic value and increased amounts of those components which ranged from less (alloy) to little (nickel bronzes) to no (currency notes) intrinsic value. This is one version of debasing the money supply in the aggregate.

Underneath the movement of these official monetary aggregates were numerous local personal decisions concerning components besides the gold and silver coinage mentioned earlier. Diffusion of that alloy coinage, the advertised replacement for the silver coinage being withdrawn, did not encounter a universally enthusiastic reaction in British West Africa. It was not only the inferior coin driving the superior out of circulation in some respects, its presence intensifying the operation of speculative and precautionary demands for money by offering a sharp contrast with a silver so prized that it was being repatriated in significant quantities. It was also in the arena of short- and medium-term business requirements, the domain encompassed by the transactions demand, that alloy coinage produced important consequences. The purchasing power of that coinage, as denominated in indigenous media with local or regional standing, was less than that of a silver. H. W. Leigh, the acting chief secretary of the Northern Territories of the Gold Coast, expanded on his 1921 observations, noted at the outset of this section, concerning the introduction of alloy in light of the fact that the "natives have a very good idea of the intrinsic value of silver and other metals." The "purchasing power of alloy coinage," he continued, was "now far less than that of British silver." An early intermedia exchange rate in the Northern Territories between cowries, an authentic currency in major areas of West Africa and elsewhere, and silver was 1000 cowries = 1 shilling silver. The exchange rate had "now dropped and varies according to local conditions and demand but for a shilling alloy it is doubtful if more than 500 cowries could be bought." For those business people and consumers with threshold transactions requirements for cowries and who employed silver and then alloy to meet them, the reduced purchasing power of alloy may have ironically increased the transactions demand for it. In fact, general transactions was likely the only growth source in demand for alloy coinage, as it was, according to Secretary Leigh, "Useless for melting into ornaments" (1921 *AR*, Northern Territories of Gold Coast, p. 3) and presumably other storage vehicles that served to hold the intrinsic value of metallic content in response to the operation of speculative and precautionary demands.

In fact, neither silver nor silver alloy coinage was denominationally apt for meeting a significant zone of African transactions requirements. The three-pence coin (3 d.) was the lowest one minted in both silver and silver alloy. This denomination was still too high in terms of prices for some local goods as expressed in such indigenous media as cowries. With respect to silver, Lt. Col. A. Morris, chief commissioner of the Northern Territories of the Gold Coast, put the essential facts concisely in 1901. The lowest silver coin in circulation, the three penny piece, was too high. It then purchased 250 cowries. Most daily purchases made by the "natives" involved sums ranging from 10 to 30 cowries. This does not mean that there was little or no demand for the 3d. silver piece. Acting Chief Secretary W. Fosbery's 1905 statement for Southern Nigeria that "3 penny silver pieces [were] especially in demand" (1905 *AR*, Southern Nigeria, p. 11) no doubt applied in many other locations.

But as the British strove to fashion a currency system that fit local price and intermedia exchange rate configurations more accurately, opinion strengthened that action should be taken to deal with the sub-3d. zone of transactions requirements. Chief Commissioner Morris wanted the early introduction of a subsidiary nickel coinage that included penny and half-penny pieces; his 1901 estimates of what the relevant intermedia exchange rates might be had the penny at about 80 cowries, the half-penny at about 40 cowries. He did not recommend a copper coinage for the Northern Territories, as "coppers would be mostly turned into rings and other ornaments," this melt-down done also as an affirmation of the intrinsic value of copper. And, most intriguingly in light of British endeavors not only to abolish barter but also to repress moneys other than their own, attempts to be discussed later in this section, Morris recommended the desirability of retaining some co-existence among the media. He believed that it was not necessary to have a nickel coin below that of the half-penny, as "cowrie coinage must remain the medium for all very small purchases in the way of foodstuffs, etc." (1901 *AR*, Northern Territories of Gold Coast, p. 12). Other officers echoed the general call for a "smaller coinage," though Morris's notion of a two-tiered "smaller coinage" in which British pennies and half-pennies covered the upper range and cowries the lower zone was a decidedly minority view. In fact, as already reported in Table 1, the nickel-bronze coinage that began to circulate in West Africa before World War I featured not only the penny and half-penny but also the 1/10 penny, or tenth. This coinage, with the tenth in particular, was designed to oust cowries, along with such other authentic indigenous media as brass rods and manillas, from their positions in the increasingly interpenetrated alien-indigenous monetary systems. As far as money was concerned, the British wanted only theirs for every use.

The introduction and diffusion of the nickel-bronze coinage did not proceed flawlessly. One preliminary problem involved composition of the coins. When first minted and issued, the pennies consisted of nickel and aluminium, the tenths of aluminium only. Reports from both Northern and Southern Nigeria at about the same time indicate that the tenth was "not satisfactory in composition" (1907–1908 *AR*, Northern Nigeria, p. 14) and was not meeting acceptance. It was re-minted and "as a result of the alteration in the composition of the tenths to an alloy of nickel a more rapid circulation is expected" (1908 *AR*, Southern Nigeria, p. 36). Why a tenth of nickel alloy was less objectionable locally than one composed entirely of aluminum is not fully clear. Perhaps a too distinctive appearance of an aluminum tenth made it seem separate from the half-penny and penny and fragmented the notion of a unified subsidiary coinage in the public mind. Perhaps comparative intrinsic values of the metals involved played a part. There are reports of the nickel coinage being melted down, but no available testimony on this point concerning the aluminum tenth during its short circulation life.

Besides the composition problem, the British also faced supply constraints. Even before the First World War disrupted nickel shipments, some local officers felt that the quantities of nickel coinage made available in their areas were not adequate. C. H. Armitage, the chief commissioner of the Northern Territories of the Gold Coast, predicted in 1913 that if a sufficient supply of nickel were provided, nickel "would completely supersede the cowrie." Amounts were not adequate, and as an example Armitage quoted a report from the provincial commissioner of the Northeast Province, who wrote that it was "too bad only £200 of nickel coin provided," as it was "very popular" (1913 AR, Northern Territories of Gold Coast, p. 5). The impact of World War I transformed inadequacy into scarcity, and Armitage observed in 1918 that since the supply of nickel was not forthcoming in war, "cowries were coming back" and cited "friction between the 'petty trader' and native over exchange rates" (1918 AR, Northern Territories of Gold Coast, p. 4).

To composition and supply problems add counterfeiting. This practice, which was a business of its own in some locations, presumably affected the entire spectrum of foreign currency. But the testimony available focuses on a scam to pass off tinned coins as shilling pieces which delayed the introduction of nickel coinage into Northern Nigeria. The officer reporting from that territory for 1906–1907 noted the presence of a "large number of counterfeit coins" which caused "incalculable harm to our coinage." He claimed that counterfeiters milled the edges of coppers for "native" blacksmiths who then tinned them. This process produced coins in the shape of pennies and half-pennies that were passed on to "more ignorant natives" as 1/- or 2/- pieces. Because of their similarity to the p. and ½p. in the new subsidiary nickel coinage, its introduction was delayed (1906–1907 AR, Northern Nigeria, p. 42).

The problems surrounding the introduction of the nickel coinage were minor in contrast with those that bedevilled paper currency. Many observers commented on the unacceptability of paper notes in most parts of Africa, for reasons of destructability by climate or insects, lack of intrinsic value to satisfy speculative and/or precautionary needs, and denominational inappropriateness for the greatest range of indigenous transactions requirements. But it is important not to write paper off as a totally failed currency from the British viewpoint, because a significant amount of paper did circulate and as such had consequences for the alien-indigenous money mix. Some British officials noted that one reason why cowries were so popular was that a number of Africans felt that they "kept prices down." Cowries did possess a greater capacity than even the expanded British currency menu with its tenth (1/10 p.) to target precise price in the lower and by all reports most common range of African daily transactions. The opposite effect, to bias prices upwards, apparently came from the circulation of paper in some areas. British paper money first officially appeared in Gambia in 1919, and the officer reporting from that territory for that year noted what was almost the universal reaction to alien paper currency in Africa: it was "unwillingly accepted at first. . ." But in Gambia, unlike in some other locations, paper "perforce circulated freely later . . . no doubt . . . considerable discounting took place . . . which had a regrettable effect on prices" (1919 *AR*, Gambia, p. 11). Presumably, the price in paper currency for a given commodity was higher than it would have been in other media. Price tiers thus complicated the possibilities for exchange already made intricate by the existence of shifting exchange rates between and among local and alien money supply components.

If exchange was rendered more difficult, one effect of introducing different elements of the official British money supply was the same. As cowries were displaced by the tenth-penny piece and a host of hostile administrative actions, prices did rise. Some writers have described an "imported inflation" which penetrated Africa more easily as a result of a currency standardization that also linked African territories to the reigning world currencies (Ofonagoro, 1979, p. 654). But local inflation, not itself exclusively caused by those sometimes ill-specified global forces, was still imported in at least one specific sense. The forced reconfiguration of local monetary systems by the colonial authorities, in these cases the British, removed indigenous media with a more refined capacity to fit price variations for most African daily transactions. So subsidiary nickel coinage, with its tenth-penny, knocked out the more calibrated cowrie currency and, not fitting prices, was a major factor pushing the prices on many daily necessities upward to conform to its denominational capabilities.

As the previous pages have tracked some of the components of the official British money supply—gold, silver, silver alloy, nickel-bronzes, and paper—the profound extent to which the colonial authorities aimed to transform the very exchange basis of African daily life has become clear. Not only did administrations everywhere enforce their own versions of money as legal tender and repress alternatives, but these also tried to stamp out what was perceived as "barter." In fact, some bureaucracies had their own rankings of the states of exchange and so converted them into evolutionary stages. One such approach placed "barter" as the first or "most primitive" phase in any society's economic evolution. The second stage was a "money economy," with a particular colonial power defining "money" mainly as its own currency and coins. The third stage was a "credit economy," the most advanced phase, which required a high degree of "economic maturity" from its participants. As some administrators attempted to reduce the incidence of perceived barter exchange, they sometimes legislated various restrictions on credit—its acceptable meanings, availability, accessibility, and permissible uses. Accelerating the arrival of stage two, the subject of this section, and forestalling the advent of stage three, the theme of the next, are understandable for financial reasons: stage two was also the bureaucratic bedrock. The "money economy" had one simple but crucial administrative definition: most Africans paid their taxes in those official coins.

Remaking local exchange arenas did not follow the same scenario everywhere. Barter remained a "most primitive" form of exchange, an obstacle to administrative "progress" (a.k.a. tax collections), even when the transaction was actually monetized from one or more African viewpoints, as economic anthropologists have reported again and again,[1] though not recognized officially as such. Suppressing barter was sometimes more a series of ad hoc administrative actions than a concerted policy, depending on time and place. And bureaucrats took different attitudes towards moneys not their own but which they acknowledged as valid media of exchange. Less repressive outlooks on non-official money sometimes produced a less hurried approach to the enforcement of a limited and limiting local money supply. The more comprehensive a particular administration's definition of money and the less forceful its attempts to suppress barter, the less severe was the short-run damage bureaucratic action inflicted on the evolution of local exchange arenas and, of course, on the opportunities for exchange and consequent economic betterment. The somewhat contrasting experiences of British Nigeria, aspects of which have already been mentioned in this essay, and British Tanganyika, which the author has detailed elsewhere, illustrate these observations.[2]

In Tanganyika the British, who took control of most of what had been German East Africa in the aftermath of World War I, moved with relative dispatch to implement a narrow conception of the money supply. This was the version that should consist mainly of East African paper and coin, as the East African Currency Board exercised official control over the money supply for what were now the three British possessions of Kenya, Uganda, and Tanganyika. The Dar es Salaam administration demonetized Indian coinage from 23 July 1921 and the German coinage from 1 April 1923. The former German administration had already repeatedly tried, with only partial success, to reduce the supply of the Maria Theresa taler (dollar or real), a silver coin used territorially for trading purposes (McCarthy, 1976b, pp. 651–52). These were the coinages, "non-official" depending on which administration, that government had acknowledged for a time as valid media of exchange. None of the commodities which local media groups employed as money, such as iron, brass wire, hoes, and cattle, had obtained even momentary official recognition as a legitimate though illegal medium of exchange, the perceptions of some bureaucrats notwithstanding (McCarthy, 1976b, p. 655). This fact meant that the administrative rubric of barter in Tanganyika was comparatively sweeping. So when bureaucrats acted to "stamp out" barter, in what must rank across the colonial spectrum as one of the more energetic campaigns against "primitivism" then defined, their gutting of many local exchange opportunities inflicted especially great harms (McCarthy, 1976b, pp. 660–62).

In Nigeria, by contrast, both official perception and toleration of indigenous moneys were greater. Professor Ofonagoro has written that "in the late nineteenth century most colonial officials responsible for managing the affairs of southern Nigeria tended to overemphasize the importance of intrinsic value, and persisted in the erroneous notion that cowries, manillas, brass rods, and such were mere items of barter. Thus they perpetuated the notion that currency was nonexistent in the country, and that in introducing British currency they were merely improving a system that was previously based on direct barter" (Ofonagoro, 1979, p. 636). Doubtlessly, "most colonial officials" did believe that "in introducing British currency they were . . . improving a system," but what majority official conceptions of "money" and "barter" were in both Northern and Southern Nigeria (not administratively unified until 1914) are other matters altogether.

Examination of published colonial reports has produced enough examples to suggest that the foregoing explanation should be refined. In the very early twentieth century various administrators in the south wrote about the existence and circulation of multiple "native" currencies and cited the rates of exchange between those and official money. This suggests either a rapid metamorphosis in official outlook from the "late nineteenth century" or an intercentury continuity of attitude. An author of the 1900 official report for Southern Nigeria did describe brass rods, manillas, brass wire, gin, cloth, and tobacco when used "in transactions between or among Europeans" as "instances of barter" and suggested that those items "can't be regarded in any way as currency" in European "transactions." But he had listed those commodities as instances of "native" currency and after noting the commonplace that in the Benin territories, as in Lagos, cowries are used for small purchases, he conceded that they "may be regarded as acting as a currency to a limited extent" (1900 *AR*, Southern Nigeria, p. 7). In that same report one notes how the "absence of coin in districts has made it necessary to recognize that orders of Native Courts [local surrogate enforcers of colonial 'justice'] can be complied with by payment of manillas, brass rods, etc. and even in 'trade goods,' except gin," a "custom" that "probably originated with the provisions contained in Sec. CXI of African Order in Court, 1889." The writer makes a clear distinction between payment-in-currency and payment-in-kind ("trade goods") and tentatively locates its legal genesis in the late 1880s. He also quotes prevailing rates of exchange between official and "native" moneys; for example, brass rods equalled 2½d., manillas, 1¼d., and wires, ⅛d. (1900 *AR*, Southern Nigeria, p. 8). Other administrative reports, for North as well as South, contain then-prevailing rates of exchange between British and indigenous moneys, sometimes with a high degree of detail (1902 *AR*, Northern Nigeria, p. 71; 1904 *AR*, Southern Nigeria, pp. 12–13).

Greater official perception and toleration of indigenous moneys in Nigeria did not alter the long-run objective of the colonial administration to impose its own narrow version of a "money economy" on the country. In multiple endeavors that quickened in the early twentieth century and accelerated thereafter the colonial administration went after cowries, manillas, brass rods, and other valid though not preferred media of exchange in various ways. Prohibitions on imports placed one type of obvious ceiling on some components of the total Nigerian money supply. Administrators sometimes pursued less direct assaults, such as declaring brass rods and manillas legal tender but only in specified "native markets" (the Native Currency Proclamation of 1902) (Ofonagoro, 1979, pp. 639–54).

So in Nigeria the costs of dogmatizing a particular version of money were imposed on the populace, though on a more lagged basis than in Tanganyika. Indeed, the costs everywhere in Africa that forcibly experienced a reconfiguration of its monetary systems and zones must have been staggering. Consider first the energies absorbed in environments in which the media themselves became the preferred and sometimes dominant vehicles of entrepreneurial opportunity. Media, of course, have always been perceived in most environments as both economic means and ends and are sometimes the objects of intense speculative/investment activity. But colonialism intensified both the risk and uncertainty inherent in business decisions, as it made government itself, always a major factor in influencing the economic and financial climate, at one and the same time a more determined extractor of the populace's assets but one with a life-span of undetermined length. No wonder the heightened operation of speculative and precautionary demands for money, which presumably benefitted individual people but in reducing the total available circulating money supply must have hampered exchange. And as alien and indigenous moneys interpenetrated more and more, arbitrage became more widespread and constituted perhaps the greatest "growth industry" for aspiring African entrepreneurs during the tortuous transition to the official "money" economy.

Officials unanimously testify that exchange rates between various components of the British money supply, on the one hand, and such staples of the indigenous money supply as cowries, brass rods, copper wires, and manillas, on the other, fluctuated, depending on time and place. Arbitrage could, of course, occur within either alien or indigenous category, or within one type, as, for example, there were at least five types of manillas (*atori, awiramu, abbie* or prince, *ama-ogono* or town, and *perkule*) (1904 *AR*, Southern Nigeria, p. 12). Let us concentrate on intersystem exchange rates and focus on one of the more arresting examples of arbitrage possibility, the Northern Nigerian experience in the early part of the twentieth century, as it concerns cowries and British silver shillings. As one officer put it in 1902, the value of cowries in silver varies from time to time and increases as they are carried further northwards (1902 *AR*, Northern Nigeria, p. 71). The following table, which reports the number of cowries needed to buy one shilling, confirms the heightened appreciation of the cowrie as it moved north. The reporting officer for Northern Nigeria in 1904 observed that some "natives think they are being defrauded" if one shilling equals 1000 cowries at Sokoto or Barrichi and 3000 at Lokoja. Others, no doubt, fully appreciated the significance of differential exchange rates and moved cowries around, notwith-

Table 4.   Exchange Rates: Cowries and British Silver in
Northern Nigeria, 1902

Location	No. of cowries = 1 shilling (1/-)
Yola	1,200
Illorin	4,000
Bida	3,000
Lokoja	2,500
Illo	1,000
Zaria	2,000
Kano	1,200
Katsena	1,200
Sokoto	1,200
Kontagora	2,500
Nassarawa	2,400

Source: 1902 *AR*, Northern Nigeria (p. 71).

standing their transport costs, to capitalize on those differences, activity which increased the transactions demand for cowries and the speculative and/or precautionary demands for silver. So the British aimed to "equalise the rate of exchange [of cowries] with silver throughout the country," a goal the pursuit of which was then complicated by the existence of Northern and Southern Nigeria as separate administrative jurisdictions. Some thought, with little attention to the unofficial market activity this plan would engender, that reserves of cowries should be established in charge of the British Residents (officers) in order to give the cowrie a fixed value everywhere (at, say, 100 per one pence) until cowries would be superseded by the subsidiary coinage (1904 *AR*, Northern Nigeria, pp. 102–103).

Meanwhile, an intriguing official interpretation of exchange rates between cowries and silver appeared. Frederick Lugard, then governor of Northern Nigeria, apparently believed that the appreciation of the cowrie promoted the circulation of coinage; the demand for cash in Sokoto had supposedly lowered the rate from 1200 cowries per shilling to 2000 and upward (1904 *AR*, Northern Nigeria, pp. 102–103). It is difficult to detect all the forces that produced the above situation. Was it only a case of an increase in cowrie exchange value promoting a demand for silver to buy more cowries, which added to the already existing demands for silver and produced a greater relative demand for silver than cowries, which caused silver to appreciate vis-à-vis cowries? If arbitrage was a major factor, which the author strongly believes it was, then perhaps an excessive supply of cowries had become available in more northern locations as a result of cowrie movement in that direction. That supply was too plentiful to sustain the then-prevailing cowrie-silver exchange rates and these then moved in favor of silver. To the interpretation of relative greater demand for silver must be added the too abundant supply of cowries created by arbitrage for even a partial explanation of Northern Nigerian monetary history in this regard. In any event, the media in Northern Nigeria as elsewhere had become the message in that they not only were a major official preoccupation in reporting, but they also had come to consume a large, perhaps the greatest share, of the population's economic and business energies.

The harms wrought by the forcible imposition of the official version of the "money economy" are significant in themselves, but all the more so as the prevailing interpretations of the results of this process accentuate its alleged positive aspects. While he does focus our attention on the hardships caused by Britain's unwillingness to redeem those local currencies it was suppressing in Nigeria (excepting manillas), Professor Ofonagoro does posit benefits from the imposition of British currency in that country:

> Certainly, no one can deny that it was beneficial in the longer run to have a modern, uniform currency system operating throughout the confines of the Nigerian market which was thereby linked effectively, albeit in a dependent capacity, with the international money markets of the twentieth century, and at par with sterling. While the British currency system reigned supreme in Nigeria, the Nigerian economy remained a ward of sterling, subject to regulation from London. But the foundation had been laid for the ultimate emergence of the *naira*, and of a relatively independent, modern Nigerian money market (1979, pp. 653–54).

This interpretation, with some names of places and coins changed of course, could apply, given the directions of current scholarship, to other colonial situations as well. So it is of the utmost importance that one be clear about the assumptions of the above reasoning and its implications. Ofonagoro's "longer run" is the same as Keynes's in that we'll all die during it. But its lack of specificity in this context incorrectly downplays the harms associated with the colonial period, a "short-run" within the millennial sweep of African history, and with the legacy of colonialism still present today.

Why is it "beneficial" to have a "modern, uniform currency system" operating within a Nigerian "market," (or any market or markets) the oneness of which as an entity with sufficient unity and/or integration is itself falsely taken for granted? In the case studies of monetary intrusion we have studied "modernity" and "uniformity" are not per se necessary or desirable attributes. Even more, the British themselves had no fixed definitions of those terms, as their continuous revisions of their coinage, the experimentations associated with different metallic contents, the withdrawal of lower denomination paper currency, and so forth, demonstrated. "Modernity," itself a vague, short-term notion, and "uniformity," a term too often employed in practice with an abstractness that does not even belong in textbooks, were rendered, even if one accepted them as monetary goals, more elusive in light of the perennial supply problems that bedeviled a number of components of the official money supply.

And when much scholarship assigns to the penetration of a "capitalist world-economy" into Africa the cause of much "underdevelopment" it is ironic to observe one arguing that even though the supremacy of the British currency system made Nigeria a ward of "London," the "foundation had been laid for the ultimate emergence of the *naira*, and of a relatively independent, modern Nigerian money market." A foundation laid in dependency is not so easily rebuilt in independence, particularly when Ofonagoro seems to assume, again falsely, that "flag" or political independence brought with it the relative economic independence of a modern Nigerian money market, again the existence of which as oneness is merely posited. As to the *naira* and its relations to colonial currency, once a ward in the British imperial monetary sense, still a ward in some respects in the realities of international money markets. However one analyzes the origins of "underdevelopment," (see pp. 128–36), the destruction of indigenous monetary systems and zones removed a shield that protected in some degree the population from the vagaries and in some instances the lesser versatilities of more internationally connected moneys. A cardinal instance of this was seen in the case of cowries versus tenth-penny and the inflationary thrust which the diminution of cowries imparted to the prices of many local commodities.

It seems that scholarship, in the case of money, endorses the rationale employed by the colonialists themselves concerning the need for a "unified, standardized, legalized" money. This is nothing more than a repetition of mercantilist notions on the subject, which, it must be remembered, construed economics from the viewpoint of enhancing state power. Clearly, it is to the advantage of a state to have within its boundaries one monetary system that it can manipulate. Competing currencies are adversarial in political terms, but not necessarily in either economic or financial contexts.

Most scholarship on African monetary history also accepts the ludicrous paradigm of economic maturity mentioned earlier, which features "barter" exchange as "primitive," if not downright "pre-historic." Barter does not deserve that stigma in either present or past. Commodity swaps of various kinds and loans that require the borrower to amortize by purchasing so much of the lender's exports have today become more common. Granted, not every colonial administration defined barter so sweepingly nor endeavored to repress it so completely as did the Tanganyika administration. But the general thrust of colonial efforts to reduce barter, however beneficial to promoting tax collections in specie and not in kind, was altogether harmful to exchange diversity. Trying to eliminate during the colonial period "crop swaps" which involved food (which may have actually been money depending on local viewpoints) surely damaged, as we have reported elsewhere, the development of more extensive internal trading patterns in life necessities (McCarthy, 1976b, p. 661).

Why must scholarship on this subject unthinkingly replicate the mind-set of colonialism in particular and state-serving economic assumptions in general? In challenging aspects of mainstream interpretation one is not suggesting multiplicity of moneys is itself inherently desirable. A sensible position is twofold. Recall the concept of optimal media mix, which involves the co-existence and preferably complementarity of certain indigenous and alien moneys. And discard the stages of economic maturity approach for one that highlights optimal exchange form mix, combining barter, money, and credit transactions in ways best suited to the needs of a given economic and business area or region. Scholarship must refine further the costs and benefits involved in the enforced transition to the official "money economy," but there is little doubt that, however arguable the benefits, the damages to productive exchange, as opposed to a money-in-and-for-itself transaction, were extensive. The "media as ends" people benefitted; the "media as means" people were not so fortunate. Productive exchange so limited and distorted and a concern with media so disproportionate and obsessive restricted, in turn, a territory's economic growth and development. Ironically, the fastening of a narrow version of "money economy" on an area constrained its capacity to produce for itself and for others which, in these cases, included extra-territorial markets. So the intrusion of official money in the ways it happened slowed the integration through intensification of trade ties of a territory into what some call the "capitalist world-economy." Productive exchange in all these local, national, and international contexts was also seriously affected by bureaucratic restrictions on African access to credit.

2. Remaking the Exchange Arena: Credit Devitalization

Access to sufficient credit in a timely manner is important for all actual and prospective economic agents, but restrictions on its availability, permissible uses, and even acceptable legal forms seem to hit many business people with special force. The subject of credit devitalization has not received the same scholarly attention as have those of African moneys and the coerced transition to the official "money economy." Economic anthropology now illuminates more the different types of African money than the related but distinct rubric of "indigenous or ethnic sources of credit."[3] One can not, therefore, integrate business and economic history with economic anthropology in the area of credit as one has endeavored to do for authentic moneys repressed as illegal tender or suppressed under the guise of barter. And the credible secondary literature on credit restrictions is most sparse. The subject is, nonetheless, of critical importance and deserving of much further study than the sources available have enabled us to give it so far. For the moment, an examination of some administrative approaches to credit limitation demonstrates the significance of the issues involved. Whatever their origins or particular language of formulation, even an incomplete enforcement of these regulations would have limited the types of exchanges that could occur, skewed those that did, and overall frustrated the emergence of peer relations between African business people and others.

Let us consider the nature of those regulations based on the partial sample at our disposal. The author has elsewhere analyzed in detail the origins of the Tanganyika administration's approach to credit restriction as well as the formulation, refinement, and impact of resulting policy. Suffice it to say that the Tanganyika bureaucracy tried to minimize the number of credit transactions of any size between "natives" and "non-natives" in order to respond to five factors that all, though in different mixes at different times, affected administrators. These were, to reprise them simply, the need to repress a "credit economy" that might undermine the diffusion of the official "money economy" which supplied the revenue, perceptions of Asiatic commercial avarice and African naîveté, the lobbying effectiveness of Indian organizations, the British Mandate for East Africa's injunctions concerning usury, and the related fears concerning agricultural debt and a landless peasantry. It is not possible to produce here the same type of "inside" analysis of policy origins for other administrations, since the author has not yet gained access to the kinds of confidential documentation necessary to recreate the realities of policy formulation as distinct from its rhetoric. But one can note the significant differences that characterize credit regulations across a range of colonial experiences. In order to limit as much as possible credit transactions the Tanganyika government required that all Africans obtain permission from a local official in writing for every specific debt assumption, a significant disincentive, unless the person wishing to obtain credit held an exemption permit or was in one of the occupations which did not "need the protection of the law" (McCarthy, 1982, pp. 37–49).

In British Nyasaland the policy was not based on exemptions for individual persons or groups but on a ceiling. There government enacted the Credit Trade with Natives (Amendment) Ordinance of 1936, which gave "effect to a recommendation of the Nyasaland Chamber of Commerce for the increase of the amount of credit which may legally be given by non-natives to natives from £1 to £10" (1936 *AR*, Nyasaland, p. 56). It is not clear from this description whether the ordinance intended to limit the total amount any one "non-native" could lend to any one "native" to 10 pounds or whether the maximum was transaction-specific. Presumably 10 pounds was the most any "non-native" could advance to any "native" during the life of a business relationship, because if the limitation were transaction-specific, its intent to control the amount of credit given to "natives" would be meaningless even on paper as the daily upper bound would then consist of how many transactions interested parties might be willing to negotiate within a twenty-four-hour period. In any event, however constrained, government had legally expanded the permissible zone of regular business behavior in the credit arena among people of different backgrounds in Nyasaland. This approach—raising the ceiling—contrasts, as noted, with Tanganyika's general exemptions from written certification for individual persons or groups. This author found no record of any individual person granted an exemption, but the general groups excluded from the written certification requirement included, from 1931 on, "trading contracts made by 'natives' holding trading licenses." So the properly licensed in Tanganyika faced neither written hurdle nor ceiling maximum, which suggests that at least in this respect business people were less fettered there than in Nyasaland.

The key enforcement provision in credit restriction legislation in Tanganyika, Nyasaland and elsewhere was legal irrecoverability. One could violate any ordinance on this matter and extend credit to "natives" either in excess of stipulated amounts or without complying with the necessary paperwork, but if the debtor defaulted or became remiss in meeting a repayment schedule, the creditor could not use the courts to recover. Legal irrecoverability probably did not deter all illegal transactions, but the strong impression is that it did largely succeed in making credit restriction effective. Legal irrecoverability also worked in ways that frustrated the emergence of peer economic relations among different groups of Africans and between Africans and others. The particular scenario varied. In the early 1900s the government of Southern Nigeria proclaimed that "no Court can enforce against a native any obligation of a commercial character based on credit, which has been incurred by him towards a person who is not a native of the Protectorate" (1900 AR, Southern Nigeria, p. 16). Removing the option of legal action delegitimized *de jure* and *de facto* whatever *de facto* mutuality of treatment had come to characterize relations between "natives" and "non-natives" both within and without Southern Nigeria as well as those between "natives" regarded as members or non-members of that Protectorate. So racial and protectorate affiliation became barriers to the conduct of business in yet more ways.

Other administrations based their targets on distinctions derived from social structures. Sierra Leone's, for instance, enacted about 1905 a Protectorate Native Law Ordinance that circumscribed legal recoverability for the following people in the manner prescribed. For paramount chiefs: "Debt cannot be recovered from a paramount chief unless it is proved by the certificate of the D.C. [district commissioner] that the principal men have assented to the debt being contracted." For everyone else, the kind of permission needed to even contract a debt was emphasized: "A native can not incur a debt save with the consent of his family or the chief of [the] town in which he resides . . ." (1905 AR, Sierra Leone, pp. 31–32). Presumably, without some colonially certified "proof" of chiefly permission or of an unspecified approval from a family unit itself vaguely defined, "everyone else" who contracted a debt would be immune to recoverability.

Immunity sometimes rested on bureaucratic position. In the late 1930s the Gold Coast government proclaimed a Public Officers (Liabilities) Ordinance which stipulated that "loans incurred by junior civil servants shall not in the future be recoverable." The background for this particular grant of irrecoverability, as the official line put it, was that arrests of public officers on debt matters were of "frequent occurrence." These arrests supposedly originated because some civil servants, under pressure from relatives to stand surety for loans as "money lenders insist on borrowers being secured," became entrapped by the improvidence of their kin (1938–1939 *AR*, Gold Coast, p. 103). The government version does not analyze the possibility that the civil servants themselves were the actual debtors in difficulty. Whatever the real nature of dereliction, junior civil servants in the Gold Coast received a special legal exemption based on bureaucratic rank that distorted in yet another way the development of peer economic relations; how this immunity affected their capacity to contract debt is unclear.

Legal recoverability, an indispensable element in promoting and regularizing peer economic relationships or those based on both equality and equity of reciprocal treatment in every respect, was thus politicized by colonial administrations in pursuit of one or another goal pertaining to stability. One can empathize in particular with fears concerning agricultural debt and the increased risk of more landless "peasants," factors operational in Tanganyika and probably elsewhere, in light of multiple debt problems—international, governmental, domestic agricultural, etc.—that increasingly cloud the 1980s. But the available evidence overwhelmingly supports the notion that legal recoverability was excessively politicized in ways that damaged the capacities of African business people and others to expand and further energize exchange.

"Protecting Africans" from the avarice, real or imagined, of others by removing them from litigation may have spared demonstrated defaulters court costs and other payments, but the overall result was to fasten on the "protected" yet another type of harmful dependency on government. In British Africa this result was poignantly ironic. Here were colonial administrations, priding themselves on implanting and nurturing what was to become a legacy of legality and constitutionalism, placing one agency of government, the central bureaucracy in a particular colonial territory, in the position of "protecting" Africans from the operation of another branch of government. This was the court system that proceeded through various local levels to the territorial High Court and on to a regional Appeals Court. Governments of all kinds everywhere sometimes speak with conflicting tongues, but certain features of colonialism, such as those just adumbrated in this section on credit restriction, made the mission and message of government especially confusing from some business perspectives. Other types of distortions and confusions resulted from government's manipulation of its own language as well as those concepts and symbols that may be regarded as forming a universal vocabulary of economic logic.

3. Manipulating the Language of Economic Logic: Gutting the Concept of Savings

All colonial administrations put their respective languages in the service of reaching their objectives, and language so harnessed was sometimes language manipulated. Government use of some words and phrases left on them an imprint, which was really a spectrum of abuse, ranging from tainting to the destruction of meaning. Language manipulation presumably affected all areas of human endeavor but has special significance in its impact on the elements of an economic behavior construed as widely as possible. These elements include the very concepts which, when yoked to goal and motivation and framed through cognition, produce the varieties of that behavior. Language manipulation and its resultant harms both during the colonial period and as a haunting legacy in the present are issues that have received insufficient attention from scholars, in part because European languages are still adjudged to be among the most positive bequests of the will of colonialism.

The author has elsewhere delved into language manipulation in its multiple senses for interwar colonial Tanganyika and its ramifications in the present. He showed how dissolving differences among a cluster of words—encouragement, exhortation, wish, order, and command—undermined government's capacity to direct economic activity with any sense of distinct priority. He demonstrated how the use of a phrase that should have retained a special meaning—"essential public service"—was so often invoked to justify the employment of "forced labor" of various kinds that its definition became "whatever government wanted," not necessarily what was either "essential" or "public" or a "service," And he examined how the bureaucracy's artificial agronomic nomenclature, which divided crops into the almost exclusively dichotomous categories of "food" or "export" (also called "cash" and "economic"), partitioned activity in a harmful way (McCarthy, 1979, pp. 9–16). All these points deserve serious study for the rest of British Africa, as well as for French, Portuguese, German, Italian, and Spanish Africa. Scholars with acute linguistic competence should pursue language manipulation in their specialties. Within its thematic framework, and given the available evidence, this essay shall focus on savings—a concept severely limited in meaning by manipulation and left with a most tainted residue. A vignette on how and why this notion was so treated will further demonstrate government's constraining impact on the business environment during the colonial period and also suggest another link with the present. That governments of today encounter problems in encouraging people to deposit funds in institutions which they own or regulate is surely related in part to how governments of yesterday conducted themselves on similar matters.

In most British territories there appeared an institution known as the savings bank. Usually associated with the government-run post office, this type of bank was supposed to act as an educational vehicle for transmitting and then inculcating a notion of savings defined in an especially Victorian way. There were even penny savings banks established in some schools. Writing about the "growing appeal to Africans" which the Savings Bank in Kenya was allegedly manifesting in the mid-1930s, one official described both process and notion in a manner remarkably concise and arresting. Since the bank's establishment in that country in 1910, there had been occurring "an inoculation of thrift" (1935 *AR*, Kenya,

p. 37). Other territories started having that experience earlier, but officials played the same theme though the orchestration was somewhat different. In the mid-1890s, a bureaucrat in the Gold Coast wrote that "some progress" had been made in the "great thrift lesson which since 1888 the Government has undertaken to give natives of the Gold Coast" (1894 *AR*, Gold Coast, p. 22). In the same territory later in the 1890s an unidentified official, perhaps the same one who earlier addressed the question, gave some definition to the kind of thrift most British officers had in mind. Of the Africans using the bank, "most" regard it as a "convenient place for brief periods"; a "few" will acquire a "notion of the real importance of thrift and of gradually accumulating a sum which will be available in time of need" (1896 *AR*, Gold Coast, p. 7).

A conception of "frugality" or "economical management" is here so inter-twined with various biases concerning time and quantity. Those who deposit funds only for an unspecified 'brief' period receive no plaudits, while those who slowly and incrementally build a sum treated as a reserve will have learned well. Those who withdraw later in the future than nearer in order to meet a need that arises in that long term will have acted properly, while the short-termers have not allowed themselves sufficient time to grasp the essentials of this particular brand of thrift. Needless to say, the microeconomic, in this case personal, definitions of what short, middle, or long term mean on an individual's time horizon may vary from the macroeconomic, in this case bureaucratic, imposition of temporal differentiation. Some administrators did not see it that way, of course, and reprised the educational motif. Acting Colonial Secretary Frank Rohrweger of Lagos Colony noted that the number of depositors in the Government Savings Bank there had risen from 416 to 543 during 1895, "a most satisfactory increase, indicating amongst other things that the schoolmaster is abroad" (1895 *AR*, Lagos, p. 4).

The "schoolmaster" encountered various reactions from Africans to the implementation of this particular aspect of the British colonial educational mission. Some show that apparently numerous Africans had already mastered other principles adumbrated by other "schoolmasters," this time in courses in intro-ductory economic logic. These reactions relate sometimes to the existence of non-bank financial opportunities, sometimes to inter-bank "comparison shop-ping," facilitated by deposit ceilings and lower interest rates associated with the Government Savings Banks, and sometimes to a risk-aversion against an agency connected with a government the intentions of which were rendered even more than normally suspect by its colonial essence. This variegated behavior caught the attention of some reporting officers, whose own actions in moving against the tide of a common economic logic did not prevent them from noting the facts of life. Sometimes the facts themselves may have received some embellishment, as in the following estimate of some prevailing interest rates in Uganda in 1908–1909. In that territory, the official observer wrote, the Savings Bank "is not yet regarded with much favour by the natives of the Protectorate. This is due to the fact that they expect to get at least 100 percent per annum on any money lent. Indeed, 1,200 percent per annum is no uncommon rate on monthly loans among themselves.'' Whatever the going rates were there at that time, local officials continued to promote an institution that supposedly paid a yearly interest rate of 2½ percent: "Endeavours are being made to explain that a savings bank is for the encouragement of thrift, and that they [the African residents] should not look on deposits as money loaned to the Government, but rather that the Savings Bank is a place where they can put their money for safety, with the power of withdrawal at any moment if they require it" (1908–1909 *AR, Uganda,* pp. 9–10). Preferably for the longer "moment" than the shorter, but such were the obstacles facing the bank at that time in Uganda that officers emphasized more the convenience and safety aspects, the latter most necessary in view of the fact that the primary definition of "to save" in this fashion was becoming for most Africans "to lend money to the Government."

Experience elsewhere enriches the themes of risk aversion and inter-bank opportunities (for more on non-bank avenues, see p. 114). Some bureaucrats persisted in explaining the savings bank's difficulties in terms of their own educational mission: "[The] Nyasaland native has yet to recognize the value of thrift" (1912–1913 *AR,* Nyasaland, p. 20) and "the natives of the Protectorate [Uganda] have not yet learnt to appreciate the objects of the bank" (1911–1912 *AR,* Uganda, p. 5). Others noted telling anecdotes. In 1901 in Gambia only one African had opened an account in the Government Savings Bank, then under control of the territory's Treasury Department. He soon closed it; he had deposited 10 shillings for six weeks, but according to a report signed by Colonial Secretary H. M. Brandforth Griffith, "He was afraid the Treasury officers might have 'chopped' it" (1901 *AR,* Gambia, p. 15). To be sure, African risk aversion applied to some banks other than the government-associated savings banks. This reaction seems stronger in the earlier phases of the colonial period, and some groups more than others receive special attention in the official reports.

Take the Gold Coast experience. Officers there in 1908–1909 focused on the Ashanti people, who were then under a separate administrative jurisdiction in the interior prior to later subsumption under the entity "Gold Coast." The reporting officer quoted the unidentified manager of a branch of the Bank of British West Africa, which had been established in Coomassie (Kumasi) towards the end of 1907. The manager noted that the "ignorance of Ashanti regarding objects of bank, together with their innate conservatism, are still matters to be reckoned with . . . "and predicted that they will in time with the spread of "commerce and education" recognize that a bank "affords them a safe and convenient method of saving money" (1908 *AR,* Ashanti, p. 25). One year was not enough for the upcountry Ashanti, as the savings banks at Coomassie and Obuasi "are only made use of by coast natives" (1909 *AR* Ashanti, p. 12) during 1909, but the

British bureaucrat and bank officer had somewhat different perspectives on the rationale for Ashanti aversion. The bank manager focused on the more narrow question of comparative advantages for different modes of savings without reference to the broader environmental context. The Ashantis still prefer, he supposedly said, "Their crude native methods of utilising and keeping their savings to the up-to-date facilities afforded by the bank" (1909 *AR*, p. 22). The British official gave a wider definition to risk aversion in this environment: "The Ashanti proper is still too suspicious of our methods to confide his savings to strangers" (1909 *AR*, Ashanti, p. 12).

As colonial time went by, Africans decided some strangers warranted more suspicion than others, and Government Savings Banks experienced stiffer competition from other types of banks and economic opportunities. Differential interest rates were always a problem for the savings banks. In the early 1900s in Lagos Colony, for instance, the savings bank posted a per annum interest rate of 2½ percent. The Bank of British West Africa there, in an ironic demonstration that it knew how to use incentives to encourage its own version of thrift, had implemented a two-tier two-time period schedule of interest rates: 3 percent on deposits of six months; 4 percent on yearly deposits (1900–1901 *AR*, Lagos, p. 9). Savers voted with their money. A 1917 report on the by now unified Nigeria evidenced the contention that the savings bank business continues to decrease, "due in large measure to higher rates of interest offered by commercial banks on small deposits" (1917 *AR*, Nigeria, p. 14). Gold Coast rates about the same time were even starker, though without the two-tier structure. The Government Savings Bank there also paid an annual interest rate of 2½ percent, which the Bank of British West Africa had doubled to 5 percent (1900 *AR*, Gold Coast, p. 17).

Government savings banks not only experienced heightened competition from without, but also operated under internal constraints that limited and perhaps even undercut their capacities to "educate" Africans in official versions of thrift. Some banks imposed ceilings on the amount any one saver might have on account; in Zanzibar into the 1930s the total a depositor could have to his credit, excluding interest, could not exceed Rs (rupees) 1,500 (or 100 pounds). Other banks restricted withdrawal procedures. A 1935 Nigerian regulation made provision for the "speedy withdrawal by a depositor in Lagos of a sum exceeding 2 but not exceeding 10 pounds" from the Post Office Savings Bank there, an intriguing exercise in presumably enforcing the longer-term dimension of bureaucratic thrift by targeting a withdrawal maximum and minimum (1935 *AR*, Nigeria, p. 87). The official numbers for the savings bank and its branches in Nigeria indicate increases in every reporting category for the years 1936, 1937, and 1938, a portrait of growth quite unlike the situation that prevailed two decades earlier.

Evidently that withdrawal restriction did not impede the bank's overall expansion and those increases might suggest some success in the British colonial thrift "inoculation." But how much is impossible to say, since these numbers,

Table 5. Expansion of Nigerian Savings Bank, 1936–1938
(amounts in £)

	1936	1937	1938
branches	77	86	95
depositors	29,291	35,043	39,830
individual transactions (deposits and withdrawals)	85,065	100,707	109,915
deposits paid in	86,617	118,001	120,393
deposits withdrawn	61,429	83,866	98,032
on deposit, 31 December	115,443	149,578	171,939
average deposit	3.941	4.268	4.316

Source: 1938 *AR*, Nigeria (pp. 81-82).

unlike some of those presented in other reports, do not distinguish "African" and "non-African" users of the bank. Nor can one infer, of course, motivation or mode of use, since how long those withdrawals had remained in the bank is not reported. The average deposit increased just a little over one-third of a pound during the two-year period (.375), which does not indicate that more users were saving more, but almost the same average amount. This suggests perhaps that the bank was still perceived by most as a "convenient place for brief periods" rather than a longer-term incremental incubation depository for a growing sum "which will be available in time of need" and that the 10 pound maximum in that "speedy withdrawal" regulation may have operated to retard the growth in that average.

The most constraining governing principle imposed on savings banks was a version of the perennial British imperial notion of local self-sufficiency. The maxim that every overseas colony or territory should "pay its own way" or "pull-its-own-weight-in-the-boat" found a particular translation in the case of the savings banks. An implicit attitude received written formulation in the 1930s. The secretary of state for colonies had appointed a committee to examine the savings bank systems in the colonies. This committee proposed a series of recommendations to implement its broad objectives—to make the savings bank financially sound and self-supporting independently of general local (colonial, territorial, or protectorate) funds (1936 *AR*, Zanzibar, p. 34). The local units then enacted decrees to reflect their specific circumstances. The banks then presumably became even more cautious and, as far as the official record to 1940 goes, never experimented with techniques that might have significantly increased average deposits over a longer term, such as the two-tier two-time period structure of interest rates employed by the Bank of British West Africa in what used to be Lagos Colony.

The image of the savings bank as a financial pit-stop rather than long-term partner in economic betterment was a reality that delimited, even within British frames of reference, the meaning of "savings." This term, as a result of manipulation during the British colonial experience, also acquired a set of connotations that went beyond British and conventional textbook denotations. Savings as "lending money to the government" is not the best public-relations strategy for encouraging people to think of themselves, their heirs, and their country as the primary beneficiaries of systematic accumulation sustained over a longer time horizon. This was surely one universal connotation associated with the Post Office Bank experience, but there were others that varied according to the kinds of local restrictions on deposit maximums and access to funds. Ironically, perhaps the most damaging aspect of government-run savings ventures lies in the way the greater security that supposedly explains part of the differential between interest rates paid by the Post Office Banks and others was shattered in public perception by the facts of colonial life. So it was really a world of multiple economic contradictions that featured banks that paid less for more insecurity. Colonial governments were no financial rocks of gibraltar for their depositors. And the mutilation, even severing of the link between government and provider of security in the arena of savings and investments is part of the colonial legacy that should especially concern contemporary development planners as they more intensively investigate the greater local generation of loanable funds to reduce international debt dependency.

The concept of "savings" received a different type of abuse but with similar implications in the colonial experience of French tropical Africa. If the operation of the Post Office Banks caused some Africans in British Africa to construe savings as "lending money to government," then the activities of agencies known as indigenous provident societies in French West Africa no doubt caused many to equate savings with taxation. *Les sociétés indigènes de prévoyance, de secours et de prêts mutuels agricoles* began to emerge from the beginning of the twentieth century and developed their blended functions over a period of two or more decades in a process lucidly portrayed by Jean Suret-Canale which we shall place in our analytical framework. Those societies originated as reserve granaries, "collective granaries where, under threat of punishment, each peasant had to deposit a part of his harvest. He was not allowed to touch it until the following year" (Suret-Canale, 1971, pp. 235–36). To the extent that savings is postponed consumption, then the reserve granaries represented savings, albeit of an involuntary sort. This was theory. In practice, "left to an uninterested administration—preoccupied merely with preventing the peasant from going near the granaries—the 'reserve' were often destroyed by rats or insects. The district officers and agents of the administration regarded this as an additional means of fleecing the peasant and, through advance deductions, the peasant rarely recovered even the approximate amount of his deposit'' (Suret-Canale, 1971, p. 236). The result was not savings with interest, but with disinterest or negative interest.

To the function of involuntary savings was added that of loans of seeds to cultivators. Just as the notion of savings as systematic accumulation was burlesqued by eaten grain, so also was the concept of a loan as a beneficial extension of credit ridiculed by its almost complete identification with usury. Even after the provident societies began making seed loans to farmers, their rates of interest, extracted in kind, remained extortionate (some charging 25 percent), although the percentages were less rapacious than those sometimes charged by private traders, who in the best loan-sharking tradition demanded interest in kind at an annual rate equivalent to 200 to 300 percent (Suret-Canale, 1971, pp. 236–37). The functions of the provident societies expanded during the 1930s to include a range of activities associated with the promotion of agriculture;[4] for one thing, the societies were legally empowered to become producers' cooperatives, which acknowledged an already existing state of affairs in some locations. The term cooperative was misleading, because membership for all indigenous cultivators was compulsory in many cases. Details concerning the diffusion and fate of the provident societies can be found elsewhere (Suret-Canale, 1971, pp. 240–44).

Our concern here is preeminently with the provident societies as perpetrators of multiple language abuses. The abuses inflicted upon savings and loans have already been mentioned. The concept of time horizon, basic to decisions that affect the economic future, did not escape unscathed, as the *prévoyance* embodied in the societies' official title became distorted versions in practice of "foresight" or "caution." Many cultivators must have wondered as well over the real meanings of *secours*: government-sponsored "assistance" or "help" turned out to be nothing more than various ways of "fleecing the peasants" (Suret-Canale, 1971, p. 236) for the benefit of the "public sector," which was, of course, the fleecers themselves, their constituents, and turfs. Reversing the usual meaning of a word is one of the most perverse types of language abuse, and that is what apparently happened here: assistance became extraction; to give became to take. And, finally, consider another meaning reversal. The *mutuels* or cooperative aspect of the provident societies was only rhetorical: voluntary became compulsory; cooperation became coercion. This last meaning reversal also took place in British Africa, as in selected cases government compelled producers to join cooperatives (McCarthy, 1982, pp. 93–109).

Business people faced not only an environment complicated by official monetary intrusion, credit devitalization, and language manipulation and their results, but also one containing more specific and at times more quantifiable fetters, such as trades licensing fees, market dues and regulations, railroad rates, and tariff and non-tariff barriers.

B. More Immediate Measures

1. Trades Licensing Fees and Market Regulations

Trades licensing fees constrained the business and wider economic environment in several ways. For those already conducting trade, the fees represented another annual cost of doing business, passed on to the final consumer. For those wishing to trade, the fees may have acted as effective entry barriers, depending on personal financial circumstances. Even more, the particular structure of licensing fees in specific territories, as well as the very definitions of the types of trade and the kinds of traders legally permissible, affected entrepreneurial response and initiative in the microcosm and territory-wide economic change in the macrocosm.

An East African profile demonstrates that the Tanganyika fees for trading licenses were higher than in neighboring dependencies but not in all cases.

Table 6. Comparative East African Trades Licensing Fees in Early 1940s
(in shillings/pence)

	Tanganyika	*Kenya*	*Uganda*	*Zanzibar*
Lowest Retail Trading Fee				
for non-natives	50/-	10/- to 30/-	45/	7/50 to 45/-
for natives	20/-			
License to purchase				
"native" produce	100/-	30/- to 75/-	45/- to 150/-	45/- to 150/-

Source: Tanzania National Archives Secretariat File 30272.

The governments of Kenya, Zanzibar, and Uganda had reduced certain fees during the 1930s; Tanganyika's did not. The 1936 Trades Licensing Ordinance in Kenya "reduces fees to figures more in keeping with those in force before enactment of the Licensing Ordinance, 1933" (1936 *AR*, Kenya, p. 54). In Zanzibar, which like Kenya and Uganda and unlike Tanganyika based in some cases the license fee on value of stock held, the minimum fee for traders holding stock not exceeding Rs. 500/- was Rs. 10, according to Trades Licensing Decree No. 5 of 1933 (then prevailing ratios had 100 cents = 1 Rupee = Sh. 1/6d.). That same decree also put the maximum fee for a banker's or general trader's license at Rs. 300/- (1933 *AR*, Zanzibar, p. 29). So by the early 1940s the minimum fee had come down from 10/60 to 7/50 in East African shillings/cents in Zanzibar.

Let us track the history of the Uganda licensing structure in more detail. In 1931 it featured some rates that had increased at least nominally from their levels

Table 7.   Selected Licensing Fees in Uganda, 1912 and 1931

	1912	1931
General trading license (wholesale and retail)	£10 (150 rupees)	£15
—each additional general trading store	£ 1 (15 rupees)	£ 5
Retail trading license	£ 3 (45 rupees)	£ 7.10 shs.Od.
—each additional retail store	£ 1 (15 rupees)	£ 3.15 shs.Od.

Sources: 1913–1914 AR, Uganda (p. 4). Licensing Ordinance of 1912.
          1931 AR, Uganda (p. 55).

about two decades before. The 1931 report noted that a hawker's license cost 48 shillings per annum, the same rate as prevailed in 1927 (Jamal, 1978, p. 425). But the 1933 Uganda report contained more detailed information concerning what was in European eyes a "racially" demarcated licensing structure. Hawkers' licenses went to "non-natives" for £6 (120 shillings) per annum, to "natives" for £3 (60 shillings) (1933 AR, Uganda, p. 58). Ginning licenses remained costly, £50 per annum in the Eastern and Buganda Provinces, £25 in the Northern and Western Provinces, as of 1935 (1935 AR, Uganda, p. 53). A key 1938 Ugandan Trading Ordinance then reenacted the territory's basic trading law, but approached the subject more from the "point of view of control and regulation rather than production of revenue." Its fees, some of which are reported in Table 6, were "considerably" lower than what prevailed before. But regulations based on location as well as background received more emphasis. The 1938 ordinance prohibited "trading by non-natives outside townships and trading centers (except in Buganda)." The law also banned "trading by natives on behalf of a non-native" and for the first time made a distinction between "commercial travellers" and "hawkers" in conformity with the practice in neighboring territories (1938 AR, Uganda, p. 36).

The Tanganyika administration also sought to control trade in a web of increasing legal intricacy, but its retention of revenue-raising as a co-equal if not more important goal in trade regulation deserves comment first. Whereas the three other British East African territories reduced their revenue dependence on licensing fees at times during the 1930s, the Tanganyika government persisted in maintaining a fee structure that, in comparative terms, seriously constrained economic operations for some and suffocated opportunity for others (McCarthy, 1982, pp. 24–36). And the government of Uganda, though lowering fees overall, still kept the lowest retail trading fee for both "natives" and "non-natives" at the 45 shilling level.

Taking relative starting positions and highlighting only one entry barrier—that of retail licensing costs—one suggests that the indigenous African appears worst off in Uganda, second worst off in Tanganyika, which had its special 20 shilling retail license for "natives," and somewhat better off in both Kenya and Zanzibar. Insofar as licenses to purchase "native" produce are concerned, the entry barrier is stiffest in Tanganyika with its 100 shilling fee per annum. In Uganda and Zanzibar a produce dealer would not approach the 150 shilling maximum until he or she had accumulated stocks of a value sufficient to kick them into the upper reaches of that tax, which would mean of course that the fee was not an entry barrier, but a cost of doing business.

Graduating fees both in relation to definitions of trade and traders as well as magnitude of stocks held had important consequences for the quantity and configuration of economic and business opportunity. The distinction between "wholesale" and "retail," and that between importing and exporting, underpinned a graduation of fee that supposedly reflected a hierarchy of economic function. This table of economic ranks placed retailing by itself on the lowest level. What determined the particular sequence of upper levels varied among territories in all parts of Africa, but the generic elements featured retailing in conjunction with importing and/or exporting, then wholesaling by itself, then in combination with importing and/or exporting. Whether these economic functions do constitute a hierarchy and can be adjudged less or more valuable or important in the economic process is questionable. That so many Africans, of those who traded, congregated, as it were, on the retail only level may have resulted partly from economic choices based on "lower fees." Of all those trading on the "upper levels," including Europeans and Indians, that so disproportionately few were Africans was no doubt connected with a discrimination that assumed many guises. In this instance, a series of rising hurdles produced by escalating fee schedules constituted a set of entry barriers of increasing magnitude.

One also wonders about the implications of fee graduation by value of stock held even within a single license category, such as the lowest retail trading fee in Kenya and Zanzibar, as reported in Table 6. To what extent this procedure may have discouraged stock accumulation by a single business person to avoid higher taxation is not known. Nor can one quantify the precise extent of a license proliferation phenomenon, though it did occur. A trader who wished to carry a stock value that would place him in a higher tax bracket but with a high propensity for tax avoidance asks his workers to take out licenses in their names and legal responsibility for the incremental stock. Many British officers wrote about "overtrading." For example, the 1938 Nyasaland (Malawi) report notes that the Licensing (Amendment) Ordinance, 1938, "is designed to ensure as far as possible uniformity of policy in the granting of licenses, and to prevent over-trading" (1938 *AR*, Nyasaland, p. 58).

"Overtrading" itself did not have a uniform meaning, but officers appear to use it most frequently when they describe an allegedly "excessive" number of Africans engaged in retailing only, beyond an implicit "optimal" trading population appropriate for the level of economic activity in any area. By economic standards, excessiveness would depend on specification of that optimal number. This is a most difficult and probably futile task, since it requires a set of assumptions about the roles of different traders in reacting to, and further stimulating, economic change, and accurate predictions about the future levels of commerce in a district so that shortages of traders would not exist in times of heightened activity. Bureaucratic standards were not so precise, however. The simple impression that there were "too many" people doing something that challenged administrative control requirements was sufficient. It is ironic that in attempting to reduce by higher fees an African presence on the "upper levels" of trade administrators exacerbated what to them was a politically destabilizing "bulge" in the service sector at the grass-roots levels of retail trade.

The "bulge" reflected to some extent the economic facts of life. Elsewhere in this essay Post Office Savings Banks were discussed. The existence of economic opportunities with rates of return higher than the P.O. Savings Banks offered was one obstacle retarding their acceptance and growth (pp. 105–07). Trading did not guarantee those returns, but the promise was alluring enough for many. Two British officers in the 1890s echoed a theme that sounded throughout the entire colonial era. In the Gold Coast one explained the "slow progress" the Government Savings Bank was making there: Petty trading absorbs what might have been deposits (1892 *AR*, Gold Coast, p. 40). In Lagos another noted that the number of bank depositors was steadily on the increase, but "it must be remembered that most natives of the Colony, especially the women, are born traders and embark the whole of their available capital in business" (1897 *AR*, Lagos, p. 4). In another and unquantifiable way the "bulge" resulted from escalating trades licensing fee structures.

The distinctions that generated fee differentiation also had significant pro-secutorial possibilities. A retailer could legally sell only to final consumers. Should that final consumer turn out to have been another trader who resold even part of that purchase to another person, the retailer would be in potential legal jeopardy. More research is needed into the whole prosecutorial issue; the available Tanganyika record is itself sparse on the number of actual prosecutions (McCarthy, 1982, p. 35). But the more compelling question involves the "chilling effects" of trade legislation, which featured more distinctions as the colonial period unfolded, such as that already cited between "commercial travellers" and "hawkers." The more legally risk-averse traders would likely deal mainly with people whose backgrounds were known to them. The more risk-averse may have found that the farther one travelled from one's community, the fewer familiar faces one encountered. So among the "chilling effects" one reckons the following constraints on business behavior: a significant delimitation of the exchange process, both with respect to the people and distances involved. The unquantifiable dimension is the extent of the freeze. Court convictions for violating the conditions of one's trade license might entail fines of tens or hundreds of shillings, plus court costs. Although the probabilities of being caught can not be established in absence of records detailing day-to-day police movements, the possibility of no-win litigation was an omnipresent specter.

While licensing fee structures worked to contract both the physical incidence and economic diversity of exchange, another group of legislative pronouncements featured a more precise attack on the economics of location. Government bureaucracies everywhere strove not just to regulate trade, but to stifle those versions of commerce that conflicted with admistrative control and/or revenue needs. Consider as demonstration of this statement official markets and their often adversary relationship with more mobile types of trading. Colonial governments everywhere promoted the establishment of official market centers as ways to raise revenue and increase administrative efficiency. Revenue came from the market dues or stall fees that merchants paid to conduct business in a presumably more strategic location, but calculated from whose perspective? Trade was clustered not on the basis of the most optimal economics of location for encouraging the growth of commerce, but on the "bureaucratics" of location for facilitating the collection of other taxes as well as the identification of more-monied Africans for political purposes. The colonial police were sometimes among the market patrons, not so much to purchase produce but to apprehend those who had evaded such direct taxes as the hut and poll levy or to give those who still had time to pay an "easy opportunity" to do so. Official markets were thus an important element in bureaucratic control strategies.

Whatever threatened or undermined their functioning had to be repressed. Besides Tanganyika rules detailed elsewhere (McCarthy, 1982, pp. 50–63), the governments of Sierra Leone and Nyasaland, to cite but two examples, tried to deal with trading practices adverse to administration. Forestalling was an increasing problem. Describing business techniques prevalent throughout colonial territory, a Sierra Leone official observed that his government's Native Produce (Itinerant Purchase) Rules of 1932 "were made to deal with a growing practice among certain traders in the Protectorate of sending out lorries along the roads for the purposes of forestalling native produce on its way to recognized markets" (1932 *AR*, Sierra Leone, p. 50). Bureaucracies faced irritating activities coming from both buyers and sellers. When "hawkers" operated too close to official market centers, many of which were located in more "urban" locations, their presence was deemed detrimental to the functioning of those centers. Administrations did not want those coming into a town to use an official market to be "tempted," a word some officials employed to describe the "allure" of non-official market opportunities, by either forestallers or hawkers. So the government of Nyasaland, in an action that typified responses elsewhere, enacted a Trades Licensing Ordinance of 1937, one rule coming from which imposed a ban on hawking within three miles of a township (1937 *AR*, Nyasaland, p. 56).

All these attempts to manipulate the economics of location for administrative purposes constrained, distorted, or eliminated some possibilities for conducting business, depending on the circumstances. Evidence on impact in Tanganyika suggests that in some locations those running afoul of the bureaucracy re-located their operations beyond the radius proscribing them. So in some areas there developed an "extra-urban" zone of commerce, with a fillip from bureaucracy. In other locations re-location proved for whatever reason not feasible, and both busines people as well as prospective patrons found a reduced exchange menu, with the presumed negative consequences for economic vitality.

As to the official markets themselves, their associated transactions costs were not incidental. Official markets were not uniform everywhere in the African colonial experience, and even within one territory significant differences in procedure existed. One such variation arose from how markets used prices and disseminated price information. Another source of differentiation was how user fees were assessed. Some markets charged stall fees based on time, *per diem*, *per mensem*, or annually. Others levied charges calculated on some percentage of the monetary value of total sales, but how this sum was computed varied. On whatever basis, market fees were not a negligible cost of doing business. Vali Jamal has estimated that for a certain portion of Uganda's colonial history "at 5 percent of *sales*, the market fee could easily have amounted to 10–15 percent of *net income*" (Jamal, 1978, p. 425). When fees were computed as a percentage of sales, the five percent figure was not a ceiling. In certain circumstances in Tanganyika the percentage was 6 (McCarthy, 1982, p. 126); in some cases in Zanzibar, it hit 10 (1936 *AR*, Zanzibar, p. 35).

2. Railroad Rates

Colonial railroads enjoyed a special status as an administratively protected mode of transport. The attractiveness of constructing railroads as the primary transport engine of "economic development" had gained strength, of course, from memories of their roles in the economic and business histories of England, the United States, and some continental countries. This knowledge might have assisted in the formulation of transport policies that while according to railroads a crucial role, recognized the importance of fostering other modes as well. In fact, imitation of the railroad experience of the 'more developed countries' became exercises in slavish mimicry, with profound consequences for business people in particular and economic activity in general.

Many territories endeavored not just to promote railroads, but to stifle other potentially or actually competitive forms of transport, particularly motor vehicles, through a series of devices that varied in repressive intensity. Depending on particular circumstances, a colonial bureaucracy may have striven to prevent some commodities from travelling by road, to restrict "uneconomic" or sometimes just plain competition from motor vehicles to railroads, or to eliminate altogether intermodal competition. A range of examples demonstrates the contents of the legislative arsenal. Fearing that competition from new roads might cause losses of revenue to the railroad, the Gold Coast[5] enacted the Carriage of Goods by

Road Ordinance of 1936 "to prevent carriage of certain goods" along roads (1936–1937 *AR*, Gold Coast, p. 78). The prohibition applied to the "carriage of cocoa (the colony's no. 1 export) in the direction of the coast and to the carriage of imported goods from the coast to the interior" (1937–1938 *AR*, Gold Coast, p. 86). The government of Sierra Leone had already authorized itself in the Public Transport Services Ordinance, 1928, to run public transport on such routes as the governor-in-council may determine and to "restrict competition on the routes used" (1928 *AR*, Sierra Leone, p. 26). It further bolstered its regulatory power with its own Carriage of Goods by Road Ordinance, 1937, in order to "control competition with the railroad" (1937 *AR*, Sierra Leone, pp. 51–52). The government of Nigeria did not employ the tactic of commodity prohibition followed in the Gold Coast, but used licensing fees in an attempt to limit competing motor vehicles. A 1933 regulation required commercial vehicles in certain areas where they may compete with the railroad pay an increased fee for their licenses (1933 *AR*, Nigeria, p. 83).

East African governments were also concerned with protecting their railroads. The Tanganyikan administration used costly motor vehicle licensing fees and disbursed infrastructure funds far more to railroad maintenance and upgrading than to improving the territory's various categories of roads. To the extent that it serviced roads the Tanganyika government concentrated on those that "fed" the rail network rather than providing alternative transport routes. The Kenyan bureaucracy, using language that recurs in the transport ordinances of some other territories, increased its legislative assault on motor vehicle traffic deemed threatening. Its Carriage of Goods (Control) Ordinance, 1931, "regulates the hitherto indiscriminate competition with the railway by the carriage of goods by motor vehicles" (1931 *AR*, Kenya, p. 49). "Regulation" of "hitherto indis-criminate competition" was apparently insufficiently biting, because one year later the Kenyan administration enacted another ordinance, advertised as a "limited duration" law, that "on certain roads prohibits uneconomic motor competition" with the railroads (1932 *AR*, Kenya, Ord. 46). "Regulation" escalated to "prohibition" and "indiscriminate" acquired the more administratively useful designation of "uneconomic." In the bureaucrat's book of helpful catch phrases "uneconomic" meant whatever activity was harming the revenue position of the railroad or might in the future undermine its revenue intake, whereas "indiscrimi-nate" was, even for a bureaucracy, not even tactically vague. "Discriminate" motor competition might possibly have been revenue-threatening but not illegal under the first ordinance.

Some railroad systems needed more protection than others for various reasons. One major factor that sometimes necessitated such administrative intervention against other transport modes was self-induced. In some cases railroads charged high rates that rendered them unable to compete in an environment free of bureaucratic interference. This subject—comparative railroad freight and passenger rates—illuminates differences in bureaucratic approaches to finance and economics with a starkness not frequently found. Consider as a start Tanganyikan-Nigerian contrasts. The author has elsewhere presented the essential facts concerning the Tanganyika Railway Administration (McCarthy, 1982, pp. 22–23). It had achieved considerable autonomy, though technically an agency of the Tanganyika administration, and got its way on most rate increases, which produced a schedule of transport charges that almost everyone thought excessive. The salient principle here was a rate-making philosophy that construed the railroad and its revenue position as a separate matter from general administrative revenues and overall territorial economic growth and development. The railroad itself, in a particularized version of the British imperial dictum that each colonial territory should pay its own way, had to become self-supporting. This approach reversed the notion that railroads were parts of an economy's infrastructure; they had themselves become structures guarded by a rate armor that constrained trade, a conclusion supported by ample contemporary testimony but difficult to quantify.

The government of Lagos Colony in southern Nigeria followed a different rate-making philosophy in the early 1900s. There the Lagos Government Railway had fixed freight and passenger rates at levels ''unremunerative on present volume of traffic''; these were, according to Acting Colonial Secretary W. Fosbery, ''much lower than customary on West African lines.'' And in an explanation that clearly distinguishes the Lagos approach from that of Tanganyika he noted that government was not willing to raise rates directly in order to bolster revenue but looked ''more to indirect revenue receipts owing to the development of the country by means of the railroad than to direct railroad receipts'' (1905 *AR*, Southern Nigeria, p. 45). Lower railroad rates would stimulate more traffic and multiply economic activity which would in turn increase the revenues obtained from a battery of indirect taxes fastened on production, distribution, and exchange. This philosophy made especially good sense if an administration depended greatly on customs duties for its revenue. Nigeria and the Gold Coast did; in the latter, customs duties accounted for 78.3 percent of total revenue in 1936–1937, up from 67.9 percent in 1933–1934. Tanganyika obtained 31.6 percent of its revenue from import duties, a category of customs duties, in 1936, but this fact still does not exonerate the Tanganyika Railway Authority from its ''tunnel vision'' approach to rate-making. The Lagos case not only contrasts sharply with a Tanganyikan approach that ignored the wider economic and financial benefits of reasonable rates, but also stands out as an exception to the general thrust of the varieties of legislation designed to protect the railroad adumbrated above. When the Lagos Government Railway announced that it had adopted the ''principle of low freights'' in the early 1900s, it stressed the already mentioned rationale: ''To facilitate agricultural development and capabilities of the country.'' But another reason involved dealing with a threat from competitive river transport, which existed from Lagos to Abeokuta, about one-half the length of the railroad line, a challenge which had become ''somewhat serious'' (1903 *AR*, Lagos, pp. 10–11).

A detailed examination of some railroad freight and passenger rates will heighten contrasting administrative approaches to transport and economic activity in general and begin to clarify in particular which business people in what aspects of their activity were most affected. Most colonial administrations acted on the correct assumption that business people were acutely sensitive to transport costs and did enact periodic rate reductions in an endeavor to stimulate increases in trade. The fact of these rate adjustments is indisputable. What is a matter of argument is whether African and expatriate business people shared proportionately in any benefits accruing from these reductions and how various types of economic activity fared in this arena of government intervention.

As the usual design of a colonial railroad network aimed far more to connect a territory with agents and agencies outside its borders than to promote an interior exchange of commodities locally produced, it is not surprising that most colonial governments paid special attention to rates for various imports and exports. The Gold Coast, for example, revised its Class II rates downward from 1 July 1905, from a flat charge of 2s.6d./ton-mile to a sliding scale that ranged from 2s.6d. to 1s.9d/ton-mile (fees in shillings/pence). Beyond a certain level heavier cargoes travelled for proportionately less and indeed this revision was acknowledged as "a concession which benefitted the importers of machinery" (1905 *AR*, Gold Coast, p. 40). More freight reductions followed in 1906 (1906 *AR*, Gold Coast, p. 45), but a bureaucrat intriguingly noted in the 1908 official report that these did not "stimulate development" and as a matter of fact there had occurred some shrinkage of traffic (1908 *AR*, Gold Coast, p. 47). As the global storm of depression organized itself in the late 1920s, the Gold Coast administration again reduced rates, "mainly for imports" from 17 November 1929 and then "considerably reduced" in January 1930 central province cacao (cocoa) rates, the territory's key export as noted (1929–1930 *AR*, Gold Coast, p. 26).

At about the same time as the Gold Coast was going to a sliding scale for its Class II commodities ostensibly to benefit the "importers of machinery," the government of Sierre Leone was abolishing wagon-rates based on any classification of goods. The new rate, 2s.63d. per ton per mile, was a wholesale one based on an entire eight-ton wagon, filled or not, and when full, the total transport cost was about one-third cheaper than before. Both the rationale and result of this abolition are arresting. Classification was abandoned in order to place the "small trader, as far as possible, on the same footing as the wholesale firm." Described as the "advance agent of trade," the small trader could really benefit from the wholesale rate, assuming that he or she "can carry heavy inventories" (1905 *AR*, Sierra Leone, pp. 55–56). And just how many "small traders" in Sierra Leone were in a position to do that? Probably not many in the absence of cooperation. This is yet another instance of laudable intent gone awry. Striving to promote a reduction in user fees from which all traders might realize proportionate gains, government couched its revision in the very categories—be able to fill a whole wagon to get the biggest savings—of the more powerful. Although the new system was supposedly "regarded with equal disfavour by larger firms and small traders alike," one suggests that such government action clearly favored not only already established "wholesale firms" but also worked to differentiate the group of "small traders" (1908 *AR*, Sierra Leone, p. 55). Not everyone was equally "small" and those on the upper financial rungs of that group were better positioned to try to take advantage of whole wagon rates, thereby further segmenting that group.

The railroad experience of a *unified* Nigeria (at least on paper from 1 January 1914) speaks to all the major themes of this section. It demonstrates a continuity of rate reductions, interrupted only by the exigencies of World War I, that goes back to the old Lagos Government Railroad days. It reveals a government willing to use rate reductions to help those associated with exporting and importing, but indicates as well an administration concerned with assisting more domestic economic groupings. It shows a bureaucracy perhaps more than most not so much committed to repressing competition with the railroad as enhancing intermodalities of transport. Let us begin with the history of rate changes and their implications.

In 1914 the Nigerian government enacted several large reductions in railroad rates, advertised as "temporary" and publicly acknowledged as made in the "interests of the mercantile and mining communities," which included of course significant but unspecified numbers of both Africans and expatriates. These cut the rates on palm kernels by 10 percent and lowered the per ton charge from Kano on groundnuts and shea nuts by 30 shillings/ton, among the various commodities affected (1914 *AR*, Northern Nigeria, p. 30). In 1915 the administration did not raise the general basis of rating, as was done "more or less generally on other railroads elsewhere and on the only steamship line serving Nigeria," but did impose a war surcharge of 10 percent on certain goods from 10 March 1916. As an exception to this general picture rates on fuel oil and kerosene were in fact reduced in 1915, for the "benefit of the minefields" (1915 *AR*, Nigeria, p. 24). And a list of goods had been exempted from that war surcharge; these included building material, cotton (ginned and unginned), machinery, tin, and country produce, the last item indicating an administration not wholly insensitive to a "local trade" that operated mainly within the territory itself (1916 *AR*, Nigeria, p. 31). These exemptions were short-lived; on 1 August 1917 the war surcharge rose to 30 percent and the exemptions were eliminated (1917 *AR*, Nigeria, p. 21).

The mining industry still continued to receive favorable consideration even in the midst of wartime austerity. The government replaced the sliding scale rate on tin with fixed rates that featured a two-tiered reduction possibility. In an intriguing demonstration of government rewarding higher metals prices rather than just using rates to "compensate" businesses in times of lower prices the Nigerian administration mandated that if the price of tin went below 190 pounds per ton, the rail rate from Bukuru to Iddo decreased by 1 pound 5 shillings/ton. If tin's price exceeded 190 pounds per ton, that same rate diminished by 6 pounds, 3 shillings and 6 pence. Since tin was then consistently over 190 pounds per ton, the companies got a "material advantage." The rates on machinery and mining tools were also reduced from third to first class for the "benefit of mining" (1916 *AR*, Nigeria, p. 31).

After World War I ended, the Nigerian government maintained its stance towards the mining industry, but returned to its pre-war position of more generalized reductions for goods associated with the "import-export" economy and to a lesser extent those commodities involved principally in intra-territorial commerce. In addition, government implemented more rate reductions for coinage shipments. As already reported (pp. 87–90), the British government was systematically debasing its own official money supply by withdrawing West African silver coins and increasing the amount of alloy in circulation. All the while, the railroad remained profitable in its own terms. Consider a few instances from the 1930s. Rate reductions affected cocoa, tin, and kerosene from 1 July 1931; a large number of commodities went into a lower (less expensive) class at that time (1931 *AR*, Nigeria, pp. 44–45). From 1 October 1931 special rates applied to groundnuts and ginned cotton (between certain stations only) and from 21 December 1931 special return (round-trip) wagon rates went into effect for certain imports and exports (between certain stations) (1931 *AR*, Nigeria, p. 45). This downward trend gained strength in 1932, when government cut rates on "many of the principal export and import commodities," with some of the reductions made station-to-station, such as cocoa from Itori to Lagos, benniseed from Makwadi to Port Harcourt, and salt from Apopu and Port Harcourt to Sokoto. "Substantial reductions" applied to freight charges on specie or bullion (silver and mixed metal) from 1932 (1932 *AR*, Nigeria, p. 58), and rates for shipping copper and nickel coins went down in 1935 (1935 *AR*, Nigeria, p. 69). Railroad-rate and money-supply policies were clearly operating in tandem in Nigeria. Throughout the 1930s government refined its rate structures for Nigeria's items of commerce. Further reductions affected in 1935 "staple commodities, such as cotton, palm oil, and palm kernels" (1935 *AR*, Nigeria, p. 69), a revision of both rates and classifications applied to country produce in 1937 (1937 *AR*, Nigeria, p. 68), and "through rates" for certain fruits, import and export traffic were introduced in 1938. In that year also occurred a reduction in the basis of first class freight fares from 4d to 3d./mile (1938 *AR*, Nigeria, p. 69).

One striking fact, insofar as the comparative history of colonial railroad operations is concerned, is that here was a rate-reducer that was self-sustaining financially. This contrasts sharply with a Tanganyika Railway that raised rates in a struggle to approach solvency. In 1937 the Nigerian Railroad carried a surplus balance forward of £2,612, an appropriation of £70,000 having been made to the Reserve Fund (1937 *AR*, Nigeria, p. 67). In 1938 the picture was not as sanguine but nevertheless solid given the strength of the Reserve Fund. Revenues of

£2,337,424 did not quite match expenditures of £2,344,288, exclusive of a contribution of £429,387 to the Renewals Fund (1938 *AR*, Nigeria, p. 68). The Nigerian Railroad did not attempt to subsidize commodity transport through unduly high passenger rates. It was, in fact, committed to reducing both freight and passenger charges, though not necessarily in every class. As early as 1911 Acting Colonial Secretary Donald Cameron was observing in Southern Nigeria that the "policy of reducing 3rd class passenger fares has been justified in a remarkable manner." Some 510,501 passengers purchased third-class tickets in that year, which represented an increase of 130,677 over 1910 (1911 *AR*, Southern Nigeria, p. 26). So whereas in its freight reductions the Nigerian government seemingly favored more what some call the "export-import" economy, its agents, and participants, in its passenger fare decreases the administration necessarily affected far more people originating and disembarking within the country than either entering or leaving it. The bureaucracy thus promoted a personal movement, though not to the same degree material circulation, within a nascent domestic version of economy.

3. Tariff and Non-Tariff Barriers

The general subject of tariffs in economic and business history has proved among the most intractable areas of research. One can explain, in theory, the various rationales for government taxation of exports and imports, the merits and demerits of different types of tariffs from the perspectives of major economic ideologies, and the distinction between tariffs levied for revenue purposes only and those the function of which is to protect domestic goods from "harmful" foreign competition. In practice, one encounters especially acute problems in assessing the impact of tariffs. Nonetheless, this section broaches the basic question of "winners" and "losers" from tariff legislation.

Even colonial railroads perceived as charging the least extortionate freight rates followed those practices so that governments could maintain and increase their revenue share coming from tariffs (and the battery of other taxes that affected goods in movement). Let freight rates not operate as insuperable barriers to movement so that we can tax in transit and at the ports. This strategy represents a more rational bureaucratic approach, as it recognizes a hierarchy of taxes based on blends of financial and economic logics, than a tactic of maximizing all types of taxes, regardless of their economic impact (as in Tanganyika's "tax, tax, whatever the tax"). From some business viewpoints, the concept of *rational government bureaucracy* may be an oxymoron, and a tax deferred to port collection rather than levied prior to loading was an extraction that affected overseas marketability ultimately and decisions to produce and then ship in the first place. Without access to sufficient business records at the present time, one must defer to a future date consideration of business perceptions of, and reactions to, the range of import and export levies as well as such non-tariff barriers as quotas, shipping and inspection procedures. Now one can offer a few vignettes of the actions of some governments with respect to import and export duties (for Tanganyika, McCarthy, 1982, pp. 18–22).

Zanzibar illustrates an inverse relationship between the levels of import and export duties that pivots on that island's principal article of both production and export, cloves and clove-related manufactures. The government of Zanzibar successively raised its ad valorem percentage on imported goods as it attempted to reduce the financial burden of export duties on clove producers and others associated with that industry. In 1921 government raised general import duties from 7½ percent to 10 percent ad valorem and added an extra 15 rupees per gallon to the already existing levy on distilled liquors. From 1922 it introduced a 5 percent rebate of the export duty on cloves, which then stood at 25 percent and was paid in kind. On 28 October 1927 import duties rose from 10 percent to 15 percent ad valorem in order to broaden the "basis" of taxation and lighten the "burden borne for so long by producers of cloves" (1927 *AR*, Zanzibar, p. 4). Then in 1928 the bureaucracy substituted a cash ad valorem duty on cloves for the previous duty in kind, to be collected "immediately prior to shipment," reduced the percentage from 25 to 20, and abolished the system of rebated duty. In August 1928 the government, "with the object of retaining an important market for cloves," implemented a "system of drawbacks of duty with respect of cloves used in the manufacture of clove oil vanillin" (1928 *AR*, Zanzibar, p. 4). Differentiation by clove product type crystallized in the 1930s, as the 20 percent export duty applied to cloves and mother of cloves, while clove stems were assessed at 10 percent (1937 *AR*, Zanzibar, p. 36). These legislative changes obviously raised the costs of doing business for everyone associated with the import trade and affected consumers, if the costs were passed through.

The impact on different constituencies connected with all aspects of clove production and distribution may not be so straightforward. Those 1928 actions that reduced the export duty from 25 percent to 20 percent but changed its basis from in kind to in cash and insisted on instant collectibility may have, instead of lessening the "burden" on clove exporters, intensified pressure on cash flows and actually generated more difficulties than benefits. Everything else remaining the same, cash payment may also have created deflationary tendencies within the Zanzibari economy, the extent varying according to how much of the money government collected it then actually spent locally. If prices did decline, then the problem of impact becomes even more intricate: which goods and what business people were most affected. Without more evidence on the workings of the clove industry, the financial profiles of particular clove entrepreneurs, the various versions of the Zanzibari money supply, and actual movements of specific prices, these propositions remain prima facie logical but unverifiable.

Not every territory levied export duties and some that did abolished the practice at various times during the colonial period. Kenya, for instance, had eliminated them by the early 1920s (as well as canceling an income tax in 1922). The inverse relationship that existed in the Zanzibar case between levels of import and export duties applied in Kenya even more forcefully. As it abolished export duties, Kenya, to "assist local production," placed "protective tariffs" on rice, grains, timber, ghee, butter, and cheese. "To increase revenue tariffs were raised against wines, distilled liquors, tobacco, motor cars, etc."; there being no local motor car industry nor, in British eyes, any significant local liquor, wine, or tobacco production to protect, these tariffs were exclusively revenue-raising (1922 AR, Kenya, p. 9). At about the same time, the Gold Coast government abolished export duties on kola nuts and palm kernels, while it retained one on cocoa (1922–1923 AR, Gold Coast, p. 22). And Sierra Leone removed those levies on palm oil and gum copal. In the latter case import duties were not trending upwards generally to compensate. In fact, in November 1923 when those export levies were eliminated, the import duty on "provisions" was reduced by one-half, from 25 percent to 12½ percent (1923 AR, Sierra Leone, p. 6). One reason why the export-import relationship was not as inverse in Sierra Leone as it was in Kenya and Zanzibar was that Sierra Leone retained some of its export duties on such products as palm kernels and kola nuts.

As an important example of another kind of inverseness characterizing the movements of different types of taxes consider the case of Gambia. In 1931 that territory reduced the export duty on groundnuts from £1 to 10/- a ton, an apparent benefit for those associated with groundnuts and their export (1931 AR, Gambia, p. 36). But what government gives it can take away, though not necessarily to or from the same people or groups. In 1933 the yard tax went up. This tax, Gambia's version of a "hut and poll tax," had levied four shillings on "every yard containing no more than four huts," with extra fees for extra dwellings that charged more if a "hut" were occupied by a "non-family of the owner or occupier" than if a dwelling were inhabited by kin (1931 AR, Gambia, p. 39). So within Gambia's revenue calculus any money lost through the reduction of the groundnuts export duty was to come from the increase in the yard tax. This levy, to paraphrase a rationale employed earlier in the Zanzibar case, was more "broadly based" and hence distributed the cost of government more widely, though not necessarily with greater equity.

Nigeria's experience with export duties gains added importance in view of the earlier analysis of its usually cost-cutting railway. During the First War, from 7 October 1916, Nigeria imposed export duties listed in Table 8. This was an administration with some grasp of basic economics and so the tax was applied with attention to current business conditions. "In view of the large stocks on hand," it was decided to charge only half-rates until 31 March 1917 (1916 AR, Nigeria, p. 5). From 1 January 1918, however, export duties were levied on additional commodities: 10 shillings/ton on groundnuts; 3 pence/pound on tanned hides and skins; and 2 pence/pound on untanned or haired hides and skins (1918 AR, Nigeria, p. 3). Then in October 1922 Nigeria abolished the differential

Table 8.   Nigerian Export Duties, 1916, 1932, and 1936

Product	1916 duty			1932 duty			1935 duty		
	Pounds	Shillings	Pence	Pounds	Shillings	Pence	Pounds	Shillings	Pence
Cocoa/ton	2	6	8	1	3	4	Same as 1932		
Palm kernel oil/ton				2	0	0	Same as 1932		
Palm oil/ton	2	0	0	1	4		11	6	
Palm kernels/ton	1	2	6	0	18	0	10	6	
Tin/ton (from 1933)					3	4	Same as 1933		
Fresh bananas							1½d. per count bunch		
Dry bananas							2d. per 10 lbs.		

Sources: 1916 *AR*, Nigeria (p. 5); 1932 *AR*, Nigeria (p. 73); 1933 *AR*, Nigeria (p. 86); 1935 *AR*, Nigeria (p. 90).

export duty on palm kernels exported to places outside the British Empire and British Africa (1922 *AR*, Nigeria, p. 16). This move presumably cost government some revenue in the short run, but made kernels in non-British markets more competitively priced and perhaps encouraged greater aggregate exports and hence produced an overall higher revenue take from export duties in the longer run.

In the 1930s the configuration of export duties changed in only a few instances. In nominal terms the cocoa duty in the 1930s was half what it had been from 31 March 1917, and the same as it was from October 1916, until 31 March 1917. Palm oil rates declined in all three readings; likewise for palm kernel fees. Resolution and Order No. 2 of 1934 gave a mid-1930s fillip to this trend, as it directed that the export duty on palm kernels and palm oil be considerably reduced. In yet another instance of revenue inverseness it imposed those above noted duties on fresh and dried bananas and fastened a "new import duty on dried fish" (1934 *AR*, Nigeria, p. 89). In another matter that concerned those associated with palm products the Nigerian Tariff (Amendment) Ordinance No. 6 of 1932 exempted from export duty palm produce exported direct from the Cameroons under British Mandate across the frontier into the Cameroons under French Mandate (1932 *AR*, Nigeria, p. 69). (The British and French each took administrative responsibility for one of the two League of Nations mandates into which German-ruled Cameroon had been divided in the aftermath of World War I.) The seemingly minor export duty on tin, a relatively light degree of taxation that parallels the Nigerian Railway's schedule of less than onerous tin freight rates, apparently became more biting if some basic facts about points of origin and destination did not apply. Regulation No. 18 of 1934 specified that the export duty on tin equal 50 percent of the maximum royalty payable "except if ore is from Cameroon under British Mandate or is to be smelted in the UK or British possessions'' (1934 *AR*, Nigeria, p. 90).

Non-tariff trade barriers also affected business people and consumers. Insofar as quotas mattered, the most important legislative action was meant for the Japanese though not aimed only at them. Concerned at the extent of Japanese textile imports into West Africa (and elsewhere) and the threat these posed to U.K. manufactured items, the governments of the Gold Coast and Nigeria imposed quotas on Japanese textiles coming into their territories. In 1934 the Gold Coast, as well as the proximate administrative divisions of Ashanti, the Northern Territories, and Togoland, enacted importation of textiles (quotas) ordinances phrased in general language that included any country but was in fact directed against the Japanese. In 1934 Nigeria prescribed that 1935 Japanese textile imports not exceed 2,430,000 sq. yards and, to strengthen enforcement, required that one purchase and hold a specific trading license created for those wishing to import "regulated textiles" (1934 *AR*, Nigeria, p. 89). These actions prima facie benefited those associated with U.K. produced textiles and penalized those connected with Japanese product, which in some cases may have involved the same people, such as retailers handling multiple country cloths. Precise specification of impact remains elusive without more evidence concerning the textile trade in these countries. Nor is one able to offer concrete information about the effects of these quotas on textile prices, although the simple proposition is that if nothing else happened and quotas limited supplies, prices would rise, presumably helping merchants and irritating consumers.

4. Other Taxes, Other Laws

The previous sections have begun to cover systematically most of the more noticeable extractive devices fastened by bureaucracies upon businesses and business people. Trades licensing fees, market dues, railroad rates, and tariffs were among the most significant government-imposed costs of business, but these do not exhaust the contents of the administrative extractive arsenal. The most apparent omission here has been government-established marketing boards, created in a number of African territories. Unlike some of our other subjects, there is an extensive secondary literature on these agencies, which set producer prices lower than prevailing export ones and so accumulated surpluses (see Grier, 1981, pp. 41–42).

Consider briefly the Ugandan experience, which Vali Jamal put so succinctly (Jamal, 1978, pp. 433–35). There government established marketing boards for cotton and coffee in the early 1940s to meet wartime exigencies. At first the administration argued that the boards contained inflation, because without their price-dictation, shortages would drive prices up. Later the rationale broadened; a major function of the boards was price stabilization: when prices fell, government would use the accumulated surpluses to subsidize declining prices. Jamal notes that "from the point of view of the farmers," a major group of African business people from this author's perspective, "the marketing boards were just additional tax-gatherers—and indeed that is exactly what they were. For fifteen years or so marketing boards extracted huge sums of money from farmers, then for the next five to seven years they repaid a small part of this by way of price stabilization." Government had defended the surpluses partly on the basis that it would get greater value for money in the future as prices fell, but "prices of consumer goods had increased considerably so that the money the marketing boards doled out in the late 1950s and early 1960s was worth only two-thirds its value in the period it was collected" (Jamal, 1978, p. 434). The marketing boards were more than "just additional tax-gatherers" probably from the viewpoints of affected farmers and surely from our perspectives. Here was government acting not only as extractor but also as meddler, manipulating the price mechanism, a major vehicle of economic communication, and in so doing damaging its communicative capacities. This is yet another instance of how bureaucracy distorted economic communication during the colonial era and provides further evidence of the harmful language manipulation discussed earlier [see pp. 104–08].

Besides other taxes, there were other laws that impinged on business and business people. Taking farmers again as important groups of business people not always appreciated under the business rubric, one notes the fashioning by administrators of sometimes extensive commodity regulations that cover with varying intensities all phases of the production process and frequently involved cesses or levies, depending on the particular crop and colony. These economic regulations have received attention from this author and others, although the literature is still not as full nor based in every case on the kinds of heretofore classified evidence that might permit a more probing examination of origins and impact. A systematic profile and analysis of comparative crop regulation in all its dimensions is a task that remains for another time and place, just as is the comparative study of the varieties of protest and political action associated with those regulations that occurred in a number of African locations (McCarthy, 1982, pp. 79–109).

As the preceding sections have begun to demonstrate, the "view of the state," to correct a statement of W. G. Clarence-Smith (Clarence-Smith, 1983, p. 10), is *not* "easy to reconstruct," when done comprehensively or in a framework that aims ultimately for completeness. Having assembled the rudiments of our comparative regulatory profile in a manner that relied heavily on available primary sources, we now offer a more systematic theoretical analysis of the concepts central to a discussion of bureaucracy and business in Africa. This semantic section, along with the empiricism of Part I on comparative regulation, will give the second section of Part II, which highlights selected case studies of government-business relations based on secondary sources, greater perspective.

II. WHAT BUSINESS DID TO BUREAUCRACY AND AFRICA: GOVERNMENT-BUSINESS RELATIONS

A. Vocabulary

The vocabulary of scholarship first requires comment. As they trace the activities of foreign (construed as originating extra-continental) businesses in Africa itself, some scholars use the term *economy* in several senses, write about *public* and *private sectors*, and discuss the roles of *the state* and *business* in *underdevelopment* and *development* processes themselves variously defined or ill-explained. Let us consider each key term in turn.

The concept of economy has itself received much abuse in scholarship. An economy is not just any economic grouping, but one that exhibits at least some minimal integration and/or unification. The types of integration and unification and indeed the very definition of minimal are all matters for discussion in particular cases. However, without some organization partaking of unification and/or integration the concept of economy would lack a threshold coherence and blur indistinguishably into the less rigorous rubric of economic grouping. Yet some invoke economy so casually, even ritualistically, that its multiple loose uses have devalued its worth as a construct with meaning.

One reads about the European world-economy becoming a capitalist world-economy or system. To be fair, those operating under the influence of one or another version of the world-economy paradigm now dominating much scholarship[6] would find this author's definition of economy too narrow for their global, holistic methods and purposes. But why does purported comprehensiveness, embodied in the sociologizing of the concept of economy into socioeconomic system, have to become a huge transdisciplinary, ill-defined incubus? This is what has happened. When asked to give the addresses of the various headquarters of the ''capitalist world-economy,'' the true believers, if taking so pedestrian and empirical a question seriously, would probably list governments, multinationals, etc. Then why not jettison the notion of *one* capitalist world-economy to study the existence of multiple economic groupings, clustering some businesses in some locations, that might have been economies rigorously construed? Why not consider the actions of governments and other agents from particular countries that may have achieved or been in the process of fashioning a truly national economy? And why not investigate particular examples of government-business cooperation and conflict? Some scholars do seek the macrocosm through the microcosm, the reverse of world-economy practitioners, but it is imperative that everyone use the term economy with precision in all senses.

One further reads about the allegedly harmful impact of the agents and agencies of the capitalist world-economy in originating and then entrenching various forms of underdevelopment in the Third and Fourth Worlds. Scholars developing these themes often write about the impact of one or another action upon a particular *territorial economy*. They falsely assume that the existence of internationally recognized borders around a territory, themselves a legacy of imperialism becoming colonialism in Africa, creates a territorial economy. So the capitalist world-economy, itself an amorphous socioeconomic premise of ill-specified capitalistic, global, and economic elements, contains levels of fictive economies. These descend, in the fashion of the great chain of being but without its spiritual and logical persuasiveness, through what were at best during the colonial period territorial *economic groupings*, down into local versions of economic activity that may have constituted economies, depending on circumstance (McCarthy, 1977, pp.573–77).

World-systems practitioners and people using other forms of economic globalism uncritically are not alone in their loose use of economy. The literature of economic development features a family of kindred concepts that designate more function than express an organized entity. These are: the *dual economy*, made up of an *export economy* and a *traditional or subsistence* version. Some use the notion of *enclave economy* to designate the export economy cum those elements of traditional economy now oriented more towards servicing exports by providing food and labor than meeting indigenous needs in what remained of the traditional setting. All these concepts of economy are more analytical constructs than articulations of reality, the degree of divergence between theory and fact varying according to the type of economy under discussion. While one can speak about particular cases in which all the activities associated with exporting did constitute an economic grouping that may have been an authentic manifestation of an export or enclave economy, there rarely was in practice just one traditional or subsistence economy in an area. Besides, it is erroneous to equate traditional with subsistence, wrong not to acknowledge the important variations in meaning of tradition and subsistence, and false to write as if traditional precludes change, sometimes of a dynamic type. So the notion of dual economy is especially theoretical, and shakily so at that, since it includes one type—the export economy—that sometimes approached and even reached actualization in fact and another—traditional or subsistence—confusingly used in theory and never actualized, in the sense that the traditional economy was the other single economy in a given area in addition to the export type.

One should, therefore, be especially wary about sectoring economies that may be fictive. The territorial economy has often been divided by writers into *public* and *private sectors*, but how can one segment what does not exist as a whole? Even without sector terminology, the more accurate expressions "public elements" and "private aspects" still require great care in application. Whether, and if so how, the constructs "public" and "private" have meaning in the many different cases of ethnic economic activity during the colonial period still requires more ethno-anthropological research. And since colonial governments arrogated to themselves "guardianship" of all land within a territory and thereby placed the land and by extension everything in or on it in their ultimate version of public domain, perhaps the more relevant yet difficult questions concern de jure and de facto public elements, but mainly de facto albeit attenuated private ones. To begin to answer these questions one would have to know, as noted, much more about indigenous constructs of public and private and what private had come to mean in fact from the perspective of colonial bureaucracy that reserved the right to deprivatize whatever threatened its stability. Whatever the outcome, one should no longer sector the imaginary but try to present multiple perspectives and realities on the terms "public" and "private."

Public sector has also been used inauspiciously by some as another way to analyze the *role of the state*. In this case one inapposite term is equated with another. When the subject is phrased as the role of the state, readers receive far too stereotypical an impression of the colonial state and may falsely conclude, if you have seen one bureaucracy in action, you have seen them all. Insofar as specific policies and actions are concerned, there were important differences in bureaucratic behavior, as the previous sections on comparative economic regulation have demonstrated. Yet difference resides not only in policy, action, and impact, but also in structure, formulation, and type and degree of bureaucratization.

The state was, under colonialism, de jure the particular territorial bureaucracy backed ultimately by the European country of imperial origination, but de facto that territorial administration itself in all its agencies and manifestations. The concept of nation-state can not be applied at all, since the cartographical partition of Africa by the European powers in the 1880s and beyond created paper territories, composed of many ethnic groups in varying degrees of cohesion or mini-nations or communities but hardly amalgamating into one nation that coincided with those boundaries. And the concept of the state in some of its denotations must be used with caution. To conceive of a state as an administration with certain relations with the land and its people seems correct. But these connections resulted so much from unilateral arrogation of right by people who could at best be called semi-indigenes that one thinks it best to concentrate on presenting as detailed a portrait of what bureaucracy was and what it meant. This entails analysis of a particular bureaucracy's internal structure of a kind already done for Tanganyika elsewhere (see McCarthy, 1982). Key points include: What agencies or departments constituted the central administration in its capital city or up-country; what relations these may have had with metrocentric bureaucracy; what non-governmental interests influenced administration and in what ways or through what agencies of that bureaucracy; and the roles of law in the articulation of a bureaucracy's decisions.

The metrocentric question is also important from the standpoint of world-systems and other Marxist-influenced perspectives. Some grant the "semi-autonomy" of territorial colonial administrations from the metropolis (Whitehall, Paris, etc.), but insist that the zone of semi-autonomy was secondary to the central fact that colonial administration still reflected imperial purpose. Moreover, whatever local variation exists, bureaucracy was mainly an intermediary of the agents and agencies of the capitalist world-economy or, if one prefers unadulterated Leninism, of imperialism. These views do not sufficiently distinguish de jure from de facto conditions, nor analyze enough the specific ways in which different legal systems influenced or provoked areas of action that were far more than zones of semi-autonomy. British and French administration, for example, operated on two distinct legal corpora, Anglo-Saxon common law and Gallicized Roman law, respectively. These different legal matrices were more than casual factors in influencing the articulation of imperial chains of command that varied considerably with respect to degree of centralization, the French being more tightly controlled from the center in theory than was the British. So even de jure and placed in the language of those we query the prefix in "semi-autonomy" has no fixed meaning across the colonial experience nor does "autonomy" itself yield a standardized definition. More case studies of particular territorial bureaucracies along the lines mentioned above should enrich our patterns of both practical and theoretical complexity, sharpen the distinction between imperialism and colonialism, and thus render even more unwise the unrefined slotting of the role of the state in any great chain of world-economy paradigm or imperialist schemata.

Business also requires a more comprehensive and balanced treatment than much of the literatures of African business and economic history, economic development, and world-systems scholarship have so far accorded it. The definitions of businesses and business people must, as noted in the introduction, expand to include institutions, groups, and individual people not heretofore appreciated under the business rubric or acknowledged only fleetingly or otherwise insufficiently. These include the range of farmers, from what some term the agrarian haute bourgeoisie or kulaks, through the middle levels of agrarian bourgeoisie, to the smallest-scale or size operators in a given area, sometimes called peasants, as well as the institutions or agencies integral to their "ways of life." A partial list of the latter would feature the variety of ethnic means for generating indigenous forms of credit, mechanisms for re-allocating or re-distributing usufructuary rights where ownership as land possession itself did not exist, and commodity exchange rates in different areas. These subjects, as well as numerous others, have been left for investigation by those interested in economic or business anthropology, but it is essential that one integrate them more directly into economic and business history.

Indigenous agribusiness also needs more extensive delineation. One problem that delimits some scholarship is an association of business with manufacturing or extraction of a sort marked by western forms of factory industrialization. This attitude has not only been partly responsible for an unappreciation of agriculture as business, but also for an incomplete understanding of agribusiness. It was sometimes connected with an industrialization or at least a capital-intensification of seemingly small dimensions of agriculture, but not usually with an industrialization of the factory mode so often erroneously termed an "advance" from more rurally decentralized home or cottage industry in the experiences of some western countries. Add to this attitude the appearance in yet another way of surrealistic sectoring and one can gauge the strength of the mental blinders inhibiting a panoramic perspective on business of and in Africa. Some divide the fictive *territorial economy*, uncritically applying a tripartite terminology articulated mainly at first in connection with western development, into *manufacturing*, *agriculture*, and *service sectors*. Whatever the demerits of another sectoring of an imaginary whole, thinking of activity only as this tripos has constrained scholars from examining the range of action that represents a hybridization of those categories in modified ways, as, for example, *agri-service* is in one major way *agri-business*.

Though seen properly by some as a multiplicity of activities under an umbrella rubric of service rather than as a sector of behavior, the full sweep of indigenous services still requires a more systematic and thorough examination than scholarship concerned with business has produced to date. What has limited research in this area, as in some others, is a search for class that has in effect placed a threshold of numbers on kinds of activities before these trigger the really heavy analysis associated with application of class or group categories. So when apparently "few" people become engaged in some activity servicing agriculture or mining, for instance, their actions are adjudged significant, if at all, in the context of an embryonic or pre-class formation petite-bourgeoise, and not so much as important in themselves as manifestations of a particular business ethos and entrepreneurship.[7] African business history would benefit from a reconsideration of the corpus of entrepreneurial scholarship[8] that surged in the 1960s and 1970s and is often one of the factors associated with the emergence of African economic history as an authentic field. This reexamination should not be done through class lenses alone, nor accept as complete the ways in which scholars have treated entrepreneurship up until now. It should seek to appreciate even more African business in its own terms—from the viewpoints of its own practitioners, their business forms and stuctures analyzed not reflexively and totally in relation to western ones, and their relations with other businesses, governments, and consumers presented from all different points of view.

Both indigenous and foreign businesses must be appreciated in all their shapes and sizes. The size or scale question needs special emphasis. There is a tendency on the part of some to track mainly the penetration of large-scale foreign business enterprise in Africa. While oligopoly (few sellers) and oligopsony (few buyers) are increasingly important phenomena in the latter decades of the nineteenth century and throughout the twentieth, one should not lose sight of small- to medium-size business activity in Africa from outside Africa. Nor should one forget the pervasive commercial significance of various groups of immigrants into Africa, such as the Indians in East Africa, about whom a substantial literature already exists.[9]

The immigrant theme deserves much further study. Some business people came to Africa as immigrants; other immigrants became business people once in Africa. These facts characterize the experiences of nationals from the countries that physically administered much of the continent as well as the records of those who came from the non-colonizing powers, such as Greece and the United States. Under the rubrics of immigrants as or becoming business people one should not leave out people whose activities, in a fashion reminiscent of the way colonial bureaucracies are treated by some scholarship, are too often seen only through world-systems or imperialist constructs. The usually stereotyped group of white settlers must be reevaluated dispassionately in the context of business practices—their colonial impact and continuing legacy. Some engaged in the kinds of manufacturing that everyone defines as business; others got involved in agribusiness; but many became farmers, such as the Afrikaners, and their activities should be appreciated under business categories just as those of African farmers must. Not all white settlers, perhaps not even the majority, became large-scale operators defined in their respective crop and environmental contexts. There were distributions of wealth and income, endowment and skills, successes and failures, positive and negative contributions to Africa among all types of farmers, whatever their background, and indeed among traders, bureaucrats, and all other economic and business agents and agencies on or associated with the continent. Defining those successes and failures and identifying positive and negative contributions to Africa both bring up the final set of terms in our present consideration of the vocabulary of scholarship.

Development and *underdevelopment* are much used words in the language of international affairs and in some writing about roles of business and bureaucracy in colonial Africa. These terms, when applied, must be invoked with great precision. Too often scholars and others treat development as an un- or ill-specified better state of affairs. At the hands of some the term has become a mantra, the repetition of which will itself produce meaning. It is hard to say whether development or underdevelopment is the more abused term. Some write about underdevelopment more as a state of being or becoming than an empirically verifiable or logically explicable set of harms. What is more, underdevelopment supposedly implies a kind of development, else to what does the prefix relate? Yet much writing on underdevelopment does not specify the types and degrees of development that have been repressed or distorted. Not all writers exhibit such a metaphysical approach to matters that involve health, food, life, and death. But it is still necessary to propose some caveats concerning the uses of development and especially underdevelopment.

When employing the notion of underdevelopment, always specify the kind of development one has in mind. This choice will always be ideological and often tendentious, no matter who makes it. But frank recognition of these facts may reduce one of the barriers that obstructs communication on these matters between Marxists and kindred souls, on one side, and various "non-Marxists" on the other. The former are usually scholars with a keen sense of ideology and its uses but who often view non-true believers as crude empiricists without moorings. The latter are usually also scholars but many perceive themselves as non-ideological or at least non-tendentious and view their opposite numbers as little more than propagandists.

These attitudes have hampered deep analysis of perhaps the central question in both development and underdevelopment debates, which is, put simply, relations between governments and markets. Others would put the general issue as follows: What should be in the public and private sectors, what should be their relationships, and what is the optimal sectoral mix for a particular country? Public-private sector distinctions may acquire more meaning, depending on the country, as "flag independent" governments have striven to transform territorial economic groupings into nascent versions of national economies. Whatever the conceptualization, the question of relations between governments and markets includes the key points that all who contemplate Africa's future as shadowed by its past and present must address. These are: The roles of imperial governments and their colonial bureaucratic transformations in market definition, creation, development, distortion, or destruction during the colonial period itself and as haunting present-day legacy; the roles of various businesses and business people from Africa as well as outside it in those same market processes mentioned above in both the past and as continuing influences; the relations between governments and businesses in and to those aforementioned market processes over time.

All five market phenomena—definition, creation, development, distortion, and destruction—are important for considering government and business, in situations of both single and joint action. Defining the particular market under analysis is critical, since *markets* are a huge set of varying ways of aggregating exchanges that also differ among themselves. One must appreciate foreign and indigenous perceptions of what markets were and how they functioned. Not all markets consist even partly of visible structures with fixed headquarters or nuclei. And relations among price, exchange-value, and use-value are not treated with the same type of rationality in every instance. In short, one can use neo-classical economic analysis to provide one major angle of insight into markets created, distorted, or destroyed by foreign and indigenous agents and agencies. But market is a construct that transcends any one mode of economic thought or ideology. There are markets in Africa created by Africans themselves that are best understood first in their own terms before their efficacy is adjudged, if at all, in the degree to which they approach neo-classical market models, as the research of some prominent ethno-scientists and substantivists has revealed. [10]

Definition is essential to assessing impact. When looking at foreign business involvement in an area, some scholars properly attempt to distinguish investments in relation to objectives. [11] One such distinction is that between market-oriented investments and supply-oriented investments. The former, as the name indicates, focus on developing in some way a market of some kind for a particular product the company sells. Such market-oriented investment is thus influenced by the general level of income in a country or territory and "rarely involves enclave development." Supply-oriented investments pertain to raw material or precious metal extraction and often share no community of interest with a host state; the situations resulting from extraction are frequently only enclaves "without substantial interaction with the surrounding domestic economy" (Carstensen, 1984, p. 236 [n.8]). This is a useful exercise in investment differentiation, even though one is back in the thicket of terminology concerning economy. It presents market definition, creation, and development from the perspectives of businesses. It requires determining the nature of a specific government-business relationship. It places investment in multiple economic contexts, which one can make more precise by examining the relations among markets created or at least defined by local and foreign business and by bureaucracies themselves. These relations sometimes partake of the processes of distortion and destruction, specification of which will illuminate aspects of the underdevelopment question. Whether and to what extent different market experiences or outcomes were good or bad, positive or negative contributions to Africa, depends on one's own ideological perspective, which every scholar necessarily has and must acknowledge.

This extended discussion of the main concepts and issues that pervade analysis of business and bureaucracy in Africa comes not only from a strong preference that scholars and others use a more precise vocabulary in discussion. Driving this search for more rigorous articulation is also the realization that those proposing revisions in global economic relations, under the rubric of suggestions for a New International Economic Order, begin with the notion of the capitalist world-economy in its present and past manifestations. This construct has, as noted previously, fatal fractures that proceed in part from a gross confusion of the concepts of economy and socioeconomic system. Yet it is a controlling idea that is almost revered by some strains of scholarship on underdevelopment issues, has infiltrated other scholarly venues and gone insufficiently criticized there, and has achieved the status of a polemical rallying point for all who feel aggrieved because of past and present international economic relationships of various sorts. If it never existed, how can it be reformed? It has become a cartoon concept, one that approximates in some of its parts the realities of international economic history over five centuries but as a summation burlesques what themes unite that field of inquiry.

World-systems research that wishes to partake of rigor in the application of economic and business concepts should focus more on those aforementioned market processes of definition, creation, development, distortion, and destruction as these occurred on all the "levels" of activity featured in its great chain of economy paradigm. Of course, during the nineteenth century authentically global markets in and for capital of various types took more integrated and unified shapes. But one set of factor markets does not any economy make, let alone a version that purports to occupy or at least influence much of the globe. Nor do bilateral or multilateral relations between or among particular countries or even continents in themselves constitute an international version of economy, although they certainly require analysis as a type of economic grouping. Nor does the increasing importance of international business, variously defined as multinational, transnational, international, and global corporations, ipso facto crystallize a global or semi-global version of economy.

Business activity abroad often seems more correctly understood as the definition, creation, development, and where necessary the distortion and destruction of various markets—of, by, and for international business, constrained by a number of factors. These include constraints internal to a specific firm's structure, endowment, and resources, but also feature those originating in the external environment. Among the latter are reckoned actual and potential income levels of the population that would support a market. And influencing income levels as well as standing as possibly the greatest actual or potential external constraint on business is government. All these observations suggest the desirability of reformulating that major issue in contemporary debate concerning underdevelopment and development. It is not only relations between governments and markets nor the optimal definitions of public and private sectors. Duality has become tripos, as there are at least three major forces to be considered—governments, markets, and businesses, as comprehensively defined in the previous pages. Those who prefer to list labor[12] as a separate force are certainly entitled to do so, although we consider laborers as consumers as key aspects of market processes and laborers as producers, savers, and investors under our expanded rubric of business.

B. Case Studies

With all these considerations concerning vocabulary in mind, readers can better appreciate the problems involved in analyzing actual cases of business-government relations and impact. Recall the general approaches to those relationships mentioned at the very outset of this essay. Some write about government and business as cooperating and/or conflicting; others talk about zones of convergence and divergence. Still others use the images of government as collaborator and/or spectator in a business abuse of Africa, or track how government and business together abused Africa, or note how business was sometimes a collaborator and/or spectator in a government abuse of Africa. These are the major thematic possibilities that characterize a literature that has become more extensive as African business history has emerged over the last decade or more as a distinctive field of inquiry.

This final section examines some of the works that have refined the above framework of possibilities and endeavors to use their limitations as frontiers of opportunity to give "state of the art" in this area a more rigorous meaning. It spotlights studies that seek to disaggregate the categories of state and business because this thrust yields the most probing and realistic results. As he studied the history of large corporations, Raymond Vernon observed that as they articulated their separate manufacturing, marketing and financial bureaucracies, they became "a group of cooperating semi-independent forces with distinguishably different goals," objectives other than simple or even intricate profit maximization and often in conflict with one another (Vernon, in Carstensen, 1984, pp. 5–6). This key insight applies in modified forms to "small" and "medium" businesses and to government itself, however its size is quantified, the scale of its operations measured, the scope of its impact assessed. It is thus necessary to explore which part of a government is in what specific relationship with which portion of a business at what time.

This approach produces greater intricacy of possibility. The notions of cooperation and conflict, convergence and divergence apply within as well as without. But each government bureaucracy and business bureaucracy exhibited different modes and degrees of sub-bureaucratization. That is, the rate at which constituent agencies, departments, or divisions articulated themselves as more distinctive centers of semi-independent power varied considerably. In some cases, it did not happen at all. In others, "semi-independence" meant, for all practical purposes, functional autonomy. Vernon's insight modified for other circumstances raises yet another set of problems. The constructs "view of the state" and "view of business" have already been proved deficient over-simplifications, which was an easy task. Not so readily accomplished is demonstrating what the concepts of cooperation and conflict meant to government and business on all macro- and micro-levels. Cooperation and conflict may have acquired different meanings in specific contexts of relations between a government and a business and within the organization of each. Goal discovery and specification should cast partial illumination on the problems of cognition and perception. But this is one area where the retrospective investigator really "sees through a glass darkly." What one may interpret as different agencies of the same organization pursuing "distinguishably different goals" may strike others as the same overall objective sought in nuanced fashions.

Some scholars more than others have demonstrated greater awareness of multiple perceptions and manifestations of conflict and cooperation between and within governments and businesses appropriately disaggregated into their constituent elements. Jean-Philippe Peemans has analyzed "Capital Accumulation in the Congo Under Colonialism: the Role of the State" with some terminological imprecision and under the less than cogent influence of the great chain of world-economy paradigm but with great realism concerning specific bureaucratic interactions on the spot. He writes:

> The state is never a pure reflex nor a simple, docile tool. One cannot deny to the state a priori a certain degree of autonomy within a system whose global coherence must be assured by the state. It seems therefore appropriate to speak of interdependence between the state and financial groups rather than of dependence of the state. Through its relative autonomy, the

state has to arbitrate between conflicting interests, between various sectors of capital, between short-term and long-range interests of the system. Above all, the state has the responsibility to ensure the expansion, the stability and the continuity of the predominating economic and social patterns (1975, p. 201).

One shall not dwell on his sectoring of a capital that was not unified to begin with, nor linger long on the problems for his analysis that use of the great chain of world-economy paradigm presents, since these are instances of generic errors in scholarship already discussed. But if it is one of the functions of the state to assure the "global coherence" of the "system," then no wonder that there is no system as such nor much "global coherence" in the prevailing economic groupings. The very autonomy conceded to the state, though presented in such ambiguous terms as "relative" (to what?), permits a variegated local behavior, as readers have seen, that promotes global diversity, not coherence.

While flawed, his description of the role of the state contains three important notions that deserve recognition. These are the state as *interdependent*, as *arbitrator*, and as *guarantor*. Interdependence implies that reciprocal needs produce some situations that are inherently ambiguous. In those instances neither government nor business can be adjudged the more influential or powerful. Acceptance of this ambiguity and the fact situations that create it are important points. Describing the state as an arbitrator is also significant, because it acknowledges that one of the participants or players is also a judge or referee, with a power that goes beyond the mediation of disputes. To be an arbiter of "conflicting interests," when some of those involved are your very own, is power indeed, especially when the definitions of "the system's" interests and of what is "short-term" and "long-term" are all at stake.

The state as guarantor intersects with its role as arbitrator. The state endeavors to guarantee a "stability" that implies both continuity and enhancement of "the predominating economic and social patterns," but this statement really means something more and involves techniques analagous to those five market processes mentioned earlier. The state has the power to *define* and thereby ratify those already existing "economic and social patterns" it prefers as conducive to stability as "the predominating" ones. The state can attempt to *create* and *develop* other patterns it requires to implement its conceptions of stability and include those among the "predominating." The state can also try to *destroy* a pattern or patterns that may in fact predominate from the viewpoints of others but which threaten(s) stability. And in situations that necessitate power as finesse and not as bludgeon the state can strive for the most efficient *distortion* of already existing patterns or those it is creating, in accordance with its stability requirements. Of course, the items involved in all these processes may not constitute "patterns," in Peemans's word, but nascent or incomplete evidence of what is to come or be manipulated.

When he analyzes specific instances of interaction between government and business bureaucracies, Peemans becomes most compelling, nowhere more than in his treatment of transport (1975, pp. 201–10). Only a hint of how he handles the sometimes subtle realities of government-business relationships can be given here. The Congolese state "created the conditions for profitable exports from the mines controlled by the financial groups. But this does not mean that the transportation policy was oriented entirely in favour of the mines." The Matadi–Leopoldville railway was built "in order to export animal and vegetable products from the Upper Congo." Relations between the state and the transport companies then began to exhibit a "certain ambiguity," which partly came from different notions concerning appropriate tariff levels. The CFML company, which constructed the railway and to which the state had already heavily contributed, took advantage of its monopoly position and tried to fix tariffs "at a level almost as high as the portage tariffs." The company sought thereby to maximize its rate of return; the state "wished to develop exports to the maximum, and thus to reduce the tariff." And so Vice Governor-General Moulaert came into conflict with the private river-transport companies, which wanted a cartel "aiming at tariff increases." The state obtained a "progressive decrease in tariffs" through the application of "sustained pressure" (Peemans, 1975, p. 202). The term "tariff" here refers to transport rates levied by private carriers, is a technically correct usage, but should not be confused with the taxes or tariffs assessed by governments on imports and/or exports, analyzed elsewhere [see pp. 122–26].

Though the term "tariff" is used in multiple senses, the Congolese case gains a comparative richness against the background of our earlier discussions of railroad rates, tariffs and public-private terminology. Not every government bureaucracy operated on the same revenue calculus and mix of objectives, exhibited same degree of sub-bureaucratization, nor confronted the same configuration of privatization. These facts go far in explaining the array of factual outcomes portrayed in this extended essay. Juxtapose the Congolese case with that of Tanganyika insofar as trunkline transport is concerned. In the Congo the state faced a constellation of transport interests which were essentially privatized; in Tanganyika, government owned and operated the railroad. There were significant conflicts in the Congo between the state and those private companies, which pivoted on the pursuit of "distinguishably different goals," to recall Vernon's phrase. In Tanganyika conflict in this area was more within the state itself, as already noted [p. 118]. There sub-bureaucratization had produced a Railway Administration which, while still officially part of the territorial bureaucracy, had achieved sufficient functional autonomy to get its way on requests for upward revisions of rates. Here was an administration also pushing most exports in one or another version of its "plant-more-crops" campaign in the late 1920s and throughout the 1930s (McCarthy, 1982, pp. 64–78) so that it could reap more revenues from indirect taxation of trade and the direct taxation of producers with supposedly more money to be extracted.

But the critical question for some bureaucrats was when do taxes and freight rates move from economic irritant to suffocator. The level of railroad rates had clearly tilted toward the latter in Tanganyika, because of "distinguishably different" formulations of the administration's twin goals—maximization of exports and revenue—by different agencies of that bureaucracy. Faced with two goals the equally zealous pursuit of which would create contradictions, the Railway Administration emphasized increasing its revenue share, rather than promoting expanded aggregate exports through lower rates. And whatever its short-term financial gains were, this approach laid the basis for slower long-term export growth through confiscatory rates.

While Peemans proposed a conception of the colonial state that contained the elements of a greater departure from metrocentricity than he envisioned and analyzed transport in a way that invited contrasts with Tanganyika, David K. Fieldhouse in his study of *Unilever Overseas* has deftly probed business perceptions of actual and potential markets as constrained by government action. Black Africa "was clearly one of the least attractive regions in the world for any multinational whose overseas subsidiaries made goods for local consumption." The reasons for this unattractiveness were several. Poverty "inhibited demand," as "very few of the vast range of Unilever products were within the capacity of most Africans to buy." Soap was, but most of it "had to be of the cheapest type that offered very low profit margins." Besides poverty, "political and economic structures" posed obstacles to market development. "Apart from Nigeria and Zaire, most political units formed by the colonial powers, though large in comparison with the preceding indigenous units, were far too small in population and resources to constitute viable markets for modern consumer industries unless these were given heavy protection." Decolonization exacerbated market unviability, since "three relatively large common markets—French West and Equatorial Africa and British East Africa—subsequently broke up into their component parts" (Fieldhouse, 1978, p. 417).

This situation in "Black Africa" is interesting both in itself and for how Fieldhouse analyzed it. Here was a business accepting a definition of poverty and a notion of economic limit associated with state action and its interests. The conventional notion of African poverty is often based on per capita income statistics monetized in terms of an official "money economy." Government-sanctioned legal tender was only part of an area's real money supply, a fact the forms and consequences of which were detailed in an earlier section (see pp. 84–100). Narrow monetization of income overstates the extent and depth of poverty, which is another example of an abused word in scholarship. Poverty can encompass any or all of the following deficiencies—of money, or goods, or means of subsistence. None of these, when comprehensively construed, was as pervasively present during the colonial period as Fieldhouse and others take for granted. What is more, any definition of poverty must include wealth as well as income. Failure to take the former into account compounds an analytical imprecision already present in monetarily biased conceptions of income.

The preceding discussion of misconstrued and over-stated poverty is not the prelude to an indictment of Unilever behavior in Africa as such, because its perceptions, indeed modus operandi on the continent were not unique. But one wonders what would have happened had companies operating in Africa taken a more imaginative and accurate approach to the exchange process. Other firms in other climes accepted the necessity of "barter" arrangements in order to "jump-start" more integrated exchange circuits, as the experience of International Harvester and Singer in Late Imperial Russia demonstrates, a story so ably told by Professor Carstensen (1984). Whether the goods involved were "barter" or really monetized from local viewpoints is not the issue. The fact is that when placed in an international comparative perspective, Unilever and others took a less than perceptive approach to unlocking African market potential. And when firms were less successful in Africa than elsewhere and sometimes failed there, these outcomes reinforced the notion of a limited market potential as rooted in African poverty.

Market potential was delimited in a second artificial fashion. Just as Unilever operated within a rubric of "money economy" that did and does Africa's exchange flexibility and market potential a grave disservice, so also did it almost entirely accept political definitions of economic opportunity. To think of a market only as a "political unit formed by the colonial powers" or as common market aggregations of those units demonstrates the extent to which government's boundary dictation had stifled business perspectives. Taking the entire land-mass occupied by a particular administration or even just one of its regional or provincial sub-divisions as minimal market spatial size might make the thresholds of market viability unnecessarily high. Fieldhouse himself never specified what minimum number of people or amounts of resources might have served as triggers of potential market viability.

All these themes—the roles of the state, business-government interactions and their impacts, and market perceptions and processes—receive various treatments in perhaps the most valuable compendium issued to date, *Business Empires in Equatorial Africa*. This work embodies much of a May 1982 workshop held at the School of Oriental and African Studies in London and was published as the 1983 edition of *African Economic History*. The approaches to those themes taken by the authors exhibit a stimulating blend of realism and refinement but provoke questions that originate in the concerns of this parvum opus. To the extent that the workshop did reveal an overall conception of the state it resembled in some ways that proposed by Peemans, although the state was described in terms of less potential power. The state "in its different guises" was described as *mediator* "between different capitalist groups and in response to pressures from other classes," not as a more formidable arbitrator (Clarence-Smith, 1983, pp. 5–6). The state's role as *guarantor* was acknowledged, but the notion of *interdependence* seemed to take second place to a debate over the "relative power and autonomy of state and companies" (Clarence-Smith, 1983, p. 6).

Government is disaggregated: "There were differences and contradictions between the metropolitan state in Europe, central governments in the various territories, local administration, and the chiefly hierarchies.'' And some of the implications of disaggregation receive recognition: ''Far from being the obedient servants of large companies, these different levels of government had interests of their own and imposed compromises on firms'' (Clarence-Smith, 1983, p. 5). Both disaggregation and its implications can be carried much farther, as earlier suggested. There were ''differences and contradictions'' not only between the aforementioned administrative ''levels,'' but within them as well. This more comprehensive disaggregation should also apply to business, but the papers in this volume that treat the internal organization of several firms do not system- atically examine intra-firm cooperation and conflict, in part because of evidentiary constraints, in part because the possibility of sub-bureaucratization was not seriously considered. The state is thus more internally differentiated than business, an imbalance which should be corrected in future scholarship.

The central contribution of this workshop, insofar as general conceptions of the role of the state are concerned, may well be a periodization that invites careful scrutiny. It is ''necessary to specify what state apparatus a firm might be dealing with in what period. Chronologically, this meant distinguishing between the phases of 'robber colonialism,' mature colonialism of the interwar years, reformist colonialism after 1945, and independence'' (Clarence-Smith, 1983, p.5). In the ways and with the examples used therein the periodization seems illuminating, on the surface. ''Robber colonialism'' is most graphically embodied in the Congo Free State (a.k.a. Leopold II of Belgium), ''almost a company itself and without the backing of a metropolitan state.'' France mimicked Leopold and handed over much of French Equatorial Africa to the ''same kind of concession company'' (Clarence-Smith, 1983, p. 6). During ''mature colonialism'' companies gained more oligopoly power and the state provided a wider range of facilities and services for firms: ''Investing in transport and other infrastructures, controlling labor through coercion and taxation, forcing peasant production of certain commodities, fixing prices, and guaranteeing interest payments to railway companies. The level of public investment was remarkably high, whether in the form of direct inputs or in the form of large state shareholding companies'' (Clarence-Smith, 1983, p. 6).

During ''reformist colonialism'' post-1945 ''the close alliance between the state and big business began to come under pressure. A more autonomous and interfering state flirted with white settler demands in the Belgian Congo and Angola, while simultaneously exploring the strategy of focusing both economic and political activities on the African peasant masses.'' Recognizing the need to disaggregate busines more thoroughly, W. G. Clarence-Smith further observes that ''altered relations between state and companies may in part have reflected changes in the corporate structure of big business and its tendency to concentrate more on the western world than the third world after 1945, a question which needs to be addressed'' (Clarence-Smith 1983, p. 7). Independence ''marked a sharp break in the interplay between the state and large corporations . . . the weakness and instability of the post-colonial state resulted in a sudden and sometimes forced change of strategy on the part of large companies . . . the weakness and corruption of the state has encouraged the emergence of a new kind of 'rip-off' capitalism, which acts in the role of asset-stripper and leaves nothing behind'' (Clarence-Smith, 1983, p. 7).

Even for Equatorial Africa, let alone elsewhere, this periodization must be used with caution for several reasons. It tends to homogenize the concept of colonialism during certain time periods, because it retrogresses into over-generalizations about the roles of the state and business. Consider the period of so-called ''mature'' colonialism as a glaring instance of the lack of refined comparative perspectives. The ''state,'' to use once again an intermediate category of analysis between metropolis and locality in frozen fashion, provides a ''wider range of facilities and services for firms'' listed above. The enumeration is correct, but the types and degrees of what was provided, indeed its very mix, varied in important ways from territory to territory, as our continuing research on comparative economic regulation is decisively demonstrating. How a bureaucracy tried to ''control labor through coercion and taxation,'' how it endeavored to ''force peasant production of certain commodities,'' and ''how it fixed prices,'' to cite three of the examples used here and only a few of the instances of germane state action that affected all sizes of business, had great consequences for the configuration of economic activity at the time and in the future. Colonialism, as noted, was actually the beginning of a transformation of imperialism, which produced such varied outcomes.[13]

So any periodization that homogenizes colonialism and especially one that sequences change based on notions of time as chronology and structuralism as impressionism is bound to encounter problems. For instance, achievement of ''flag independence'' did mark a ''sharp break in the interplay between the state and the large corporations'' in the ways heretofore cited, but one major reason for the ''weakness and instability'' of some post-colonial states is rooted deeply in the colonial legacies each faced in somewhat different ways. Put too simply, here were administrations in the process of Africanizing their personnel trying to use structures that had been fastened upon their countries not primarily for the purposes of ''development'' or ''growth,'' but for control and extraction. To seek development and growth through structures designed to promote stability and stasis was like trying to turn around a tanker on a dime. Though many ''flag independent'' administrations mandated ''reforms'' in bureaucratic structures, these were most often cosmetic and superficial, not underlying. So there is a great continuity in the colonial and post-colonial administrative spheres that a periodization of this sort elides.

It does have some shafts of illumination. The call to analyze in more detail changes in business structures should apply not only to the post-1945 ''reformist'' period but also to the other eras. This investigation of internal structures should include state bureaucracies as well, because neither state nor business was ever totally static. Even if no changes were consciously made by business or government administrators in the designs of their organizations, the relations between personnel and those structures are inherently dynamic in either a retrogressive or progressive sense, depending on one's viewpoint. What is more, the multiple relations between a business and government bureaucracy and its operating environments are also inherently conducive to change of some sort.

One has more general reactions to the major approaches of both workshop and periodization, but these would replicate in several ways our earlier analysis of the vocabulary of scholarship. The concentration on "business empires," for instance, is another example of scholarship paying insufficient attention to small- and medium-size business both from within and from without Africa. The very last essay in the volume provides a beginning corrective to this imbalance. One hopes that H. Laurens van der Laan's study of a Swiss family firm in West Africa, A. Brunnschweiler and Company, 1929–1959, will inspire other research on other firms not reckoned in the major leagues in conventional terms (van der Laan, 1983, pp. 287–97). There are many other positive features of this seminal volume, but we shall continue concentrating on distinctive contributions to analysis of business-government relations.

In "European Planters, African Peasants, and the Colonial State: Alternatives in the *Mise en Valeur* of Makaland, Southeast Cameroun, During the Interbellum" Peter Geschiere has treated conflict between government and business over labor in an especially arresting fashion. Open to the applicability of a "functionalist teleology" which explains development "only by the functional logic of a mode of production," he avoids a facile use thereof and insists that one must "analyze the political level as well: the reality of actors, strategies, and decisions, their intended and unintended consequences." What was "the outcome of the process of articulation in Makaland" was "the exploitation of small-scale peasant production through capitalist market relations." This result was not "preordained," though it is "functional." A "real alternative" to this outcome existed: "The appropriation of surplus value from Maka wage laborers on large-scale European plantations." This alternative became "secondary," because administrators and also "peasants" made decisions that greatly influenced actual "articulation." What Geschiere terms the "short-term interests" of the administration—the "fear" that "not enough labor would be left for the administration itself"—made it "intervene against further extension of the European economy" (Geschiere, 1983, p.101). "Not enough labor" means that administrators preferred "cash-crop production by the villagers themselves," since these situations were more amenable to direct bureaucratic "supervision" than those on large-scale European plantations. The state dominated in Makaland because capital was "weak" in the region and there was little "regular surplus labor in the old mode of production." The state, therefore, "had to play a crucial role in mobilizing the labor of the Maka for the exploitation of the region" (Geschiere, 1983, pp. 101–102).

This case study stands on the merits of its facts, whether or not one accepts the entire fabric of its interpretative language. But its importance extends into areas that the author could not, because of space, or would not, because of ideological orientation, confront. Who or what has more control over the "extraction of surplus capital," in the author's own words, is critical in determining the destination(s) of what is extracted. Specification of destination must go beyond "the demands of capital" or the "needs of capital," abstract language which Geschiere himself chided the distinguished French anthropologist P-Ph. Rey for using, or the vaguely defined apparatus of the "capitalist world-economy," on which this author has earlier commented. Colonial states often preferred all-African production situations, because these internalized returns more than expatriate enterprise, with its greater propensity to repatriate. Greater internalization meant increased exposure to the tax net, and revenue so obtained underpinned and perhaps strengthened the state apparatus, the particular configuration of stronger and weaker state agencies depending inter alia on patterns of budgetary appropriations over the years. Specification of destination must thus occur within our frameworks of state and business differentiation. What specific agencies or divisions or parts thereof, the language of differentiation varying according to context, received disproportionate shares of a state's or a business's "expropriation of surplus value" is also integrally connected with the phenomenon of sub-bureaucratization analyzed earlier.

Barbara J. Heinzen has contributed an elegantly thoughtful vignette in her study of "The United Fruit Company in the 1950s: Trusteeships of the Cameroons." She has examined the UFC operating through its British and French subsidiaries in what were then the two separate United Nations Trusteeship territories of British Cameroons and French Cameroons. She, more than some other authors in this volume, systematically takes into account local business structures, including plantations and smallholders' cooperatives, and their evolving relations with both government and the respective subsidiary of the multinational UFC. She demonstrates in particular "the manner in which a multinational company will adapt its operations—is, in fact, obliged to adapt its operations—to local definitions of how the trade should be organized." This emphasis on discovering those "local definitions," from the multiple perspectives of government agencies and local businesses, is one of the major keys to writing the history of business and bureaucracy in Africa more effectively (see McCarthy, 1982, pp. 24–36).

Her "case study would tend to support company executives' claims that their subsidiaries are subject to pressures from, if not always directly the nation-state, certainly from the social and commercial organization of businesses within that state." The Compagnie des Bananes and Elders and Fyffes, the companies involved, did have some "bargaining levers," such as "a high level of control over shipping and sales and to a lesser extent over the quality of production" (Heinzen, 1983, p. 151). The language of her conclusion is most refreshing: "The nature of any company/host relationship is less likely to have been defined by the dominance of one party over another than it is the product of an evolving process of pressure and adaptation that shapes both sides" (Heinzen, 1983, pp. 151–52). Put another way, those who debate the "autonomy of the state" issue by taking points in linear chronological time and arguing that at one point the state was "more autonomous" and at another a business was "more powerful" are misconstruing the issue. To appreciate that "evolving process of pressure and adaptation" one must put particular business-government relationships in the context of a more secular historical version of time and consider the evolution of the "bargaining levers" each possessed throughout an association of whatever kind. She does momentarily descend into the linear point mode, when she notes that "such a process might at any one point favor one party over the other," but recovers to make one of the most important points in the entire volume: "Any long-term involvement . . . is bound to create a hybrid organization that in some way should have satisfied the legitimate aspirations of both company and host country" (Heinzen, 1983, p. 152).

The concept of transformation is another major key to writing the history of bureaucracy and business in Africa more effectively. It has many dimensions. Heinzen here correctly applies one such aspect, when she highlights organizational hybridization as it related to a subsidiary becoming neither just a semi-autonomous stand-in for its international progenitor nor an authentically indigenous business enterprise but a cross-blend. Transformation applies in multiple senses, as noted throughout, to the experiences of particular colonial bureaucracies in general and their relations with business in particular.

Ulrich Stürzinger has furnished the last distinctive approach to business-government relations to be considered here in "The Introduction of Cotton Cultivation in Chad: The Role of the Administration, 1920–1936." In an area with what some considered a sparse resource endowment the government itself took the initiative in starting cotton cultivation as a cash crop (1920–1928) and then remained the driving force at least through 1936, the somewhat abrupt termination date of his essay. Development of cotton cultivation was an ongoing series of acts of *force majeure* by government, whatever the specific language of administrative implementation, and Stürzinger documents this theme with acute detail.

How he interprets the colonial administration's cotton policy offers another angle of vision on state action and relates to some of the central linguistic concerns of this essay. Two goals "determined" that policy: "self-preservation and strengthening of power." Although "the choice of cotton as a cash crop can be explained by the demand of French industry as well as by the lack of any indigenous minerals," its "cultivation was very helpful in building up an administrative system that integrated colonial and traditional structures" (Stürzinger, 1983, p. 220). Stürzinger details this "hybridization," to use Heinzen's arresting phrase in yet another way, of structures and underscores how important cotton cultivation was in a fiscal sense. Chad was able to meet its direct administrative costs internally from 1900, when the French officially established their rule in the terrritory, until the 1930s. About 80 percent of those revenues came from the head tax, and "a rise in head tax revenues gave more freedom of action to the Governor of Chad. This explains why the administration was interested in creating certain economic activities which facilitated the levying of taxes." The "tax potential" of these activities was "the critical criterion"; whether farmers received remuneration "was never seriously discussed."

As he examines the dubious contributions of cotton policy to the "economic development of Chad" and notes that in an accounting sense the "only winner" was the company known as Cotonfran, Stürzinger makes several important points. The first concerns the jargon of various "economies" dissected throughout this paper. "Neither the idea of an integration into the world economy as an autonomous economic unit," he argues, "nor the goal of a rather dissociated self-reliant economy correspond to the imperatives of those years when colonial economies had to complement those of the mother country" (Stürzinger, 1983, p. 221). Even in its own terms, the suspect patois of world-systems analysis, this argument points in at least one right direction. Bilateral relations between a colony and its home country were more controlling than multilateral associations with transnational agents and agencies in this particular case study. The argument becomes valid when shorn of the questionable constructs of "colonial economy" and a "world economy" now rendered even more metaphysical in its wraith-like presence as "autonomous economic unit."

A second major point is his interpretation of state action, which pivots on too delimited conceptions of economics and economic rationality. He concludes that "the cotton policy in Chad was not guided by *economic conceptions*." It was "rather" central to strengthening the administration:

> Therefore economic weaknesses of the system were not corrected in an economically rational way, but compensated for by administrative measures that were at the disposal of the colonial service in Chad. Rather than market forces based on a coherent long-term economic policy, it was the administrative imperatives of the day which led to the establishment of a cotton economy in southern Chad (Stürzinger, 1983, p. 223).

He creates a disjunction between state action and market forces and equates economic rationality with the latter. There are different types of economic rationality and various modes of economy (see McCarthy, 1976b, pp. 647–48), and their origins do not reside exclusively in the logic of market forces, which are here imperfectly specified. The author has elsewhere detailed the construction of a *bureaucratic economy* by Tanganyikan colonial administrators and argued that their action and inaction produced "an economy in the most basic sense: an organization of the forms, contents, and locations of production, distribution, and exchange in ways that supplied the revenue and order the bureaucracy demanded" (McCarthy, 1982, p. 5).

Stürzinger's study of a regional commodity policy does not in itself demonstrate state action of a breadth and depth necessary for the creation of a bureaucratic economy coterminous with the administrative boundaries of Chad and meaningful in territorial terms. But his evidence is highly suggestive of an increasingly pervasive bureaucratization of economic structures which partook of that hybridization quoted above: "building up an administrative system that integrated colonial and traditional structures." These "structures" were in key dimensions economic and so perhaps here one can speak of an emerging regional version of a bureaucratic economy. Not all bureaucratic economies are identical in origins, forms, and consequences, of course. But it does seem, based on the available evidence, that the origins and entrenchment of bureaucratic economies in the colonial experience involve, in part, hybridization of various kinds, which are aspects of the key concept of transformation.

III. RETROSPECTIVE AND PROSPECTIVE

The complete story of bureaucracy and business in Africa from the 1880s into the 1960s and beyond remains to be written, but this extended essay has laid a foundation for such an endeavor. Its first major part addressed the subject of comparative economic regulation, because of the compelling necessity to differentiate state action in a manner too much scholarship ignores or does not carry sufficiently far. The very definition of state action should be as comprehensive as possible. It should include what was directed at, or impinged upon, the general economic environment as well as what was aimed at particular agents and agencies within that general setting. The series of vignettes presented in Part I featured the media of exchange, credit, savings, trades licensing fees, market regulations, transportation with emphasis on railroads, tariff and non-tariff barriers, and an addendum mentioned government marketing boards and other commodity regulations. In all these areas there were, to be sure, similarities in bureaucratic conduct, but the differences that emerged went considerably beyond the cosmetic. Governments were affecting the basics of economic and business life in profoundly varying ways, with consequences that pervade both past and present and shackle the future. Regulations were *ipso facto* restrictive, but their designs differed in important ways, as those vignettes demonstrated. The degree to which state actions in all areas thus constrained or repressed behavior varied significantly across the colonial spectrum, which means that there is a distinctive history of abuse for each territory, not just for African colonialism in general.

While the present profile of comparative economic regulation has begun to assemble relevant differences in systematic fashion and differentiate consequences analytically, there are at least two major questions that require much deeper investigation and more evidence not currently at our disposal. These are origins and impact. The kind of "inside" study of the origins, forms, and effects of decision making, based on the unpublished and sometimes confidential documentation of government on every level, done for interwar Tanganyika (see McCarthy, 1982) should be conducted mutatis mutandis for other territories. More complete attention to the "political level," as Peter Geschiere earlier termed it, will show how complex was "the reality of actors, strategies, and decisions, their intended and unintended consequences" in multiple colonial environments.

Part II spotlighted government-business relations. It began with an examination of vocabulary, because linguistic imprecision or incompleteness on the ABCs of any analytical framework—such terms as economy, public sector, private sector, development, and underdevelopment—is widespread. The aim was not to produce one vocabulary becoming dogma, but to question so forcefully the existing uses of some terms that these will be used with much greater care in the future. Even if the only result of semantic analysis is to define the ambiguities inherent in the application of terms, any framework that employs those constructs with an awareness of their shadows will possess greater realism. A number of approaches to business-government relations then received scrutiny. Two major concepts seem to guide analysis in the most probing directions: differentiation and transformation. *Differentiation* applies to the structures and powers of both state and business internally and externally, including which agency of government is in what kind of relationship with what part of business, and encompasses the key notion of *sub-bureaucratization. Transformation* is in one major way differentiation in the multiple dimensions of time, simple chronology viewed as a necessary adjunct to an analysis based in historical time. *Hybridization*, one type of transformation, is casting special illumination on such subjects as the local adaptations of international corporations and the official bureaucratization of local economic structures. All these concepts in the presence of a richer evidentiary base of primary sources will make more feasible the writing of that complete story of bureaucracy and business in Africa from the 1880s into the 1960s and beyond.

ACKNOWLEDGMENTS

This extended essay formally began as a semi-vaudevillian conference paper presented at the behest of Fred Carstensen to the Business History Conference in Hartford, Connecticut, in March 1984. Parts of the introduction and the money section received an appropriate response from the audience, which included Chairperson William N. Parker and critic Jeremy Atack. In its longer incarnation it has received constructive criticism from Hamilton Cravens, Robert E. Schofield, Richard Lowitt, Richard Kirkendall, John Dobson, Alan Marcus, and Greg Sanford. These people, especially Hamilton Cravens and Robert Schofield, helped the author eliminate some of its flaws. The author thanks Iowa State University for furnishing financial assistance on two occasions that made full-time research on this project possible. He is deeply indebted to the editor of this series for his continuing encouragement and patience.

NOTES

1. For a fascinating account of local monetary evolution that embodies the approaches of both archaeology and ethno-economics and deserves the widest possible audience, please see Pierre de Maret (1981).

2. For an analysis of the introduction of French currency in central Niger which corroborates for part of French Africa some facts of our analysis but which does not use our particular framework, please see Stephen Baier (1980, pp. 105–10).

3. It is important to know as much as possible about "indigenous or ethnic sources of credit" in both past and present, as some so-called "less developed countries" seek to reduce their international debt dependencies. While they continue to refine economic development models, some economists openly acknowledge the need for more information about "traditional capital markets" so that their specifications of K (capital) and M (various versions of the money supply) in those models might be comprehensive. A forthright recognition of this necessity in an overall totally arresting interpretation of money and capital in economic development can be found in Ronald McKinnon (1973, p. 38).

4. For a discussion of one version of the provident societies in the latter colonial era, when their functions and workings seemingly became more constructive, please see Jane Guyer (1980).

5. For more details on the Gold Coast's approach to transport, please consult G. B. Kay (1972, pp. 135–98). This book, with its mix of commentary, original documents, and statistical abstract, is also exceptionally useful in the areas of general economic policy, finance, general agriculture, agriculture with emphasis on cocoa, and education.

6. For a review of the literature on Africa and the "world economy" that approaches comprehensiveness in some respects but remains too much within the construct itself and does not really challenge its language, premises, or logic, please see Frederick Cooper (1981). A companion piece on states and social processes in Africa also covers some of the same historiographical ground, but is useful for both its bibliographical contribution and its synthesis of academic jargon. It, too, does not really query the basic vocabulary of economies, sectors, and underdevelopment. Please see John Lonsdale (1981).

7. In a tome otherwise distinguished by its wealth of information and clear presentation Gavin Kitching at times exhibits this tendency. His concern is admittedly class formation, but this special emphasis should not preclude similarly inclined scholars from considering the implications of their evidence in multiple business contexts. Please see Kitching (1980).

8. Of the many works that constitute this corpus, two can be recommended unhesitatingly to newcomers as excellent introductions to the genre. Please see Polly Hill (1970) and Sara Berry (1975).

9. Please see Floyd Dotson and Lillian O. Dotson (1975); their bibliography is most helpful (pp. 629–31).

10. The research of ethnoscientist Dennis M. Warren, though not primarily ethno-economic or ethno-business, has implications for these areas as well: Ghana market information in author's possession. For an introduction to the ABCs of ethnoscience for historians, please see D. M. P. McCarthy (1976c). For a brief discussion of the need for both multiple epistemologies and taxonomies of underdevelopment in the past as well as present, see D. M. P. McCarthy (1976a).

11. For a discussion that takes Professor Reuber's tripartite classification of "export-oriented," "market-development," and "government-initiated" and modifies it to distinguish "four main motives for making a productive investment overseas," three of which are "exported-oriented," and the fourth for "market-development," please see D. K. Fieldhouse (1978, pp. 9–23).

12. For a review of the literature on labor and labor history in Africa, please see Bill Freund (1984).

13. For a brief analysis of the relations between the economics of penetration and formal imperialism in the case of the Gold Coast, please see D. M. P. McCarthy (1975).

REFERENCES

Annual Reports. These are sometimes entitled *The Social and Economic Progress of the People of . . .*
Their official place of publication is listed as London. Their official date of publication is one year
after the one noted, with exceptions given in parentheses. In cases of reports that cover parts of two
years the date of publication is always placed in parentheses.

  Ashanti. 1908, 1909
  Gambia. 1901, 1919, 1931.
  Gold Coast. 1892(1893 or 1894), 1894(1896), 1896, 1900, 1905, 1906, 1908, 1913, 1921(1923),
      1922–1923(1924), 1929–1930(1930), 1936–1937(1938), 1937–1938(1939), 1938–1939
      (1939).
  Kenya. 1922(1924), 1931(1933), 1932, 1935, 1936.
  Lagos. 1895, 1897, 1900–1901(1902), 1903.
  Nigeria. 1915(1917), 1916(1918), 1917(1919), 1918(1920), 1921, 1922, 1923, 1924, 1925,
      1926, 1927, 1928, 1929, 1930, 1931, 1932, 1933, 1934, 1935, 1936(1938), 1937(1939),
      1938.
  Northern Nigeria. 1902, 1904, 1906–1907(1907), 1907–1908(1909). 1914(1916).
  Northern Territories of the Gold Coast. 1901, 1913, 1918, 1921.
  Nyasaland. 1912–1913(1913), 1936, 1937(1939), 1938.
  Sierra Leone. 1905, 1908, 1923, 1928, 1932, 1937.
  Somaliland Protectorate. 1905–1906(1906), 1906–1907(1907), 1907–1908(1908).
  Southern Nigeria. 1900(1902), 1904, 1905(Southern Nigeria[Lagos]), 1908, 1911.
  Uganda. 1908–1909(1910), 1911–1912(1913), 1913–1914(1915), 1931, 1933, 1935, 1938.
  Zanzibar. 1927, 1928, 1933, 1936, 1937.

* * *

Baier, Stephen (1980), *An Economic History of Central Niger*. New York: Oxford University Press.
Berry, Sara S. (1975), *Cocoa, Custom, and Socio-Economic Change in Rural Western Nigeria*.
    London: Oxford University Press.
Carstensen, Fred V. (1984), *American Enterprise in Foreign Markets: Singer and International
    Harvester in Imperial Russia*. Chapel Hill: The University of North Carolina Press.
Cooper, Frederick (1981), "Africa and the World Economy." *The African Studies Review* 24,
    2/3(June–September 1981): 1–86.
Clarence-Smith, W. G. (1983), "Business Empires in Equatorial Africa." *African Economic History*,
    12: 3–11.
de Maret, Pierre (1981), "L'Evolution Monetaire du Shaba Central Entre Le 7ᵉ et Le 18ᵉ Siecle."
    African Economic History, 10: 117–49.
Dotson, Floyd, and Lillian O. Dotson (1975), "The Economic Role of Non-Indigenous Ethnic
    Minorities in Colonial Africa." In Peter Duignan and L. H. Gann (eds.), *Colonialism in Africa,
    1870–1960, IV: The Economics of Colonialism*. Cambridge: The University Press, pp. 565–631.
Fieldhouse, D. K. (1978), *Unilever Overseas: The Anatomy of a Multinational, 1895–1965*. London:
    Croom Helm.
Freund, Bill (1984), "Labor and Labor History in Africa: A Review of the Literature." *The African
    Studies Review*, 27, 2(June): 1–58.
Geschiere, Peter (1983), "European Planters, African Peasants, and the Colonial State: Alternatives
    in the *mise en valeur* of Makaland, Southeast Cameroun, During the Interbellum." *African
    Economic History*, 12: 83–108.
Grier, Beverly (1981), "Underdevelopment, Modes of Production, and the State in Colonial Ghana."
    The African Studies Review, 24, 1(March): 21–47.
Guyer, Jane I. (1980), "The Provident Societies in the Rural Economy of Yaounde, 1945–1960."

Working Paper No. 37, African Studies Center, Boston University.

Heinzen, Barbara J. (1983), "The United Fruit Company in the 1950s: Trusteeships of the Cameroons." *African Economic History*, 12: 141–56.

Hill, Polly (1970), *Studies in Rural Capitalism in West Africa*. Cambridge: The University Press.

Jamal, Vali (1978), "Taxation and Inequality in Uganda, 1900–1964." *The Journal of Economic History*, 38, 2(June): 418–38.

Kay, G. B. (1972), *The Political Economy of Colonialism in Ghana: A Collection of Documents and Statistics, 1900–1960*. Cambridge: The University Press.

Kitching, Gavin (1980), *Class and Economic Change in Kenya: The Making of an African Petite Bourgeoisie, 1905–1970*. New Haven: Yale University Press.

Lonsdale, John (1981), "States and Social Processes in Africa: A Historiographical Survey." *The African Studies Review*, 24, 2/3(June/September): 139–225.

McCarthy, D. M. P. (1975), "Imperialism." *The Journal of Economic History*, 35, 1(March): 134–37.

(1976a), "History of Under-Development in the Third World." *The Journal of Economic History*, 36, 1(March): 41–4.

(1976b), "Media As Ends: Money and the Underdevelopment of Tanganyika to 1940." *The Journal of Economic History*, 36, 3(September): 645–62.

(1976c), "How Can An Historian Use Ethnoscience?" Unpublished conference paper, African Studies Association, Boston, Massachusetts, November.

(1977), "Organizing Underdevelopment From the Inside: The Bureaucratic Economy in Tanganyika, 1919–1940." *The International Journal of African Historical Studies*, x, 4: 573–99.

(1979), "Language Manipulation in Colonial Tanganyika, 1919–40." *Journal of African Studies*, 6, 1(Spring): 9–16.

(1982), *Colonial Bureaucracy and Creating Underdevelopment: Tanganyika, 1919–1940*. Ames: The Iowa State University Press.

McKinnon, Ronald I. (1973), *Money and Capital in Economic Development*. Washington: The Brookings Institution.

Ofonagoro, Walter I. (1979), "From Traditional to British Currency in Southern Nigeria: Analysis of a Currency Revolution, 1880–1946." *The Journal of Economic History*, 39, 3(September): 623–54.

Peemans, Jean-Philippe (1975), "Capital Accumulation in the Congo under Colonialism: The Role of the State." In Peter Duignan and L. H. Gann (eds.), *Colonialism in Africa, 1870–1960, IV: The Economics of Colonialism*. Cambridge: The University Press, pp. 165–212.

Stürzinger, Ulrich (1983), "The Introduction of Cotton Cultivation in Chad: The Role of The Administration, 1920–1936." *African Economic History*, 12: 213–25.

Suret-Canale, Jean (1971), *French Colonialism in Tropical Africa, 1900–1945*. New York: Pica Press.

Tanzania National Archives (Dar es Salaam) Secretariat File 30272.

van der Laan, H. Laurens (1983), "A Swiss Family Firm in West Africa: A. Brunnschweiler & Co., 1929–1959." *African Economic History*, 12: 287–97.

Warren, Dennis M. Unpublished research material in author's possession.

SPECIAL INTERESTS AND
THE NINETEENTH-CENTURY
ROOTS OF THE U.S.
MILITARY-INDUSTRIAL COMPLEX

Ben Baack and Edward John Ray

ABSTRACT

The U.S. military-industrial complex has its roots in the late nineteenth century. Prior to then American military history was characterized by buildup during war followed by demobilization. During the 1880s, however, the United States for the first time undertook a major peacetime military buildup. Between the near total demobilization following the Civil War to the outbreak of World War I the size of the U.S. Navy became second only to the British fleet. The determinants of America's first peacetime military buildup and the development of a military-industrial complex can be traced to a confluence of economic events and special political interests.

Research in Economic History, Volume 11, pages 153–169.
ISBN: 0-89232-677-8

I.

In 1960 President Eisenhower issued the following warning in his farewell address to the American people: ''We must guard against the acquisition of unwarranted influence, whether sought or unsought, by the military-industrial complex. The potential for the disastrous use of misplaced power exists and will persist'' (U.S. Presidents, 1961, pp. 1039–40).

Eisenhower's depiction of powerful special interest groups each with vested interests in the development and purchase of complex and expensive weapons has led to a growing number of investigations into the peacetime military establishment (Pursell, 1972; Rosen, 1973; Koistinen, 1980). Despite the increased attention given to the phenomenon of the peacetime military buildup in the United States, few studies have attempted to pinpoint and explain its origin. One popular view is that it was a product of the Cold War of the 1950s while other studies traced its history back to the period between the two World Wars (Nelson, 1972). In fact, we first observe the coalescing of business, military, and political interest groups in support of a peacetime military buildup during the years between the Civil War and World War I. It was during this period that we first observed institutional arrangements between the military and industry for the purpose of large-scale weapon acquisitions with the focus on the construction of a new navy.

Following the Civil War the navy had been reduced to a few squadrons of wooden sailing vessels which provided at best a limited coastal defense. Beginning in the 1880s, the United States became a participant in what was to become a major international naval arms race. The weapons system involved was the large and expensive, steel-plated, steam-propelled, and heavily armed warship. By the time President Roosevelt sent the Great White Fleet on its voyage around the world in 1907, the steel battleship strength of the American navy was the second largest in the world. Never before had a weapons acquisition program of this magnitude been undertaken during peacetime in American history.

The purpose of this paper is to provide some insight into the first peacetime military buildup in the United States. In doing so we will examine the economic and political interests which combined to undertake and sustain a rapid growth of the American navy during the late nineteenth and early twentieth centuries. In the following section of the paper we will trace the rise of the new navy from its origin to the end of the Teddy Roosevelt era. In the subsequent section we assess the development of the institutional environment within which the new navy emerged. The final section offers statistical evidence on the formation of political and economic interest group alignments which contributed to the naval buildup.

II. RISE OF THE NEW NAVY

The heritage of the peacetime military buildup can be traced directly to the construction of the new navy during the late nineteenth and early twentieth centuries. Up to that point the history of the U.S. military had been one of buildup during each war followed by demobilization after the war ended. The War of 1812, the Mexican War, and the Civil War were all followed by periods of very low levels of military spending. During the Civil War, for example, the navy had reached a strength of nearly 700 ships, aggregating 500,000 tons, mounting 5,000 guns, and manned by 51,500 officers and men. Shortly after Lee's surrender at Appomattox, however, all work on new ship construction was suspended. Fifteen years later the navy had only 45 ships (Navy Report, 1880, p. 3; La Feber, 1963, p. 58).

Within two decades after the Civil War demobilization a fundamental change in this pattern began to emerge. Between 1880 and 1905 the share of the federal budget spent on the military went from 20 percent to over 40 percent. Whereas federal expenditures doubled during this period the budget of the army tripled and the naval budget increased nearly eightfold. The navy's share of the federal budget went from less than 6 percent in 1880 to over 20 percent in 1905 (Table 1).

While expenditures rose for both the army and navy, it was the buildup of the navy which provided the incentives for a coalescence of business, military, and political interests. The reason was simple. Throughout this period the army spent very little for manufactured goods. A full two-thirds of its budget was spent on paying its troops, having its corps of engineers clear rivers and harbors, and hiring private firms to transport men and material. Less than 2 percent of its budget went to the purchase of arms (Table 2).

The navy, on the other hand, began to devote a growing share of its budget for manufactured goods. In 1880 it spent over half its budget on pay and nothing for the construction of new ships. By 1905 pay accounted for only 17 percent of its budget while ship construction had reached nearly 40 percent of the budget (Table 3). To enable the navy to build and maintain a fleet of steel warships required large investments in shipyards and steel plants by businessmen and

Table 1.   Naval Share of the Federal Budget

Year	Total Federal Expenditures	Total Naval Expenditures	Naval Share of Federal Budget
1880	267,643,000	14,864,148	5.6%
1885	260,227,000	16,021,080	6.2%
1890	318,041,000	22,006,206	6.9%
1895	356,195,000	28,797,796	8.1%
1900	520,861,000	55,953,078	10.7%
1905	567,279,000	116,655,827	20.6%

Sources: Historial Statistics of the United States, Colonial Times to 1970 (Washington, D.C., 1975), Pt. 2, p. 114. *Annual Report of the Navy Department* (Washington, D.C., 1918) Statement 2, p. 276.

Table 2.   Share of Major Entries in Army Budgets

Entry	Share of 1885 Budget	Share of 1895 Budget	Share of 1905 Budget
Pay	32.3%	27.6%	27.7%
Transportation	8.1%	4.8%	10.7%
Harbors and Rivers	23.0%	36.8%	32.7%
Arsenals	.7%	.6%	1.6%
Purchase of Arms	.9%	1.4%	1.9%

Sources: Annual Report of the War Department (Washington, D.C., 1905) Vol. I, pp. 55–61; (1895) Vol. I, pp. 40–59; (1885) Vol. I, pp. 40–56.

Table 3.   Share of Major Entries in Naval Budgets

Entry	Share of 1880 Budget	Share of 1885 Budget	Share of 1895 Budget	Share of 1905 Budget
Pay	52.1%	43.1%	26.2%	16.6%
Ordnance	1.8%	1.5%	1.2%	3.4%
Equipment	4.0%	4.8%	3.9%	2.6%
Steam Machinery	5.4%	5.8%	3.2%	3.7%
New Steel Ships	0%	13.4%	35.1%	38.9%

Sources: U.S. Congress. Senate. 65th Cong. 3rd sess., S. Doc. 418, Table 1, pp. 643–68. *Congressional Record*, 57th Cong., 1st sess., pp. 5382–92. *Report of the Secretary of the Navy* (Washington, D.C., 1880, 1917).

long-term financing by the government. In effect, it meant putting together a production team of businessmen, naval officers, and politicians.

Between 1883 and 1898 the United States built 110 ships including 12 battleships, 33 torpedo boats, 18 cruisers, and 16 destroyers. By 1902 the United States was fourth in world battleship strength and sixth in overall fleet size with 140 ships. By 1908 the United States was second only to Britain in total warship tonnage (see Tables 4, 5, 6).

To the extent that the United States was committed to build a first-class naval fleet requiring substantial amounts of long-term investment one would expect ideally that such an undertaking would commence during a period of prolonged peacetime. But, that does not explain why the U.S. naval buildup took place during the period 1883–1910. Nothing similar had occurred during any of the previous postwar peacetime periods in U.S. history. Two questions that we address in this paper are relevant to an understanding of the emergence of the military-industrial complex in post-World War II America: Why did the United States embark on a peacetime naval buildup during the late nineteenth century? And, what were the elements of the political and economic coalition that successfully sustained a national commitment to a massive military buildup over a period of almost 30 years?

Table 4. Warships Authorized Each Year by Congress to be Built for the United States Navy Since the Commencement of the New Navy

Year of Authorization	Type of Ship	Number
1883	Cruisers	3
1884		
1885	Cruisers	2
	Gunboats	2
1886	Monitors	4
	Second-class Battleships	2
	Cruiser	1
	Gunboat	1
	Torpedo Boat	1
1887	Monitors	2
	Cruisers	2
	Gunboats	2
1888	Cruisers	7
	Gunboat	1
1889	Gunboats	2
	Ram	1
1890	Battleships	3
	Cruiser	1
	Torpedo Boat	1
1891	Cruiser	1
1892	Battleship	1
	Cruiser	1
1893	Gunboats	3
	Submarine	1
1894	Torpedo Boats	3
1895	Battleships	2
	Gunboats	6
	Torpedo Boats	3
1896	Battleships	3
	Torpedo Boats	10
1897	Torpedo Boats	3
1898	Battleships	3
	Destroyers	16
	Torpedo Boats	12
	Monitors	4

continued

Table 4 continued

1899	Battleships	3
	Cruisers	9
1900	Battleships	2
	Cruisers	6
	Submarines	6
1901		
1902	Battleships	2
	Cruisers	2
	Gunboats	2
1903	Battleships	5
1904	Battleships	1
	Cruisers	5
	Submarines	3
1905	Battleships	2
1906	Battleship	1
	Destroyers	3
	Submarines	8
1907	Battleship	1
	Destroyers	2
1908	Battleships	2
	Destroyers	10
	Submarines	8

Sources: Congressional Record, 57th Cong., 1st sess., pp. 5388–89. 61st Cong., 3rd sess., U.S. Congress. Senate. S. Docu. 666, pp. 700–05.

Table 5.   Fleet Size of Major Naval Powers
1902

	Armored Warships			Total Fleet Size
	Battleships	Cruisers	Total Armored	
Austria	14	3	21	63
France	20	22	56	447
Germany	27	10	37	125
Great Britain	53	24	104	447
Italy	6	10	23	219
Japan	6	5	18	172
Russia	14	12	50	341
United States	17	9	36	140

Source: Congressional Record, 57th Cong., 1st sess., p. 5389 (Washington, D.C., U.S.G.P.O., 1902)

Table 6. Fleet Size of Major Naval Powers
1908

	Armored Warships			Total Fleet Size
	Battleships	*Cruisers*	*Total Armored*	
Austria	3	9	17	58
France	18	32	76	420
Germany	22	16	75	183
Great Britain	52	35	173	409
Italy	11	6	27	110
Japan	11	14	44	172
Russia	5	9	29	204
United States	25	23	87	147

Relative Warship Tonnage	
Great Britain	1,669,005
United States	685,426
France	628,882
Germany	524,573
Japan	371,891
Russia	240,943
Italy	220,458
Austria	114,250

Source: Annual Report of the Secretary of the Navy (Washington, D.C., U.S.G.P.O., 1908), pp. 12–13.

III. DEVELOPMENT OF THE INSTITUTIONAL ENVIRONMENT

In 1880 President Hayes made the first request by a chief executive since the Civil War for a larger navy. In his annual message to Congress he argues that building a large and modern navy would help protect the nation's growing commerce. In a subsequent series of events we see the beginning of a new navy during peacetime. One year after Hayes' address the Secretary of the Navy established the Naval Advisory Board to study the number and type of new ships needed for the fleet and to propose a comprehensive building program for submission to Congress. Made up of naval officers, the board in its final report asked Congress to commit itself to an eight-year 68-ship building program costing nearly 30 million dollars (U.S. Congress, H. Doc., 32, p. 29). President Arthur urged Congress to give special attention to the board's recommendations arguing nothing was more vital to the defense of the United States than a strong navy (Richardson, 1898, p. 51).

In January 1882, the House Naval Affairs Committee began hearings on the board's recommendations. It called upon both naval officers and businessmen to assess the fleet's condition and American industry's capacity to build new ships. The iron and steel executives who testified before the committee argued that the new navy should be built of steel. In response the committee's chairman expressed the hope that in letting contracts for steel ships, the national government would be encouraging the steel industry to expand its facilities. For their part, the naval officers argued that expansion would happen only if a major shipbuilding program were undertaken (U.S. Congress, H.R. 653).

In the following year Congress approved funds for the navy's first steel ships. The Naval Appropriation Bill of 1883 did more, however, than initiate a navy shipbuilding program. It also set the foundation of an institutional structure which for the next 25 years encouraged the interaction of business, naval, and political groups involved in building the new navy.

The first step taken under the bill was the establishment of what was called the Gun Foundry Board. During the congressional hearings steel executives had pointed out that the Europeans were far ahead of the Americans in the technology of producing the armor, heavy steel, and ordnance required for the navy's new ships. The board was charged with the task of making a technical evaluation of the European armaments industry and recommending to Congress how a comparable effort could be undertaken in the United States. Under the auspices of the board, armor and steel experts were sent on tours of the major European armament plants. In its first report the board recommended further assessments of European technology and generous government contracts to stimulate an American naval arms industry (Gun Foundry Board, 1884).

After receiving the recommendations of the Gun Foundry Board, Congress took up the questions of how the manufacture of heavy masses of steel could be inaugurated in the United States. The Senate directed the appointment of a Select Commission on Ordnance and War Ships. The House established a Commission on Ordnance and Gunnery. Both commissions heard testimony from the major American ship and steel makers and sent staff members to tour European armaments plants. Their final recommendations were essentially in accordance with those of the Gun Foundry Board (U.S. Congress, H.R. 1450,).

Each submission of a final report seemed to increase the number of people interested in naval armaments. What started out with the appointment of the Gun Foundry Board in the 1883 Naval Appropriations Bill led to the creation of dozens of boards of inquiry, commissions, and special congressional committees during the 1880s. Members of American industry were hired by government commissions and committees to tour European plants, study their technology, and then testify before naval budget hearings. An increasing number of navy officers also toured European plants on behalf of congressional committees, gave their testimony before budget hearings, and all the while served as consultants to U.S. ship and steel companies. The day of double dipping had arrived. In short, an institutional framework was being formed which promoted the coalescence of military and industrial interests in the expansion of the navy. The transfer of foreign technology on ship and heavy steel manufacturing to American industry was being subsidized by the government (Allard, 1959). American firms were getting more and larger contracts. The navy was getting more ships.

By 1890, 10 years after President Hayes had first argued the case for a larger navy, Congress had authorized 33 steel warships. As the Secretary of Navy pointed out, however, the fleet still only ranked 12th among the navies of the world behind even Turkey and China let alone the super powers of England, France, Russia, and Germany. (Navy Report, 1889). Yet from the navy's point of view, 1890 was a benchmark year. Congress authorized the construction of the first American battleships. In addition, in a series of tests conducted by the navy it was discovered that a process of adding small amounts of nickel to steel produced a metal of spectacular strength and therefore ideal for armor. Since all nickel was imported at the time, Congress appropriated one million dollars for the navy to purchase its own supply (Navy Report, 1890, p. 20–21). Despite the passage of the highly protective McKinley Tariff Act of 1890, Congress put nickel on the free list.

From 1890 to the Spanish-American War the condition of the fleet was considerably enhanced. Congress authorized on average at least one battleship per year. The rate of ship tonnage built increased. The navy began to run its first trials of a submarine. The American process of making nickel-steel armor became so highly rated that both Carnegie and Bethlehem steel companies began to win contracts to provide armor for foreign navies.

Not surprisingly, the onset of the Spanish-American War resulted in an acceleration of the rate of ship construction. This expansion followed a decade during which naval expenditures had increased 128 percent. During the war Congress authorized a long list of new ships. Contrary to the experience of previous wars, however, the navy was not demobilized following the end of conflict. Naval expenditures decreased for only one year after the war. During that one year the level of expenditures was still at a rate nearly twice the immediate pre-war rate.

By the time Teddy Roosevelt came into office, America had become a major naval power. Its battleship fleet was the fourth largest in the world. Both the naval and industrial segments of the defense establishment increased their pressure on Congress for an even larger fleet. In 1903 the Navy's General Board called for the construction of a battleship fleet second only to Britain's. That same year the Navy League of the United States was formed to pool the resources of civilian advocates of naval expansion such as the ship building and metallurgical industries. Among its founding members were former secretaries of the navy as well as prominant industrialists and financiers such as J. P. Morgan. Like its counterparts in Britain and Germany, the Navy League set out to operate as a pressure group. While its primarily lobbied Congressmen, the League also attempted to "educate" writers and editors of newspapers of the need for a larger navy. Some historians have attributed a critical role to the Navy League in helping the Roosevelt administration achieve its goal of an unprecedented peacetime increase of U.S. naval power (Rapport, 1962; Sprout, 1939). Between 1902 and 1908 naval expenditures nearly doubled as Congress authorized an average of two battleships per year. The previously separate interest groups acting to increase the navy were now working together within an institutional framework.

IV. THE COALESCENCE OF ECONOMIC AND POLITICAL INTERESTS

A. Protection of U.S. Commerce

There were several themes which developed during the course of the late nineteenth and early twentieth centuries around which arguments were made for the construction of a new navy. One of the major ones was the need for a larger navy to protect the nation's growing commerce. During the period of rapid expansion of naval expenditures U.S. exports expanded more than 75 percent from $696 million in 1888 to $1,231 million in 1898 and an additional 51 percent to $1,861 million in 1908. Exports of manufactured goods increased from 20.4 percent of total exports in 1878 to 40.9 percent by 1908. The U.S. share of world exports of manufactured goods increased from 4.1 percent for the period 1886–1890 to 11.7 percent by 1899 and 13 percent by 1913.

In conjunction with the rapid expansion in U.S. trade between 1888 and 1910 came a dramatic shift in the geographical pattern of trade. The share of U.S. exports to Europe declined from 86 percent in 1880 ($719 million) to 65.1 percent in 1910 ($1,136 million). During that same interval, the share of U.S. exports to Canada, Central and South America, and Asia and the Pacific all increased. Clearly, as the geographic scope of our commodity trade expanded the need to develop substantial naval power became more credible.

Financial investments invariably follow international trade. The United States experienced net capital inflows amounting to $287 million in 1888 but net capital outflows amounting to $279 million in 1898. U.S. investments abroad increased 257 percent from $700 million in 1897 to $2,500 million in 1908. Income from investments abroad increased 185 percent from $38 million in 1900 to $108 million in 1910.[1]

B. International Power Politics

As American trade expanded so did the nation's participation in world affairs. This was a second theme around which arguments were made for a larger navy.

Following the Civil War the American government gave little attention to international relations. With the onset of the 1880s, however, the United States began to implement an active policy of foreign intervention. In 1882 the American navy participated in a British bombardment of Alexandria, Egypt. U.S. Marines assaulted the city along with the British Royal Marines. Three years later U.S. Marines were sent to Columbia to help suppress a rebellion in the Panama area. By the late 1880s and early 1890s the United States was actively intervening in many of the countries in both Central and South America.

While America increased its intervention abroad so did the major European powers. Britain, France, Germany, Italy, Portugal, and the Netherlands partitioned Africa. Britain acquired a substantial empire during the period we are focusing on. France took control of all of Indochina and the European powers established leaseholds and spheres of influence in China. Not suprisingly, one of the arguments put forth by naval advocates was that in such a hostile world a powerful navy was necessary for national security. Few suggested that America might be invaded, rather the concern was over the economic cost to the country of a foreign power blockading U.S. ports.

C. Finances

A final point should be made before we turn to our assessment of congressional support for the expansion of the Navy. The coalescence of economic and political forces for a new navy emerged during a period when the federal budget was running a surplus. Each year from the end of the Civil War to the mid-1890s government revenue which was generated mainly from tariffs exceeded expenditures. Those interests who favored protection were able to maintain the relatively high "war tariff" rates through to the end of the century. As a result, one of the continuing issues before Congress was how to deal with the surplus.

Politically unwilling to reduce its revenue the government proceeded to increase expenditures. "Pork barrel" legislation was passed with relish. Congress liberalized the veteran's pension program. A massive public works program for local improvements was undertaken. In what was in effect a revenue sharing program, Congress in 1889 granted a lump sum payment of over 15 million dollars to the northern states in partial repayment of the income taxes collected during the Civil War. Not to be left out, naval advocates argued that Congress could well serve the nation if it reduced the surplus by voting larger naval appropriations.

V. THE VOTING RECORD, 1882–1908

In order to assess whether any of the forces we have been discussing played a significant role in explaining growth in naval expenditures between 1882 and 1908, we collected data on congressional votes on key military procurement bills and on amendments to bills and attempted to explain those votes in terms of state-based economic interest groups. Based on our earlier observations regarding international trade and finance, we would expect manufacturing and perhaps steel-producing interests to favor the naval buildup and agricultural interests to oppose the buildup.

We argued in an earlier paper on the income tax that the Democratic party quickly allied itself with anti-big business, low income, agrarian interests (Baack and Ray, 1983). Therefore, we would expect to find in general that the Democratic party voting strength in the House and Senate to be united in opposition to naval spending.

The Naval Appropriations Bill of 1882 was passed by the House on a vote of 119-76. The bill provided money to complete construction of three monitors and agreed in principle to construct two steel cruisers. In a sense therefore this bill was the first to contain language indicating a commitment to build a modern navy (Cong. Rec., 47th Cong., 1st sess., p. 5608). Using Tobit analysis for appropriate estimation associated with limited dependent variables, we obtained the voting regression results for the Naval Appropriations Bill of 1882 indicated in Eqs. (1) and (2) below:

$$Y_{82} = 0.78 + 0.02M_{80} - 0.01A_{80} - 2.2 \times 10^{-9}S_{80}, \qquad (1)$$
$$\phantom{Y_{82} =} (1.45) \quad (2.67) \quad (0.13) \quad (0.19)$$

$$R^2 = 0.1933$$

where Y_{82} represents the percentage of support for the bill in the House by state and M_{80}, A_{80}, and S_{80} represent the relative importance of manufacturing, agricultural, and steel production by state in 1880.[2] Absolute t-values appear in parentheses. As expected, state manufacturing interests were positively and significantly related to military support in 1882. When party voting behavior is taken into account we obtain the following:

$$Y_{82} = 3.36 + 0.07M_{80} - 0.060A_{80} + 3.0 \times 10^{-9}S_{80} - 0.02D^H_{82} \qquad (2)$$
$$\phantom{Y_{82} =} (4.07) \quad (0.81) \quad (0.74) \quad (0.26) \quad (4.19)$$

$$R^2 = 0.5116$$

where D^H_{82} represents Democratic voting strength in the House by state in 1882. Clearly, the vote was along party lines. The high-income, Republican, manufacturing states of the Northeast and North Central regions were the backbone of congressional support for naval spending in 1882. While the other independent variables are correctly signed, they are not highly significant.

One theme we will want to follow throughout the voting analysis is whether or not the party vote variable continues to render the manufacturing vote relatively insignificant. If so, we will be unable to determine if naval spending support is incidental to differences in political ideology or if it is grounded upon economic self-interest (the simple correlation between M_{80} and D^H_{82} is -0.54).

The Naval Appropriations Bill of 1890 contained money for three of what were to become America's first steel battleships. The votes analyzed here are on an amendment to strike out all three of those battleships. The amendment failed 181 to 105 in the House (Cong. Rec., 51st Cong., 1st sess., pp. 3395, 3396). The dependent variables, Y^H_{90} and Y^S_{90}, represent House and Senate support at the state level to keep the battleships in the appropriations bill (the Senate beat back the amendment by a vote of 33 to 18) (Cong. Rec., 51st Cong., 1st sess., pp. 5297).

$$Y^H_{90} = -0.83 + 0.03M_{90} - 0.27A_{90} - 5.4 \times 10^{-10}S_{90} - 0.02D^H_{90}$$
$$\quad\quad (0.92) \quad (2.26) \quad\quad (2.84) \quad\quad\quad (0.09) \quad\quad\quad\quad (3.71)$$

$$R^2 = 0.6114 \tag{3}$$

where M_{90}, A_{90}, and S_{90} are the 1890 state-based measures of manufacturing, agricultural, and steel-producing interests at the state level and D^H_{90} is Democratic voting strength in the House of Representatives by state in 1890. Except for the insignificant steel variable, each of the independent variables are highly significant and signed as expected.

The successful Senate vote to defeat the amendment to cut military spending on battleships looked as follows:

$$Y^S_{90} = -.51 + 0.02M_{90} - 0.14A_{90} + 7.5 \times 10^{-8}S_{90} - 3.9 \times 10^{-3}D^S_{90}$$
$$\quad\quad (0.23) \quad (1.35) \quad\quad (1.14) \quad\quad\quad (0.92) \quad\quad\quad\quad (0.81)$$

$$R^2 = 0.2566 \tag{4}$$

where D^S_{90} represents Democratic voting strength in the Senate by state in 1890. All of the variables are signed as expected but only the state manufacturing interests variable is significant at the 5 percent level.

The next major effort to take the steam out of the navy buildup for which the vote was recorded came in 1895. The Naval Appropriations Bill of 1895 contained funding to build three more steel battleships. An amendment introduced in the House proposed to eliminate funding for all three ships. That amendment to cut naval spending failed by a vote of 202 to 67 (Cong. Rec., 53rd Cong., 3rd sess., pp. 2468, 2469). The Senate also voted on an amendment to cut back funding from three battleships to two and succeeded by a vote of 33 to 29 (Cong. Rec., 53rd Cong., 3rd sess., pp. 3124). The dependent variables Y^H_{95} and Y^S_{95} represent votes in opposition to the cuts in naval funding by state in the House and Senate respectively.

$$Y^H_{95} = -0.65 + 0.02M_{90} - 0.21A_{90} - 1.2 \times 10^{-10}S_{90} - 5.3 \times 10^{-3}D^H_{94}(5)$$
$$\quad\quad (0.76) \quad (2.10) \quad\quad (2.20) \quad\quad (0.02) \quad\quad\quad\quad (0.99)$$

$$R^2 = 0.2836$$

$$Y^S_{95} = -0.02 + 0.02M_{90} - 0.07A_{90} + 8.9 \times 10^{-9}S_{90} - 1.48 \times 10^{-3}D^S_{94}(6)$$
$$\quad\quad (1.60) \quad (1.65) \quad\quad (0.70) \quad\quad (0.76) \quad\quad\quad\quad (0.33)$$

$$R^2 = 0.1254$$

where D^H_{94} and D^S_{94} represent Democratic voting strength by state in the House of Representatives and Senate, respectively. The state manufacturing interests variable is positive and significant in both the successful House defeat of the cut in shipbuilding and in the failed attempt to stop the Senate cutback. The agricultural variable and party affiliation are signed as expected but relatively insignificant in the Senate vote compared to the House vote. This is no doubt related to the fact that the Senate amendment was less dramatic in its proposed cuts than the House amendment and probably was the product of some degree of compromise among the contending factions.

Following the success of limiting new battleship construction to two rather than three ships in 1895, the anti-military forces attempted further cutbacks in 1896. The Naval Appropriations Bill of 1896 contained funding for two steel battleships. The House vote for which we have data was on an attempt through amendment to strike both battleships from the budget. The effort to vote down the battleship expenditures failed on a vote of 141 to 81 (Cong. Rec., 54th Cong., 1st sess., pp. 4856). Again we measured support for naval expenditures by the percentage of votes in the House by state that prevailed in defeating the amendment to cut battleship expenditures, Y^H_{96}. The Tobit regression results we obtained were as follows:

$$Y^H_{96} = -2.03 + 0.03M_{90} - 0.17A_{90} - 3.1 \times 10^{-11}S_{90} - 3.48 \times 10^{-3}D^H_{96}$$
$$\quad\quad (2.17) \quad (2.69) \quad\quad (1.90) \quad\quad (0.01) \quad\quad\quad\quad (0.06)$$

$$R^2 = 0.3502$$
$$\tag{7}$$

where D^H_{96} represents Democratic strength by state in the House of Representatives. Both state manufacturing interests and agricultural production interests have significant coefficients and were signed as expected. It is quite interesting that holding economic interest effects constant, political affiliation is quite insignificant in all of the anti-navy votes during the 1890s. Yet, the anti-naval spending position of congressional representatives in the Democratic party was the dominant explanatory variable in congressional votes on naval appropriation bills in the early 1880s. These results suggest that by 1890 the driving forces favoring and opposing expansion of naval budgets closely paralleled economic self-interests and cut across political party lines. The weakening of the link between political party affiliation and votes on naval appropriations by Congress help to explain how it was possible for naval expenditures to continue expanding dramatically during the 1890s despite the fact that the Democratic party made huge gains in national and local elections.

Following the Spanish-American War the political division over the size of the military budget re-emerged with Democrats strongly opposed to naval spending. The regressions below reflect the division of interests regarding the Naval Appropriations Bill of 1908. Y^H_{08}, which passed in the House by a vote of 139 to 124 (Cong. Rec., 60th Cong., 1st sess., pp. 6163, 6164).

$$Y^H_{08} = 1.13 + 2.49X10^{-2}M_{10} - 0.15A_{10} + 2.44X10^{-9}S_{05} - 1.25X10^{-2}D^H_{08}$$
$$\quad\ (1.28)\quad (2.30)\qquad\quad (1.96)\qquad (0.87)\qquad\qquad (2.46)$$

$$R^2 = 0.4942 \tag{8}$$

where M_{10}, A_{10}, and S_{05} represent the manufacturing, agricultural, and steel-producing interests for 1910, 1910 and 1905, respectively, D^H_{08} represents the House of Representatives voting strength of Democrats by state for 1908.

There are three primary observations to be made based upon our empirical analysis of seven different congressional votes on naval appropriations spanning the 26 years from 1882 to 1908 during which America emerged as a major military power. First, from the outset states with significant manufacturing interests and, therefore, substantial and rapidly expanding direct trade and investment interests abroad, were strong supporters of naval expenditures. It was this early marriage of naval and industrial economic interests in the United States that sustained the massive naval buildup during the late nineteenth and early twentieth centuries.

The leading agricultural states consistently opposed money for the navy. Throughout the period considered, a vote for naval spending was a vote to continue to maintain high tariffs, the primary source of government revenues, in order to subsidize the overseas business activities of manufacturers who were principally located in the northeastern and north central states.

Secondly, the Democratic party, which allied itself early in the 1870s with agrarian, anti-tariff, anti-eastern establishment interests in low-income states consistently opposed the naval buildup. Political party affiliation in Congress was most significant in explaining voting patterns in the 1880s.

Finally, the acceleration in the naval buildup after 1890 and the failure of the opposition to trim naval budgets significantly was directly related to the decline in concerted Democratic opposition to naval spending during the 1890s. Without a weakening of Democratic opposition to naval appropriations during the 1890s, it is doubtful that the size and quality of the U.S. naval machine could have improved at the pace observed at the time. After the Spanish-American-War,

Democratic support was again solidly against military spending. But, by that time domestic and overseas manufacturing interests appear to have become sufficiently strong to fend off Democratic opposition. In a sense, the close but successful vote on the Naval Appropriations Bill in 1908 may have signaled that almost 10 years prior to our entry into World War I the development of a peacetime military buildup had come of age and could withstand partisan political opposition.

NOTES

1. All foreign investment and trade data were taken from *Historical Statistics of the United States, Colonial Times to 1970*, Part 2, Chapter U, *"Analysis of the Foreign Commerce of the United States,"* (Washington, D.C.: Dept. of Commerce and Labor, Bureau of Statistics, 1975); and, Exports of Manufactures from the United States and Their Distribution by Articles and Countries, 1800 to 1906 (Washington, D.C.: G.P.O. 1907).

2. The sample size is 32. For the regressions in this paper the critical values for a one-tailed significance test on the coefficients is 1.31 for the 5 percent level of significance.

REFERENCES

Analysis of the Foreign Commerce of the United States, (1906), Washington, D.C.: G.P.O.
Annual Report of the Secretary of Navy. (1884, 1889, 1890, 1918), Washington, D.C.: G.P.O.
Baack, B., and E. Ray, (1983), "Special Interests and Constitutional Amendments: A Study of the Adoption of the Income Tax in the U.S." *Ohio State University Working Papers in Economics*, No. 84–5.
Congressional Record, 47th Cong., 1st sess., p. 5608.
Congressional Record, 51st Cong., 1st sess., pp. 3395, 3396.
Congressional Record, 51st Cong., 1st sess., p. 5297.
Congressional Record, 53rd Cong., 3rd sess., pp. 2468, 2469.
Congressional Record, 53rd Cong., 3rd sess., p. 3124.
Congressional Record, 54th Cong., 1st sess., p. 4856.
Congressional Record, 57th Cong., 1st sess., p. 7604.
Congressional Record, 60th Cong., 1st sess., pp. 6163, 6164.
Exports of Manufactures from the United States and Their Distribution by Articles and Countries, 1800 to 1906. (1907), Washington, D.C.: G.P.O.
Historical Statistics of the United States, Colonial Times to 1970, Pt. 2, Ch. U. (1975), Washington, D.C.: Department of Commerce and Labor, Bureau of Statistics.
House Executive Document. No. 32. 47th Congress, 2nd Session.
Recommendations of the Naval Advisory Board: 29.
House Report. No. 653. 47th Congress, 1st Session.
House Report. No. 1450. Report of the Commission on Ordnance and Gunnery. 49th Congress, 1st Session.
Koistinen, P. (1980), *The Military-Industrial Complex*. New York: Praeger.
La Feber, W. (1963), *The New Empire*. Ithaca: Cornell University Press.
Nelson, K. L. (1972), "The Warfare State: History of a Concept." Reprinted in Pursell, *The Military-Industrial Complex* New York: Harper and Row pp.15–30.
Pursell, C. W. (1972), *The Military-Industrial Complex*. New York: Harper and Row.

Rappaport, A. (1962), *The Navy League of the United States*. Detroit: Wayne State University Press.

Report of the Secretary of the Navy. (1880), Washington, D.C.: G.P.O.

Richardson, J.D. (1898), *A Compilation of the Messages and Papers of the Presidents, 1789–1897*, Vol. VIII., Washington, D.C.: G.P.O.

Rosen, S. (1973), *Testing the Theory of the Military-Industrial Complex*. Lexington: Lexington Books.

Sprout, H., and M. Sprout (1939), *The Rise of American Naval Power*. Princeton: Princeton University Press.

U.S. Congress. House. 47th Cong., 2nd sess., H. Doc. 32.

U.S. Congress. House. 47th Cong., 1st sess., H. R. 653.

U.S. Congress. House. 49th Cong., 1st sess., H.R. 1450.

U.S. Navy, Gun Foundry Board. (1884), *Report of the Gun Foundry Board*. Washington, D.C.: G.P.O.

U.S. Presidents Public Papers of the United States: Dwight D. Eisenhower, 1960–61. (1961), Washington, D.C.: G.P.O.

A NEW LOOK AT FISCAL POLICY IN THE 1930s

Thomas M. Renaghan

ABSTRACT

Past authors have utilized the full-employment surplus to conclude that fiscal policy was not expansionary in the thirties, relative to 1929. This paper relies upon more relevant weighted standardized surplus as the correct indicator of fiscal activity. It is concluded that the overall thrust of federal fiscal policy was more expansionary than past authors suggest, relative to 1929. This paper also examines the course of combined government fiscal policy. In this case the results are mixed with expansionary shifts in 1930 and 1931, contraction in 1932 and 1933, and expansionary shifts in 1936, 1938, and 1939.

Few economists would quarrel with the conclusion that fiscal policy was not expansionary in the thirties. E. Cary Brown's 1956 classic article concluded that relative to 1929, the expansionary thrust of federal fiscal policy was offset by contractionary shifts at the state and local government level, when measured at full employment.

Research in Economic History, Volume 11, pages 171–183.
Copyright © 1988 by JAI Press Inc.
All rights of reproduction in any form reserved.
ISBN: 0-89232-677-8

The federal government's fiscal action was more expansionary throughout the 'thirties than it
was in 1929 . . . state and local government's fiscal policy was expansionary through 1933
but decreasingly so . . . The federal government's policies were little more than adequate in
most years of the 'thirties to offset these contractive effects of state and local government . . .
(pp. 866–67).

Based on these findings, Brown offered his often-quoted conclusion that:

Fiscal policy, then, seems to have been an unsuccessful recovery device in the 'thirties—not
because it did not work but because it was not tried. (p. 863).

This accepted view of fiscal policy was modified by Larry Peppers a decade
ago. Restricting his analysis to federal fiscal activities, Peppers argued that
Brown underestimated full-employment tax receipts and hence: "there was an
expansionary bias introduced into his figures that led him to conclude that federal
fiscal policy was more expansionary than it was in 1929" (1973, p. 209).

I will show, however, that Brown's and Pepper's reliance upon the full-
employment surplus led them to misjudge the course of thirties fiscal policy.
Specifically, utilizing the weighted standardized surplus, which gauges the impact
of fiscal policy at the actual level of national income, I conclude that the overall
thrust of federal fiscal policy was more expansionary than Brown's and Pepper's
results suggest, relative to 1929.

This paper also analyzes the course of combined fiscal policy. In 1930 and
1931, the expansionary activities of state and local governments reinforced the
expansionary thrust of federal fiscal policy. In 1932 and 1933, federal shrinkages
coupled with those of state and local governments caused combined fiscal policy
to reach very contractionary levels relative to 1929. In 1934 federal expansion
offset the contractive effects of state and local governments. In 1936, 1938, and
1939 federal expansion caused combined government fiscal policy to reach the
expansionary levels obtained in 1930 and 1931.

Yearly shifts in fiscal policy are also relevant to the course of 1930s fiscal
policy. In this case, the findings are supportive of the notion that thirties fiscal
policy was not expansionary. Federal and combined government fiscal policy
emerges as expansionary in only four years—1930, 1931, 1933, and 1939. The
results differ because measuring yearly shifts in fiscal policy requires a different
methodology from that used to gauge the effects of fiscal policy relative to 1929.

I. MEASURING FISCAL POLICY

It is well established that the actual budget is an inappropriate measure of fiscal
policy because it is endogenously determined. A decline in economic activity
will, for example, produce an actual budget deficit. It would, however, be
incorrect to cite an actual budget deficit as evidence of an expansionary fiscal
policy. Discussions of fiscal policy avoid this drawback of the actual budget by

focusing on the weighted full-employment surplus as the correct indicator of fiscal policy. By measuring tax receipts and government expenditures at full-employment GNP the weighted full employment surplus avoids the pitfalls in the actual budget, that is, the weighted full-employment surplus successfully distinguishes automatic from discretionary fiscal action. In order to insure consistency with the balanced budget theorem, tax receipts are weighted by the marginal propensity to consume. The weighted full-employment surplus is shown in Eq. (1).

$$WFES = adtY_{FULL} - dG \tag{1}$$

where:

WFES = The weighted full-employment surplus.
a   = The marginal propensity to consume.
dt   = The change in tax rates.
Y_{FULL} = Full-employment GNP.
dG   = The change in government expenditures.

The weighted full-employment surplus, of course, is not the only exogenous measure of fiscal policy. Consider, for example, the weighted standardized surplus shown in Eq. (2).

$$WSS = bdtY_o - dG \tag{2}$$

where:

WSS = The weighted standardized surplus.
b   = The marginal propensity to consume.
dt   = The change in tax rates.
Y_o = The actual level of GNP.
dG   = The change in government expenditures.

The weighted standardized surplus is defined as the change in tax receipts attributable to changes in the tax code (dtY_o) weighted by the marginal propensity to consume (b) less the change in government expenditures (dG). In contrast to the weighted full-employment surplus, both the weighted change in tax receipts and the change in government expenditures are evaluated at the actual level of GNP. Clearly, then, the weighted full-employment surplus and the weighted standardized surplus differ only by the level of GNP at which fiscal policy is measured.

Neither the full-employment surplus nor the weighted standardized surplus can answer the question of what is the most appropriate level of national income at which to evaluate fiscal policy. The point is that they answer different questions. The weighted full-employment surplus is a guide to how much work fiscal policy must do to reach full employment while the weighted standardized surplus gauges the current strength of fiscal policy.

If actual GNP were close to full-employment GNP, one might expect the weighted full-employment surplus and the weighted standardized surplus to yield similar results. For the postwar period, W. H. Oakland (1969) compared quarterly changes in the weighted standardized surplus to changes in the full-employment surplus and found that discrepancies were largest in periods of recession. This suggests that the weighted full-employment surplus tends to overstate the effect of changes in tax rates when the economy is far from full employment.[1] Moreover, when national income is depressed, the information conveyed by the weighted full-employment surplus is of limited relevance. As Blinder and Solow (1974, p. 17) point out: "The weighted FES (full-employment surplus) is a true measure of the impact of budgetary changes in a full-employment economy; but such information may be of limited interest if the unemployment rate is 6 percent."

In short, the weighted standardized surplus provides a different and potentially more relevant measure of fiscal policy in the 1930s than that suggested by past authors. Quantifying the weighted standardized surplus is the task of the next section of this paper.

The weighted standardized surplus is defined as the change in tax receipts attributable to changes in the tax code weighted by the marginal propensity to consume less the change in government expenditures. Following G. E. Corrigan (1970), P. H. Hymans and J. P. Wernette (1970), and W. H. Oakland (1969), who present estimates of the weighted standardized surplus for the postwar period, government expenditures are assumed exogenous with respect to fluctuations in GNP. Eq. (3) demonstrates the calculation of the weighted standardized surplus.

$$S_t^{y*} = a(TR_t^{y*} - TR_{t-1}^{y*}) - (TE_t - TE_{t-1}) \tag{3}$$

where:

S_t^{y*} = The weighted standardized surplus in calendar year t, at the actual level of income y* prevailing in calendar year t.

a   = The marginal propensity to consume .[2]

TR_t^{y*} = Total federal tax receipts in calendar year t, at the actual level of income y*, and tax rates prevailing in calendar year t.

TR_{t-1}^{y*} = Total federal tax receipts at the actual level of income y* prevailing in calendar year t and tax rates prevailing in calendar year t–1.

TE_t = Federal government purchases of goods and services, transfer payments, and grants-in-aid to state and local governments in calendar year t.

TE_{t-1} = Federal government purchases of goods and services, transfer payments, and grants-in-aid to state and local governments in calendar year t–1.

The central element in Eq. (3) is that in comparing the fiscal impact between two years income is held constant at the current year's level. Consider, for example, fiscal policy in 1933 relative to 1929. In this case Eq. (3) becomes:

$$S_{1933}^{y=1933} = a(TR_{1933}^{y=1933} - TR_{1929}^{y=1933}) - (TE_{1933} - TE_{1929}) \qquad (4)$$

Further, suppose one is interested in measuring the change in fiscal policy between 1933 and 1934, this would be measured by:

$$S_{1934} = a(TR_{1934}^{y=1934} - TR_{1933}^{y=1934}) - (TE_{1934} - TE_{1933}) \qquad (5)$$

In short, I compare the shift in fiscal policy between two years at the level of national income prevailing in the current year.

The impact of revisions in the tax code are quantified by regressing total federal tax collections on personal income (a GNP proxy) and a series of intercept and slope dummy variables representing alterations in federal tax laws.

To measure their impact with regressions on monthly data between 1929 and 1939, I introduce intercept and slope dummy variables for each of the Revenue Acts shown in Table 1. The intercept dummy variables, on the other hand, capture the effect of increases in personal income, estate and gift, social security, and corporate tax rates. Hence, the tax function shown in Eq. (6) allows for both intercept and slope shifts.

Table 1. Federal Tax Law Revisions 1929–1939

Revenue Act	Years Covered	Major Provisions of the Act
Revenue Act of 1932	1932, 1933	Raised Personal Income, Corporate Profits, Estate and Gift, and Excise Tax Rates
Revenue Act of 1934	1934	Raised Personal Income, Corporate, and Capital Gains Taxes
Revenue Act of 1935	1935	Raised Personal Income Tax Rates
Revenue Act of 1936	1936, 1937, 1938, 1939	Raised Personal Income, Corporate, and Estate and Gift Tax Rates
Social Security Act	1937–1939	Established Social Insurance Contributions
Revenue Act of 1938	1938–1939	Eliminated the Undistributed Corporate Profits Tax and Reduced Capital Gains Tax Rates

Source: U.S. Bureau of Internal Revenue, *Statistics of Income 1940,*Part I. (Washington D.C.: U.S. Government Printing Office, 1943).

$$TR_t^{y*} = a_0 + a_1Y + a_2t + a_3t^2 + a_4d32 + a_5d34 + a_6d35 + a_7d36 \quad (6)$$
$$+ a_8 \text{ SOCIAL SECURITY} + a_9d38 + a_{10}QY32 + a_{11}QY34$$
$$+ a_{12}QY35 + a_{13}QY36 + a_{14} \text{ SOCIAL SECURITY}$$
$$(x) Y + a_{15}QY38$$

where:

TR_t^{y*} = Total federal tax receipts (seasonally adjusted).
Y = Monthly personal income (seasonally adjusted).
t = Time trend (January 1929 = 1.0).[4]
t^2 = Time trend squared.
d = Intercept dummy for a particular Revenue Act, e.g., d32 is the dummy for the Revenue Act of 1932.
QY = Slope dummy for a particular Revenue Act, e.g., QY32 = d32 (x) Y.

The regression results are reported in Table 2. The large number of statistically significant coefficients and the good fit (high adjusted R^2) shows that Eq. (6) successfully captures the tax structure of the 1930s.

Table 2.   Revenue Act Regression Results

Variable	Coefficient (Billion of $)	Standard Error	t Statistic
Constant	−.6498	.133	−4.865
Personal Income	.01125	.0014	7.761
time	.00459	.0015	2.890
time squared	−.00006	.00001	−0.533
d32	.5168	.103	5.000
d34	1.6602	.737	2.251
d35	.8400	.246	3.410
d36	.6845	.173	3.934
dSS	−.4283	.351	−1.218
d38	2.3177	.484	4.784
QY32	−.0090	.0019	−4.710
QY34	−.0298	.0138	−2.154
QY35	−.0143	.0042	−3.358
QY36	−.0117	.0027	−4.251
SSY	.0072	.0048	1.503
QY38	−.0359	.0073	−4.909

R^2 = .9265   Durbin-Watson Statistic = 2.0161 rho = .06698
$F_{15,116}$ = 100.57   Standard Error of the Regression = .03238
Number of observations = 132

Source: Monthly personal income is taken from Moore, *Business Cycle Indicators,* Vol. II (1961). Monthly tax receipts are taken from Firestone, *Federal Receipts and Expenditures During Business Cycles 1879–1958* (1960).

Eq. (6) served as the basis for the calculation of the change in tax receipts attributable to changes in the tax code. Consider, for example, the change in federal tax receipts between 1929 and 1932 shown in column (1) of Table 3. The change in tax receipts between these two years was calculated by substituting personal income in 1932 into the 1929 and 1932 tax equations and subtracting tax receipts in 1932 from those in 1929. This procedure serves to isolate fluctuations in tax receipts produced by changes in national income from those explained by legislative changes in the tax code. An analogous procedure was used to calculate yearly shifts in tax receipts resulting from alterations in the tax code. For example, the change in tax receipts between 1934 and 1933 was calculated by substituting the value of personal income in 1934 into the 1934 and 1933 tax equations and subtracting tax receipts in 1934 from those in 1933.

Estimates of the federal weighted standardized surplus, relative to 1929, in billions of current dollars and as a percent of actual GNP for the period 1929–1939. are shown in columns (3) and (4) of Table 3. The weighted standardized surplus, relative to the previous year, in billions of current dollars and as a percent of actual GNP is shown in columns (3) and (4) of Table 4. Government fiscal activity on all levels, relative to 1929, is shown in column (6) of Table 3. Column (6) of Table 4 shows combined government fiscal policy relative to the previous year.

Data limitations prevented deriving separate estimates of state and local fiscal activity at prevailing levels of GNP. As a result, combined fiscal activity, relative to 1929, was derived by expressing the change from 1929 in Brown's state and local weighted full-employment surplus and coupling it with estimates of the weighted standardized surplus.[5] A similar procedure was used to calculate the estimates of combined fiscal activity relative to the previous year. Since Brown found that state and local government fiscal policy was not expansionary in the 1930s, the estimates of combined government fiscal activity shown in Tables 3 and 4 may well contain a contractionary bias. In other words, the thrust of combined government fiscal activity may well have been more expansionary than the results in Tables 3 and 4 suggest.

Tables 5 and 6 compare the results obtained here with those of Brown and Peppers. Table 5 shows the percentage point deviations from 1929 in the weighted standardized surplus and Brown's and Peppers' estimates of the full-employment surplus. Columns (3) and (4) of Table 5 compare the deviation from 1929 in my measure of combined fiscal policy with Brown's. Table 6 compares yearly percentage point deviations in the weighted standardized surplus with Brown's and Peppers' measures of the full-employment surplus.

The percentage point deviation from the previous year in Brown's measure of combined fiscal policy is compared with my estimate in columns (3) and (4) of Table 6.

It is clear that both Brown and Peppers underestimated the combined deflationary impacts of termination of the 1931 Veterans' bonus and passage of the Revenue Act of 1932. In 1933, for example, Brown shows an expansionary shift of 0.90

Table 3.   Measures of Fiscal Performance Relative to 1929

Year	(1) The Weighted Change in Tax Receipts (Billions of $)	(2) The Change in Government Expenditures (Billions of $)	(3) The Weighted Standardized Surplus (Billions of $) (1)–(2)	(4) The Weighted Standardized Surplus (%of GNP)	(5) Brown's State and Local Full-Employment Surplus (%of GNP)	(6) Combined Government Fiscal Policy (% of GNP) (4)+(5)
1929[a]	3.156	2.629	0.527	0.50	−2.37	−1.32
1930	—	0.135	−0.135	−0.14	−0.32	−0.46
1931	—	1.552	−1.552	−2.03	−0.05	−2.08
1932	2.544	0.556	0.795	1.36	1.47	2.83
1933	3.224	1.356	1.868	3.34	2.77	6.11
1934	3.441	3.765	−0.324	−0.49	3.41	−1.55
1935	3.094	3.906	−0.812	−1.12	2.90	1.78
1936	2.887	6.024	−3.137	−3.79	2.25	−1.54
1937	3.294	4.768	−1.474	−1.62	1.85	0.22
1938	3.642	5.980	−2.338	−2.75	1.98	−0.77
1939	2.827	6.301	−3.474	−3.82	1.28	−2.54

Note: [a]The weighted standardized surplus in 1929 is calculated by subtracting total federal government expenditures from weighted tax receipts in 1929.

Source:

Column (1): The weighted change in tax receipts is calculated from the regression in equation (6).

Column (2): The change in government expenditures is taken from *The National Income and Product Accounts of the United States 1929–1974.* (U. S. Department of Commerce, 1974).

Column (3): Column (1)–(2).

Column (4): Actual nominal GNP is taken from *The National Income and Product Accounts of the United States 1929–1974* (U. S. Department of Commerce, 1974).

Column (5): All relevent data are contained in Brown (1956, pp. 864–65). Columns (5) and (3) contain full-employment estimates of taxes and government expenditures, respectively. Brown's full-employment tax receipts were converted to current dollars and weighted by a marginal propensity to consume of 0.762 and subtracted from government expenditures. The result was then expressed as a percent of actual GNP.

percentage points in the full-employment deficit, while Peppers argues that 1933 was contractionary with the full-employment surplus shifting by 0.70 percentage points over its 1929 level. By contrast, Table 5 shows that between 1929 and 1933 the weighted standardized surplus rose by 2.84 percentage points to reach 3.34 percent of actual GNP. Federal fiscal contraction reinforced state and local shrinkages resulting in a contractionary shift of 7.98 percentage points in combined fiscal policy between 1929 and 1939.

Table 6 shows yearly shifts in fiscal policy. Again, the findings reported here contrast sharply to those of Brown's and Peppers'. In 1933, for example, the weighted standardized budget registered a very expansionary shift of 11.0

Table 4. Measures of Fiscal Performance Relative to the Previous Year

Year	(1) The Weighted Change in Tax Receipts (Billions of $)	(2) The Change in Government Expenditures (Billions of $)	(3) The Weighted Standardized Surplus (Billions of $) (1)–(2)	(4) The Weighted Standardized Surplus (%of GNP)	(5) Brown's State and Local Full-Employment Surplus (%of GNP)	(6) Combined Government Fiscal Policy (% of GNP) (4)+(5)
1929	3.156	2.629	0.527	0.50	–2.37	–1.32
1930	—	0.135	–0.135	–0.14	–0.32	–0.46
1931	—	1.417	–1.417	–1.86	0.22	–1.64
1932	4.632	–0.996	5.628	9.65	1.55	11.20
1933	—	0.800	–0.800	–1.43	1.23	–0.20
1934	4.969	2.409	2.560	3.92	1.04	4.96
1935	6.506	0.141	6.365	8.77	–0.17	8.60
1936	6.087	2.118	3.969	4.79	–1.20	3.59
1937	8.016	–1.256	9.272	10.22	–0.19	10.03
1938	7.568	1.212	6.356	7.47	0.00	7.47
1939	—	0.321	–0.321	–0.35	–0.56	–0.91

Source:

Column (1): The weighted change in tax receipts is calculated from the regression in equation (6).

Column (2): The change in government expenditures is taken from *The National Income and Product Accounts of the United States 1929–1974.* (U. S. Department of Commerce, 1974).

Column (3): Column (1)–(2).

Column (4): Actual nominal GNP is taken from *The National Income and Product Accounts of the United States 1929–1974* (U. S. Department of Commerce, 1974).

Column (5): All relevent data are contained in Brown (1956, pp. 864–65). Columns (5) and (3) contain full-employment estimates of taxes and government expenditures, respectively. Brown's full-employment tax receipts were converted to current dollars and weighted by a marginal propensity to consume of 0.762 and subtracted from government expenditures. The result was then expressed as a percent of actual GNP.

Column (6): Columns (5) + (4).

percentage points over the level obtained in 1932, while combined government fiscal policy witnessed an expansionary shift of 11.40 percentage points. By contrast, Brown and Peppers show contractionary shifts of 0.74 and 1.03 percentage points, respectively, in the full-employment surplus.

By 1934 and 1935, the findings reported here are similar to those of Brown's and Peppers'. For 1936, however, Brown and Peppers have underestimated the expansionary impacts of the second Veterans' bonus bill, relative to 1929. They show, respectively, fiscal expansions of 2.70 and 1.77 percentage points between 1936 and 1929. Table 5, on the other hand, shows the federal weighted standardized deficit rising by 4.29 percentage points over the level obtained in 1929.

Table 5. Deviation from 1929 in the Weighted Standardized Surplus and the Full-Employment Surplus (Percentage Points)

Year	Weighted Standardized Surplus (1)	Combined Fiscal Policy (2)	Brown's Full-Employment Surplus (3)	Brown's Combined Fiscal Policy (4)	Peppers' Full-Employment Surplus (5)
1930	−0.64	1.41	−0.54	−0.56	−0.30
1931	−2.56	−0.21	−2.55	−2.51	−1.74
1932	0.86	4.70	−1.64	−0.05	−0.33
1933	2.84	7.98	−0.90	1.80	0.70
1934	−0.99	0.32	−2.20	0.97	−1.06
1935	−1.62	3.65	−2.16	0.75	−0.44
1936	−4.29	0.33	−2.70	−0.27	−1.77
1937	−2.12	2.09	0.13	2.62	1.62
1938	−3.25	1.10	−1.21	1.40	1.72
1939	−4.32	−0.67	−1.43	0.66	1.01

Source:
Column (1): Table (3) − column (3).
Column (2): Table (3) − column (6).
Column (3): Derived from Brown (1956, p. 865).
Column (4): Derived from Brown (1956, p. 865).
Column (5): Taken from Peppers (1973, p. 201).

Table 6. Deviation from the Previous Year in the Weighted Standardized Surplus and the Full-Employment Surplus (Percentage Points)

Year	Weighted Standardized Surplus (1)	Combined Fiscal Policy (2)	Brown's Full-Employment Surplus (3)	Brown's Combined Fiscal Policy (4)	Peppers' Full-Employment Surplus (5)
1930	−0.64	1.41	−0.54	−0.56	−0.30
1931	−1.72	−1.18	−2.01	−1.95	−1.44
1932	11.51	12.84	0.91	2.46	1.41
1933	−11.08	−11.40	0.74	1.85	1.03
1934	5.35	5.16	−1.30	−0.83	−1.76
1935	4.85	3.64	0.04	−0.22	0.62
1936	−3.98	−5.01	−0.54	−1.02	−1.33
1937	5.43	6.44	2.83	2.89	3.39
1938	−2.75	−2.56	−1.34	−1.22	0.10
1939	−7.82	−8.38	−0.22	−0.74	−0.71

Source:
Column (1): Table (4) − column (3).
Column (2): Table (4) − column (6).
Column (3): Derived from Brown (1956, p. 865).
Column (4): Derived from Brown (1956, p. 865).
Column (5): Taken from Peppers (1973, p. 201).

The yearly shifts in fiscal policy presented in Table 6 stand in stark contrast to the findings of Brown and Peppers. Between 1934 and 1933, for example, Brown and Peppers show expansionary shifts in federal fiscal policy of 1.30 and 1.76 percentage points, respectively. By contrast, Table 6 shows a large contractionary shift of 5.3 percentage points in the weighted standardized surplus between 1933 and 1934. The weighted standardized surplus rose by 4.8 percentage points between 1934 and 1935. By contrast, Brown and Peppers show, respectively, small contractionary shifts of 0.04 and 0.62 percentage points in the full-employment surplus. Brown and Peppers conclude that, relative to 1935, 1936 was a year of fiscal expansion. Yet, they underestimate the expansionary impact of the 1936 Veterans' bonus. Again, in Table 6, I show federal fiscal expansion of 3.98 percentage points, while Brown and Peppers show, respectively, small expansions of 0.54 and 1.33 percentage points. In short, the results presented here indicate that both, relative to 1929, and relative to the pervious year, Brown and Peppers have underestimated the strength of the 1936 Veterans' bonus legislation.

For the period 1937–1939, the results reported here contrast sharply to Brown's and Peppers' findings. Again, in Table 5, in 1937, 1938, and 1939, the federal weighted standardized deficit rose bt 2.12, 3.25, and 4.32 percentage points, respectively. While Brown documented expansionary shifts in federal fiscal policy in 1938 and 1939, the magnitude of the shifts shown in Table 6 are much larger. Peppers, on the other hand, suggests that federal fiscal policy in 1937, 1938, and 1939 was very restrictive, relative to 1929. Peppers shows respective shifts of 1.62, 1.72, and 1.01 percentage points in 1937, 1938, and 1939, respectively. Peppers attributes the restrictive fiscal policy of 1937–1939 to the introduction of social security taxes. As he (Peppers, 1970, p. 206) explains: "After 1935, however, there was a great relative and absolute growth in social insurance contributions. While they had comprised less than 2 percent of potential receipts in 1935, they made up over 20 percent in 1938. This introduced a tax source which was quite sensitive to variations in the level of economic activity." While the regression results reported in Table 2 confirm that the introduction of social security taxes had a statistically significant effect upon total tax collections, the social security legislation did not produce a contractionary shift in federal fiscal policy. In short, by concentrating on the full employment surplus, Peppers overstated the contractionary impact of social security taxes at the actual level of national income.

The yearly shifts in fiscal policy shown in Table 6 indicate, with the exception of 1937, a pattern of fiscal expansion. Between 1937 and 1938, for example, there was an expansionary shift of 2.75 percentage points in the weighted standardized budget. This was followed by a further expansionary shift of 7.82 percentage points between 1938 and 1939. Table 6 also shows a pattern of combined government fiscal expansion. Between 1937 and 1938, combined government fiscal policy registered expansionary shifts of 2.56 and 8.35 percentage points, respectively. Brown also finds evidence of federal and combined government fiscal expansion. The magnitude of the shifts reported in Table 6 are, however, much larger. Peppers shows a small contractionary shift of 0.10 percentage points between 1937 and 1938 and a slight expansionary shift of 0.71 percentage points between 1938 and 1939 in the full-employment budget.

II. CONCLUSION

This paper has presented a different perspective on thirties fiscal policy from that offered by past authors. The evidence indicates that, relative to 1929, federal fiscal policy was very expansionary in 1931 and from 1936 to 1939 and only marginally expansionary in 1930, 1934, and 1935. Further, federal fiscal policy was clearly contractionary in 1932 and 1933, relative to 1929. Yearly shifts in federal fiscal policy have also been quantified. In this case, federal fiscal policy was expansionary in 1930, 1931, 1933, 1936, and in 1938 and 1939.

The pattern of combined government fiscal policy has also been documented. From 1930 to 1933, the fiscal impact of all levels of government followed a pattern similar to that of the federal government. It was expansionary in 1930 and 1931 followed by contractionary reversals in 1932 and 1933. For most of the remaining years of the 1930s, however, state and local shrinkages more than offset federal expansion, relative to 1929. It was not until 1939 that combined fiscal activity surpassed the expansionary level obtained in 1931.

ACKNOWLEDGMENTS

The author wishes to thank Peter H. Lindert, Thomas Mayer, Alan L. Olmstead, and Michael N. Hayes for helpful comments and suggestions on earlier drafts of this paper. The assistance of the editor of this volume is also recognized. Any remaining errors are, of course, the responsibility of the author. Please address comments to Thomas M. Renaghan, California Public Utilities Commission, Rate Design and Economic Branch, Room 4002, 505 Van Ness Avenue, San Francisco, CA 94102.

NOTES

1. See Blinder and Solow (1974, p. 25).
2. Temin's estimate of the marginal propensity to consume of 0.762 was used to weight tax receipts (see Temin, 1976).
3. Federal government expenditures are taken directly from U.S. Department of Commerce (1974).
4. The time trend variables have been included in the regression to capture the cyclical trend in tax receipts. Fitting a polynomial time trend to a series is common procedure to detrend a series (see Maddala, 1977, pp. 334–337).
5. Brown's state and local full-employment surplus was derived from his Table 1 (1956, pp.

862–63). Subtracting column (5) from column (3) in his Table 1 yields the state and local full employment surplus in billions of 1947 dollars. These estimates were then converted into current dollars and expressed as a percent of actual GNP.

REFERENCES

Blinder, A. S., and R. M. Solow. (1974), "Analytical Foundations of Fiscal Policy." In A. S. Blinder (ed.), *The Economics of Public Finance*. Washington D.C.: The Brookings Institution.

Brown, E. C. (1956), "Fiscal Policy in the Thirties: A Reappraisal." *American Economic Review*, 46, 857–879.

Corrigan, G. E. (1970), "The Measurement and Importance of Fiscal Policy Changes." *Monthly Review Federal Reserve Bank of New York*, (June); 25–40.

Firestone, J. M. (1960). *Federal Receipts and Expenditures During Business Cycles 1879–1958*. Princeton: Princeton University Press.

Hymans, P. H., and J. P. Wernette (1970), "The Impact of the Federal Budget on Total Spending." *Business Economics*, 5; 29–34.

Maddala, G. S. (1977), *Econometrics*. New York: McGraw-Hill.

Moore, G. H. (1961), *Business Cycle Indicators*. Princeton: Princeton University Press.

Oakland, W. H. (1969), "Budgetary Measures of Fiscal Peformance." *Southern Economic Journal*, 35; 347–358.

Peppers, L. C. (1973), "Full-Employment Surplus Analysis: The 1930s." *Explorations in Economic History*, 10; 197–210.

Stein, H. (1969), *The Fiscal Revolution in America*. Chicago: The University of Chicago Press.

Temin, P. (1976), *Did Monetary Forces Cause the Great Depression?* New York: W. W. Norton.

U. S. Bureau of Internal Revenue (1943), *Statistics of Income 1940*. Washington D. C.: U.S. Government Printing Office. Part I.

U. S. Department of the Commerce (1974), *The National Income and Products Accounts of the United States 1929–1974*. Washington D. C.: U. S. Government Printing Office.

THE USE OF COMPLICATED
MODELS AS EXPLANATIONS:
A RE-EXAMINATION OF WILLIAMSON'S
LATE 19TH-CENTURY AMERICA

Charles M. Kahn

ABSTRACT

Multisector simultaneous equations models pose a dilemma for economic historians because they requires us to rethink our notions of using models to "explain" history. This paper demonstrates the proper technique for evaluating and understanding the results of large-scale models: employing pencil-and-paper submodels and sensitivity tests to determine the minimal sets of assumptions which yield the results of interest.

We use this technique to evaluate the findings of Jeffrey Williamson's model of late nineteenth-century America, particularly his conclusions about the effects of improved transportation on social savings. We show that when properly handled,

Research in Economic History, Volume 11, pages 185–216.
Copyright © 1988 by JAI Press Inc.
ISBN: 0-89232-677-8

his model yields social savings comparable to those of simpler models in the literature, but for different reasons. Simpler models have overestimated social savings by ignoring the supply response of transported goods to changes in transportation price. These errors have been offset by ignoring the "dynamic" component: increases in the rate of investment due the lower relative prices of transported investment goods. Estimates are given for the significance of these and other factors.

I.

Complicated simultaneous equations models have long been used in pure economic theory and in macroeconomic prediction. Jeffrey C. Williamson's *Late Nineteenth-Century American Development* (1974) attempts to employ this type of model as an explanation of a particular phase of American economic history. Despite the path breaking nature of the project he has undertaken and provocative results he achieves, the work has to date generated relatively little response.[1] Part of the reason may be the perceived difficulty (and expense) inherent in reconstructing and rerunning his simultaneous system. The difficulty is not as great as might be imagined[2] and as we argue below, it is not even absolutely necessary to rerun a computer simulation in order to make a constructive assessment of it.

Nonetheless, part of the silence may be due not to technical problems but to methodological ones, because this use of a complicated model as explanation poses a considerable dilemma, requiring us to rethink our notions of what constitutes an "explanation" in economic history. This paper argues that complicated computer models make their contributions in relation to and must constantly be viewed in comparison with the simpler pencil-and-paper models of the sort quantitative economic historians have been using for some time now.

Complicated and simple models are designed to meet different objectives. On the one hand, we fear that simple models may leave out important, but complicated interactions. If we rely on the conclusions of such models, we are forever subject to the nagging doubt about taking into account one or another of the inter-relationships that were excluded might reverse our findings. Thus if we are solely interested in predicting the future (or replicating the past) as accurately as possible, we want as complicated and complete a model as we can achieve. We are limited only by the amount of data at our disposal and the sheer cost of constructing and running the model.

However, accuracy is not the only goal; simplicity is also a virtue. When we merely cite a 72-equation model as the explanation of some phenomenon, it is difficult to argue that we understand any better than when we started. Without further analysis it is not clear which of the 72 equations is crucial for the results we achieve and which are peripheral.

The standard technique for determining which assumptions are crucial—and thus, the central step in using a model as an explanation—is a sensitivity analysis, that is, altering one or another assumption and seeing if the results change. For normal-sized models, this step ought to be explicitly performed at the same time that the counterfactual experiments are run.[3] But for a model as big as Williamson's, a complete sensitivity analysis would take (as he notes) far more computer time than any research project can afford. Part of the solution is a division of academic labor resembling a game of "King of the Hill": One person develops a model, takes a position and establishes a challenge to all comers to knock him off. Williamson plays the game fairly: he provides his explicit model, adequate for any skeptic to alter and rerun at will. He even specifies those equations whose defenses he feels are weakest. We therefore have a ready-made procedure for reviewing and criticizing complicated models; that is, to participate in just this sort of sensitivity analysis—separating the important assumptions from the unimportant ones, and substituting alternate formulations of the important ones.

Although our goal is now clear, the means of achieving it are not. How will we be able to tell which of the assumptions are likely to be crucial, which of the parameters are worth varying in order to rerun the model? The key lies in simplifying the model—that is, making a "model of the model" which is small enough to handle with pencil and paper. Although Williamson's general equilibrium model is complicated, it is (like the economy it attempts to mirror) reasonably stable in the face of marginal changes of the sort economic historians consider. Therefore, as we will demonstrate, carefully chosen simplifications of the model can be used to predict the effects of altering the complicated model. In fact, we may be said to understand the complicated model when we are able to predict with reasonable accuracy (leaving that term suitably elastic, of course) the outcome of a counterfactual experiment before we run it. Such understanding will allow us to pick and choose among the myriad of possible adjustments a subset most likely to yield interesting results.

After an outline of the structure of the Williamson model and our attempts to replicate it, the body of this paper will be devoted to just this sort of examination of two particular topics that Williamson discusses: the Great Depression (chap. 5) and the effects of transportation on midwestern development (chap. 9). In each case we will examine the major determinants in the model of the effects of any change we make and compare the size of the effects in the simulations with what a simpler pencil-and paper model would have predicted. In the case of aggregate growth rates, our conclusions are largely negative: the Williamson model adds little that was not predicted in simpler frameworks. In the case of interregional transportation, the model provides a way to examine the magnitude of several potentially important effects hitherto uninvestigated.

Structure of the Williamson Model.   The model specifies Cobb-Douglas production functions for three sectors: midwestern agricultural goods, midwestern industrial goods, and northeastern industrial goods. Industrial goods are produced with capital and labor; agricultural goods are produced with capital, labor, and land. Technical progress in each sector is neutral and exogenous. There is also a transportation sector with production function unspecified. The model takes the relative price of manufactures and agricultural products in the Northeast as fixed by world conditions. Adding or subtracting the exogenous transportation cost yields the relative prices in the Midwest.

The growth of the land stock is exogenous, as is, for all practical purposes, the growth of the total labor force. Savings is a fixed proportion of income; the decay rate of the capital stock is fixed; and capital, once in place, cannot be moved between sectors. In the short run, the supply of each factor to each sector is fixed. Perfect competition is assumed, so that in any sector each factor receives its marginal revenue product. In the longer run, labor moves between sectors in response to relative wages, the rate of migration varying with the magnitude of the wage differential. New Investment is also distributed according to relative returns, provided that the difference in returns rises above a certain threshold, representing the information costs of moving funds between sectors.

Domestic demands are calculated for both agricultural and industrial goods in both regions. Since prices of outputs are determined by exogenous world demands and exogenous international and interregional transportation costs, domestic demand cannot affect prices or factor mobility. Instead, domestic demand determines the quantities of goods that will be shipped interregionally and internationally. For example, at the ruling prices in the Midwest, any surplus of agricultural supply over midwestern demand is presumed to be shipped to the Northeast. Any excess over northeastern demand is presumed to be shipped abroad.

For this paper we have attempted to reconstruct Williamson's model as closely as possible. This is not as straightforward an exercise as it might sound. Those who have worked with large-scale econometric models will realize that there is always an error hidden somewhere in the bowels of a program and that even the difference between the ways two computers round numbers can affect the result in a simulation of 40 years. Nonetheless we believe we have in fact achieved a fair approximation; our calculations compared Williamson's for 1890 (a particular year of interest) will allow the reader to judge this for himself.[4]

The model we have used is the same as that reported in Williamson, with the correction of certain typographical errors.[5] The corrected equations are shown in Table 2 (notation is the same as Williamson's). It should be noted that Eqs. 19, 64, and 66–69 of the original are redundant, and were originally included in the model solely for double-checking.

One difficulty with the model as it stands is the assumption that eastern relative prices are fixed on a world market (less the exogenous cost of international transportation). This assumption is consistent as long as the United States continues to export agricultural and import industrial goods. But the model in effect assumes that trade flows can be reversed at the same relative prices, ignoring the price wedge caused by cost of transportation. In several years, given the relative prices, the model predicts that the United States *imports* agricultural goods; in

Table 1. A Comparison of Williamson's Original Run with the
Replication of the Model Used in this Paper[4]

Replication		Original
258.308	Q_{IE}	257.937
108.143	Q_{IW}	116.104
256.245	Q_{AW}	250.953
1651.086	K	1645.673
817.482	K_{IE}	803.393
347.880	K_{IW}	373.287
485.724	K_{AW}	468.993
157.807	L	158.906
57.387	L_{IE}	58.057
74.834	L_{AW}	73.367
25.587	L_{IW}	27.483
280.680	Y_E	278.871
425.736	Y_W	427.049
2.352	w_{IE}	2.321
2.849	w_{IW}	2.847
2.397	w_{AW}	2.394
.135	r_{IE}	.137
.171	r_{IW}	.172
.106	r_{AW}	.107
706.416	Y	705.919
72.250	T	67.641

fact, what should happen in these circumstances is that eastern relative prices readjust until international trade is eliminated. The problem is actually less serious since the model ignores eastern production of agricultural goods, and in any event the situation does not occur often. Thus we can be reasonably confident that the simplification does not affect results as long as we are not interested in a question directly focusing on international trade.[6]

Two other limitations to the model should be noted: First, the domestic demand functions are not homogenous in prices—theoretically troublesome, but not likely to be of great importance since the demands are largely passive. Secondly, there is an odd feedback in the investment function. As Wiliamson specifies the model, there is no lag between the time an investment good is ordered and its installation for the purposes of production. Normally a model adds current investment into production next period. Here current investment affects this period's capital stock. However, some preliminary runs determined that including the lag had little effect on the model for most purposes (although it did reduce the total capital stock) and so the non-lagged version was retained.

A modification we have made to the transportation sector will be noted in Section III.

Table 2.

$$L_{AW}(t) = L_{AW}(t-1) \left\{ n_W(t-1) - \hat{m}_{IA}(t-1) + \frac{m_{WE}(t-1)L_E(t-1)}{L_W(t-1)} - \right.$$
$$\left. - m_{EW}(t-1) \right\} + \hat{m}_{AI}(t-1)L_{IW}(t-1) \tag{17}$$

$$d(t) = P_{AW}(t)\beta_R \frac{Q_{AW}(t)}{R(t)} \tag{28}$$

$$I_{IWE}(t) + I_{AWE}(t) = s\phi_{WE}(t)Y_E(t)/P_{IW}(t) \tag{32 1/2}$$

$$I_{AWE}(t) = \frac{\{I_{IWE}(t) + I_{AWE}(t)\}}{[1 - \phi_{EW}(t)]} \left\{ \frac{P_{IW}(t)I_{AWW}(t)}{S_{AW}(t) + S_{IW}(t)} \right\} \tag{33}$$

$$I_{IWE}(t) = \frac{\{I_{IWE}(t) + I_{AWE}(t)\}}{[1 - \phi_{EW}(t)]} \left\{ \frac{P_{IW}(t)I_{IWW}(t)}{S_{AW}(t) + S_{IW}(t)} \right\} \tag{34}$$

$$\phi_{WE}(t) = \max\{0,1 - e^{-\mu[i^*(t)-\tau]}\} \tag{39}$$

$$\phi_{EW}(t) = \max\{0,1 - e^{\mu[i^*(t)+\tau]}\} \tag{40}$$

$$\hat{\phi}_{IA}(t) = \max\{0,1 - e^{-\mu[\hat{i}^*(t)-\tau]}\} \tag{41}$$

$$\hat{\phi}_{AI}(t) = \max\{0,1 - e^{\mu[\hat{i}^*(t)+\tau]}\} \tag{42}$$

$$COL_E(t) = P_{AE}(t)\left[\frac{P_{AE}(t)D_{AE}(t)}{(1-s)Y_E(t)}\right] + P_{IE}(t)\left[1 - \frac{P_{AE}(t)D_{AE}(t)}{(1-s)Y_E(t)}\right] \tag{51}$$

$$COL_W(t) = P_{AW}(t)\left[\frac{P_{AW}(t)D_{AW}(t)}{(1-s)Y_W(t)}\right] + P_{IW}(t)\left[1 - \frac{P_{AW}(t)D_{AW}(t)}{(1-s)Y_W(t)}\right] \tag{52}$$

$$s = \{P_{IW}(t)[I_{IWE}(t) + I_{IWW}(t) + I_{AWE}(t) + I_{AWW}(t)] + $$
$$+ P_{IE}(t)[I_{IEE}(t) + I_{IEW}(t)]\}/\{Y_E(t) + Y_W(t)\} \tag{66}$$

$$T(t) = [Z_A(t)P_{AW}(t)\{D_{AE}(t) + EX(t)\}] + $$
$$+ [Z_I(t)P_{IE}(t)\{D_{IW}(t) + I_W(t) - Q_{IW}(t)\}] \tag{72}$$

II. THE WILLIAMSON MODEL AND OUTPUT GROWTH RATES

Williamson's model succeeds in replicating an important fact of American economic history: the decline in the growth rate of GNP per worker during the "great depression" of the late 1800s. On the basis of Gallman's national income figures and Lebergott's labor force estimates, Williamson calculates average annual changes in per worker GNP.[7] Between the decade 1869–1878 and the decade 1884–1893 (henceforth "the first period") the record shows GNP per worker growing at 1.71 percent per annum. For the period 1884–1893 and 1899–1908 (henceforth "the second period") the growth rate is 1.24 percent per annum. Actually Williamson's model seems to overstate this decline, yielding an estimated decline from 2.39 percent to 1.33 percent when calculated in 1870 prices.[8] Our replication obtains even larger decline: 2.63 percent to 1.33 percent.[9] However, since the calculation ignores transportation resources and labor productivity in that sector (see Section III), a more appropriate measure of the decline in per worker growth is the output valued at location of production—that is, omitting value added in transit. Valued at these "manufacturers prices" in 1870 the per capita GNP growth rate declines from 2.47 percent per annum to 2.06 percent, that is, approximately 0.4 percentage points. Using other base year prices we find a range of decline from 0.3 to 0.6 percentage points.[10]

There are two standard, simple frameworks in which growth rates are analyzed. Denison's "sources of growth" framework and the one-sector growth models. In this section we will pick specific topics Williamson examines and compare his results with those from these simplified models.

The "sources of growth" framework starts with the equation

$$Y^* = T^* + \alpha_K K^* + \alpha_L L^* + \alpha_R R^* \tag{1}$$

In one sense this is an identity: if we take weighted growth rates of inputs (K = capital; L = Labor; R = Land; stars denote growth rates) and subtract them from growth rate of output (Y), we are left with the "residual" (T) which is a measure of increased factor productivity—that is, of precisely the excess of output growth over input growth.

In another sense, however, this is a simple theory of economic growth, one which assumes the share of output obtained by the various factors (which are the appropriate weightings in the above equation) are constant, and the growth rates of productivity and of these inputs are exogenous. Thus we can say that growth rates fell in period two relative to period one "because" productivity growth fell or "because" of retarded growth of the capital stock. Table 3 provides a summary of such a source of growth estimate, based on the simulation of Williamson's model. (The final entry, "Residual due to reallocating factors," is the only one that cannot be estimated without a multisector model; it will be explained in detail on pp. 193–194.)

While the sources of growth framework treats these variables as strictly exogenous, Williamson's model includes numerous relationships between them. Thus it can be used to examine the effects of movements in any one variable upon the others and ultimately upon the rate of growth of output.

In this way, Williamson uses the model to examine more completely the effects of several counterfactual experiments. For instance, he considers the

Table 3.   Summary of Sources of Growth Estimates

	period 1 (1870–1878 to 1884–1893 in 1881 prices)		period 2 (1884–1893 to 1899–1908 in 1896 prices)	
Factor productivity growth in agriculture	0.7%		0.4%	
x share of agriculture in total output	x.52	0.4	x.32	0.1
Factor productivity growth in manufacturing	1.6%		1.0%	
x share of manufacturing in total output	x.48	0.7	x.68	0.6
Growth due to factor productivity		1.1%		0.8%
Capital Stock Growth rate	5.9%		4.6%	
times share in income	x.32	1.8	x.37	1.7
Labor Force Growth rate	2.2%		1.5%	
times share in income	x.63	1.4	x.60	0.9
Land Stock Growth rate	2.7%		1.6%	
times share in income	x.05	0.1	x.03	0.0
Growth due to input growth		3.4%		2.7%
Residual due to reallocating factors from low to high productivity sectors		0.1%		0.3%
Output Growth Rate		4.7%		3.7%

Note: Discrepancies in totals due to rounding errors.

effect of the decrease in the rate of growth of land, which he equates with the hypothesis that growth declined due to the "disappearance of the frontier."

As he notes, the sources of growth framework demonstrates that the closing of the frontier should have had little effect on output growth rates. The growth rate of land in the first period averaged 2.7 percent and in the second period 1.6 percent. If we consider a counterfactual experiment in which the stock of land grew at 4 percent each period, we would expect almost negligible effects. Since land's share of national income in this model is never above 6 percent, the sources of growth framework would predict for the first period an increase in per capita growth rate of less than .06 x (4 percent - 2.7 percent)—or less than a tenth of a percent. Moving from the original decline in the growth rate of land between the two periods to the counterfactual constant rate of growth of land would stem output growth rate by less than .06 (2.7 percent – 1.6 percent)—or less than a tenth of a percentage point.

Williamson notes that when the growth rate of the stock of land is altered, his model can trace the following interrelationships which the sources of growth framework ignores: (1) Induced changes in the growth rates of other factors; and

(2) induced changes in total factor productivity growth due to changes in the mix of output from low to high productivity growth sectors. However, it is not necessary to run his model to predict the effects of these extra factors. To test their likely importance, we can examine submodels which include each of the complications in turn. The appendix demonstrates this technique, comparing pencil-and-paper estimate of the consequences of each interrelationship that Williamson mentions with the magnitude of the effect of that interrelationship found by actually running the counterfactual model. In general the estimates are good, indicating that, for this particular counterfactual, the complications added by the Williamson model make little difference. And in fact, when we run the counterfactual simulation with 4 percent land stock growth rate, we find, no matter which price weighting is used, or which period we examine, that the change in per capita growth rate in the counterfactual simulation is never more than 0.1 percent. Similarly, the change in the decline between periods is never more than 0.1 percent.[11]

However, we will not always be able to generate simplified submodels to handle these interrelationships. In the case of growth rate estimations there is an additional interrelationship in the model, one which Williamson does not mention explicitly. Economy-wide productivity is a weighted average of sectoral productivity growth. This weighted average equals the whole of the residual only under one of two assumptions: that the return to factors is the same in all sectors or that factor supply in any particular sector grows at the same rate as the total supply of that factor.[12] If a factor of production is shifting from low to high productivity uses, the residual is boosted—the size of the boost depending on the speed of the shift. Suppose, for example, n% of the capital stock is shifted from agriculture to industry in a period (presumably by depreciation without replacement). Then

$$\Delta Y/Y \cong (r_{IW} - r_{AW}) \; n\% \cdot K/Y \qquad (2)$$

How important is the sectoral shift of factors of production in determining growth rates? The question cannot be answered without resort to a model like

Table 4. Per Capita Output Growth in Original Simulation and Counterfactual with Constant Growth of Land Stock

| | *Original Model* | | *Land Growth at 4%* | |
	Period I	*Period II*	*Period I*	*Period II*
Prices of				
1870	2.47	2.06	2.52	2.13
1881	2.38	1.74	2.45	1.84
1888–1889	2.44	1.97	2.50	2.05
1896	2.49	2.14	2.54	2.20

Williamson's. The final entry of Table 3 reports the effects as measured in the basic simulation. In the first period, factor shift is of minimal importance, since average migration of labor during the period is very small. In the second period, however, about 1 percent of the western labor force per year leaves agriculture for industry—an amount greater than the natural increase in the agricultural labor force. Since there is a fairly large difference between the agriculture and industrial returns in both capital and labor in this latter period, this mobility is sufficient to add about 0.3 percentage points to the growth rate. However, the *difference* in mobility from the original to the counterfactual model appears to be small— causing less than a 0.1 percentage point shift.

In sum, the sources of growth framework adequately predict the results of the Williamson model in this particular counterfactual.[13]

Since the Williamson model treats as endogenous factors that the sources of growth framework treats as exogenous, the Williamson model can be used to go behind proximate causes in attempts to explain growth rates. In particular, Williamson examines the "ultimate" causes of the decline in capital stock growth.

One-sector growth models provide a particularly simple framework for analyzing growth rates. Most such models predict that in the long run the capital stock tends to some constant "natural" rate of growth. In models without technological progress the growth rate of the capital stock eventually approaches the growth rate of the other factors. In a model such as this one, with Hicks neutral technological progress,[14] the capital stock will grow asymptotically at a rate different from that of other factors; in a one-sector model this rate approaches $n + TFPG/(1-\alpha_K)$, where n is the growth rate of the other factors and TFPG is total factor productivity growth.[15] Using the Williamson parameters, a simple model would predict a constant long-run rate of growth of capital stock equal to $1.5 + (.8/.63) = 2.77$.

In the short run, however, the size of the capital stock is given by historical circumstances and the rate of growth varies. To analyze short-run growth, Williamson makes use of the following expression from one-sector growth theory models:

$$K^* = (sY/P_IK) - \delta \tag{3}$$

Williamson argues that the Civil War decade left a low capital stock and high savings rate, temporarily driving up the rate of capital formation. The supposed slowdown is thus in reality a return to the longer run rate of growth as the size of the capital stock adjusts.

Note the structure of the argument: Williamson has appealed to a submodel—and a very simple one, consisting of a single equation—as the explanation of the results of the more complicated model. In particular he argues that it is the interrelationships of this particular equation that are the vital ones for understanding the decline in the rate of growth in his model. Thus the following technique provides an immediate test of the argument: alter one or another of the parameters of the simple equation and compare with a change of the same parameter in the complicated model.

Two such tests are examined in Appendix B. The first assumes a larger initial capital stock (25 percent larger than the actual 1870 level); the second assumes the savings rate to be 8 percentage points lower, bringing it in line with the pre–Civil War levels. Neither alteration should affect the long-run rate of growth, but both should affect initial growth for both counterfactuals. Simulations are compared with pencil-and-paper predictions of the effects. Both estimates support Williamson's explanation of the behavior of the model. Increasing the capital stock by 25 percent significantly reduces the decline in investment growth; lowering the savings rate over the whole period is sufficient to "eliminate" the fall in productivity growth. (See Table B1, Appendix B.)

To summarize: Our experiments tend to confirm Williamson's explanation of the decline in capital stock growth rates in his model as stemming from a distinction between long-run "natural" rates of growth and a short-run higher rate of growth caused by special conditions in the post–Civil War United States.

III. THE WILLIAMSON MODEL AND TRANSPORTATION SOCIAL SAVINGS

In Williamson's model, transportation improvements account for a significant amount of the economic growth of the Midwest and of the United States as a whole. This conclusion appears to contradict Fogel's[16] findings on the magnitude of the social savings of railroads, but, as Williamson notes, the two investigations examine distinct questions: Fogel sought to estimate the effect of the reduction in transportation costs achieved at any time by a substitution of railroads for canals; Williamson's concern is the effect on the economy of the reduction in all interregional transportation costs over time.

Williamson argues that the observed convergence of eastern and western agricultural prices is due to a decline in transportation costs. Consequently, he calculates agricultural transportation costs, not directly, but by means of this difference. The reductions are dramatic. In the 1870s, New York agricultural prices are 80 percent higher than Iowa prices; by 1910, they are only 20 percent higher. For industrial goods, however, Williamson accepts a direct calculation of transportation costs from railroad charges, which did not decline over the period. This asymmetric treatment creates anomalies. Although industrial transportation costs include only the railroad's charges, agricultural transportation costs include all middlemen and marketing services. Williamson's model thus classifies improved storage, better communication, and growth in arbitrage as "improvements in agricultural transportation." In 1870, value added in transportation accounts for about 17 percent of GNP in the model.[17] In 1890 transport is about 10 percent of GNP in the model.

Williamson compares a simulation using the historically observed relative prices in the two regions to a counterfactual simulation in which the transportation costs remain constant, so that the percentage differentials between eastern and western prices remain at the 1870 level. He finds three particularly striking effects of high transportation costs:

1. Per capita GNP would have grown more slowly—mainly because of a 1 percent decline in the growth rate of capital stock.

2. By 1890 the social savings would have been 21 percent—that is, without the decline in transportation costs, real GNP would have been 21 percent less.

3. The West would have specialized more in industrial goods—so much more that western agriculture would have fallen from 36 percent of GNP to 25 percent (and, as a proportion of Midwest production, the decline would have been much more dramatic.)

In general, upon replicating Williamson's model, we arrive at similar results, summarized below. Our social saving estimate for 1890 in the replication is smaller than Williamson's estimate, but nonetheless hefty. Another indication of the dramatic nature of the change in production is the fact that transportation of goods interregionally falls by two-thirds in the counterfactual.[18]

Table 5. Estimate of the Impact of Declining Transportation Costs; a Replication of the Williamson Model

		simulation observed costs of transportation	simulation assuming no reduction in transport costs	
Capital stock growth rate (% per annum)		5.90	5.34	
Growth of per capita GNP (% per annum)		2.61	2.11	
		(1)	(2)	social savings [(1)-(2)]/(1)
GNP (1870 prices)	1870	100.0	100.0	
	1871	103.3	99.5	3.7%
(index: 1870 GNP	1880	170.0	154.0	9.2%
= 100)	1890	253.3	220.8	12.8%
Share of agriculture	1870	.358	.358	
in GNP	1871	.366	.373	
	1880	.403	.384	
	1890	.363	.305	
Share of agriculture	1870	.713	.713	
in midwestern	1871	.717	.715	
production	1880	.704	.642	
	1890	.655	.511	

What causes these dramatic results? Can they be understood in terms of a simpler model? The candidate, of course, as Williamson notes, is Fogel's social savings framework. Figure 1 illustrates the standard social savings calculation. Q_1 represents the quantity of services actually purchased and Q_2 the reduced quantity that would have been purchased had the marginal cost of transportation not fallen.

The shaded area represents the social savings; it is less than Q_1P and greater than Q_2P. Thus an upper bound on the social savings in the Williamson model can be estimated without rerunning the simulation at higher transportation prices, by multiplying the quantity of transportation services observed in the initial run by the change in transportation costs for the second run. Such a calculation is outlined in Table 6; it yields a "naive" upper bound to social savings of 3.9 percent.

This bound exceeds actual social savings because demand for transportation services is not inelastic. Increases in transportation costs cause producers, consumers, and investors to initiate adjustments in resources and demands to reduce the burden—adjustments simpler models cannot take into account. The main such adjustment would be Williamson's "static effect": If the cost of shipping to and from the Midwest increased, the Midwest would reduce its specialization in export goods. The burden to the society of increased transportation costs would be partially offset by a switch to non-transported production and a resultant decline in demand for transportation.

In Williamson's model, the quantity of transportation services demanded is equal to the excess supply of the commodity in the given region. For example, suppose the cost of transporting agricultural goods rises by P. Then the price of farm goods in the Midwest will, according to the assumptions of the model, fall

Figure 1.

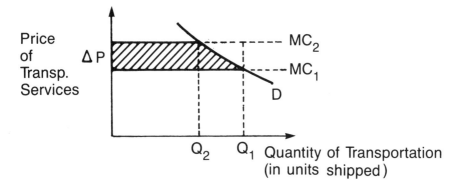

Table 6.   A Naive Estimate of the Social Savings of Transportation
Based on Data from the Initial Simulation

Quantity of agricultural goods shipped east (1890)	104.7		
1890 agricultural transport cost in initial simulation		0.40	
1890 agricultural transport in counterfactual model		0.70	
$Q_1 \Delta P$ in agriculture			31.4
Quantity of industrial goods shipped west (1890)	110.3		
1890 industrial transport cost in initial simulation		0.28	
1890 industrial transport cost in counterfactual models		0.24	
$Q_1 \Delta P$ in industry			−4.0
			27.4
GNP (1890)		÷	706.4
Social Savings			3.9%

Note: Costs are exogenous data in the simulation; in the model they are normalized so that agricultural goods
in the Midwest in the initial simulation have a price of 1. Quantities shipped and GNP figures are taken
from the replication of the Williamson initial simulation and are in the units used in the Williamson
model. Thus only the final social savings, normalized by GNP, is directly comparable with other studies.

by the same amount. The resultant surplus of agricultural goods in the Midwest
depends only on prices in the Midwest. Figure 2 represents the market for
western agricultural goods.

Figure 2.

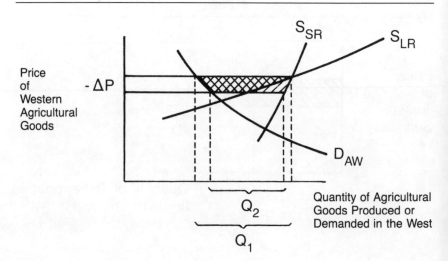

In the short run, transportation social savings corresponds to the shaded area. In the long run, the elasticity of supply of agricultural goods increases, because labor and capital can be moved between sectors. Thus long-run social loss from increased transportation costs (the cross-hatched area) should be less than the short-run social loss.

The Williamson model takes account of these supply responses. Why then is Williamson's calculated social savings not smaller than the naive estimate? A considerable portion of the effect comes, in fact, from an inconsistent assumption of the model: that transportation services can be treated as a free good. Williamson assumes that the supply of transportation can increase without diverting resources from other sectors. Rather than assuming the marginal social costs of transportation is equal to the price, Wiliamson implicitly assumes it always equals zero.

There are two sorts of circumstance under which increases in the quantity of transportation services would indeed be costless. The first possibility is that there are large economies of scale in transportation. However, Williamson himself describes the simulation as assuming constant costs in transportation.[19] The second possibility is that increased demand for transportation services could pull extra resources into utilization. Since Williamson bills the model as a full employment one[20] we should not expect to find these additional resources available domestically. Increased demand for transportation services could pull in additional labor and capital from abroad. However, this assumption is inconsistent with the exogenous factor flows from abroad assumed in the rest of the model. Moreover, if one were to modify the model (as Williamson later does) to endogenize international factor movements, flows should be determined by average factor returns throughout the economy, not just by the much more volatile conditions of the transportation sector.

To take resource costs into account, I have made simple adjustments to the model, chosen partly for ease of construction and interpretation, and partly to keep the model as close to Williamson's original as possible. The added equations are listed in Table 7. I have assumed that transportation is produced entirely by industrial labor (in equal amounts from east to west) and in a competitive market. Thus the ratio of wage rate to the price of transportation is equal to the productivity of labor in transportation.

Given this opportunity, I determined how much industrial labor would be necessary to run the observed transportation system of the original simulation. I added this amount of labor to the industrial labor supply. Then when the simulation was rerun, this labor was available as part of the total labor supply.

Higher transportation markups in the rerun were interpreted as correspondingly lower productivity of labor in transportation. Demand for transportation is derived endogenously as before, in turn generating the derived demand for labor in transportation. If demand for labor in transportation turned out to be less than in the initial simulation, the excess labor was diverted to industrial production; if demand for labor turned out to be greater in the rerun, than labor was drawn from industrial production.

Table 7.   Modification to Williamson Model Taking Account of
Resource Costs in Transportation

(73) $L_{IE}(t) = L_E(t) - L_{ER}(t)$

(74) $L_{IW}(t) = L_W(t) - L_{AW}(t) - L_{WR}(t)$

(75) $C_A(t) = (w_E(t) + w_{IW}(t))/(Z_A(t) P_{AW}(t))$

(76) $C_I(t) = (w_E(t) + w_{IW}(t))/(Z_I(t) P_{IE}(t))$

(77) $L_{ER}(t) = L_{WR}(t) = Q_{AT}(t)/C_A(t) + Q_{IT}(t) /C_I(t)$

Note: L_{ER} is eastern labor employed in transportation; L_{WR} is western labor employed in transportation; C_A is productivity in agricultural transportation; C_I is productivity in industrial transportation; Q_{AT} is quantity of agricultural goods shipped; Q_{IT} is quantity of industrial goods shipped; all other notation corresponds to Williamson (pp. 45–46).

There are numerous limitations to this approach. I have continued, for example, to assume that no extra capital is necessary to run the transportation system. I have made labor completely mobile between industry and transportation, rather than assuming the stickiness found elsewhere in the model. I have not allowed for the possibilities of economies of scale (but see Appendix C). Ideally, it would be more instructive to make productivity rather than transportation cost the exogenous variable in the counterfactual.

Table 8 gives resultant social savings in three different years for our initial replication of the Williamson model, and for the modified version to take account of resource costs. Since social savings is subject to the same index number problem as in any other aggregated economic measurement, we have calculated social savings based on three different price weightings. The first calculation weights the components in 1870 prices, the second in the prices of the year for which the calculation was made, and the third in what would have been current year prices had transportation costs not declined. The two current price weightings rarely differ by more than a percentage point. The constant price weighting gives different results, but it is a theoretically less satisfactory measure. Since social savings are already calculated as a ratio, and year-to-year variations in social savings are of no particular interest, there is no need to "deflate" a social savings estimate. Instead current relative prices are the proper weighting.[21]

As Williamson notes, the increase in transportation costs will induce changes in the model that the above static analysis does not take into account. Among the effects is one Williamson calls the "dynamic effect": as the cost of transportation increases (in effect increasing relative prices of industrial goods in the Midwest) the rate of accumulation is reduced, since a given level of midwestern agricultural savings can now buy fewer investment goods. In our model corrected for resource costs, this phenomenon still occurs; the rate of accumulation decreases from 5.9 percent to 5.5 percent.

Table 8. Social Savings in a Model with or
without Resource Costs

	Year	Weighting I calculated in 1870 prices	Weighting II calculated in current year prices with actual transportation costs	Weighting III calculated in current year prices assuming no reduction in transportation costs
replication of Williamson Model	1871	3.7%	2.7%	3.4%
	1880	9.2%	7.0%	8.0%
	1890	12.8%	8.7%	9.6%
model corrected for resource costs	1871	3.4%	2.3%	3.0%
	1880	7.6%	5.3%	6.4%
	1890	7.9%	3.2%	4.2%

An estimate of the importance of the dynamic effect can be obtained by measuring the changes in the total capital stock of 1890 in the counterfactual simulation and multiplying by the marginal productivity of agricultural capital. The result is a cost of nearly 2 percent of GNP. The product of capital actually falls by slightly less because of a long-run shift in the sectoral composition of the capital stock. Table 9 compares the observed fall in GNP (under weighting II) with the sum of the naive estimate and the estimated dynamic effect. Note that our estimates indeed bound the observed shift. Similar results occur under weighting III.[22]

To investigate the magnitude of the static effect, an alternate counterfactual experiment was performed in which the transition to counterfactual markups occurs only in the final year. Thus, there is almost no elasticity of supply for agricultural goods, and the dynamic effect only takes place in the final year, where its impact is negligible.[23]

In this case, agricultural production is virtually unaffected (corresponding to S_{SR} in Figure 2); and industrial production is altered only to the extent that it is necessary to move labor from industry into providing extra transportation. But because demand for goods by midwesterners is not completely inelastic, as the price of industrial goods rises there is a degree of substitution into agricultural goods and a somewhat lower quantity of them shipped out of the region.

Although the total of the social savings is not greatly affected by this alternate experiment, the causes of the social savings in this case are quite different. Here the loss due to the dynamic effect is less than 0.2 percent. In addition, the naive bounds are much closer together and observed social savings is much closer to

Table 9.   A Comparison of Simulated and
A Priori Estimated Social Savings

Estimation of Bounds:	Upper	Lower
naive estimate	3.9% ($=Q_1\Delta P$)	1.2% ($=Q_2\Delta P$)
adding in estimate of dynamic effect	1.8%	1.5%
	5.6%	2.8%
Result of simulation (Weighting II):	3.2%	

the upper bound, as we would expect, since short-run demand for transportation is more inelastic than long-run demand.

In sum, between two-fifths and three-fifths of the observed loss of GNP in the basic model is due to reductions in investment over time, because of the change in relative price of agricultural goods. For the remaining, static effect, a naive estimate assuming inelastic transportation demand overstates the true social savings by between 1 percent and 14 percent if factors are supplied inelastically (so that elastic commodity demand is the only source of elastic transportation demand). It overestimates by between 39 percent and 64 percent if we allow the factor mobility of the Williamson model.

The conclusion is that decreased investment could be a major component of the cost in the transportation social savings, and factor mobility could have an important role in offsetting those costs.

Having gained some understanding of the various components of the transpor-

Table 10.   A Comparison of Simulated and A Priori Estimated
Social Savings for a Counterfactual Experiment in Which Cost of
Transportation is Higher Only in 1890

Estimation of Bounds:	Upper	Lower
naive estimate	3.9%	3.4%
adding in estimate of dynamic effect	0.2%	0.1%
	4.0%	3.5%
Result of simulation (Weighting II):	3.5%	

tation social savings in Williamson's model, we next investigate the robustness of the social savings estimate to several alterations to the model.

Our first alteration was to smooth transportation markups. The agricultural markup is based on the difference between wheat spot prices in Iowa and New York. During the period, year-to-year variations in the difference are large, indeed comparable with the trend reduction.[24] Although it is likely that on average this difference represents transportation costs, in any given year shortages or excesses in local supplies will upset this relationship.[25] For instance, the regional price differential falls 40 percent in Williamson's model between 1870 and 1871. Williamson's 1871 figures illustrate what the effect would have been from a 40 percent decline in transport costs, but they almost certainly overstate the effect of the true decline in transport costs in that year. A smoothed markup corresponds to an assumption that the decline in underlying transport costs stemmed from numerous technological advances occurring steadily through the period.

From 1870–1875 to 1885–1890, the transportation markup falls by an average of 2.2 percent a year. Therefore, we have assumed a constant decline of this amount over the two decades. The biggest effect of this smoothing is to reduce the extreme agricultural transportation markup in 1870 from 101 percent to 83 percent.

The actual industrial markup *increases* over the period 1870–1890. In order to bias our procedure against understating the magnitude of the social savings, we have smoothed industrial transportation costs on a trend to 1910. On this longer trend industrial transportation costs still increase, but at a reduced rate; the 1870 markup becomes 21 percent instead of 25 percent.

Table 11 compares a simulation using these smoothed markups to one in which the markups remain constant at 83 percent and 25 percent respectively. The results is a further, but less marked, decline in the size of the social savings (compare with Table 8).

Next we consider the effect of using the ''Wisconsin differential'' calculated by Williamson rather than the ''low differential'' as the indication of agricultural transportation costs.[26] Wisconsin prices are preferable since Iowa was on the edge of the country in 1870 and, even as of 1910, was likely to be less representative of midwestern transport costs.

A priori it would seem likely that such an alteration would reduce the social savings still further, since the costs of transportation would fall less. As Table 12 indicates, the lower markups actually *increase* the social savings. This anomalous result may be due to the manner of stating the counterfactual. In this simulation, we have recalculated the initial demand for transportation based on lower Wisconsin prices. Consequently, initial demand for transportation is higher in this simulation and transportation is a correspondingly larger portion of the economy—so that increases in its cost would have greater impact. This hypothesis could be checked by estimating the impacts in simplified models, as in the previous section. Before doing so, it would be desirable to modify the Williamson model

Table 11.   Social Savings with Smoothed Transportation Markups

	Weighting I (1870 prices)	Weighting II (current year prices; actual transport costs)	Weighting III (current year prices under high transport costs)
1871	0.1%	0.1%	0.1%
1880	2.0%	1.6%	1.7%
1890	4.5%	2.4%	2.6%

Table 12.   Social Savings with Wisconsin Markups

	Weighting I	Weighting II	Weighting III
1871	0.1%	0.1%	0.1%
1880	2.2%	1.9%	2.0%
1890	4.9%	3.4%	3.6%

to include explicit estimates of transportation resources and an empirically tested production function for that sector.

In one sense, the results thus far argue less that transportation cost decreases had no effect than that social savings are only one measure of the effect. In other words, our figures show the robustness of social savings calculations to most occurrences short of reductions of the factor supply. In all the above accounts, although total output remains virtually unchanged, the composition of that output varies considerably.[27] Figure 3 graphs the growth path of midwestern production in the factual and counterfactual runs of the final version of the model (with Wisconsin markups).

Table 13 compares the quantities of goods transported in the two cases, demonstrating that, even though the effect on social savings of increased transports is small, the effect on the composition of the economy's output is great.

As we have noted before, factor mobility within the West is a major reason why the social savings is as low as it is. On the other hand, this mobility is a long-run phenomenon; in the short run factors are fairly *immobile* in the Williamson model. Capital once in place cannot be moved and its decay rate is low.[28] It would be worthwhile to see if the results are significantly affected by moving to the other extreme and assuming perfect mobility of capital within the Midwest. Table 14 describes the results of such a modification; again we use the smoothed Wisconsin markups.

There is little effect on the magnitude of the social savings, because there is very little difference in the size of national income. Since we have recalculated labor requirements in these simulations, the results are not exactly comparable, but a reasonable estimate is that making western capital perfectly flexible increases

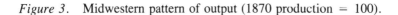

Figure 3. Midwestern pattern of output (1870 production = 100).

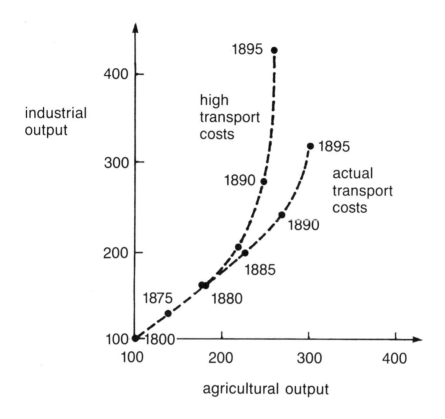

agricultural output

Table 13. Goods Transported in Counterfactual as
Percentage of Goods Transported in Original
(Model with Smoothed Wisconsin Markups)

	Agricultural	*Industrial*
1871	99.6%	99.2%
1880	95.0%	91.9%
1890	82.7%	77.5%
1894	69.4%	64.4%

GNP by 1.2 percent in the initial run and by 1.0 percent in the counterfactual
with no decrease in transport costs.[29]

Although the increased flexibility reduces social savings hardly at all, it greatly
increases the variation in the pattern of trade and production. Indeed, in the

Table 14.   Social Savings with Flexible Capital Stock

	Weighting I	Weighting II	Weighting III
1871	0.2%	0.1%	0.1%
1880	2.4%	1.9%	1.9%
1890	5.7%	2.5%	2.7%

model with flexible capital, high transportation costs cause interregional trade to cease entirely before 1890. In short, further investigation of factor mobility is likely to have little effect on social savings calculations, but will be important if we are interested in the causes of regional specialization.

IV. SUMMARY

If to understand a model is to be able to predict the results of changing any particular assumption in any particular instance, then we are still some way from a full understanding of the Williamson model. Still, considerable progress has been made. In this paper, I have examined two sets of issues addressed by Williamson, attempting to identify the equations on which each result depends. The basic technique involved building pencil-and paper submodels which yielded the same conclusions using the results to predict which new simulations were most likely to yield different results.

In the case of aggregate growth rates, we established that most of the effects of changes in the stock of land can be understood in a sources of growth framework, a simplification which yielded predictions accurate to a couple of tenths of a percentage point. Two counterfactual simulations demonstrated the validity of Williamson's intuition that the reduction of capital stock growth rates during the Great Depression could be attributed in his model to an initial shortage of capital and abnormally high savings rates followed by a return of the system to its long-run rate of growth—just as a one-sector growth model would predict.

In the case of transportation social savings, we found that the naive model gave fair predictions as to the results of the more complicated counterfactual— for the effects that it included. The extreme values of social savings initially found by Williamson were due to a simplifying assumption of zero resource cost for additional transportation and the use of 1870 prices in calculating GNP. Specific choices of smoothed or unsmoothed markups. or Iowa or Wisconsin prices as an indicator of western relative prices, or of short run flexibility or inflexibility of factors made relatively little difference to the calculation. Nor have any of the adjustments examined affected Williamson's finding that the pattern of production varies considerably in response to transportation markups. With high transport costs there is indeed considerably less interregional trade and specialization.

Our modifications to Williamson's model reduce the social savings estimate to about the level calculated by other studies for railroad social savings alone.[30] However, it must be emphasized that the factors underlying the social savings in the Williamson model are quite different than those in previous studies. On the one hand, simple static models underestimate the social savings by ignoring the resultant slowdown of capital formation due to a rise in the price of transported industrial goods—a cost which becomes fairly important in the course of twenty years. This underestimate is offset by the overestimate due to the assumed inelastic demand for transportation. This assumption is invalid not so much because it requires inelastic demand for the goods transported (after all, final Midwest demands in Williamson's model are not very elastic), but for the long-run elasticity of *supply* of transportable goods. As transportation costs rise, the Midwest shifts to the production of non-export products.

This paper has also attempted to indicate the strengths and weaknesses of the use of complicated simultaneous equation models in the study of economic history.

First of all, such models are not a substitute for improved data. For any given estimate on any particular question, Williamson's model is not necessarily more accurate than a simpler model with better data. By the same token, of course, it is also misguided to dismiss estimates from the Williamson model simply because one or another parameter is of uncertain accuracy. Here, as we have emphasized, it is a sensitivity analysis that is the key to using the model. Although there is a risk that efforts at complicated modeling may be substituted for the quest for improved data, there is a greater potential for this work to complement the search, by indicating those parameters for which improved accuracy really makes a difference.

But for all the concern both in this paper and in Williamson's book, with numbers and calculations to three decimal places, the point of this sort of modeling is not so much numerical accuracy as conceptual clarity. In a sense, a model like this one is an accounting device, a means—like pencil and paper in smaller cases—of remembering the plethora of factors which may (or may not) be involved in whatever topic we are investigating but which our limited brains may not be able to keep track of.

As such, this sort of model often will not lead to dramatic results if it is at all stable (and we wouldn't have much confidence in it if it weren't). That is to say, much of the time we will, based on experience with previous models, have been able to keep track of all the important considerations; and the extra interactions of the complicated model will not change the result significantly.

Of course, occasionally the questions we ask may be themselves too complicated so that there isn't a way of phrasing them in anything but a complicated model. Some economic historians may feel that most of the really interesting questions in economic history are grand and simple ones. Nonetheless, this paper discussed two interesting questions addressed in the Williamson model, which could not be asked in much simpler words: the first is the importance of the rate of factor migration, interregionally or intersectorally, as a determinant of growth rates. The second is the set of questions about regional patterns of trade, investment, and specialization in the absence of transportation improvement.

However, in most of Williamson's book—and, one would expect, in most cases where such models are used in the future—modeling will be directed towards an established debate rather than towards defining new debates. When so used, the models will often demonstrate that the sources of growth accounting or the partial equilibrium social savings model—or whatever simple model we started with—was indeed sufficient. Moreover, when the complicated model does reverse the results of the simpler model, a listing of the equations of the model and the results of the computer run will not in and of itself provide a convincing argument; someone on the other side of the debate, confronted with results contradicting his or her prior beliefs can just as well conclude that it is some error within the black box which is yielding these off-the-wall results. Unusual results are insufficient unless they themselves can be explained—which again means cutting through the complicated model to find a simple submodel yielding the same results.

Thus, paradoxical as it may seem, a complicated model may sometimes provide the shortest route to finding simple explanations of complex historical phenomena. It is in this respect that I feel Williamson's model makes its major immediate contribution for the two topics we have examined. It is well known that in the simplest growth models, long-run and short-run rates of capital stock are dependent on different sorts of factors. It is equally clear that increasing the cost of capital goods should reduce investment. With hindsight, it is obvious that the former factor could be important in explaining the slowdown in productivity growth of the late 1800s and the latter could be a factor in the social savings from transportation. What was not so obvious beforehand is that these two factors out of the hundreds of also seemingly unrelated possibilities were the ones with sufficient clout to require our attention. But the computer's attention is not so limited; it can obligingly point out to us the ''obviously'' important factors we may otherwise fail to notice.

APPENDIX A

In this appendix submodels are used to examine the importance of the extra interrelationships Williamson cites as distinguishing the late nineteenth-century model from a Denison sources-of-growth framework. The goal is to estimate the likely importance of these interrelationships without having to run the counterfactual simulation. These estimates are then compared with the results of the counterfactual simulations. The agreement is close, demonstrating that this technique can be useful as a first pass in determining which particular modifications are likely to be important to examine in a sensitivity analysis.

Williamson lists several arguments as to why the exogenous change in growth rate of land will change other factors that the simpler theory holds constant. The first effect cited is an induced growth in the capital stock. The greater the stock of land, the greater the level of national income and thus the greater national investment. Starting with a given level of capital stock, we would observe a short-term increase in the growth rate of the capital stock.

To estimate the likely magnitude of the effect note that under the more rapid counterfactual growth rate of 4 percent, the land stock is 17 percent larger than the initial simulation after 10 years and 52 percent larger after 30 years. Call this increase $\Delta R/R$.

In any year excess income in the counterfactual is approximately equal to the difference in the land stock times the marginal product of land. Thus investment increases by sd $\Delta R/P$, where s is the savings rate (never assumed greater than 20 percent in the model); P is the relative price of western machinery (averaging about 1.15) and d is the marginal product of land. For a given capital stock this implies

$$\Delta K^* = \frac{sd\Delta R}{PK} = \frac{s\alpha_R}{P}\frac{\Delta R/R}{K/Y} < .01\frac{\Delta R/R}{K/Y}$$

(remembering that α_R never rises above .06)—an amount which is second-order small within our 40-year time frame.

Of course, this induced increase in K causes further increases in Y (ΔY is approximately $d\Delta R + r\Delta K$) but with changes in k of second order, these second round effects on ΔY are even more minor and can be safely ignored. In the early years K/Y is about two, in the later years it is about three. Thus by using information from the original run only, we can estimate that the induced effect on capital stock growth rate is less than a tenth of a percentage point for the first period; less than two-tenths for the second. And when we run the counterfactual model we find the change in the growth rate of the capital stock are indeed insignificant—0.03 of a percentage point for the early period and 0.10 of a percentage point for the latter. By our original sources of growth argument the effects of these changes in the capital stock growth on the per capita growth rate can indeed be safely ignored.

The second effect that Williamson postulates is an induced variation in the growth of the labor force. The sole channel for this effect in the Williamson model, however, is variation in natural rates of labor force growth in various parts of the country. These differences are small; migration in response to the wage differentials is slow; and the wage differentials themselves are small. Thus this induced effect on labor growth should be even tinier than the induced effect on capital growth. And in the simulations, the counterfactual growth rate for the total labor force are indistinguishable from the original rates.

The other two postulated effects operate through induced changes in shares of output. Both total factor productivity and total factor shares are weighted averages across sectors, and in both cases the weights are dependent on output shares. Indeed, Williamson argues that rather sharp observed sectoral productivity declines over the period were offset by increased importance of the higher-productivity-growth sector.[31]

However, in any particular counterfactual, the importance of this effect depends on the magnitude of the anticipated shift. If V_{AW} represents the share of agricultural goods (Q_{AW}) in GNP, then, using the approximation $\Delta Q \sim \Delta R \cdot d$,

$$\frac{\Delta Vaw}{Vaw} = \frac{\Delta Qaw}{Qaw} - \frac{\Delta Y}{Y} = \frac{[Rd}{Qaw} - \frac{Rd]}{Y} \frac{\Delta R}{R}$$

In model with Cobb-Douglas production, the first term within the brackets is a constant—here it equals 10 percent. Since agricultural land's share of output is never less than 2 percent, the upper bound on the percentage change in share of agriculture is 1.4 percent for the first period; 4.2 percent for the second. In the computer simulation, the second period has a 4.0 percent increase; and for the first, the shares are indistinguishable.

There are two effects to be considered from an increase in the share of agricultural production in the counterfactual.

First, it should change the share of capital in the initial sources-of-growth equation: Capital receives a higher share of output from manufacturing than from agriculture; therefore, an increase in the importance of agriculture decreases capital's share in the total economy. But capital's share will change by only slightly more than a percentage point—and the induced effect on total growth rates will be negligible.

Second, since productivity growth in agriculture is lower, we would expect a lowering of average rate of technological progress by 5 percent times the difference in the rates in the two sectors, or less than one one-hundredth of a percentage point. And indeed the residuals in the first period are indistinguishable to the hundredth of a percentage point. For the second period, this estimate is off by a factor of 10—but the differences in the residual are below the level of significance—i.e., less than one-tenth of a percent.

The reason for this discrepancy is the final extra interrelationship included in the Williamson model, the effect on TFPG of the speed of moving factors from low to high productivity sectors mentioned in the text (pp. 193-194).

APPENDIX B

This appendix demonstrates the testing of a putative explanation of the working of a complicated model. In this case, the explanation is one given by Williamson for the behavior of the growth rate of capital stock in the model, in particular that the decline can be understood in terms of Eq. (3) of the text. If this is true, then altering one of another factor of the full model should produce the same results as altering the factor in this equation. Thus a comparison of the two constitutes a test of the adequacy of the submodel as an explanation of this particular aspect of the full model.

The first test we make is to suppose that the initial capital stock had been increased by 25 percent. To estimate the magnitude of the impact of this alteration, take proportional differences in Eq. (3) of the text:

$$\Delta K^*/K^* = \frac{K^* + \delta}{K^*} \left(\frac{\Delta Y}{Y} - \frac{\Delta K)}{K} \right) = \frac{K^* + \delta}{K^*} \left(\frac{r\Delta K}{Y} - \frac{\Delta K)}{K} \right)$$

$$= \frac{K^* + \delta}{K^*} (\alpha_K - 1) \frac{\Delta K}{K} = \frac{.06 + .03}{.06} (-.68) \times .25 = -.25$$

From 1870 to 1871, the capital stock in the original model grows by 5.53 percent; in the counterfactual it grows by 4.32 percent—a fall of 22 percent, comparing favorably with the above estimated fall of one-fourth. Other results are indicated in Table B1.

Over time, of course, the original 25 percent advantage in the counterfactual capital stock will not last because of diminishing returns. Rather, the model would be expected to converge to the original growth path. For the first period as a whole—that is, for a period centering on 1881, about a decade into the run—the fall is 13 percent. For the second period—that is about 3 decades after the simulation begins—the fall is only 6 percent.

In sum, increasing the initial capital stock by 25 percent significantly retards the slowdown in capital growth rates between period one and period two.

The second counterfactual we examine assumes savings rate at the pre–Civil War level, 8 percentage points lower than observed levels. We would expect that

Table B1. A Comparison of Capital Stock and
Per Capita Income Growth Rates

	Original Simulation	1870 Capital Stock Increased 25%	Savings rate lowered by 8 percentage points
Capital Stock 1870–1871	5.53	4.32	1.60
Capital Stock Period I (1870/78–1884/93)	5.90	5.12	3.16
Period II (1884/93–1899/1908)	4.58	4.29	3.71
Per Capita Income Period I in 1891 prices	2.39	2.20	1.54
Period II in 1896 prices	2.14	2.05	1.59

this cut into the savings rate by 44 percent would result in a decline of the gross capital stock by about three-halves of this amount[32] or 66 percent. Across the computer simulations it falls 71 percent in the first year.

Again this is a short-run effect. By the last decade of the computer simulation, the difference between factual and counterfactual growth rates of the capital stock has been reduced to less than 0.5 percentage points and continues to fall. Indeed, in this counterfactual, rate of growth of capital is *higher*—over the second period than over the first period, and the increase is sufficient to "eliminate" the Great Depression (see Table B1).

Thus, our experiments tend to confirm Williamson's explanation of the decline in capital stock growth rates in his model stemming from a distinction between long-run "natural" rates of growth and a short-run higher rate of growth caused by special conditions in the post–Civil War United States.

Although the one-line equation accurately predicts the changes in capital stock growth rates one year in advance, it does not predict the change 10 or 30 years into the simulation. The steady state equation in the text is also not a good predictor of period two growth rates in the simulations. Thus the pencil-and-paper models examined so far do not explain long-run growth rates in the Williamson model.

APPENDIX C

In this appendix we will use techniques similar to those in the preceding appendices in order to make a preliminary estimate of the potential error involved in assuming that there were not economies of scale in the transportation sector.[33] Suppose the sector exhibited 20 percent economies of scale—a figure well above any estimates. How would his affect the social savings estimate?

Consider the following graphical depiction of the transportation market:

Figure C1.

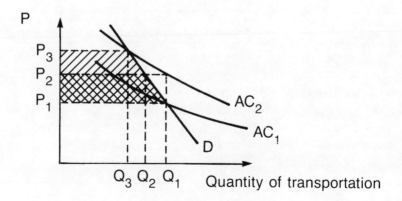

The counterfactual experiment described in the text may be regarded as an increase in the price of transportation by a factor γ, for all levels of transportation output. $P_2 = \gamma P_1$; and Q_2 is the equilibrium quantity of transportation services in this counterfactual experiment. But this experiment neglects the possibility of scale economies. Suppose the industry is subject to economies of scale. Let AC_1 represent the original average cost curve for the industry, and AC_2 those costs increased by γ at every scale of production. γ is thus the ratio of old to new price of transportation only if the quantity of transportation services demanded remains unaffected. We expect that the increased cost decreases transportation demand, further increasing the average observed cost of transportation. (P_3, Q_3) represents the equilibrium in the properly formulated counterfactual experiment. Support that demand function for transportation can be represented as $eP^{-\varepsilon}$, where ε is the elasticity of transportation demand. Then our incorrect estimate of the social savings is $\int_{P_1}^{P} 2\, eP^{-\varepsilon}\, dP/GNP$, represented by the cross-hatched area; and the "true" social savings is $\int_{P_1}^{P} 3\, eP^{-\varepsilon}\, dP/GNP$, represented by the entire shaded area. Thus the percentage error in the social savings estimate is

$$E = \frac{P_3^{-\varepsilon+1} - P_2^{-\varepsilon+1}}{P_2^{-\varepsilon+1} - P_1^{-\varepsilon+1}} = \frac{(P_3/P_1)^{-\varepsilon+1} - Y^{-\varepsilon+1}}{Y^{-\varepsilon+1} - 1}$$

Let the initial cost curve be $AC^1 = cQ^{1/\eta-1}$ where η is the scale factor. Thus $AC_2 = \gamma cQ^{1/\eta - 1}$. By hypothesis

$$P_3 = eQ_3^{-1-\varepsilon} = \gamma cQ_3^{1/\eta - 1}$$

$$P_1 = eQ_1^{-1-\varepsilon} = cQ_1^{1/\eta - 1}$$

These equations can be solved for P_3/P_1 in terms of γ, ε, and η. Tedious algebra yields:

$$P_3/P_1 = \gamma^{\kappa}$$

where $\kappa = \eta/(\eta + \varepsilon - \eta\varepsilon)$. Let $\gamma = 1.248$ and $\varepsilon = .769$ (both calculated from simulation runs). If we assume 20 percent economies of scale, ($\eta = 1.2$) then $E = 15$ percent—that is, there is a 15 percent understatement of social savings. If 10 percent economies of scale are assumed $E = 7.7$ percent.

ACKNOWLEDGMENTS

I am grateful to Robert Fogel, Stanley Engerman, Jeffrey Williamson, David Galenson and participants in the economic history workshops at Harvard University and the University of Chicago.

NOTES

1.   Among the reviews that have appeared are those by S. Engerman (*Economic History Review* [February 1976]: 191–93); Lance Davis (*History and Theory*, [1976] vol. 3, pp. 322–28); and Gavin Wright (*Journal of Politcal Economy*, [February 1976] pp. 201–205). A recent analysis of the question is by John James (*Exploration in Economic History*, 21, No. 3 [July 1984] 231–53).

2.   And, for the Williamson model, the difficulty should have be even less in the future, since the program used here to replicate the model is available from the author on request at the cost of mailing.

3.   In fact, there is a very close relationship between the two processes. We call an adjustment of the model a counterfactual experiment when we change an interesting assumption, which we believe to have been true, into another interesting assumption, which we believe not to have been true. The experiment is particularly successful when it reverses (others') previously held conclusions. We call an adjustment of the model a sensitivity analysis when we change a not-particularly-interesting assumption, to which we don't feel particularly committed, for another which we find no more attractive. The experiment is successful when it fails to reverse (our own) just established conclusions.

4.   The original figures are from Williamson, Late Nineteenth Century American Development (1974) Cambridge University Press. Appendix B.

5.   Wiliamson (pp. 45–50). It should be noted that most of these discrepancies are typos occurring in publication, not in the original running of the Williamson models.

6.   However, the same difficulty occasionally occurs with interregional trade: when we raise transportation cost in some of the counterfactual simulations in Section III, trade occasionally flows backwards (that is, the Midwest imports grain). When this happens we simply have to stop running the model; the correct alteration would have to be western relative prices adjust until there is no trade between the regions.

7.   Robert E. Gallman. "Gross National Product in the United States, 1834–1909," In *Output, Employment and Productivity in the United States after 1800* New York: Columbia University Press 1966 (National Bureau of Economic Research Studies in Income and Wealth, No. 30, p. 26); S. Lebergott, *Manpower in Economic Growth; the United States Record Since 1800*, New York: McGraw-Hill 1964 (Table A.1, p. 510).

8.   Williamson, (p. 95).

9.   Since we are unable to calculate 1869 figures, our averages start from an 1870–1879 base.

10.   Although we will continue to report our estimated growth rates to two decimal places, it must be emphasized that rounding errors (apart from index number problems) mean that significance should only be attributed to the first position after the decimal point.

11.   That Williamson finds the counterfactual experiment to make .2 percentage points difference in the second period is due to his use of nominal rather than real GNP and his inclusion in GNP of transportation income achieved without a resource cost- again see Section III.

12.   The discrepancy is thus in fact a kind of "aggregation bias" (see, for example, H. A. J. Green. *Aggregation in Economic Analysis*, chap. 12 Princeton NJ: Princeton University Press 1964); it disappears when we deal with factor stocks in different sectors as distinct, each with its own return and growth rate.

13.   Williamson also examines the results of a counterfactual experiment in which the sectoral decline in productivity growth does not occur. In the original industrial productivity growth falls by 0.6 percent: agricultural by 0.3 percent. Our sources of growth estimate is that if neither fell and if agriculture's share remained constant at about .45 of output (which is its mid-period value) the fall in growth rate would be reduced by the same amount as the reduction in the fall in total factor productivity growth—slightly less than one-half of a percentage point. In Williamson's simulation, however, the decline is less than one- one-hundredth of a percentage point. He attributes this lack of change to the fact that agriculture's share moves—but the change in share is likely to be second order as before. Whether this is in fact the correct explanation, or whether this difference is due to induced

changes in the rate of factor migration or to WIlliamson's calculation of GNP in this section in current rather than constant prices, or to some other explanation still, would be worth examining through the same techniques as above.

14. For a more detailed discussion see Edwin Bermeister and A. Rodney Dobell, *Mathematical Theories of Economic Growth* (New York: The Macmillan Company, 1970), especially chapter 3.

15. The equation holds, for example, if growth rates of land and labor are constant and all sectors have identical Cobb-Douglas production technologies.

16. Robert W. Fogel, *Railroads and American Economic Growth: Essays in Econometric History*, (Baltimore, 1964), John Hopkins University Press.

17. Although this figure is close to Kuznets' estimate of 18 percent for the 1870s (Simon Kuznets, *Modern Economic Growth*, cited in Williamson, p. 52), Williamson's figure does not include intraregional transportation costs.

18. Cf. Williamson, chapter 9, Tables 9.1, 9.2, and 9.3. Growth rates are computed between averages for 1870–1878 and 1884–1893. Shares of agricultural production in GNP are computed in current prices and transportation markups. This procedure is in contrast with (and, I believe, preferable to) Williamson's in Table 9.3, where GNP in the original simulation is valued in the original current prices, and GNP in the counterfactual simulation is valued in counterfactual prices.

19. Williamson (pp. 185–86). The effects of assuming economies of scale in the transportation sector are examined in Appendix C.

20. Williamson (p. 31).

21. Otherwise put, if we wanted to calculate as a percentage of GNP the social costs of increases in the current price of oil, we could argue for weighting plastics into the calculation at either pre- or post-increase price; but it would be difficult to justify using 1960 relative prices for the estimation. This argument explains why, of the various weightings, it is the current price weightings that should be trusted. It does not explain why the discrepancy between weightings is so large. The divergence is due to the enormous difference between eastern relative prices in the simulation. The price of agricultural goods relative to industrial goods is one-third higher in the East in 1870 than in 1890.

22. The slightly different estimates of the dynamic effect are due to the use of actual and counterfactual estimate, respectively, of the marginal productivity of agricultural capital. In estimating the bounds social savings is calculated as a percentage of GNP measured in the current year prices of the original simulation (weighting II). Using current year prices with higher transportation costs (weighting III) would make all estimates approximately .4 percentage points higher.

23. Indeed, the only reason for the dynamic effect is the investment accelerator mentioned in Section I .

24. From 1870–1875 to 1855–1890, Williamson's figure for the agricultural transportation markup (p. 260) declines by 30 percent. In these two decades, the average absolute change year-to-year for this markup is 18 percent.

25. For the differential to be solely the result of transport price, there must be arbitrageurs at each end of the transportation system always ready to supply agricultural goods from their own stocks whenever the price differential is exceeded. Even between New York City and Chicago, each a communication center, each well stocked with both brokers and grains, the correspondence of price differential to transportation is imperfect. The correspondence works well on average, but divergences are not uncommon due to "special circumstances" (e. g., a fire destroying stocks). See Paul W. MacAvoy, *The Economic Effects of Regulation* (Cambridge, Mass.: MIT press, 1965). Such special circumstances should be even more important in explaining any given difference between New York and Iowa or Wisconsin prices.

26. Williamson (p. 260). These markups were calculated as the difference in New York wheat spot prices and those in N.V. Strand, "Prices of Farm Products In Iowa, 1851–1940" (Research Bulletin No. 383, Iowa Agricultural Experiment Station) or W. P. Mortenson, H. H. Erdman and A. H. Drazler, "Wisconsin Farm Prices, 1841–1933," (Research Bulletin No. 119, University of Wisconsin Agricultural Experiment Station, 1933).

27.   International trade models often show gains from trade to be second-order effects and the pattern of trade to be a first-order effect.

28.   The reasonableness of this assumption depends on whether we see the capital stock of the late 1880s as characterized by fixed investment or circulating capital.

29.   For completeness, we have also tried making labor mobile. In doing so, we increase the social savings calculations slightly. The explanation for this perverse effect seems to be the following: *ceteris paribus*, having one factor mobile causes greater divergences in the returns to the other factor, causing greater flows of investment (in this case from industry to agriculture). However, by the end of the period, relative returns to the sectors have reversed—thus with hindsight we see the economy would have been better off if the capital flow had never occurred. Again this explanation must be considered tentative until it too is made into a simple model and tested. (An indirect test would be to see if the results can be reversed in a model with both capital and labor mobile.) In any event, the effects on social savings are small:

Table 15.   Social Savings in A Model with Perfectly Mobile Western Labor

	Weighting I	Weighting II	Weighting III
1871	0.3	0.2	0.2
1880	3.6	2.9	2.9
1890	6.4	3.7	3.8

30.   For a summary see Robert W. Fogel, "Notes on the Social Savings Controversy," *Journal of Economic History*, 39 (March 1979).

31.   Williamson (p. 114).

32.   By the same argument as before:

$$\frac{\Delta K^*}{K^*} = \frac{K^* + \delta}{K^*} \quad \frac{\Delta s}{s}$$

33.   The importance of this issue is emphasized in Paul A. David, *Technical Choice, Innovation, and Economic Growth* (Cambridge University Press, 1975, chap. 6, pp. 301–307).

JOHN BEVERLEY ROBINSON
AND THE COMMERCIAL EMPIRE
OF THE ST. LAWRENCE

Peter J. George and Philip J. Sworden

ABSTRACT

As the staple economy of Upper Canada developed in the first half of the nineteenth century, the courts were called upon to decide cases in vital economic areas such as contracts, property, corporations, and transportation development. This paper focuses on the career and decisions of Sir John Beverley Robinson, a major public figure in Upper Canada and Chief Justice of the Court of Queen's Bench, 1829–1862. Robinson's decisions helped to define a legal framework within which Canadian businessmen became more aware of the law and its implications for the conduct of business.

Research in Economic History, Volume 11, pages 217–242.
Copyright © 1988 by JAI Press Inc.
All rights of reproduction in any form reserved.
ISBN: 0-89232-677-8

I.

The chain of lakes and rivers, from Lake Superior downwards, comprises the noblest inland channel of fresh waters on the globe; and it is, I think, no extravagant pretension to challenge for the St. Lawrence the pre-eminence over every other river in the world. . . . it pursues its majestic course through fertile lands. . . which are distinguished by the language, the laws, the freedom, and the enterprize of the British race. John Beverley Robinson (1840)

The relationship between the law and economic development has developed rapidly as a field of historical study in the United States, where discussion has centered on whether the legal system was an active or passive agent in the process of economic growth. Willard J. Hurst, for example, has assigned primary significance to underlying American economic values and the legislative process in shaping the law and the legal system (Hurst, 1982). Morton J. Horwitz has instead emphasized the emerging concept of "instrumentalism" whereby, especially in the first half of the nineteenth century, legal institutions were remade through an "alliance" of business and judicial interests to expedite America's economic transformation (Horwitz, 1977; Flaherty, 1981).

For Canada, the debate is barely joined; in particular, the relevance of "instrumentalism" is much less clear. Very little Canadian historical work has been done on the relationship between the law and the economy, except for a series of articles by R. C. B. Risk on Canada West, 1841–1867, in which he examines the early development of the business corporation, the law of markets, including contracts and commercial paper, property law, and the courts' interpretation of economic aspects of the common law (Risk, 1973, 1976, 1977a,b).[1] But, the study of law is only part of the picture; the other major institution influencing the colonial economy was the legislature and its statutes. Both legislative acts and, to a lesser extent, judicial interpretation of the common law reflected public attitudes towards economic activity. By 1860, according to Risk, there was a widely held consensus in Canada West that economic progress, especially resource exploitation, was a public "good" and was to be achieved primarily by private initiative supported where possible by government. To that end, Risk concludes, the Canadian legislature aggressively promoted economic growth, but the Canadian courts, based in the English common law, were reluctant to change the law to facilitate economic development, unlike courts in the United States (Risk, 1977b, pp. 420–25).

In examining these issues, we focus on the judicial career and decisions of Sir John Beverley Robinson who was a major public figure in Upper Canada from 1812–1863. At the beginning of his career, Upper Canada was a newly developing territory. It had no tribunals or administrative boards, few large corporations, and no routine standards with respect to contracts and other legal forms. Robinson, as Chief Justice of the Court of Queen's Bench from 1829–1862, enjoyed a remarkable degree of influence over the economy and society through his legal decisions. He dominated the court and wrote the majority of its decisions. Robinson was a Loyalist, with strong views on the type of society he wished to see implanted in Upper Canada. He believed that commercial prosperity was the cornerstone of social progress, and a crucial determinant of Canada's happy existence within the British Empire. Indeed, in an aspect little recognized by Creighton and others, Robinson was in fact a crucial (yet almost unattributed) factor in the success of the St. Lawrence commercial system (Creighton, 1956; Tucker, 1964; Tulchinsky, 1977).

II.

Robinson remains one of the least known of Canada's great judges. Born in 1791, Robinson's career as a lawyer, politician, Chief Justice and elder statesman spanned almost the entire history of Upper Canada until its disappearance under Confederation in 1867. Although he was one of Upper Canada's leading figures, his judicial decisions and political writings have been little studied (Brode, 1984; Robinson, 1904; Read, 1888; Jarvis, 1967; Saunders, 1976; Cook, 1977).

Robinson's career was remarkable. He was left fatherless at the age of seven. He quickly rose to become attorney-general of Upper Canada in 1812, while only 21. At 38, he was appointed Chief Justice of the Court of King's (later Queen's) Bench for Upper Canada, the youngest Chief Justice then ever to sit in a British court of law. Why did Robinson rise so quickly in the normally slow-moving judicial hierarchy? Does an examination of the Upper Canadian society that produced him, and necessarily affected his decisions regarding the economy, shed any light on his judicial mien?

Robinson was born of a United Empire Loyalist father, who had fought for maintaining the British tie and was involved in Simcoe's first term as lieutenant-governor of Upper Canada. When Robinson's father died in 1798 at York, his father's Loyalist comrades delivered him to John Strachan, brought over from Britain to teach the colony's Loyalist sons. Through friendship with Strachan (the two took an immediate liking to each other), Robinson's good fortune continued. He studied law with Solicitor-General Boulton, and when the War of 1812 interrupted his studies, served gallantly under Brock. His legal training, his baptism under fire, his connections with Strachan, and his obvious abilities were enough to secure Robinson's appointment as acting attorney-general, although he had not yet been called to the bar. Later in the decade, he took leave of absence to continue his studies in England.

Once attorney-general, Robinson came inevitably to politics, and in 1821 he was elected a member of the Legislative Assembly for York where he served until 1829. During the 1820s, Robinson acted as government leader in the Assembly, drafting much of the legislation and speaking publicly on important issues as chief spokesman for a coalition of like-minded conservatives known collectively as the Family Compact.[2] In 1829, Robinson resigned his seat in the

Assembly to become Chief Justice of the Court of King's Bench. As Chief Justice from 1829–1862, he presided over the court with jurisdiction over the fastest growing colony in British North America and, although he rendered decisions on many different subjects, many of his judicial decisions bore directly on the Upper Canadian economy. Moreover, by virtue of his office, he was also Speaker of the Assembly and Chairman of the Governor's Executive Council, and continued to draft much of the government's legislation. But his political influence waned as Reform elements strengthened, and after the Act of Union in 1840 he was relegated to the background of public affairs. As a Loyalist, a prominent member of the Family Compact, and Chief Justice, Robinson was determined to maintain a politically and economically independent British-based society on the borders of America.[3]

During his government leadership in the 1820s, Robinson was active in the promotion of public works construction in Canada and of immigration from Great Britain. He drafted a report on internal navigation which recommended road and highway construction, and was himself an investor in the Welland Canal project. He was quick to recognize the commercial importance of the railroad and the telegraph. He helped to develop British policy favoring assisted immigration while he was in England pursuing the Canada Trade bill in 1822, and again in 1825, for only through British immigration could American influences in Canada be dampened. He was an early advocate of British North American federation as a viable device for submerging the French-Canadians, whom he regarded as pro-agrarian, anti-commercial conservatives opposed to English-Canadian, pro-development forces. Later, he would oppose the Union of 1840 on the same grounds.

Robinson's letters and published pamphlets clearly reflect the primacy of his concerns for the place of the colonies in the imperial economic system and his views on the interdependence of colonial economic, political, and social affairs. The most significant surviving documents are his letters to Lord Bathurst in 1824, his letters to the Marquis of Normanby in 1839, and his tract entitled *Canada and the Canada Bill*, addressed to Lord John Russell and published in England in 1840. In all of these writings, Robinson expressed concern at the threat to Canada posed by the United States and offered proposals for enhancing Canada's future security. Essential to social and economic progress in Canada was the provision of a stable environment for British enterprise, capital, and emigration. After all, to Robinson, "Upper Canada . . . [was] indeed a magnificent territory, as regards its climate, its soil, timber, and other productions . . .," and large enough to support a substantial population (Robinson, 1840, p. 21). But, he argued, since independence was undesirable and, worse still, impractical in the face of superior American power, Upper Canada would be viable only with British support.

Owing to a serious illness in 1838, Robinson took leave of absence and travelled to England. It was during this stay in England that he wrote *Canada and the Canada Bill*, and corresponded with Normanby. Robinson was strongly opposed to the union of Upper and Lower Canada. In his view, Union would lead to political conflict and economic chaos. He preferred instead to extend the boundaries of Upper Canada to include the island of Montreal, giving Upper Canada a seaport and a source of revenues with which to improve the St. Lawrence system (Robinson, 1839, f. 32; 1840, p. 136). Only a political settlement which would promote the rapid return of commercial prosperity would ensure a British future for Upper Canada.

Robinson was unsuccessful in his efforts to reverse the British government's decision to unify Upper and Lower Canada in 1840. After Union, his active involvement in political affairs ceased, and he concentrated thereafter on his legal duties as Chief Justice.

III.

In mid-nineteenth century Upper Canada, many judges were members of powerful interest groups. Many were Loyalists, had been educated in Upper Canada, and practiced law there. More than half had been active in politics (Risk, 1977b, p. 407). As part of the local elite with strong ties in commercial as well as political and social circles, they were steeped in knowledge about the workings of the economy, and their decisions reflected their familiarity with commercial transactions and organizations, particularly in the grain trade and land dealings (Risk, 1977b, pp. 407–408). An examination of Robinson's judicial decisions confirms his awareness of commercial affairs and, even more, in some cases reveals a conscious interest in facilitating the spread of the market economy. We examine, in turn, a number of Robinson's judgments in the areas of contract law, corporation law, and property law, and then look more closely at decisions affecting transportation development.

A.   Contract Law

The judicial interpretation of contract law was very important to the effective conduct of business in a staple economy, where financing and shipping of locally produced commodities to international markets and distribution of imported manufactures were common activities. The English law of contracts was transferred faithfully to Upper Canada. At the same time as Canadian judges were wrestling with the application of British jurisprudence to Canadian circumstances, in the United States the emergence of a national commodities market in the nineteenth century was leading to a shift in the function of contracts from simply transfer of title to a specific item to the certainty of expected returns (Horwitz, 1974, p. 918).

There were many instances in which Robinson was instrumental in making contract law more effective in Upper Canada, thereby adding to the confidence of merchants that the result for which they had contracted would be achieved and lowering risk and information costs. Robinson was concerned above all to ensure that businessmen making contracts in Upper Canada were familiar with the principles of contract law. Several different aspects of contracting were affected.

(i) Parol evidence. One issue affecting certainty as a goal for contract law was parol evidence to vary the terms of a contract. Many business transactions were still based on verbal agreements, but the use of written contracts was encouraged by the court's rulings on verbal alterations of contracts. In *Bradbury v. Oliver*, Robinson held that "There is no principle of law more clearly established than the one which prohibits the terms of a written instrument adopted by the contracting parties from being changed or qualified by parol testimony where no fraud exists" (1848, 5 Q.B.[O.S.], p. 704). The court was worried about the implications of allowing verbal evidence for perjury, and the danger that the *Statute of Frauds* would be undermined. The rare exception was parol evidence to explain ambiguous terms and enforcement of independent agreements. But the position of Robinson's court was expressed clearly in *The Bank of Upper Canada v. Boulton*:

> I do not refer to any authority, for the general principle that the terms of a written contract are not to be varied or controlled by parol testimony, for there is no point that stands more clear or is sustained by more numerous decisions . . . (1850, 7 Q.B., p. 244).

Again, in *McQueen v. McQueen* (1852, 9 Q.B., p. 538), Robinson noted "the wisdom of the rule which does not allow the terms of a written instrument to be contradicted by parol evidence of something else being intended than was expressed."[4] Robinson simply believed the rule too venerable and useful to be tampered with. While this could be construed as a narrow reliance on precedent, the result was to create greater certainty in the use of contracts by enabling businessmen to rely on the terms of written contracts in an era when commodity shipments passed through many hands over long distances under the limitations imposed by poor communications systems.

(ii) Labelling and Grading. The significance of Robinson's decisions regarding a miller's responsibility for accurate labelling of his flour for market must be seen in the context of the international grain and flour trades. Several cases deserve mention. In *Bunnel v. Whitlaw*, a miller in Paris sold his flour to a flour dealer in Brantford, the dealer in turn selling it to a buyer in the United States, all the while guaranteeing the flour to be "Victoria Extra" in quality. On inspection in Buffalo, the flour was found to be low grade, superfine flour and not "extra" superfine. The Brantford dealer was required to compensate the buyer, and claimed damages against the miller in Paris. The court upheld the dealer:[5]

It is true, I have no doubt, as one of the affidavits states, that when parcels of flour are passed from one to another among merchants, the use of such words as descriptive of the article sold does not make the vendor liable as upon a warranty. The vendor is understood to sell the lot according to the designation by which he has received it; and where no description is used he is not considered liable for any deficiency in quality, unless indeed he has given an undertaking that it shall pass inspection as of the quality mentioned in the brand, or shall in truth be of that quality. But it is different in the case of a person buying from one who manufactures the article, because the quality of the article, and the use of the brand, are under his control (1856, 14 Q.B., p. 248).

Similarly, in *Bain v. Gooderham*, a miller near Toronto sold flour to be shipped down the St. Lawrence to Montreal. He guaranteed it to be "No. 1 Superfine," normally understood in the trade to be sweet flour. However, the flour was "No. 1 Superfine" in grade but sour, and in Robinson's opinion, the guarantee of a particular grade included an obligation that it be sweet. To Robinson, the "common sense of the thing" and its effect on commerce generally was important (1857, 15 Q.B., p. 33). Again, Robinson decided in *Chisholm v. Proudfoot* that a miller who manufactures flour and labels it to be of a particular quality has given a warranty, and he stated the pleadings and evidence in great detail "because the questions presented in such cases are so important to persons engaged in this branch of trade that the ground on which we decide them ought to be clearly understood" (1857, 15 Q.B. p. 210). The impact of these decisions was to clarify the obligations of businessmen to represent accurately the quality of their products, hence reducing uncertainties and information costs to their customers.

(iii) Reliance on contemporary business practice. Robinson was aware of the broader workings of the St. Lawrence trading network and often took judicial notice of business practices to support his judgments. Thus in *Tumblay v. Meyers*, for example, a case of privity of contract respecting timber, Robinson reported that:

We know, for it has been frequently proved before us in such cases, that the persons who get out timber in this country usually go down with it to market, and that their claim to be paid out of the proceeds of the timber when sold is understood to be recognized in that description of business. It is therefore an ordinary course, when the timber is transferred in this country, that the purchaser holds himself answerable for the wages due to the men who have got it out (1858, 16 Q.B., pp. 145–46).

Other cases involving the grain trade too show Robinson taking cognizance of the "general usage of trade." For example, in *Brown and McDonell v. Browne* (1852, 9 Q.B., p. 312), he said, "When we know what the general usage of trade is in regard to any branch of business, we are to look on the parties as intending to contract with reference to it, unless we have proof that they meant to deviate from it" (p. 314).[6] This partly reflects Robinson's genuine interest in and familiarity with commerce; he owned a large estate in the southern part of

Toronto Township where his tenants were wheat growers, and members of his immediate family had large holdings (Brode, 1984, pp. 240–41; Gagan, 1981, pp. 26–29). The evolution of customary practices in a particular trade represents in part an attempt by the trade to regulate itself. For Upper Canada, judicial support for the observance of customary expectations among trading parties undoubtedly contributed to the smooth functioning of the staple economy.

(iv) Unanticipated consequences.   Yet another aspect of trade along the St. Lawrence often calling for judicial solutions was the effect of unexpected events arising after a contract was made. Two illustrative cases involving transport and shipment of wheat and grain, heard by Robinson in the mid–1850s, were *Wilmot v. Wadsworth* and *Gooderham v. Marlatt.*

Wilmot v. Wadsworth was a case involving a damaged shipment of flour. Wilmot purchased 1,100 bushels of flour from Wadsworth. The shipment was soaked by rain, so that when Wilmot received it, it was in damaged instead of good condition. Wilmot sued for damages successfully because, as Robinson said,

> It was the duty of the defendants, who had engaged to deliver the flour on board in good condition at their own charge, to take care that it was either not taken from the warehouse sooner than was necessary, or that it should be protected against injury from the weather on its way (1853, 10 Q.B. pp. 594, 599).

The case of *Gooderham v. Marlatt* involved a lost shipment. Gooderham advanced money to Marlatt who, in turn, was to ship wheat to Gooderham in Oswego. The wheat was lost in passage, and Marlatt was required by Robinson to refund the sum advanced to him, for Robinson held that the wheat was still his property until delivery of the shipment was made (1856, 14, Q.B., p. 228).

A third case, *Jarvis v. Dalrymple*, is concerned with transportation. Initially, subcontractors for the Great Western Railway agreed to be paid according to the estimate of the railway company's engineer, but they subsequently refused to live up to this clause in their contract because of a dispute over unexpected construction difficulties. They were held liable, Robinson concluding that "it is of consequence that parties should be held to the terms of their contract, or no one would be able to proceed with confidence in executing the works which are now in progress, and which are so important to the community" (1854, 11 Q.B., p. 395).[7]

(v) Breach of contract.   A last group of cases involve damages for default of contract. *Hadley v. Baxendale*, decided in England in 1854, provided the general rule, applicable in Canada as well, that not all losses would be compensated, but only those reasonably expected to arise from breach of contract. Robinson was involved in deciding on the interpretation of this precedent in several Canadian cases involving the delivery of messages by telegraph. *Stevenson v. The Montreal*

Telegraph Co. was an action against the telegraph company for negligence in not sending a message by telegraph from Hamilton to New York City with sufficient speed, so that Stevenson missed an opportunity to sell his flour at a profit. Robinson concluded that, in his view, the telegraph company could not be responsible for delays beyond their own lines, and consequently that the company was not liable: "These were damages not reasonably to be supposed to have been within the contemplation of the parties in transacting the business in question . . ." (1859, 16 Q.B., p. 538). Possibly as a result of his belief that the telegraph (and the railroad) were vital communications developments of commercial importance, Robinson wanted to protect the usefulness of telegraph companies, and not burden them with costly lawsuits. In *Kinghorne v. The Montreal Telegraph Co.*, another case involving failure to deliver a message, Robinson awarded no damages to the plaintiff, stating that a thirty-cent message, delivered carelessly, could not be permitted to bring negligence actions that might "swallow up the profits [of the Company] for years" (1860, 18 Q.B., p. 68).[8]

These judicial decisions respecting grades, warranties, responsibilities, and damages, met a broad range of needs of the St. Lawrence trading system. Moreover, in delivering his judgments, Robinson was clearly aware of the importance of his decisions to the business community in clarifying the contract law upon which the trading of goods over the vast distances of the St. Lawrence was based.

B. Corporation Law

As was the case in the United States, the early history of the corporation in Upper Canada revolved around the issue of special charters granted by legislatures, which contained strict provisions for guaranteeing the public interest, including carefully defined functions for the enterprise and limited scope for financial license. Many of the early corporations on both sides of the border were conceived as agencies of the state to meet community developmental needs.

The St. Lawrence trading network, with its emphasis on river travel, created an early demand for transportation improvements, and in Upper Canada, the first corporations were related to transportation: canal companies, harbor companies, road companies, telegraph companies, and support companies such as banks. Power to create these corporations rested in the Legislative Assembly, which passed first individual, then after 1850, general statutes of incorporation for transport companies, financial institutions, manufacturing and mining corporations (Risk, 1973, pp. 272–82). Most of the judicial decisions by Robinson and others addressed issues of the legitimate spheres of activity of corporations under their charters.

(i) Legitimacy of the corporation. With corporations becoming so important to the economy, any challenges to their existence would meet with strong

resistance from the government, but also from Robinson. In *Bank of Upper Canada v. Donald Bethune*, Bethune challenged the authority of the Bank to endorse promissory notes, basing his defense on the *Bubble Acts* in Britain. Robinson was adamant in holding that the *Bubble Acts* (6 *Geo*. 1 *ch.* 18, and 14 *Geo*. 11) were not in force in Upper Canada, and that the Bank of Upper Canada, chartered by the colonial government, did not come within the provisions of those Acts:

> The Bubble Acts are leveled at voluntary associations of individuals under false pretenses of public good, presuming, according to their own devices, to draw in unwary persons against dangerous and mischievous projects of persons presuming to act as if they were corporate bodies, pretending to create transferable stock without any legal authority by act of parliament or by charter from the crown; and if there are any other projects of a like nature tending manifestly to the prejudice, grievance, etc. of the public, the statutes are intended likewise to suppress them. Now the President, Directors and Company of the Bank of Upper Canada, if we must assume that there is but one such body, made use of no *false pretenses*—they *presumed* nothing, *pretended* nothing, *contrived* nothing—they *drew in no one*—they did not proceed according to their *own devices*—they did not pretend merely to act *as if they were a body corporate*. They *are* a body corporate, *created* by a *public act*, to which the King has assented (1835, K.B. [O.S.], pp. 173–74, emphases in original).

Robinson had been a director of the Bank of Upper Canada, but he also seems to have believed the Bank of Upper Canada would necessarily play an important part in the economy's progress. This conviction was enhanced by competition from America, especially after the completion of the Erie Canal in 1825; any financial institution that could help develop Upper Canada's economy was to be protected (Vaughan, 1968, p. 186).[9]

As the legislature was empowered to create corporations in Upper Canada, so the task of defining the legal nature and consequences of departing from the specific terms of statutes of incorporation and company charters rested with the courts. Statutes of incorporation usually required a registration document listing important information respecting the corporation. Failure to comply might impair the ability of a corporation to function.[10] To Robinson, the capacity of a corporation to carry on its business was determined by its charter, and any attempt to do something not authorized by the charter was *ultra vires*.

(ii) Geographic limits of the corporation.

In *Bank of Montreal v. D. Bethune*, Bethune pleaded that, as a resident in Upper Canada, he was not required to repay his loan from the Bank of Montreal, which was incorporated to do business only in Lower Canada. Robinson accepted this argument to a degree, holding that corporations existed only by virtue of their charter and that "when they attempt to act beyond and out of their charter, they can, in my opinion, acquire no right or interest by virtue of such act." The Bank of Montreal's charter clearly confined its activities to Lower Canada: "The facts then are, that this Banking Company are incorporated in Lower Canada, under a charter which cannot give them a right to extend their business to this province, further than our laws may allow . . .'' (1836, 4 K.B. [O.S.], pp. 347, 352). However, Robinson noted that the defendant received large sums of the bank's money, and he considered it "contrary to equity and good conscience" that Bethune should be allowed to retain the money borrowed even though he could not legally be compelled to repay the debt.

Genesee Mutual Insurance Company v. Westman was a similar instance; the case was complicated by the fact that the Genesee Mutual Insurance Company was a foreign company. Westman, a British subject resident in Upper Canada, entered into an insurance contract with Genesee Mutual, incorporated in New York State to carry on insurance business in Genesee County. Westman defaulted on his payments, and the issue arose whether Genesee could impose a mortgage on Westman's property. Robinson, regretting that English case law was silent on the ability of a foreign corporation to sue, decided that the insurance company, from the very nature and object of its charter, was incapable of conducting business, and hence suing in Upper Canada (1852, 8 Q.B., pp. 487, 498).[11] Interestingly (and perhaps because it was an *American* company involved), Robinson did not raise issues of "equity" or "good conscience" and make the defendant repay his debts.

(iii) Limitations on corporate functions.   Corporate activities were narrowly circumscribed by the terms of their charters, and judges, Robinson among them, tended to take a dim view of corporate efforts to exceed their licensed activities. In events leading up to *McDonnell v. The Bank of Upper Canada*, the bank seized a ship belonging to McDonnell as security for debt. Robinson noted that the bank's charter prevented it from holding ships or vessels for any purpose whatever, and he concluded that allowing the bank to hold the ship would be "a plain overriding of an act of parliament by a judgement of the court." He continued:

> "Whenever we can see that a motive of public policy must have led to some particular restriction which is imposed in the charter, it is our duty to give effect to the intention of the legislature when plainly expressed, and to hold that the corporation cannot legally apply its corporate powers and capacity in a manner totally and unequivocally forbidden by its charter" (1850, 7 Q.B., pp. 278–79).

Lyman v. The Bank of Upper Canada, decided two years later, was a case in which the directors committed bank funds to a contract with a ship charterer. Robinson again noted that the Bank of Upper Canada was prohibited by statute from holding ships, either in absolute property or as mortgages, and consequently no contract could arise against them as shipowners. Robinson summarized his reasons as follows:

> The Legislature incorporated the Bank with particular powers and privileges necessary for carrying on a certain description of business, quite distinct from the business of shipowners,

and those who deal with them, may know, and are bound at their peril to take notice, what it is that their charter enables them to do; otherwise all the funds which have been contributed by a body of shareholders for one purpose, might be squandered in an application to other purposes to the injury of all embarked in the undertaking; and in the case of a bank which it is intended shall have power to issue bills to circulate as money, the whole public have an interest in their being confined to the business for which they were incorporated; for, in case of their becoming insolvent by engaging in affairs foreign to their charter, thousands are involved in the loss, as being holders of their bills (1852, 8 Q.B., p. 358).

These decisions reflect some of the competing influences on Robinson and require some explanation. Given the importance of shipping in the Upper Canadian economy, restrictions on the ability of banks to mortgage ships might be construed as anti-commercial. Rather, Robinson attributes them to a real concern for the "public interest" because of the sensitive role of banks in the financial underpinnings of the economy, and to a strict constructionist interpretation of the law on corporations which, in these instances, took precedence over his affinity to commerce.

(iv) Authority and use of the corporate seal. In a major case, *Hamilton v. The Niagara Harbour and Dock Co.*, Robinson held that a corporation could only contract under its seal. The case is important in two respects. First, in views similar to those held on the parol evidence rule, Robinson declared that the assent of a corporation to a contract could be determined only by use of the seal; to conclude otherwise "would be to set at nought one of the oldest, clearest, and best established principles in our law" (1842, 6 Q.B.[O.S.], p. 388). Second, faced by counsel's argument that this principle had been eroded in America, Robinson responded by citing *stare decisis*, stating that since "the courts of justice in England have not, on any occasion, departed from the principle in question," he felt himself constrained to hold against counsel's argument. Here is another instance of Robinson inveighing against American law and insisting that Upper Canada follow British law where there was a clear British ruling.

(v) Elections of directors. Cases involving abuses in the election of company directors provide additional instances of Robinson's insistence on British precedent. In *The Queen v. Hespeler*, Robinson decided that a directorship in the Galt and Guelph Railway Company was not an office for which a *quo warranto* would apply, since the remedy was not applicable to the case of a trading corporation. Robinson noted that counsel "refer us to a passage in the very comprehensive American work of *Angell and Ames on Corporations* . . . which shows that in some of the courts in the United States this remedy has been extended to the case of officers in banks, insurance offices, railway companies, and would, no doubt, be, upon the same principle, extended to officers in other trading corporations." But Robinson could not accept their argument "for obvious reasons": it was contrary to the decisions of English Courts by which he considered himself bound (1854, 11 Q.B., p. 227).

The insistence on English case law is evident too in the case of *In re Moore and The Port Bruce Harbour Co.*, in which Robinson refused to interfere with an illegal election of directors by a writ of *mandamus* for a new election, largely because, "If we were to do so, I have a strong conviction that we should be taking a course not warranted by any English authority" (1857, 14 Q.B., p. 368).

In his decisions on corporation law, Robinson's insistence on Statutory Authority and the use of the corporate seal may be viewed as conservative. But they are consistent with his concern that businessmen have complete information about the legal scope of business activity, and confidence in the limits that the law would prescribe. Moreover, in his view, Canadian law should acknowledge the rights awarded to corporations by their charters, but avoid the excesses permitted in the United States. Any liberalization of corporate powers would have to come from the legislature. The general acts of incorporation after 1850 moved the corporate form further in the direction of an American model. (We will return to this issue in 4. *Transportation*, below.)

C. Property Law

As an area of long-established settlement, Great Britain passed on to Upper Canada a well-defined body of property law. But English law was no longer expected to cope with problems endemic to an area of recent settlement and continuing immigration, with both grants and sales by the Crown and an emerging private land market. By 1840 most of the arable land in Upper Canada had been alienated. Security of land tenure and ownership and the ability to sell and buy land with assurances about title transfer were important subjects for referral to the courts.

(i) Doctrine of estoppel.   Confirmation of title by letters patent and transfer of title were the subject of *Hennesy v. Myers*. The original holder of the land from the crown, Abbott, "sold" the land to Hennesy *before* receiving letters patent. When Abbott finally received letters patent confirming title, instead of assigning them to Hennesy, he conveyed the land to Myers. Myers argued the land was his, not Hennesy's. Faced with this situation, Robinson concluded that, after Abbott conveyed the land to Hennesy, he was estopped from any further transactions in that land, and that the letters patent, once awarded, confirmed the vesting of title in Hennesy (1832, 2 K.B. [O.S.], p. 458). The later case of *Tiffany v. McEwan* confirmed the *Hennesy* decision (1837, 5 Q.B. [O .S.], p. 598).[13]

The doctrine of estoppel was seen clearly too in the case of *Irvine v. Webster*, a case like the two above, where the second claimant was estopped by the first deed from claiming the land. Robinson expressed concern that the practice of switching titles was "notorious." Yet, what makes *Irvine* so important is the fact that it is one of the few cases where Robinson differed from English authority. As he noted, England had not been in a similar situation to Upper Canada, a new territory granting land titles, for centuries. "Estoppel by title" was something uniquely necessary to Upper Canada, but only the "peculiar circumstances" of Upper Canada allowed him to rule differently from English cases (1846, 2 Q.B., p. 24).[14] In *McLean v. Laidlaw*, another estoppel case, Robinson showed his concern over disagreeing with English cases by mentioning to the parties that he always wished someone to take his decision to the Privy Council for absolute clarification (1846, 2 Q.B., p. 224). These cases were among Robinson's most important decisions, because the colonial economy and society were vested in the land, and reliability of title was essential when land was constantly being granted and withdrawn by the Crown.[15]

(ii) Chattel mortgages. In holding or acquiring land other than by a direct grant, personal property was often used as security in the form of chattel mortgages. A mortgage of this kind was a conveyance by the borrower to the lender of his chattels, with the exception that the borrower would keep possession of the chattels until the loan was repaid or in default. Formally, the mortgage had to conform to the *Chattel Mortgages Act* of 1849, 13 & 14 *Vic.* ch. 62, as amended.

Cases under the Act gave Robinson much concern. In *Holmes v. Vancamp*, the mortgagee used an agent to file an affidavit of mortgage debt. The Act required the mortgagee himself to make an affidavit, so that the affidavit filed by the mortgagee's agent rendered the mortgage invalid (1853, 10 Q.B., p. 510). Robinson's insistence on compliance with the letter of the Act showed up again in *Armstrong v. Ausman* and *Boulton and McCarthy v. Smith (Sheriff)* (1854, 11 Q.B., p. 498, and 1859, 17 Q.B., p. 400). When moving from problems involving the requirements of a chattel mortgage *per se* to the adequacy of the description of the chattels in the mortgages, Robinson was also true to the Act.[16] Again he wished to make the law certain.

(iii) Suretyship. A surety was a person who engaged himself under a contract of suretyship to answer the debt, default, or miscarriage of another. While the contract of a surety is, in a sense, collateral to the principal obligation contracted by another person, the surety's obligation to the creditor is direct and absolute. This form of security was, like chattel mortgages, important for financing many ventures in Upper Canada. Although Robinson was preoccupied with the formalities of chattel mortgages, he appeared to be concerned in how a surety could escape his obligation. In general, any variation by which the surety might be prejudiced, if made without his consent, was regarded by the courts as an effective discharge of the surety to the creditor.[17]

Perhaps Robinson's most important surety case was *McPherson v. Dickson*. McPherson, a Quebec merchant, financed timber cutting by William Dickson, who had timber licenses in the Ottawa Valley. Dickson's brother Andrew, became surety. William was to cut the timber and raft it to McPherson at Quebec. McPherson's advances were to be repaid when the timber was sold there, no later than September 1847, when the shipping season was closing. But the market price for timber had dropped since summer and the timber was not sold at all. McPherson sued Andrew, as surety, for the advances made to William. Andrew cited a variation in the original contract to William, alleging that McPherson's agent at Quebec had entered into a new agreement with William to gain control over the timber and to get rid of the raftsmen who had brought the timber downriver to Quebec. Robinson held that Andrews' plea depended upon a parol agreement, which was unacceptable to Robinson (1852, 8 Q.B., p. 29).[18] Andrew then appealed successfully to Chancery, where Chancellor Blake viewed the subsequent deal between McPherson's agent and William Dickson as a variation of the obligation which discharged the surety (*Dickson v. McPherson*, 1852, 3 Ch., p. 185).[19]

(iv) Economic development and changing interpretations of property law. The common law conferred on a property owner the right to seek redress for any use of his neighbor's land that conflicted with his own quiet enjoyment. As the United States became more industrialized, the judicial interpretation of property rights evolved a pro-development bias in which "the relative efficiencies of conflicting property uses" took precedence (Horwitz, 1977, p. 38). This emphasis on productive use of property, consistent with economic development, confronted the traditional anti-developmental premises of the common law.

Conflicts between the forces of economic development and the older views of Blackstone on property occurred in Upper Canada as well. By nature, Robinson preferred the traditional English ideas and took pains to protect the rights of property. These contending influences came to the fore in cases involving the impact on landholding rights of growing economic activity incidental to the St. Lawrence trading system, in situations where milling, logging, river travel, and railways conflicted with "quiet enjoyment."

Consider cases arising from the conflict between milling and the concept of riparian rights. The traditional law was based on the doctrine of strict prior use. In the case of *Applegarth v. Rhymal*, Applegarth had for many years occupied a mill on the stream in question. A second mill was erected on the stream by Rhymal, five miles above Applegarth's, and its operation subsequently interfered with Applegarth's mill. The court, citing Blackstone, held that "the common law rule is that a prior occupancy does give a right and property in a current of water to the first occupant, and every subsequent occupant must exercise his right so as to not injure the first occupant" (1827, 1 K.B. [O.S.], p. 431).[20]

As society became more and more industrialized, judicial interpretations began to reflect the change. In the United States, by 1825, Joseph Story and James Kent were beginning to articulate a new riparian doctrine, based on reasonable use; that is, each owner had the right to make reasonable use of the water in a stream flowing past his mill (Lauer, 1963, p. 60). Later, in Upper Canada, this

American development was paralleled in the case of *McLaren v. Cook* heard in 1847. Although the facts were similar to *Applegarth v. Rhymal*, Robinson held that the principle of reasonable use was "well settled" in conflicts between proprietors on rivers or streams, ruling that "nothing short of a grant, or use for such length of time as will support the presumption of a grant, will entitle the proprietor of land on a stream to divert or pen back the water in such a manner as to occasion damage to those being above or below in the same stream" (1847, 3 Q.B., p. 300). Robinson was expressing the reasonable use test that was incidental to economic development. However, this did not mean that he would subsequently ride roughshod over property rights in favor of economic development and, indeed, he was never indifferent to proprietors injured by economic development.

One issue that presented complications involved the precedence of public or private rights on rivers. This issue arose most often when proprietors dammed rivers, thereby blocking navigation. *The Queen v. Myers* concerned the construction of such a dam on the North Sydenham River. Vessels had previously been able to navigate the river, but the dam prevented them from doing so. The Court of Common Pleas ruled against Myers, since public rights to navigation existed on all rivers "naturally adopted to purposes of navigation," and he had clearly interfered with a navigable water course (1854, 3 C.P., p. 305).

Robinson also examined this issue in *Snure v. The Great Western Railway Company*. Snure sued because the railway's bridge prevented ships from ascending the river to his tannery. Robinson's rejection of the company's plea of Statutory Authority in deciding in favor of Snure showed his unwillingness to sacrifice the sanctity of private property to the interests of promoting economic development, when there was a clear violation of legal principles (1856, 13 Q.B., p. 376).

Conflicts between property and development interests also arose in cases involving lumbering. An important source of wealth, logging required the uninterrupted use of rivers, often over long distances, so that logs could be floated to market. As dams proliferated in order to generate power to operate mills, the legislature passed a statute to provide for the construction of aprons around the dams to facilitate the passage of logs.[21] This Act created many problems for the courts, especially when loggers damaged a dam which had no apron. In *Little v. Ince*, for example, Ince cut away some of Little's dam to get his logs downriver, and Chief Justice Macaulay agreed he acted within his rights (1854, 4 C.P., p. 95). But when faced with a similar case, *Shipman v. Clothier*, Robinson expressed a different view:

> Then the question is—if the proprietor shall obstruct the stream at any time contrary to the statute, does it follow that any person having occasion to float timber down it, and finding it unlawfully obstructed, is at liberty to remove the obstruction, as he might abate a nuisance upon the Highway? I should say not, as a consequence of the general provisions of the act, in any case in which the stream does not appear on the pleadings to be a navigable river, and, as

such, a common and public highway. (1852, 8 Q.B., p. 593).

Thus, Robinson was not disposed to permit loggers to tear down a dam, especially on a non-navigable river, in order to ease their transportation problems. This does not necessarily reflect his belief that milling should take precedence over logging. In fact, the lumber merchants of Upper Canada were strong supporters of close economic ties with Great Britain, in large part because the British preferential tariff on timber gave them assured markets until 1848, and the British market continued to be important under free trade (Cross, 1970, pp. 226–32). In short, their political and economic views of Empire were similar to Robinson's.

D.　Transportation

The cases examined so far in the areas of corporation and property law suggest that Robinson favored controlled growth. Often the legislature appeared anxious to promote rapid growth, especially in its conferring of special charters to transportation companies. Transportation improvements were regarded by politicians and businessmen alike as public investments critical to the future development of the colony. In the enthusiasm for development, many of the political problems associated with large-scale enterprise were often overlooked or dismissed. In fact, the legislature even passed statutes protecting transportation companies against legal action from would-be plaintiffs seeking damages. The courts were soon called upon to rule on cases of the liability of transportation companies for damages caused by external effects associated with their construction and operation.

In *Griffiths v. Welland Canal Co.*, the canal company was sued for damages caused by surplus water released during a flood. Robinson cited Statutory Authority: ''For anything that may be thus done in strict pursuance of the power of the statute, no action can be maintained, for the statute makes it legal, and is a perfect defense under the general issue.'' Thus, the company's charter gave it the power to release water, and exempted it from legal recourse by those harmed by its actions (1839, 5 Q.B. [O.S.], p. 686). Similarly, Robinson's decision in *Young v. The Grand River Navigation Company* absolved the company from damages, because its act of incorporation empowered it to work on the Grand River without regard for the consequences for others of the proper conduct of its duties under the charter (1854, 12 Q.B., p. 75).

The defense of Statutory Authority was used frequently after the coming of the railway. *McDonell v. The Ontario, Simcoe, and Huron Railroad Union Company* was a case involving obstruction by the railway of McDonell's access to a public highway. Robinson denied the action, because the railway's act of incorporation bound it to obstruct McDonell in the public interest; moreover, the act did not provide for compensation (1854, 11 Q.B., p. 271). Similarly, in the case of

Wallace v. The Grand Trunk Railway, Wallace alleged that, by blocking a stream, the railway's tracks flooded several acres of his land. The railway's defense of Statutory Authority was successful (1858, 16 Q.B., p. 551). However, according to Robinson, the defense of Statutory Authority carried with it an obligation on the part of a company to exercise due care in the pursuit of its legitimate activities. For example, in *Anderson v. The Great Western Railroad Company*, Robinson insisted that although the company was empowered to divert the stream supplying Anderson's mills, it was obliged to give him notice of their plans and to complete the construction of railway works as quickly and carefully as possible:

> Then, we cannot say that the statute 4 Wm. IV., ch. 29, sec. 9, gives authority to the company to stop or divert at their pleasure, and without necessity, and as long as they please, the flow of any stream of water over which they have occasion to construct their railway. If it was necessary to do so in this instance for a time, while they were constructing their road, they should have set forth the necessity and admitted they did stop or divert the stream, and should have averred that they were proceeding with all reasonable diligence in the completion of the road, so as to show that they were continuing the obstruction no longer than was necessary. It was indispensable, also, that they should have averred that they gave that notice to the plaintiff of their intention to interfere with the flow of water to his mill which the statute requires (1854, 11 Q.B., p. 128).

The statute which placed limits on a railway's liabilities also provided for compensation to property owners who were harmed by the railway. The court appointed arbitrators to assess all damage done and to advise on compensation of the property owner. The main problem here was amounts of compensation. In *Great Western Railroad Company v. Baby*, Robinson made suggestions as to the proper form of award:

> It is on this ground that we make the rule absolute in this case; but, to avoid occasion for question upon any future award, we would suggest that it should be clearly expressed, in the first place, that the sum awarded is given for the value of the lands and tenements or private privileges proposed to be purchased, or for the amount of damages which the claimant is entitled to receive in consequence of the intended railroad in and upon his lands (as the case may be); and that the award should either be silent in regard to any other matter on which the statute gives no authority to the arbitrators to give a direction; or that, if the estimate has been influenced by anything which the company has engaged to do in order to lessen the inconvenience, it should be plainly expressed that the company have undertaken to do it; and the particular thing should be defined as to leave no uncertainty, and no room for future litigation as to what is to be done or allowed by the company, and at what particular point in their work, and in what manner it is to be done (1854, 12 Q.B., pp. 106, 121).

Furthermore, if the statute did not authorize some types of complaints, an aggrieved party could always invoke the general law of torts, especially trespass and nuisance, as long as the action was initiated within the statutory six-month period of limitation.

The defense of Statutory Authority was disallowed by Robinson, however, in cases where railway companies were careless or negligent. Flooding because of improper construction and dead livestock because of excessive operating speeds were the major complaints. When the Hamilton and Toronto Railway covered up drainage ditches after building its tracks across Alton's land, flooding resulted. Alton sued successfully in *Alton v. The Hamilton and Toronto Railway Company* because Robinson found the company guilty of "neglect of proper precautions" (1856, 13 Q.B., p. 598). Careless construction of a bridge by the Great Western Railway Company led to a similar outcome in *Moison v. The Great Western Railway Company* (1856, 14 Q.B., p. 102). Robinson's unwillingness to condone a railway's negligence was made clear too in his dissenting opinion in *L'Esperance v. The Great Western Railway Company*; the majority found for the railway under the authority of its statute of incorporation, but Robinson believed the company had been negligent, and hence was responsible for the damages caused by flooding (1856, 14 Q.B., p. 173).[22]

Livestock deaths often precipitated legal actions when the defense of Statutory Authority might be set aside. In *Renaud v. The Great Western Railway Co.*, Robinson found the railway was negligent because it had not properly fenced a crossing and because its train was operated at excessive speed through the crossing, killing several of Renaud's livestock (1855, 12 Q.B., p. 408). And in *Campbell v. The Great Western Railway Company*, Robinson extended the company's responsibilities for safe operation even further, by concluding that, even though Campbell's cattle had escaped onto the track, the railway was obliged to try to avoid collisions by employing ordinary care and skill in train operation (1858, 15 Q.B., p. 498).

This last case is important too, because Robinson explicitly mentions the changing nature of property rights with economic development in the United States. Faced with counsel's argument that American law should be applied, Robinson noted that "American decisions on the subject are not uniform, but that many of them take ground more in favour of the railway companies than is upheld in England, holding that they are entitled to their track, and may use it regardless of any one . . ." (1858, 15 Q.B., p. 503).[23] In the presence of solid English precedent, Robinson was not inclined to permit this American interpretation to influence the Court of Queen's Bench. Robinson persisted in articulating a Canadian attitude to law and economic development that was more restrained than in America, and included a greater respect for private property. Again, this is partly explained by the greater influence of English law in Upper Canada, where the formal obligations of *stare decisis* and appeals to the Privy Council made the law more conservative, a practical complement to Robinson's emotional preference for continuing allegiance to English law.

E.   British Versus American Influences

By descent, upbringing, and association, Robinson favored close ties with Britain, and he consistently cited British law over American. Many of his cases can be interpreted, then, as demonstrating Robinson's commitment to keeping Upper Canada British, and hence a society distinct from American society. On the other hand, this explanation may somewhat oversimplify the complex influences to which he was subject. In the face of the overwhelming significance of the English common law as the basis of Canadian law, a judge had little scope for initiative, but was mainly a creature of opportunity. Robinson himself remarked that, "It is the business of courts only to dispose of such questions as are brought before them; and in all countries much that is irregular may pass without being objected to" (1852, 8 Q.B., p. 498). Only as circumstances arose which permitted clarification of the law, would Robinson seize upon those opportunities.

The traumatic experience of the Loyalists in being evicted from their homes in America during the Revolution undoubtedly led them to be especially conscious of property rights, once they had re-established themselves in Upper Canada. This concern was aggravated by the fact that there were many Americans living in Upper Canada—that Upper Canada was, in fact, riven by contending American and British influences. Burnet strongly suggests that the American population of Upper Canada were least amenable to discipline by the Compact and members of the government, and contributed more than any other group to the prison population of Kingston Penitentiary (Burnet, 1972, pp. 72–75). In the 1830s and 1840s, when overseas immigrants were flooding into Upper Canada and the province itself was becoming more urbanized, a prominent social issue was law and order. There was a call for greater protection of the property rights of the "good citizens" of Upper Canada (Bellomo, 1972, pp. 11–26; Wise, 1970, p. 231).

The Family Compact stressed the insecurity of property in America as part of their basic anti-American stance, so that conscious protection of property rights in Upper Canada might be seen as a moral duty by important figures such as John Beverley Robinson. Yet the social issue of law and order was not the only thing inclining Robinson to protect property rights after the British model. Important too were the obligations of precedent and of *stare decisis*, and that Upper Canada was not then independent from British laws.[24] This fact left little room for improvisation or modification of law in Upper Canada. In *McCuniffe v. Allen*, he stated that the law and "the rules which have governed for more than a century, in respect to commercial transactions and securities of this kind, should not be treated as fluctuating and uncertain, when they have so long been certain and fixed . . . The legislature may of course place the law on a different footing, if they think it proper to do so, but we have no authority to change it" (1850, 6 Q.B., p. 382).[25] Furthermore, in *Wilcocks v. Tinning and Hornby*, when counsel relied on American authority to help plead his case, Robinson specifically disapproved, stating that his plea had to be sustained by English authority (1851, 7 Q.B., p. 372). Pleading in Upper Canada, then, had to be according to strict English authority. American influences were not helpful and were actively discouraged.

In no instance where the circumstances were covered by British precedent did

Robinson ever consider even the most persuasive aspects of American law. Whenever he was confronted with it by counsel under these conditions, he rejected it. Conversely, he exhibited a persistent tenacity to cling to English law and customs, and a reverence for established English authority. Love of order, method and punctuality, strict impartiality, respect due the court, a feeling of anti-Americanism, a duty to country, and above all duty and loyalty to the Queen and Empire were principles shown in Robinson's early life that were conspicuous in his judgments to the last.

IV.

The economic development of the St. Lawrence basin during the pre-Confederation era was closely identified with agriculture and natural resources. Lumber, wheat, and flour were the principal staple commodities produced for intercolonial and international markets, primarily in Great Britain, and merchants, farmers, and government officials attached great importance to questions of landholding, transportation development, and commercial policy. These were all concerns of practical significance to increasing the flow of international commerce. In these areas, colonial businessmen looked to the state for assistance, both to help establish an economic and political climate within which the uncertainties and costs of doing business could be reduced, and to initiate and, if necessary, undertake transportation and other large-scale projects promising significant externalities.

The legislature and the courts were the state institutions which existed, in part, to try to meet the demands of businessmen for improved investment opportunities. Most economic legislation emanating from the Legislative Assembly in Upper Canada concerned financial institutions, transportation developments, and access to the natural resource base, and often reflected Canadian geographic or environmental conditions. For the courts, however, the situation was different. Upper Canada was constitutionally obliged to copy English common law, and consequently there was less scope for the courts to consider peculiar Canadian conditions. Only where there was no appropriate English case law or where English conditions were markedly different from those in Canada did Canadian judges invoke local conditions or practices, or refer to the experience of American courts. Acts of the legislature, not court decisions, were the normal channel through which Canadian environmental conditions were advanced (Risk, 1977a, pp. 237–39). Yet, limited though they were, Canadian judges did have opportunities to bring their personal backgrounds and knowledge of Canadian business conditions to bear on judicial decision making.

From his important post as Chief Justice of the Court of Queen's Bench, John Beverley Robinson was well placed to influence the development of the Upper Canadian economy. His belief in the need for, and feasibility of, economic development, and his belief that the law could help achieve it, were compatible with the type of society he wanted to see implanted in Upper Canada. Because of his position, his longevity, and his close ties with political and economic leaders in Canada, and because of the relatively early stage of Upper Canada's economic development, Robinson's legal decisions had a visibility and an impact that are beyond the reach of present-day jurists.

In this paper, we have reviewed many of Robinson's major judicial decisions in several areas having, as their background, the conduct of business in the St. Lawrence commercial system. Of particular importance are his cases in contract law respecting grades, warranties, responsibilities and damages, his decisions on Upper Canadian transportation corporations and challenges to their authority, his decisions relating to the development of lumbering, milling, and railway building vis-à-vis settlement, his transformation of the riparian and prior-use doctrines and judgments respecting "public" and "private" rivers.

Robinson's decisions were not consistently pro-development. On the contrary, his belief that commercial prosperity underlay Canada's future in the British Empire must be weighed against his legal obligation to the abstract, conservative weight of English common law. Canadian judges, Robinson among them, fell far short of accepted judicial interpretation in the United States in their encouragement to business. Even if Robinson was sympathetic to the needs of businessmen and often rendered decisions conducive to the successful conduct of business, he cannot be labelled an "instrumentalist." Nevertheless, he did facilitate business by helping to define a legal framework within which businessmen became aware of the law and more confident about its implications for business operations. Moreover, his belief that brighter business prospects were vital to Upper Canada's future comes through clearly in both his published tracts and his written judgments. While railways might have been McNab's politics, commerce and the St. Lawrence might be thought of as Robinson's law.

ACKNOWLEDGMENTS

This is a revised version of a paper presented at the Annual Meeting of the Canadian Historical Association, Vancouver, June 6–8, 1983. We gratefully acknowledge the helpful comments on the earlier version of Professors F. T. Denton, D. P. Gagan, Douglas McCalla, Donald McCloskey, and R. C. B. Risk.

GLOSSARY OF TERMS

K.B.—Upper Canada Court of King's Bench
Q.B.—Upper Canada Court of Queen's Bench
Ch.—Upper Canada Court of Chancery
C.P.—Upper Canada Court of Common Pleas

NOTES

1. The British colony of Quebec was divided into Upper and Lower Canada in 1791 under the Constitutional Act. Upper Canada was renamed Canada West after the Act of Union in 1841, and since Confederation in 1867 has been known as Ontario.

2. The Family Compact was a Loyalist elite of professional men, career soldiers, bureaucrats, and Anglican churchmen, whose hard core had fought in the War of 1812. They shared a common ideology, composed of elements of anti-Americanism, adherence to the British connection, and conservative political, social, and religious principles. Craig (1963, pp. 110–11) notes a conscious design or plan by Compact members to use the state, the Church, the press, education, political patronage, and the law to control immigration, ensure loyalty and stamp out treason, and promote economic progress. Also, see Saunders (1957).

3. Risk has noted that "the common law . . . has generally expressed the values of the judges, and these values have been the values of powerful social groups. The values expressed by judges are likely to be shaped by the society in which they live" (1977b, p. 420). Cook (1977, pp. 91–93) concludes that Robinson did try to achieve the Compact's goals, but does not cite any of Robinson's cases to confirm this point.

4. Also, see *Mason v. Brunskill* (1857, 15 Q.B., p. 300), and *Logan v. Stranahan* (1854, 12 Q.B., p. 15).

5. See also *George v. Glass* (1857, 14 Q.B., p. 514).

6. *Tilt v. Silverthorne* was a case involving a contract to deliver flour (1854, 11 Q.B., p. 619). Robinson said,

> Being aware, as we are, from what has often been proved before us in relation to contracts in this description of business, that it is the usage of the trade, and the common understanding of the parties, that wheat delivered in large quantities at a mill, as this was, is not expected or intended to be kept apart and ground for the person delivering it . . ." (p. 620).

See also, *Reynolds v. Shuter* (1847, 3 Q.B., p. 377).

7. Also, see *Johnson v. Crew* (1835, 5 K.B., [O.S.], p. 200), *Barton v. Fisher* (1846, 3 Q.B., p. 75) and *Elliott v. Hewitt* (1854, 11 Q.B., p. 292). These cases involved unexpected events respecting house building and labor generally.

8. See also, *Lane v. The Montreal Telegraph Co.* (1857, 7 C.P., p. 23).

9. Vaughan (1968) notes that originally the bank was to be chartered in Kingston, but Robinson was instrumental in having the bank's charter changed to the "Seat of Government" at York.

10. *Niagara Falls Road Company v. Benson* (1851, 8 Q.B., p. 307) involved a corporation suing for the non-payment of calls upon the defendant's stock. Robinson took the position that the Niagara Falls Road Company, not having done everything that was required to be done by them in the Road Act, 12 Vic. ch. 84, was *not* entitled to sue. See also, *Nelson and Nassagaweya Road Company v. Bates* (1854, 12 Q.B., p. 586).

11. According to Robinson,

> This description of insurance by mutual insurance companies does, indeed, give occasion for contracts of a prospective kind, which parties insured may have an interest in endeavoring to evade; and this case shows that whether justifiably or not, they may be disposed to do so. It is better, therefore, that the ground on which such contracts stand should be at once settled and known. In our opinion, a foreign mutual insurance company founded on such principles as the Genesee Company is, cannot carry on business in this province under their foreign charter. If the Legislature should think that either justice or policy points to a different course, they can apply a remedy. We have no discretion to say that the law is different from what we consider it to be.

12. Robinson also said: "To say that the principle or maxim of our law, which requires that a corporation should bind itself by its seal, as the only legal evidence of its will, is absurd and senseless, and may be therefore rejected, is not what I can subscribe to. There are not a few principles of our law, which are open to similar objections, and yet are too firmly established to be shaken by anything less than a statute" (1842, 6 Q.B. [O.S.], p. 397). The only difficulties lay in exceptions to a corporation using its seal, and in this regard Robinson wavered. In *Blue v. The Toronto Gas and Water Co.* (1849, 6 Q.B., p. 174) the majority in the Court held that an action of assumpsit would be against the Company for damages in not fulfilling a parol contract with the plaintiff to supply water to the Toronto baths. The majority seemed to feel that a corporation was exempted from using its seal where acts of such ordinary occurrence were a daily necessity for the corporation or so insignificant as to be not worth the trouble of affixing their seal. Robinson dissented that to hold as the majority did went against all authority. However, this issue still raised doubts and Robinson reversed his position later in *Clark v. The Hamilton and Gore Mechanic's Institute* (1854, 12 Q.B., p. 178).

13. Said Robinson, "The case turns upon a principle which may have a very extensive and important application in this province, where lands are in a constant course of grant by the Crown, and have been so from the first settlement of the country" (1837, 5 Q.B.[O.S.], p. 600).

14. Robinson wrote,

The same state of things has not existed in England, in any of those cases in which the principle of estoppel has been applied, at least I am aware of no such case; and we have therefore to consider in the absence of authority, whether in reason and upon legal principles, the doctrine of estoppel can be applied under such circumstances, or whether its application is excluded (1846, 2 Q.B., p. 227).

Indeed, only in one other case does Robinson seem to go against English law, and that where also the "peculiar circumstances" of Upper Canada required him to do so. *Dean v. McCarty* (1846, 2 Q.B., p. 448) was a case involving owners of land who were burning bush on their own land, and as a result a neighbor's fence was burned. Robinson felt that in Upper Canada, where such fires were useful and necessary to clear the land, owners were responsible for injury to their neighbors *only* where negligent.

15. Even with his innovative ruling in "estoppel" cases, however, Robinson was not as forceful as Chancellor Blake in stressing that Canadian property law be adapted to Canadian conditions. For example, in *O'Keefe v. Taylor*, Blake decided as follows:

We are not dealing with the casual transfer of real property in a fully occupied and thoroughly cultivated country, but we are about to define the position of multitudes by whom a country is being peopled—by whose enterprise and labor the wastes of this vast province are rendered subservient to the purposes of civilization with unexampled rapidity. Under such circumstances, where the habit of holding land for considerable periods, under contracts similar to the present, so extensively prevails, and where the value of the soil so materially depends upon the labor of those who occupy under that sort of tenure, it is of vital importance, not only to the attainment of justice in particular cases, but to the general welfare, that, in this court, where alone such contracts can be enforced, the numerous titles which depend exclusively upon this jurisdiction for their validity, should not be shaken by the introduction of doctrines, which, however suited to other states of society, have no application in our present social condition, but that they should be shown to rest upon settled and solid foundations. But were we to apply the rule to be deduced from some of the English cases which were cited, especially some of the latter cases, upon the subject of delay without reference to the totally different social condition of this country, we should not only produce great practical evil and injustice, but should also, in my opinion, very much misapply a doctrine which in England injustice, but should also, in my opinion, very much misapply a doctrine which in England would never have been laid down under the circumstances in which we are placed (1850, 2 Ch. pp., 98–99).

16. See *Harris and Woodside v. The Commercial Bank of Canada* (1858, 16 Q.B., p. 437), *Rose v. Scott* (1859, 17 Q.B., p. 385), *Moffatt v. Coulson* (1860, 19 Q.B., p. 341), and *Fraser v. The Bank of Toronto* (1860, 19 Q.B., p. 381).

17. See *O'Neil v. Carter* (1852, 9 Q.B., p. 470), *William Darling, Executor of David Darling v. Allan Neil McLean* (1861, 20 Q.B., p. 372), and *Grieve v. Smith* (1863, 23 Q.B., p. 23 [Draper, Chief Justice]).

18. Robinson argued as follows: "If the defendant relies upon his discharge from his covenant resulting from his parol agreement to discharge, there is no doubt that a court of law cannot sustain such a defence . . . The principle is a clear one, that a contract under seal can neither be discharged, varied, or abated by parol" (1852, 8 Q.B., pp. 40-41).

19. Blake concluded that "any variation, by the defendants, or any of them, by which the surety might be prejudiced, if made without his consent, will be regarded by this court as an effectual discharge. If that be a correct statement of the law, it is not to be doubted, I think, that the variations in this contract were such as might have been prejudicial to the surety" (1852, 3 Ch., p. 205).

20. Robinson was then attorney general and counsel for the defendant on appeal from a trial at Gore District Assizes.

21. *An Act . . . To Provide for the Construction of Aprons*, Stat. Can. 1849, c. 87.

22. See also, *Vanhorn v. The Grand Trunk Railway* (1859, 18 Q.B., pp. 356, 360). Vanhorn successfully sued the railway for negligently building a bridge over a stream on his land, causing flooding; to Robinson it was "an alleged injury not foreseen, and first experienced long after the railway was completed and an injury attributed solely to the unskillful and negligent manner of constructing a culvert."

23. To back up his statement, Robinson cited several American cases.

24. As Allen remarks,

By the end of the eighteenth century, all the foundations of the modern doctrine of precedent were laid, but it could not reach its final development until certain changes, especially in the system of judicature and in the nature of the law reports, had been fulfilled. By 1833 it is recognized that the decisions of higher tribunals are binding on lower tribunals, unless "plainly unreasonable and inconvenient", and that no judge is at liberty to depart from a principle once laid down merely on the ground that it is not "as convenient and reasonable as he himself could have devised" (Allen, 1964, p. 362).

25. Robinson also said, "The legislature may of course place the law on a different footing, if they think it proper to do so; but we have no authority to change it, by departing at our pleasure from a principle uniformly acted upon for more than a century and a half" (1850, 6 Q.B., p. 382).

REFERENCES

Allen, Sir C. K. (1964), *Law in the Making*, 7th ed. Oxford: Oxford University Press.

Bellomo, J. J. (1972), "Upper Canadian Attitudes Towards Crime and Punishment." *Ontario History*, 64: 11–26.

Brode, Patrick (1984), *Sir John Beverley Robinson: Bone and Sinew of the Compact.* Toronto: University of Toronto Press.

Burnet, J. R. (1972), *Ethnic Groups in Upper Canada.* Ontario Historical Society Research Publication No. 1. Toronto: Ontario Historical Society.

Cook, Terry (1972), "John Beverley Robinson and the Conservative Blueprint for the Upper Canadian Community." *Ontario History*, 64: 79–99.

Craig, G. M. (1963), *Upper Canada: The Formative Years, 1784–1841.* Toronto: McClelland and Stewart.

Creighton, Donald (1956), *The Empire of the St. Lawrence*. Toronto: Macmillan.

Cross, Michael (1970), "The Lumber Community of Upper Canada, 1815–1867." *Ontario History* 62: 221–31.

Flaherty, David H. (1981), *Essays in the History of Canadian Law*, Vol. 1. Toronto: University of Toronto Press.

Gagan, David P. (1981), *Hopeful Travellers: Families, Land and Social Change in Mid-Victorian Peel County, Canada West*. Toronto: University of Toronto Press.

Horwitz, Morton J. (1974), "The Historical Foundations of Modern Contract Law." *Harvard Law Review*, 87: 917–56.

Horwitz, Morton J. (1977), *The Transformation of American Law 1780–1860*. Cambridge, Mass.: Harvard University Press.

Hurst, Willard J. (1982), *Law and Markets in United States History: Different Modes of Bargaining Among Interests*. Madison: University of Wisconsin Press.

Jarvis, Julia (1967), *Three Centuries of Robinsons: The Story of a Family*. Don Mills, Ontario.

Lauer, T. E. (1963), "The Common Law Background of the Riparian Doctrine." *Missouri Law Review*, 28: 60–85.

Read, David B. (1888), *The Lives of the Judges of Upper Canada and Ontario*. Toronto: Rowsell and Hutchison.

Risk, R. C. B. (1973), "The Nineteenth-Century Foundations of the Business Corporation in Ontario." *University of Toronto Law Journal*, 23: 270–306.

Risk, R. C. B. (1976), "The Golden Age: The Law about the Market in Nineteenth-Century Ontario." *University of Toronto Law Journal*, 26: 307–46.

Risk, R. C. B. (1977a), "The Last Golden Age: Property and the Allocation of Losses in Ontario in the Nineteenth Century." *University of Toronto Law Journal*, 27: 199–239.

Risk, R. C. B. (1977b), "The Law and Economy in Mid-Nineteenth Century Ontario: A Perspective." *University of Toronto Law Journal*, 27: 403–38.

Robinson, C. W. (1904), *Life of Sir John Beverley Robinson*. Edinburgh: Morang.

Robinson, Sir John Beverley (1825), "A Letter to the Right Hon. Earl Bathurst, K. G. on the Policy of Uniting the British North American Colonies." London. Reprinted 1967 in *Four Early Pamphlets on the Subject of Confederation and Union of the Canadas*. Toronto.

Robinson, Sir John Beverley (1839), Three Letters from John Beverley Robinson to the Right Hon. the Marquis of Normanby, Her Majesty's Secretary of State for Colonies, February 23, March 9, March 29. Public Archives of Ontario, Robinson Papers, MS4, Reel No. 5.

Robinson, Sir John Beverley (1840), *Canada and the Canada Bill*. London. Reprinted 1967 by S. R. Publishers Ltd., Johnson Reprint Corporation, New York.

Saunders, R. E. (1957), "What Was the Family Compact?" *Ontario History* , 49: 173–178.

Saunders, R. E. (1976), "John Beverley Robinson." In *Dictionary of Canadian Biography*, Vol. IX, 1861–1870. Toronto: University of Toronto Press, 668–79.

Tucker, G. N. (1964), *The Canadian Commercial Revolution, 1847–1851*. Toronto: McClelland and Stewart.

Tulchinsky, G. J. J. (1977), *The River Barons: Montreal Businessmen and the Growth of Industry and Transportation, 1837–53*. Toronto: University of Toronto Press.

Upper Canada Queen's Bench Reports (Old Series), 1831–1844. Toronto.

Upper Canada Queen's Bench Reports (New Series), 1844–1881. Toronto.

Upper Canada Common Pleas Reports, 1850–1881. Toronto.

Upper Canada Error and Appeal Reports, 1846–1866. Toronto.

Upper Canada (Grant's) Chancery Reports, 1849–1882. Toronto.

Vaughan, C. L. (1968), "The Bank of Upper Canada in Politics, 1817–1840." *Ontario History*, 60: 185–204.

Wise, S. F. (1970), "Conservatism and Political Development: The Canadian Case." *The South Atlantic Quarterly*, 69: 226–43.

WERE CHILDREN EXPLOITED DURING THE INDUSTRIAL REVOLUTION?

Clark Nardinelli

ABSTRACT

It has long been a commonplace observation that British children were exploited during the industrial revolution. Exploitation has, however, been either vaguely defined or not defined at all when used to describe the situation of children. The use of explicit definitions of economic exploitation implies that the industrial revolution created few opportunities for the systematic exploitation of children in nineteenth-century Britain. The consideration of indirect measures leads to the conclusion that industrialization probably decreased the exploitation of children.

I. EXPLOITATION

Child labor occupies an influential place in the histories of Britain's industrial revolution. To critics of industrialization it is a symbol of the social evils brought

Research in Economic History, Volume 11, pages 243–276.

about by the unregulated factory system. To defenders of industrialization child labor is a challenge, something that has to be explained and (if possible) rationalized. The debate over child labor has therefore implicitly recognized the condition of children as an important indicator of the social costs and benefits of the industrial revolution.

One of the central issues in the debate over child labor is the existence of economic exploitation. One of the difficulties in dealing with the question of exploitation is that many writers do not make it clear what they mean by exploitation; casual use of the word is ubiquitous in the literature on the industrial revolution. It is possible, however, to identify three commonly used definitions of exploitation: the hard times definition, the Marxian definition, and the neoclassical definition. I will explain each definition in turn.

To many historians and critics of industrialization it was self-evident that children were exploited during the first half of the nineteenth century.[1] The way the word was used implied that exploitation meant the use of another person for personal gain, usually in an unfair or unjust manner. The entire system of child labor was, according to some observers, one of exploitation. When used in this sense "exploitation" was used as a general perjorative term connoting, among other things, low wages, long hours, and harsh treatment. The "hard times" view of child labor can be found in many nineteenth-century works and continues to be influential.[2] One of the best expositions of this view is to be found in the early work of Friedrick Engels.[3] Engels wrote that

> it is obviously wrong that children still of an age when all their time should be devoted to bodily and mental development should be sacrificed to the greed of the unfeeling middle classes. It is wrong to take children from school and the fresh air, in order to exploit them for the benefit of the manufacturers. (1845, p. 169).

The underlying belief of the hard times definition is that child labor is a product of the greed of the middle classes. If the middle classes were not greedy, child labor either would not exist or would not be as severe. Capitalist greed rather than economic necessity put children in factories.

The hard times definition of the exploitation of child labor has been perpetuated and popularized by novels such as Frances Trollope's *Michael Armstrong, The Factory Boy* (1840) and Elizabeth Gaskell's *Mary Barton* (1848).[4] References to Charles Dickens' *Hard Times* (1854) probably exceed references to scholarly histories in the casual literature on the subject.[5] It would be a mistake, however, to see the hard times view as inhabiting only novels and other literary works. In a more moderate version, it is found in many contemporary historical works. One recent example is in a chapter on labor and the industrial revolution in the seventh volume of *The Cambridge Economic History of Europe:*

> [I]t is at least probable that women and children, by transferring from largely domestic to largely public employment, also worked much harder, and that the higher family money

incomes, where indeed they were found at all, were generally achieved because of their work. The factories multiplied the social costs of the child work which had always existed, while they removed its positive aspects (Pollard, 1978, p. 162).

The continuing belief that the social costs of child labor were unnecessarily high is one of the legacies of the original hard times view.

One of the important and influential definitions of economic exploitation was that of Karl Marx (1867, pp. 186–230). According to his labor theory of value, all exchange value (or value) is created by labor. Any returns to capitalists in the form of profits must therefore have been expropriated from the workers. The expropriated product of labor is capitalist exploitation. Although Marxian models have evolved in many directions since Marx's original formulation, most retain the assumption that any returns to capital result from exploitation. Now, though the existence of exploitation is true by definition in a Marian model, the degree of exploitation can and does vary. The employment of children is one way in which capitalists can increase exploitation.[6] The capitalist can exploit child labor and increase the overall level of exploitation. According to Marx, to

purchase the labour-power of a family of four workers may, perhaps, cost more than it formerly did to purchase the labour-power of the head of the family, but, in return, four day's labour takes the place of one, and their price falls in proportion to the excess of the surplus-labour of four over the surplus-labour of one. In order that the family may live, four people must now, not only labour, but expend surplus-labour for the capitalist. Thus we see, that machinery, while augmenting the human material that forms the principal object of capital's exploiting power, at the same time raises the degree of exploitation (1867, p. 395).

When children are employed, then, the level of exploitation increases.

The implication of the Marxian model is that the exploitation of children lowers adult wages. Thus, if exploitation exists, adult wages will be lower if children are employed. Another, less explicit, implication of the Marxian model is that children are treated particularly harshly. They are virtually bought and sold in labor markets, are underpaid, and suffer from ill-health and overwork. The Marxian and hard times views of child labor are in many respects quite close.

The third definition of exploitation is what I call the neoclassical definition.[7] Under the neoclassical definition, economic exploitation exists when the value of the worker's marginal product exceeds the wage rate.[8] This is a much narrower definition than that used by the critics of child labor, but I believe that economic exploitation formed a part of what the critics meant by exploitation. For example, one of the most common indictments of child labor was the charge that it was as bad as slavery.[9] Indeed, Richard Oastler in his "Yorkshire Slavery" and other writings asserted that children in factories were worse off than American slaves (Driver, 1946, pp. 36–48). The frequent repetition of the slavery comparison indicates that it was widely believed and was an important aspect of the criticism of child labor. Now, a central economic feature of slavery was neoclassical economic exploitation. (Fogel and Engerman, 1974, Vol. 1, pp. 107–57). In other words, slaves received less in (implicit) wages than the market value of what they produced. The identification of slavery with child labor, I would argue, was an implicit recognition that economic exploitation formed at least part of the exploitation of children.

In the absence of monopoly power in goods market or monopsony power in factor markets, economic exploitation will not exist.[10] Some degree of market imperfection is therefore a necessary prerequisite for neoclassical economic exploitation. Given that markets in the real world rarely achieve perfection, this prerequisite is not stringent. Problems arise, however, when we move beyond the potential for exploitation to the attempt to measure it. The ideal procedure is to compare wages with the value of marginal product. A basic problem with the ideal procedure is that it is difficult to estimate the value of children's marginal products in nineteenth-century Britain. It is also difficult to measure the real wages of a child worker, defined as money wages deflated by a price index and adjusted for work amenities and transfers to parents.

The problem involved in measuring neoclassical exploitation can best be appreciated by attempting to do so for the cotton textile industry in 1833. The cotton industry was selected because data on cotton output, prices, and factory wages are relatively good. The year 1833 was selected because it is the earliest year for which there are good estimates of children's wages. The "children" considered were male and female workers under the age of 13, the definition of children under the Factory Act of 1833 and in much of the collected data.

Suppose that cotton textile production was characterized by a Cobb-Douglas production function of the form:

$$Q = AK^{\alpha k} L_a^{\alpha a} L_c^{\alpha c}. \tag{1}$$

where Q = output of cotton textiles,

$\quad\quad K$ = capital and raw materials,

$\quad\quad L_a$ = adult and adolescent labor,

$\quad\quad L_c$ = child labor,

$\quad\quad A$ = index of productivity

$\quad\quad \alpha_i$ = share a factor i in total revenue

If P was the price of cotton textiles and W_c was the wage rate of factory children, then

$$\alpha_c = (W_c \cdot L_c)/(P \cdot Q). \tag{2}$$

In the Cobb-Douglas production function, the marginal product of child labor is equal to the average product of child labor multiplied by its factor share. In symbols,

$$MP_c = \alpha_c \cdot (Q/L_c),\tag{3}$$

where MP_c = the marginal product of child labor. The above expression can be transformed into an expression for the value of marginal productivity by multiplying both sides by the price of cotton textiles:

$$P \cdot MP_c = \alpha_c \cdot (P \cdot Q/L_c), \text{ or}$$
$$VMP_c = \alpha_c \cdot (P \cdot Q/L_c),\tag{4}$$

where VMP_c = the value of child labor's marginal product. The estimation of the value of child labor's marginal product is therefore a matter of finding estimates of α_c, $P \cdot Q$, and L_c for 1833.

The *Reports of the Inspectors of Factories* (Great Britain, 1834–1878, 1835) and the *Supplementary Report of the Factories Inquiry Commission* (Great Britain, 1834) contain estimates of the share of children's wages in total factory wages. Both sources indicate that the share of children was around 5 percent. The share of factory wages in total wage payments (which include payments to handloom weavers) was, according to Mark Blaug (1961, p. 379), around 60 percent.[11] The share of labor in the value of gross output varies from source to source, but 25 percent is probably a reasonable estimate.[12] The share of children in the value of gross output (α_c) can now be estimated as:

(child wages/factory wages) · (factory wages/total wages) · (total wages/value of output), or

$$\alpha_c = (0.05) \cdot (0.60) \cdot (0.25) = 0.0075\tag{5}$$

The value of cotton textile output in 1833 was, again according to Blaug (1961, pp. 376–79), £36 million. To estimate the number of children employed in cotton factories in 1833, I combined G. H. Wood's estimate of total factory employment with the Factories Inquiry Commission's estimate of the proportion of children in the work force (16.8 percent) to get an estimate of 34,944 for L_c.[13]

The estimate of α_c, $P \cdot Q$, and L_c can be combined to calculate the value of child labor's marginal product in cotton factories in 1833:

$$VMP_c = 0.0075 \cdot (\text{£36 million}/34944)\tag{6}$$
$$= \text{£7.7.}$$

The estimate of the value of marginal product can then be compared to the average annual wages of children under 13 to yield an estimate of neoclassical economic exploitation. The Factories Inquiry Commission found that the average annual wage of children under 13 in Lancashire cotton factories was £7.9.[14] The gross measures, then, reveal no neoclassical exploitation of children.

The closeness of the estimates of VMP_c and W_c is, however, misleading. The most serious problem is that there is no physical measure of the marginal productivity of child labor. Since the marginal product is estimated from price, output, and factor share data, it is not entirely independent of the wage data. The comparison of VMP_c and W_c may therefore be nothing more than a check on the internal consistency of the data. Such a check is of course instructive, but does not constitute decisive evidence on the question of exploitation.

Another serious problem with the estimates is that they are highly sensitive to changes in the estimators. The substitution of Deane and Cole's 1829–1831 estimates of labor's share increases the estimate of VMP_c to £10.2.[15] The substitution of Matthews' estimate of the value of output lowers the estimate of VMP_c to £6.9.[16] An alternative estimate of the annual wage of a child is £9.1.[17] Many other possible substitutions can be made to change the results in either direction. The results of this exercise lead to the conclusion that the data can be manipulated to support any conclusion on exploitation; they can show that children were severely exploited or that children were grossly overpaid in relation to their productivity. Nor are there compelling reasons to accept any particular set of estimates. In sum, the question of the exploitation of children cannot be resolved through the direct measurement of neoclassical exploitation.

The difficulties with a direct measure of neoclassical economic exploitation make it necessary to use various indirect measures. In this paper, I will use several indirect measures in order to determine whether or not children were exploited during the industrial revolution. The neoclassical definition will be the basic definition of exploitation throughout the paper. I prefer this definition because it is the most explicit and the most amenable to empirical assessment. The use of the neoclassical definition, however, does not exclude the other definitions from consideration. Many of the indirect measures will also shed light on the Marxian and hard times theories. Furthermore, the existence of neoclassical exploitation strongly implies the existence of hard times and Marxian exploitation as well. Incidentally, a normative paradox arises when hard times and neoclassical exploitation of children coexist. The neoclassical exploitation of children in a particular firm necessarily leads to a reduction in the amount of child labor employed by the firm. If hard times exploitation (considered to be a bad thing) is present, reducing the amount of child labor is (in a normative sense) a good thing. Neoclassical exploitation is therefore a good thing if it accompanies hard times exploitation.

Market imperfections are a basic prerequisite to the market exploitation of children. As a preliminary to examining the various measures of exploitation, it will thus be necessary to examine the market structure of the British economy during the industrial revolution.

II. MONOPOLY IN THE BRITISH ECONOMY

The study of the market structure of the British economy is not sufficient to determine whether or not children were exploited. It is nevertheless a necessary starting point in that the greater the potential monopoly power in an economy, the greater are the opportunities for exploitation. The market structure, it is commonly believed, changed dramatically during the nineteenth century. Before the industrial revolution, goods were produced in small workshops, in households, and on farms. Industrialization brought with it the factory and large-scale production. Large-scale production is often thought to have created monopoly or oligopoly. In fact, the British economy was highly competitive in the first half of the nineteenth century. Moreover, in some respects industrialization increased rather than decreased the competitiveness of the economy.

Competition is characterized by—among other things—a large number of firms, no collusion, and full information on the part of market participants. The main evidence supporting the hypothesis that the economy was approximately competitive comes from census and factory returns. These returns imply that the economy consisted of an indefinitely large number of small firms. J. H. Clapham (1939, Vol. 2, pp. 33–37) used the census returns of 1851 to show that the typical unit of business was small in most of the major occupations. Few firms had more than 100 employees, even in industries where machinery was used. The small craftsman or entrepreneur with fewer than 10 employees was common in many major industries. Small size is not by itself sufficient to demonstrate the lack of monopoly power. What matters is the size of firms relative to the size of the market. By the nineteenth century most British industries were selling their products in national and in some cases world markets.[18] The small size of firms coupled with the large size of markets implies that monopoly power was negligible.

There is little statistical evidence on industrial size and concentration before 1850. Between 1851 and 1870, the average size of industrial firms increased. The growth of firm size was, however, not universal and apparently did not lead to an increase in industrial concentration. According to Leslie Hannah, though economies of scale had begun to increase the size of firms,

rapidly expanding markets were sufficient to neutralize the effects of such new scale economies, so that competition between many firms was also preserved in these industries. By 1871, then, when over half of the working population were employed in factories (and considerably more than one half of output was produced in factories), it could be argued not only that the degree of competition was no less than it had been previously, but even (given larger markets and greater competition between larger numbers of firms) that it had become more intense (1976, pp. 10–11).

The trends identified by Hannah for the period 1851–1870 may well have existed before 1851. The absence of aggregate evidence for the earlier period makes it necessary to look at the evidence from particular industries before 1851.

The textile industries, the most important industrial employers of children, were characterized by relatively large factories by the standards of the time. In 1851, 411 cotton factories had over 100 employees and 113 had over 350. (Clapham, 1939, Vol. 2, pp. 35–36). Despite the relatively large size of firms, it is doubtful that monopoly power existed. Competition among thousands of firms characterized the market. Furthermore, the belief that concentration was growing is mistaken.

The persistence of the myth of growing concentration in the textile industries defies explanation. Not only did thousands of textile firms compete with each other in product and factor markets, but also, the number of employers increased steadily throughout the nineteenth century.[19] V. A. C. Gatrell's (1977) recent paper should put the myth of increasing concentration to rest for good. Gatrell used the factory inspectors' reports and other parliamentary papers to show that the size distribution of firms in the Lancashire cotton district was changing slowly or not at all during the nineteenth century. Giant firms apparently controlled no larger a share of the industry in 1841 than they had in 1815. Moreover, entry into the industry was relatively easy. Gatrell showed that both entry and exit occurred frequently. Although Lloyd-Jones and Le Roux (1980) questioned Gatrell's conclusions about the profitability of small firms, their study (based on poor-rate assessments) corroborated Gatrell's conclusion that giant firms were not taking over the cotton industry in the first half of the nineteenth century.

The implication that emerges from the factory reports and poor-rate assessments is that the cotton textile industry was competitive and perhaps becoming more so during the first half of the nineteenth century. That the cotton industry was one of the first large-scale industries provides further evidence that the economy as a whole was competitive at that time.

The industrial evidence implies that the competitiveness of British industry extended into the market for labor. In much the same way that monopoly power is limited by competition among sellers, monopsony power is limited by competition among employers. Children, especially, were employed in sectors of the economy characterized by atomistic competition. Metal works, earthenware, agriculture, domestic service, and textiles were the main users of child labor and all were apparently characterized by competitive labor markets.[20]

Aggregate evidence, however, cannot be used to indicate the absence of monopsony power in the labor market. Firms that faced competition in national or world markets for their products may well have enjoyed local monopsonies in the market for labor. The model here is the company town, where there is only one employer. The pure company town was, however, rare and frequently temporary during the industrial revolution. Furthermore, improvements in transportation and the growth in the number of firms competing for labor would, other things being the same, have steadily eroded local monopsony. It is nevertheless true that many workers may have faced only a limited set of potential employers within a given geographical area. In most cases, migration was over relatively short distances (Redford, 1926). The casual evidence, then, cannot rule out the possibility of monopsony.

The limitations of the aggregate evidence can be clearly seen in the case of the cotton textile industry. The cotton textile industry of nineteenth-century Britain came remarkably close to the ideal of perfect competition. There were an indefinitely large number of firms and few barriers to entry. The geographic concentration of the industry in the area around Manchester reduced the costs of information and increased mobility. No one firm controlled a significant share of the labor market and, to all appearances, firms actively competed for workers.

It is said, however, that workers were in fact unable to move from factory to factory. They were forced to accept low pay and harsh conditions because they could not hope to find a job elsewhere. One implication of this hypothesis is that the factory workers suffering the most would seldom change jobs. The opposite was true. The witnesses who testified before the Select Committee on the Bill for the Regulation of Factories (1831–1832) must surely have been the most oppressed workers in Britain—at least, according to their own testimony. These witnesses were not the virtual slaves of a single cruel millowner. Indeed, their work histories show that they were highly mobile. In the 30 more or less complete histories contained in the *Report of the Select Committee* (Great Britain, 1831–1832) every worker had worked for at least two millowners. Only four of the 30 had worked for as few as two millowners and those four were all teenagers. The average age of the witnesses was 26 and the average length of working life was 17 years. Workers averaged five employers, or one every 3.4 years. Moreover, some of the work histories may have been incomplete with respect to the number of past employers, making five an underestimate. In short, the data from the report indicate that workers were mobile. Furthermore, it cannot be argued that mobility was meaningless because all millowners were equally bad. The witnesses clearly identified some millowners as "bad" and some as "good." Many claimed to have left unsafe factories or cruel masters for better conditions elsewhere. The testimony, then, shows that the forces of competition were present in the textile labor market.

The behavior of workers in the cotton textile industry is consistent with the hypothesis that the labor market was competitive in the early nineteenth century. It is nevertheless not possible to conclude from the evidence that exploitation was absent. A believer in exploitation might, for example, argue that the frequent job changes are evidence of a lack of job security, perhaps planned by capitalists as a way to keep workers at a disadvantage in bargaining. All that the evidence on market structure and mobility can establish is that exploitation may have been absent, that a competitive, non-exploitative labor market cannot be ruled out. More definite conclusions can only be based on measures of exploitation itself.

III. INDIRECT MEASURES OF EXPLOITATION

The indirect measures of the exploitation of children include health, adult wages and child employment, migration and job mobility, apprenticeship, future prospects, and compensating differentials. None of these measures will provide conclusive evidence on the existence of exploitation. Indeed, it is likely that all of the measures taken together will fail to provide definitive answers. What these indirect measures of exploitation can do is provide some evidence with which to confront the views of novelists and social critics. I will begin the review of the historical evidence with health.

A. Health

The employment of children is frequently alleged to have ruined their health. This view is common in the literature produced by the hard times school of thought. For example, an oft-quoted verse entitled "The Factory Child's Last Day" tells the sad tale of a little factory girl who is worked to death (Kydd, 1856, Vol. 2, pp. 309–11). The progressive deterioration of health was emphasized by Engels in his study of the working class and subsequently became part of the Marxian interpretation of the industrial revolution. Marx wrote of the

physical deterioration . . . of the children and young persons as of the women, whom machinery, first directly in the factories that shoot up on its basis, and then indirectly in all the remaining branches of industry, subjects to the exploitation of capital (1867, p. 397).

The neoclassical model of exploitation might use an analogy between children in factories and West Indian slaves.[21] One of the most notable features of West Indian slavery was its fearful rates of mortality. In many of the West Indian slave colonies, the death rate exceeded the birth rate; continuous imports were needed in order to maintain the slave labor force. Planters apparently found it cheaper to work slaves to death and import new ones than to pay them enough in implicit wages to allow natural increase to maintain the labor force.[22] In the case of West Indian slaves, then, exploitation took the form of exposure to unhealthy living and working conditions.

If the situation of children in factories in factories was, as many writers have asserted, analogous to that of West Indian slaves, then the exploitation of children took the form of long exposure to unhealthy working conditions. Children sacrificed their health without compensation as millowners reaped the rewards of exploitation. The evidence that children were exploited in this manner is of two kinds.

First, there is abundant anecdotal evidence of how factory work damaged health. The stories of William Dodd (1842) and Robert Blincoe (Brown, 1832) and the evidence collected in the *Report of the Select Committee on the Bill for the Regulation of Factories* (Great Britain, 1831–1832) tell a terrible tale of ill-health and ill-usage. The debilitating effects of working around machinery in poorly ventilated factories are alleged to have ruined the health of children. The problem with these anecdotes is that there are counter-anecdotes. The model factories of Henry Ashworth (Boyson, 1970), McConnel and Kennedy (Lee, 1972), and others can be cited to support the contention that children in factories were generally healthy. The reports of the factory inspectors and of various royal commissions contain many examples of factories in which children were apparently treated well. Even the opinions of doctors who investigated factories were divided. Derek Fraser, describing the medical testimony, wrote that where "some eyes saw debilitated and deformed children, others saw alert and lively youngsters doing useful, healthy work." (1973, p. 13). In short, the anecdotal evidence on the health of children is inconclusive.

The second kind of evidence on the health of children is the rate of mortality in the factory districts. Both infant mortality and total mortality are cited as evidence of the poor health of factory children. An objection to using infant and total mortality rates is that they do not necessarily reflect the condition of children in factories. Mortality rates were high for many reasons, one of the most prominent being urban disamenities.[23] Although mortality rates were higher in urban than in rural areas, urban mortality rates were nevertheless falling during the industrial revolution (Wrigley and Schofield, 1981 pp. 228–36). Moreover, the existence of high urban mortality rates does not imply that children were exploited. It implies that living in the city was not as healthy as living in the country. The existing data on mortality cannot be construed to say anything about the economic exploitation of children.

The standard evidence on mortality, then, does not say much about the relative health of children employed in factories. What is needed is some measure of relative health. The *Report on the State and Conditions of the Children Employed in the Cotton Manufactories of the United Kingdom* (Great Britain, 1819) contains an appendix on the days of work lost by cotton workers due to illness. The data were drawn from only 11 factories, so the report should not be interpreted as a survey of the health of all British workers. The report contains data on health from the years 1818–1819 for 1806 workers of all ages.[24] In Table 1, days lost by age are shown for the workers in the sample. The table shows that children under 15 were at least as healthy as older workers and may have been slightly healthier than the rest of the work force. Children under 10 missed fewer days of work than any other age group, with 89.2 percent missing less than one week, compared to 79.5 percent of the sample as a whole. Workers aged 10–14 missed more time than the youngest group, but 79.8 percent missed less than one week, a greater percentage than for the sample as a whole.

A similar survey on days of work lost by age was undertaken in 1833 by the Factories Inquiry Commission (Great Britain, 1834, Pt. 1). Data were collected on workers in cotton factories in Lancashire and Glasgow and on workers in woolen factories in northern England. Younger workers, especially males, were for the most part the healthiest members of the labor force. Workers under the age of 16 lost, on average, less than one week per year due to illness. Older

Table 1. Time Lost by Cotton Workers in 1818–1819

Time Lost	Under 10	10–14	15–19	20–29	30–39	40 and over	Total
Less than 1 week	83 (89.2%)	458 (79.8%)	337 (78.9%)	319 (76.5%)	162 (81.4%)	76 (79.2%)	1435 (79.5%)
1–3 weeks	5 (5.4%)	48 (8.4%)	28 (6.6%)	41 (9.8%)	16 (8.0%)	7 (7.3%)	145 (8.0%)
Over 3 weeks	5 (5.4%)	68 (11.8%)	62 (14.5%)	57 (13.7%)	21 (10.6%)	13 (13.50%)	226 (12.5%)
Total	93	574	427	417	199	96	1806

Source: Report on the State and Conditions of the Children Employed in the Cotton Manufactories of the United Kingdom (Great Britain, 1819).

254

workers missed slightly more time, but the differences in most cases were not large.[25]

The obvious implication of Table 1 and the 1833 survey is that there were no pronounced differences in the health of cotton workers of different ages. What differences there are seem to indicate that children were healthier than older workers. Similarities in time lost might, of course, mask significant differences in health. It is also possible that a cross-sectional analysis such as Table 1 might fail to reveal the dynamic process of deterioration and replacement described by the slavery model. These objections cannot, however, reverse the result that the health data do not support the simple exploitation model. There is in fact no evidence that children's health differed significantly from the health of older workers.[26] If children were systematically worked to death only to be replaced by new waves of exploited victims, the data do not show it. If children were exploited, the exploitation did not take the form of poor health relative to other workers.

Although the health of children employed in textile factories was not inferior to that of older factory workers, it is possible that it was inferior to the health of children not employed in factories. The factory children can be regarded as the vanguard of the transformation of childhood brought about by the industrial revolution. As the group most directly affected by industrialization, child factory workers would be expected to have poor health relative to other children, assuming that industrialization brought exploitation and exploitation brought poor health. The lack of direct estimates of the health of the general population makes comparisons such as those of Table 1 impossible for factory and non-factory children. An alternative method of comparing the health of different groups of children is to compare their heights (Eveleth and Tanner, 1976, pp. 1–14). The use of height to measure nutrition and health has long been common among physiologists, nutritionists, and others (Tanner, 1981). In recent years, economic historians have also begun to exploit this rich source of data (Fogel, et. al., 1983). Data on height contain much information on economic and social well-being and are more acceptable for long-run comparisons than national income or wage data.[27] Moreover, preliminary findings indicate that height and per capita income are correlated (Steckel, 1983). It is therefore possible to make inferences about exploitation on the basis of heights.

In a recent study, Roderick Floud and Kenneth W. Wachter (1982) used the records of the Marine Society (a London charity) to estimate the heights of London boys for the years 1770–1870. Their most important finding was that London boys aged 13 to 16 were quite short by modern standards, especially in the eighteenth century. The low stature of London boys indicates the lack of nutrition and that standards of public health were also low. The time series on heights does not, however, reveal anything about exploitation. Heights gradually rose as the industrial revolution progressed. If industrialization increased the exploitation of child labor, such a rise might not have occurred. Furthermore, the historical time series on heights corresponds reasonably well to time series on the real wages of adult males, indicating that the relative position of children did not deteriorate between 1770 and 1870. The years in which the heights of children increased slowly or not at all can be explained by the same factors—such as the French Wars—that caused the general standard of living to stagnate (Williamson, 1984).

Objections might be raised to drawing general conclusions from a London time series. Although the heights of the London poor may have been highly correlated with the heights of all British poor, they might not have been closely correlated with the heights of all British children. Moreover, the relationship between a time series on heights and the economic exploitation of children is not self-evident. The exploitation of children during the industrial revolution would be better measured by comparing the heights of factory children with the heights of a sample of children drawn from the rest of the population. Such a comparison was made by factory inspector Leonard Horner in 1837.[28]

Horner's comparison of heights was inspired by the widespread casual observation that children employed in textile factories were shorter than other children of the same age.[29] References to stunted growth and physical degeneracy are common in the hard times literature on the employment of children. Yet, Horner found that children employed in factories were not shorter than their cohorts outside the factories. The Manchester factory children aged 13 to 17 were from 3.7 to 6.2 centimeters taller than the children in Horner's national sample (Floud and Wachter, 1982, p. 445). Horner's data are marred by possible sampling error and his inability to deal with some of the peculiarities of height data, but his qualitative conclusions are not likely to be reversed. According to his study of heights, if the children employed in Manchester textile factories were exploited, the exploitation did not take the form of poor health relative to children not employed in factories. The low stature of factory children was not the result of their being exploited by other sectors of the population; it was the result of the general poverty and malnourishment of the British working classes.

B. Adult Wages and Child Employment

The ability of employers to exploit child labor would be expected to lead to the increased hiring of children. Under the neoclassical view of exploitation, the increased hiring of children reduces the demand for adult labor as children are substituted for older workers. The declining demand for their services reduces the wage rate for adults. The Marxian and hard times models of exploitation also predict that the employment of children reduces adult wages. According to Marx, the employment of children allows the capitalist to reduce the workers wage rate because his previous wages can now be spread over the whole family. In order for the employment of children to have this effect, the capitalist must be able to exploit children: that is, he must be able to pay them less than the value of what they produce. The hard times literature is also full of references to how the employment of children drives down wages and throws adults out of work. All three models of exploitation, then, predict an inverse relationship between adult wages and the employment of children.

In fact, there was no apparent relationship between adult wages and the employment of children. E. H. Hunt, in his study of regional wage variations in the second half of the nineteenth century, found that

> in the main, and for most of the period, areas where men's wages were low were distinguished neither by high activity rates nor high family earnings, while many other areas combined high wages for men with better than average opportunities for women and young people (1973, p. 126).

In 1851, the activity rate for children age 10–14 was highest in the industrial counties of the north and midlands, where adult wages were relatively high. The counties with the six highest activity rates were Bedfordshire (50 percent), the West Riding (44 percent), Northamptonshire (40 percent), Buckinghamshire (39 percent), Lancashire (39 percent), and Nottinghamshire (39 percent). The activity rate for children age 10–14 was lowest in the London area and agricultural areas, where adult wages were relatively low. The counties with the six lowest activity rates were Middlesex (13 percent), Dorset (14 percent), London (17 percent), Westmoreland (18 percent), Northumberland (18 percent), and Kent (18 percent).

The geographical pattern of children's employment therefore does not conform to the predictions of the exploitation model. On the contrary, the geographical pattern is the opposite of that predicted by the model. The geographical pattern is, however, consistent with the model of a competitive labor market. The competitive model can also be used to explain the evidence on the migration and job mobility of children.

C. Migration and Job Mobility

If the child labor market was competitive, one prediction is that children, like adults, were mobile. Scattered evidence indicates that such was the case. Children apparently migrated to those areas where their wages were highest. In particular, children came from all over to the centers of the textile industry. Although in the eighteenth century child migrants tended to be parish apprentices, by the nineteenth century they were mostly free children, migrating with their parents or on their own (Redford, 1926, pp. 20–61).

In addition to geographical mobility, children were mobile between employers. Many of the voluntary job changes described in the *Report of the Select Committee* (Great Britain, 1831–1832) had taken place when the workers were children. The children interviewed by parliamentary commissions of the 1830s and 1840s frequently had worked for two or more employers.[30] Working-class autobiographies also present childhood as a time of frequent job changes.[31] The ability and willingness to leave if wages or conditions were inadequate must have severely limited the opportunities of employers to exploit children. Potential mobility was further enhanced by the geographical concentration of most major child-employing industries.

D. Apprenticeship

Not all children were free to migrate or to change jobs at will. Apprentices were bound over to master for a usual period of seven years. The institution of apprenticeship must therefore be considered as a potential source of exploitation. During an apprentice's term of service, the master owned that apprentice's labor, creating an obvious opportunity for economic exploitation. Now, certain factors operated to reduce the potential abuse of apprentices. Custom, the Common Law, and the bargaining strength of parents all served to check the power of masters over apprentices in skilled trades.[32] Moreover, to be apprenticed in a skilled trade was generally regarded as desirable, which implies that exploitation was not severe. Despite these qualifications, the potential for exploitation remained and must have been at least occasionally taken advantage of.

In the case of pauper apprentices, the power of the masters was not checked by the parents. Pauper apprentices were children apprenticed out by parish overseers under the provisions of the Poor Law. Pauper children were not wanted in skilled trades; parish authorities therefore bound children to unskilled occupations. The coming of the factory system led to children being sent to work in cotton factories as apprentice labor, an arrangement that simultaneously relieved overcrowding in parish workhouses and problems of labor supply in factories. Although some factory owners treated parish apprentices fairly, the exploitation of children appears to have been common under this system.[33] The Factory Act of 1802, though ineffective, was an attempt to curb the exploitation of pauper apprentices.

The abuse of apprenticeship was not the creation of the industrial revolution. In his essay on England before industrialization, Peter Laslett wrote:

> Apprentices therefore, were workers who were also children, extra children, extra sons or extra daughters (for girls could be apprenticed too), clothed and educated as well as fed, obliged to obedience and forbidden to marry, unpaid and absolutely dependent until the age of twenty-one. . . We may see at once, therefore, that the world we have lost, as I have chosen to call it, was no paradise or golden age of equality, tolerance or loving kindness. It is so important that I should not be misunderstood on this point that I will say at once that the coming of industry cannot be shown to have brought economic oppression and exploitation along with it. It was there already (1965, p. 3).

I will go one step further than Laslett and argue that not only did the industrial revolution not increase the exploitation of apprentices, it reduced it.

The concentration of historians on the horror stories associated with pauper apprenticeship has, I believe, obscured the real relationship between the industrial revolution and apprenticeship. The industrial revolution ended apprenticeship. The early factory masters employed an apprentice workforce because no other was available.[34] Free children, however, rapidly replaced apprentices in the textile industries in the early nineteenth century.[35] Furthermore, as modern industry replaced handicraft industry, the institution of apprenticeship began to disappear throughout the economy. Although many observers mourned the passing of the handicraft industry, its passing did create a more competitive labor market. When the industrial revolution undermined apprenticeship, it also undermined the potential exploitation inherent in that institution.

E. The Future Prospects of Child Workers

One of the criticisms of child labor in textile and other factories was that it destroyed the future prospects of the children. It was alleged that factory children were unable to acquire skills or education. Furthermore, they could not expect to work in factories after reaching adulthood because few adults were needed in the early factories. The exploitation of children, then, foredoomed them to a life of poverty.

Upon close examination, however, the evidence does not necessarily imply that child labor destroyed children's future prospects. The opportunities for adult employment in factories have been underrated by historians; many children employed in factories eventually became adult factory workers. Although the proportion of children in the textile factory labor force was higher than the proportion in other industries, adults outnumbered children from at least the earliest factory returns.[36] Textile factories could not absorb all of the factory children because adults had longer working lives. The factories nevertheless provided many jobs to former factory children. Moreover, the importance of children in the textile industry vastly exceeded their importance in most other industries.[37] In other industries, children formed a small to negligible part of the labor force and could easily be absorbed into adult employments when they came of age. Most of the positions in non-textile factories were filled by adult males.[38]

The difference between textile and non-textile factories suggests what happened to child textile workers who left textile factories: they left to work in factories where adults dominated the labor force. Employment in a textile factory may simply have been a normal early stage in the life cycle of working-class men and women. Men worked in textile factories as children and then went on to other occupations. Women worked in textile factories as children and young adults and then left to bear children and, on occasion, pursue other occupations.

The hypothesis that working in a textile factory was a normal and benign part of the working-class life cycle is supported by evidence from Jedediah Strutt's cotton mill at Belper. From December 1805 to July 1812 the Strutts kept records of the workers who gave notice and their reasons for leaving (Fitton and Wadsworth, 1958, pp. 230–32). Of the 89 males who left, 78 left to pursue another occupation. In many cases it was explicitly stated that a young man had left to learn a trade. Of the 278 females who left, 147 were pregnant and 82 were going to work elsewhere. Only 5 males and 21 females gave notice because of general dissatisfaction with work or wages.

Although detailed surveys of working careers do not exist, various parliamentary investigations, autobiographies, and biographies provide a wealth of information on individual workers. The available information indicates that child workers later were able to enter most other occupations. As early as 1819, former factory workers were employed as tailors, shoemakers, clockmakers, blacksmiths, farmers, and merchants, as well as handloom weavers and farm and non-farm laborers.[39] Many early radical and working-class leaders had been employed as children.[40] Some former child workers even became manufacturers.[41] It appears unlikely that a large population of destitute former child workers existed in nineteenth-century Britain.

The question of education remains. The employment of children must have reduced their opportunities for education, though the Factory Act of 1833 required textile factories to provide education for child employees (Sanderson, 1972; West, 1978). Although recent research has shown that the returns to literacy were relatively high in the nineteenth century, it is not clear that employment prevented children from acquiring basic literacy.[42] Literacy rates rose rapidly after 1840, a rise that was only partly the result of government intervention.[43] The rise in literacy shows that children did have opportunities to acquire some education and that most took advantage of those opportunites. For example, children could attend school before entering the labor force. Myths to the contrary, few children worked full time before age 10 in nineteenth-century Britain. An early survey of children in Scottish textile and agricultural districts showed that by 1819, over 92 percent of children under 10 were not in the labor force (Great Britain, 1819). By 1851, 98 percent of children ages five to nine were not in the labor force (Great Britain, 1851). Education could also be obtained on a part-time basis by children already gainfully employed. Despite the barriers that child labor may have put in the way of obtaining an education, by the 1880s nearly all young people in Britain were literate (Stone, 1969). Illiteracy can therefore not be used as evidence that children were exploited in nineteenth-century factories.[44]

F. Compensating Differentials

One of the predictions of the competitive model is that, in equilibrium, compensating wage differentials will equalize the total returns in different occupations (at least for the marginal worker). Workers in particularly difficult or unpleasant occupations must, according to the theory, be paid extra in order to enter these occupations. The neoclassical model of exploitation, with its comparison of child labor to West Indian slavery, would not necessarily predict the existence of compensating differentials.[45] The hard times model would also fail to predict any compensation for harsh treatment. Although the Marxian model does not specifically imply anything about the existence of compensating differentials, they are not an explicit prediction of the model. Only the model of a non-exploitative, competitive labor market predicts that compensating differentials will be paid.

In another paper, I have shown that children were paid a compensating differential when they were subject to corporal punishment (Nardinelli, 1982). In that paper, I estimated the wage premium on corporal punishment for a sample of 261 child workers aged 14 and under. The sample was drawn from the *Report of the Royal Commission on the Employment of Children in Trades and Manufactures* (Great Britain, 1843). With age, work experience, and literacy held constant, the coefficient in a cross-sectional regression indicated that corporal punishment raised children's wage rates by 16–18 percent, a result consistent with the model of a competitive labor market.[46]

In this paper, a simple test for the existence of compensating differentials will be used: the wage rates of children employed in coal mines will be compared to the wage rates of children employed elsewhere. The historical literature usually identifies coal mining as the most miserable occupation of children.[47] The theory of compensating differentials would therefore predict that the wages of child miners would be higher than the wages of other child workers. To test this hypothesis, I compared the wages of 236 child miners with the wages of 238 children in other occupations, mainly metal-working, earthenware, paper-making, and tobacco. The data sample consisted of 474 male children and was drawn from the reports of the Royal Commission on Children's Employment (1842–1843).[48] The children in the sample were aged 10 to 14.

In the wage comparisons, only age and sex were held constant. Wages, however, also varied because of education, experience, and forms of discipline. Differences between the wages of child miners and other child workers arising from these sources were probably small. Moreover, they tended to offset one another. For example, child miners were less literate but had more work experience than other child workers.[49] The incidence of corporal punishment was approximately the same for both groups of children.[50] The small and offsetting effects of these other variables justifies ignoring them in the comparisons of wages.

The theory of compensating differentials implies that in a competitive labor market, child miners would receive higher wages than other child workers. Given the undisguised horror with which many observers described the mining industry, we might expect the difference to be large. As Table 2 shows, it was. The average wages of child miners were 54 to 86 percent higher than the average wages of other children. This large differential is consistent with the hypothesis that the child labor market was competitive.

That the child labor market behaved as if it were competitive is not, of course,

Table 2. A Comparison of the Wages of Children Employed in Mines
with the Wages of Children Employed in Other Occupations
(Average wages in pence per week in 1842)

	Miners		*Other Workers*		*% difference in wages*
Age	*Number*	*Wage*	*Number*	*Wage*	*(Miners higher = +)*
10	45	54	32	29	+86
11	48	68	47	43	+58
12	45	70	56	44	+59
13	58	84	59	49	+71
14	40	91	44	59	+54
	236		238		

Source: Mines Report of the Children's Employment Commission (Great Britain, 1842), Appendix, Pt. 2, pp.
1–878, H1–H10, h1–h41; *Report of the Royal Commission on the Employment of Children in Trades and
Manufactures* (Great Britain, 1843), Appendix, pp. b1–b66, c1–c124, f1–f308, 11–148, ml–m76,
q1–q84.

direct evidence that children were not exploited. In combination with the other
findings of this paper it does provide further indirect evidence that the exploitation of children was not the rule in nineteenth-century labor markets. The evidence is, however, subject to the limitation that only market relationships of
children have been considered. Children were not completely free agents; they
were responsible to their parents or guardians. Parents frequently received their
children's pay directly from employers and children who were paid directly
usually turned their wages over to their parents. Parents, then, may have taken it
upon themselves to prevent the market exploitation of children. Because they
controlled the life and work of the children, it was in their pecuniary interest to
insure that children were paid the market value of their marginal products.

The power of parents of children may have had important effects on market
wages. It also made it possible for parents to exploit children. No explicit market
governed the relationship between parents and children. The non-market nature
of the relationship created opportunities for exploitation whether or not parents
took advantage of them. It therefore may be the case that if free children were
exploited, it was by their own parents.

IV. PARENTS AND CHILDREN

The most likely way that the industrial revolution could have increased the
exploitation of children was by inducing more parents to exploit their children.
That many parents did indeed greedily neglect the welfare of their children is

beyond question. Michael T. Sadler described such parents as ''monsters'':

> Dead to the instincts of nature, and reversing the order of society, instead of providing for their offspring, they make their offspring provide for them: not only for their necessities, but for their intemperance and profligacy. They purchase idleness by the sweat of their infants, the price of whose happiness, health, and existence, they spend in the haunts of dissipation and vice. Thus , at the very same hour of night that the father is at his guilty orgies, the child is panting at the factory (Kydd, 1857, Vol. 1, pp. 157–158).

There are many recorded instances of the economic exploitation of children during the first half of the nineteenth century. The descriptions of underpaid and mistreated child workers are among the more familiar horror stories of the early industrial revolution. Now, it is sometimes argued that by increasing the opportunities for the profitable employment of children the industrial revolution led parents astray. The income to be gained by sending a child off to work is alleged to have dominated natural parental concern for the health and welfare of children. The hypothesis was supported by J. L. and Barbara Hammond, who wrote that the

> system imposed on children more work and longer hours than human nature could bear, and somebody had to wring it out of them. Everywhere this cruel necessity hemmed in the life of the new society, and the new system wore a more inexorable face just because it made workmen, or even parents, the agents of its iron rule. In some cases, of course, not involuntary agents for there have always been parents ready to exploit their children, and the factory system offered a powerful incentive to that spirit. One witness before a Lords Committee boasted that he had broken his child's arm for disobedience in the mill. A system such as this was bound to find parents, and bound to make parents, callous to their children's sufferings, and no charge more bitter could be brought against it (1917, p. 33).

The exploitation inspired by the factory system included, and was motivated by, economic exploitation.

Despite the anecdotal evidence that working-class parents were brutal exploiters, there is much evidence to the contrary. In his study of nineteenth-century Preston, Michael Anderson found that family poverty played a more important role than exploitation in explaining the employment of children (Anderson, 1971, pp. 111–35). Few working-class families were permanently free from poverty; the employment of children became necessary in order for families to stay above the poverty line. According to Anderson,

> again and again, parents who otherwise showed considerable affection for their children and concern to do the best possible for them were yet forced by large families and low wages to send their children to work as soon as possible (1971, p. 76).

The main exceptions to this statement involved cases of parental drunkenness.

The problem of drunkenness is difficult to quantify. As Anderson points out, data from the nineteenth century indicate that the working classes were heavy drinkers (Anderson, 1971, p. 69–71). The consumption of beer, the working classes' favorite drink, was particularly heavy. In 1830, annual beer consumption in England and Wales was 19 gallons per person.[51] Heavy drinking is not, however, the same as drunkenness. Most observers agree that, though drinking was common, chronic drunkenness occurred in a small minority of cases. Such a result is consistent with the twentieth-century incidence of alcoholism. Moreover, for most working-class families the regular consumption of beer was part of daily life and not an inevitable path to drunkenness. Furthermore, even in those instances where heavy drinking did become a problem, the result was not necessarily exploitation. The problem of drunkenness, though important, cannot in itself overturn the other evidence on the position of children in the family economy.

Frances Collier's (1964) study of the family economy of cotton operatives showed the importance of children's earnings to the welfare of Lancashire families. The earnings of children often meant the difference between a comfortable subsistence and poverty. Collier believed that the factory system improved the economic status of families because of the increased opportunities for women and children. The typical working-class family would have had difficulty supporting itself without the earnings of the wife and children.

Working-class autobiographies cast further doubt upon the hypothesis that parents exploited children. In a study of autobiographies, David Vincent found that working-class people had warm feelings toward their parents. They did not consider themselves to be exploited, economically or otherwise. Children knew that they had to contribute to the family economy; many autobiographers remember being proud and happy to be able to help out. They depended upon their parents for financial security and were not bitter towards them for having to work. According to Vincent,

> No matter how bitter the autobiographers felt about their sufferings as child labourers, no matter how wrong they thought it was that they should have had to work, they very rarely blamed their parents for their experiences. They believed that their parents made them labour because they could not afford to do otherwise, and that as children they were simply trapped in the poverty of the family and the class into which they had been born (1981, p. 82).

Vincent found that only in a few cases of habitual drunkenness did working-class fathers clearly exploit their children. The autobiographers were a select group, but it nevertheless is significant that they refused to blame their parents for having to work as children.

The relationship between parents and children was not the main concern of parliamentary investigations of child labor in the nineteenth century. Much evidence on the subject nevertheless appears in the reports of various select committees and royal commissions. There are occasional references to the exploitation of children in these reports. For example, the *First Report of the Factories Inquiry Commission* referred to some parents whose "sole consideration . . . in making choice of a person under whom to place their children is the amount of wages, not the mode of treatment to be secured to them" (Great Britain, 1833a,

p. 45). Such cases, however, were the exceptions. Most of the children interviewed by the subcommissioners of the Children's Employment Commission (1842–1843) did not think their parents exploited them. When parents were mentioned at all, it was usually in a favorable or neutral manner.

Even child miners were apparently not exploited by their parents. In the *Mines Report of the Children's Employment Commission* (Great Britain, 1842), the sordid conditions in the mines were summarized by the commissioners. Although they found much to horrify and disgust them, the commissioners nevertheless concluded that

> in general the Children and Young Persons who work in these mines have sufficient food, and, when above ground, decent and comfortable clothing, their usually high rate of wages securing to them these advantages; but in many cases, . . . the food is poor in quality, and insufficient in quantity; the Children themselves say that they have not enough to eat; and the Sub-Commissioners describe them as covered with rags, . . . in general, however, the Children who are in this unhappy case are the Children of idle and dissolute parents, who spend the hard-earned wages of their offspring at the public house (p. 258).

The story in the mines, then, is consistent with the other evidence that, except in cases of drunkenness, parents did not systematically exploit their children. Children were as well-fed and well-clothed as limited family incomes would allow.

The tentative conclusion that most parents did not exploit their children raises a further question: Was this lack of exploitation due to the triumph of parental affection over the dehumanizing industrial revolution? That is the conclusion implied by the view that the industrial revolution created greater incentives for parents to exploit their children. Vincent argued that the "early factories both intensified the hardships of child labour and emptied it of what positive value it had possessed" (1981, p. 86). The positive values Vincent referred to included both material and psychological transfers from parents to children. A reduction in these transfers combined with an increase in the amount or difficulty of the child's work clearly imply that exploitation increased. The recorded instances of exploitation can thus be interpreted as the cases in which the incentives for exploitation won out over parental affection. The theories of the Hammonds, Sadler, Vincent, and many others imply that such instances increased with the coming of the industrial revolution.

I believe that, rather than increasing the exploitation of children, the industrial revolution decreased it. The new employments created by industrialization created opportunities for children to escape exploitation. Before the industrial revolution, children had few alternatives to parental control. If they were exploited by their parents, they usually had no choice but to accept it. The factories and other new employers created alternatives to parental control. The factories made it possible for children to leave home while still in their teens. Indeed, the growing independence of children was frequently cited as one of the evils of the factory system.

Children did not have to actually leave home in order to avoid being exploited. The ability to leave was sufficient to remove the opportunity of parents to exploit or mistreat children. Though they could have been independent, Anderson found that most children did not leave home until age 20 or older. Children were able to do better by staying home than by leaving, implying that parents made it attractive to remain at home. The decisions to remain in the home as part of the family economy was not the result of coercion; it was the result of a mutually advantageous exchange. According to Anderson,

> children's high individual wages allowed then to enter into . . . bargains with their parents on terms of more or less precise equality. If, as was usually the case, a bargain could be struck which was immediately favorable to both parties, then all was well, and the relationship continued, though the degree of commitment to such a relationship must often have been low. If a better alternative was obtainable elsewhere the child could take it. The contrast between the choice element in these relationships between urban children and their parents, and the situation in rural areas . . . is very marked (1971, pp. 131–32).

The difference Anderson noted between urban and rural children was largely created by the industrial revolution. The industrial revolution, then, reduced the exploitation of child labor by reducing the power of parents over children. A free bargain between equals precludes exploitation. This conclusion is contrary to traditional beliefs but is supported by the evidence. In the absence of parental affection, narrow self-interest would prove sufficient to cause parents to treat children better in an industrial than in a pre-industrial society.

V. CONCLUDING REMARKS

Economic exploitation was, of course, not absent during the industrial revolution. Some employers exploited employees and some parents exploited children. Pauper apprentices and children whose parents drank heavily were especially likely to suffer this unfair treatment. What I have attempted to show is that such cases were aberrations or survivals from earlier times. Competition prevented the systematic exploitation of workers by their employers. The natural affection of parents and the children's ability to leave home tended to prevent the exploitation of children by parents.

The lack of economic exploitation does not imply that factories, workshops, and mines were pleasant places to work or that wages were high. It implies that given the constraints imposed by means and opportunities, children did as well as they could. Small children worked because their families were poor and needed the extra income. Industrialization did not create this situation; poverty and the necessity to work existed long before the industrial revolution. If child labor was indeed evil, the evil was caused by poverty, not by textile factories.

When one considers the experience of childhood before the industrial revolution, the identification of industrialization as the source of the exploitation of children is surprising. The history of childhood in the centuries before the industrial revolution is sometimes horrifying and always grim.[52] In the (possibly exaggerated) words of Lloyd deMause:

> ,
> The history of childhood is a nightmare from which we have only recently begun to awaken. The further back in history one goes, the lower the level of child care, and the more likely children are to be killed, abandoned, beaten, terrorized, and sexually abused (1974, p. 1).

That children would work at early ages was not questioned by pre-industrial families. The economic value of children in peasant agriculture was relatively high because of the many possibilities for specialization by age. Given the brutality and harshness of much of pre-industrial life, that the working conditions of children were particularly benign is doubtful. Furthermore, the argument that industrialization increased the economic exploitation of children by removing them from the home is questionable, particularly since children in early modern England frequently did work outside the home.[53] One of the most important changes in the centuries before the industrial revolution was a gradual increase in the age at which children left home to become apprentices or farm servants. The slow increase in real income per capita led to an increase in the time spent at home before leaving to enter the labor market.[54] The age at which children began to work outside the home continued to rise throughout the nineteenth century.[55]

The modern view of childhood is itself a result of the industrial revolution and modern economic growth. As incomes rose and child and infant mortality fell, parents invested more time and money in increasing the educational and health levels of individual children.[56] A "new world of children" emerged in the eighteenth century among the upper classes and gradually spread to the other classes (Plumb, 1982). Expenditures on education rose, new consumption goods appeared, and family life began to revolve more and more around children. Despite the continued existence of child labor, it is difficult to understand why the nineteenth century has been singled out as a time of exploitation.[57] In no previous century did transfers *to* children rise so much more rapidly than transfers *from* children. An obvious implication is that exploitation—if it continued to exist—declined during the nineteenth century.

The hypothesis that the industrial revolution did not create child labor or exploitation is not new, Many economic historians have conceded that the industrial revolution may not have altered the condition of child workers for the worse. For example, according to Carlo M. Cipolla,

> child labor is described as a ghastly by-product of the Industrial Revolution. The truth is that in preindustrial society, children were as widely employed as at the time of the Industrial Revolution . . . Life in the fields was perhaps not so unhealthy as in the factories of the early Industrial Revolution, but the hardships to which children were subjected were not more tolerable (1980, p. 71).

In his classic history of the industrial revolution, Paul Mantoux interrupted his description of child labor in the late eighteenth century to point out that the

only extenuating circumstance in the painful events which we have now to recount as shortly as we can, was that forced child labor was no new evil. In the domestic system of manufacture children were exploited as a mater of course. Among the Birmingham ironmongers apprenticeship began at seven years of age. Among the weavers of the north and the south-west children worked at five or even four years old, as soon in fact as they were considered capable of attention and obedience. Far from regarding this with indignation, men at that time thought it an admirable system (1961, p. 411).

Many historians, then, viewed the exploitation of children during the nineteenth century as a continuation of past practice. The argument of this paper goes further. The evidence, admittedly fragmentary, implies that not only did the industrial revolution not increase exploitation, it gradually improved the situation of children. The increasing competitiveness of the labor market reduced imperfections and thereby reduced opportunities for exploitation. The increasing industrial employment of children gave them the freedom to leave harsh or exploitative parents. Moreover, in the long run the industrial revolution ended child labor by increasing working-class incomes, because as family incomes rose, child labor declined. Industrialization, far from being the source of the enslavement of children, was the source of their liberation.

APPENDIX

Neoclassical economic exploitation occurs when the value of the worker's marginal product is greater than the wage rate. Suppose that the production function is of the form $Q = f (L, \text{other factors})$, where Q is output and L is labor. The value of the marginal product of labor is defined as

$$VMP_L = P \cdot MP_L; \qquad (A1)$$

where VMP_L = value of marginal product or labor,
MP_L = $\Delta Q/\Delta L$ = marginal product of labor,
P = price of the final product.

Exploitation occurs whenever the wage rate, W, is less than VMP_L.

It can be shown that if perfect competition exists in product and factor markets, exploitation will not exist. The marginal revenue product of labor is defined as

$$MRP_L = MR \cdot MP_L; \qquad (A2)$$

where MRP_L = marginal revenue product of labor,
MR = $P + Q \cdot (\Delta P/\Delta Q)$ = marginal revenue.

A general condition for profit maximization is that a factor such as labor should be hired up to the point where

$$MRP_L = MC_L \qquad (A3)$$

where $MC_L = W + L \cdot (\Delta W / \Delta L) =$ the marginal cost of labor.

Now, in perfect competition firms are price takers in all markets, implying that $P = MR$ and $W = MC_L$. The condition for profit maximization in the factor market reduces to

$$VMP_L = W. \qquad (A4)$$

There is therefore no exploitation under conditions of perfect competition.

Monopolistic exploitation occurs because of monopoly in product markets. When monopoly is present, $P > MR$ and $VMP_L > MRP_L$. Because profit maximization requires that $MRP_L = W$ (assuming monopsony is absent), $VMP_L > W$. This situation is called monopolistic exploitation and is represented by the vertical distance AB in Figure 1.

Monopsonistic exploitation occurs because of monopsony power in the labor market. Because the wage rate is not given to the individual firm, $W < MC_L$. In terms of Figure 1, the MC_L curve lies above S_L, the supply curve of labor. Since $MRP_L = MC_{L'}$, $MRP_L > W$. This situation is called monopsonistic exploitation and is represented by the vertical distance BC in Figure 1.

Figure 1. The Monopolistic and Monopsonistic Exploitation of Labor

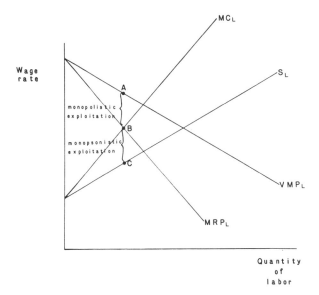

If monopoly, monopsony, or both are present, neoclassical economic exploitaton will occur. A situation in which both monopolistic and monopsonistic exploitation occur is represented by the vertical distance AC in Figure 1.

ACKNOWLEDGMENT

I wish to thank Donald McCloskey for first stimulating my interest in child labor and for his valuable comments on an earlier version of the paper.

NOTES

1. The classical statements of this belief are Hammond and Hammond (1917) and Thompson (1963). The literature on the evils of child labor is extensive. Some representative works include Kay-Shuttleworth (1832), Gaskell (1833), Fielden (1836), Cobden (1860), Hobsbawm (1967), Inglis (1971), and Thomis (1974).

2. The name for this definition of exploitation is, of course, taken from Dickens (1854).

3. See Engels (1845) for his classic description of working-class Manchester. The views of the young Engels are discussed in Marcus (1974).

4. Much has been written about the social novels inspired by the industrial revolution. Cazamian (1903) and Melanda (1970) are two useful and representative literary works. For a critical survey of the "Condition of England" novels, see Jefferson (1972).

5. For an assessment of Dickens by an economic historian, see Aydelote (1948). Given his recognized position as a severe critic of child labor, it is strange that with the exception of a brief (probably autobiographical) passage in *David Copperfield* (1850), Dickens did not write about child labor in any of his novels.

6. Marx refers to child labor often. A good summary of his general view on the exploitation of children is in Marx (1867, pp. 394–402).

7. This definition is discussed in Fogel and Engerman (1974, Vol. 2, pp. 87–90). Fogel and Engerman called it Robinsonian exploitation, after its originator (Robinson, 1969, pp. 281–304). Discussions of exploitation are relatively rare in the literature of current mainstream economics. For a useful exposition of Robinson's model, see Ekeland and Herbert (1983, pp. 488–93).

8. The value of marginal product is equal to the marginal physical product multiplied by the price of the final product. It should be noted that a wage rate less than the value of marginal product is a necessary but not a sufficient condition for exploitation. Other variables, such as training costs or compensating differentials, can reduce wages to below the value of marginal product.

9. For a critical summary of the literature comparing slavery and child labor, see Hartwell (1971, pp. 390–408).

10. The difference between monopolistic and monopsonistic exploitation is illustrated in the appendix.

11. It should be noted that Blaug's data are for the year 1834.

12. The estimate in the text (25 percent) was the average of two estimates of the share of wages and salaries in the value of output. Deane and Cole (1969, p. 187) estimate labor's share to be 24 percent in 1834–1836. Blaug (1961, p. 379) estimates labor's share to be 26 percent.

13. Wood's estimate of total cotton factory employment is reprinted in Mitchell and Deane (1962, p. 187). The percentage of children in the work force was computed from data in Great Britain (1834, p. 1, Pt. 19–37).

14. The wage estimate given in the text is that of Dr. Mitchell given in Great Britain (1834). The weekly wage data were transformed into annual data by assuming a 50-week work year.

15. Dean and Cole (1969, p. 187) estimate labor's share as 33 percent in 1829–1831.

16. Matthews' (1954, p. 151) estimate of the value of cotton output in 1833 is £32.3 million.

17. The standard wage estimates are those of Dr. Mitchell. According to Dr. Stanway's data, also reported in Great Britain (1834), wages were around 15 percent higher than implied by Dr. Mitchell's data.

18. The growth of national and international markets is one of the main themes of histories of the industrial revolution. There has been no debate about whether markets grew; the debate has been over the contribution expanding markets made to economic growth. For an important recent contribution to the debate, see Mokyr (1977).

19. The number of cotton factories increased from 1,819 in 1838 to 2,887 in 1861. The total number of textile factories (including cotton, wool, worsted, silk, and flax) increased from 4,217 to 6,378 over the same period. See Great Britain (1834–1878, 1837–1838, 1862).

20. For a recent descriptive survey of the structure of leading nineteenth-century industries, see Crouzet (1982).

21. The literature on slavery is enormous. Of particular relevance to the subject of this paper is Engerman and Genovese (1975). The contributions of Philip D. Curtin, Jack Ericson Eblen, Richard B. Sheridan, and Engerman are particularly valuable.

22. There is some question as to whether West Indian slaves died because planters worked them beyond the point of human endurance or because of the unhealthy climate. From the standpoint of the exploitation of slaves, the cause of the high rates of mortality does not matter. Similarly, if children were exploited in factories, it does not matter if their health was destroyed by extraordinarily hard work or by the unhealthy factory environment. What matters is that their health may have been destroyed.

23. The effect of urban disamenities on the standard of living has been analyzed in a series of recent papers by Jeffrey G. Williamson and Peter H. Lindert, including Williamson (1981, 1982) and Lindert and Williamson (1983). They conclude that urban disamenities had a trivial effect on the standard of living of the working class.

24. A more detailed description of the data and some of its implications is in Freudenberger, Mather, and Nardinelli (1984).

25. The only important exceptions to the statement in the text were two groups of women: Lancashire cotton workers over 40 and North England woolen workers over 30. The ill-health of these women—they lost two to three weeks of work per year due to illness—was probably the result not of factory work but of feminine afflictions.

26. The similarities in time lost among the different age groups also undermines the argument that the bad effects of factory work on children did not appear until later in life. Older workers were not as healthy as younger workers, but the differences appear to be small. One could, of course, argue that the really unhealthy workers had already left the labor force, leaving only healthy ones behind, but such an argument goes well beyond the available evidence.

27. Time series data on heights are not subject to the index number problems that plague long-run comparisons of prices, wages, and national income.

28. Horner's study is discussed in Tanner (1981). The results are summarized in Floud and Wachter (1982, p. 445).

29. See, for example, the testimony of the medical doctors in Great Britain (1831–1832).

30. The most important interviews are in Great Britain (1831–1832, 1833a, 1834, 1842, 1843). The mobility of children was increased by the unskilled nature of their work. Children moved easily not only between firms in the same industry but also between industries. Several child miners, for example, had formally been employed in textile factories. They typically reported leaving their previous employments for the higher wages in the mines. See, for example, Great Britain, (1842, Appendix, Pt. 2, pp. 206–207).

31. Vincent's (1982, pp. 62–86) description of the family economy mentions frequent changes of jobs. Charles Shaw ("An Old Potter") had worked for four different employers by the time he was 12 years old (Shaw, 1903).

32. The bargaining between parents and masters took place in a free market. It is possible that parents conspired with masters in order to exploit children. The effect of the industrial revolution on the relationship between parents and children is discussed in section IV.

33. See Clapham (1939, Vol. 1, pp. 370–374) and Mantoux (1961, pp. 408–17). The most famous description of the sufferings of a pauper apprentice is probably Brown (1832). Many of the best-known examples of the evils of child labor deal with the experiences of pauper apprentices.

34. Factory owners preferred to hire free workers. See Lee (1972, pp.114–15) and Ashton (1948, pp. 78–82).

35. For example, when Samuel Greg began working his cotton textile factory in the country at Styal in 1784, he relied heavily on apprentice labor. The wage books of Styal show the declining importance of apprentice labor in the first half of the nineteenth century. The employees at Styal were as follows:

	Wage-earners	Apprentices
1790	183	80
1831	351	100
1848	421	0

See Collier (1964, pp. 41–43).

36. By 1835, 56.6 percent of cotton factory workers and 52.3 percent of linen factory workers were over 18. See Great Britain (1834–1878, 31 October 1835).

37. The earliest detailed return on the composition of the labor force in non-textile factories is for 1867. See Great Britain (1834–1878, 30 April 1872, p. 139).

38. By 1867, over 66 percent of workers in non-textile factories were males 18 and over.

39. The Appendix to the *Report on the State and Conditions of the Children Employed in the Cotton Manufactories of the United Kingdom* (Great Britain, 1819) contains several tables showing current occupations of former factory workers.

40. One can find examples of labor leaders who began as child laborers throughout Bellamy and Savilee (1972–1984) as well as Vincent (1977).

41. The most surprising example is Robert Blincoe. See Brown (1832).

42. For some recent plausible estimates of the returns to literacy, see Mitch (1984).

43. E. G. West maintains that government intervention may have slowed down the rise in literacy. See West (1975–1978).

44. The relationship between literacy and industrialization is highly controversial, making the assertions in the text preliminary and tentative.

45. Compensating differentials are not, however, inconsistent with neoclassical exploitation. It is theoretically possible that exploited workers were nevertheless paid compensating differentials. The problem with this hypothesis is that it requires asymmetrical behavior on the part of employers. Employers compete away differential real returns by paying compensating differentials but fail to compete away exploitation. I find it more plausible to assume that competition would do away with exploitation.

46. The results of my 1982 study have been criticized on many grounds. The most important criticism, in my opinion, is that the results may be sensitive to the sample used. See MacKinnon and Johnson (1984) and Nardinelli (1984). For a theoretical explanation of the use of corporal punishment rather than other incentives, see Fenoaltea (1984).

47. The best source on the work of children in the mines is Great Britain (1842). The appendices are particularly useful. For brief summary of the evidence and the reactions to it, see Hammond and Hammond (1923, pp. 67–83).

48. The sample of children in occupations other than mining was mostly taken from the sample used in Nardinelli (1982).

49. Of the 236 children in the mines, I was able to measure the literacy of 193 and the work

experience of 188. I was able to measure these variables for all 238 of the other children. Of the children miners 36 (19 percent) were literate. The average age for beginning work was 8.8. Of the other children, 79 (33 percent) were literate and the average age for entering the work force was 9.7. Because the work of the children was unskilled, the effect of experience on wages was probably small.

50.   I could determine whether or not corporal punishment was used in the cases of only 64 child miners, of whom 35 (55 percent) suffered it. Of the 238 other children, 143 (60 percent) experienced corporal punishment. Because corporal punishment tended to increase wages, ignoring it in the wage comparisons may impart a slight downward bias to the measure of compensating differential associated with coal mining.

51.   The estimate of beer consumption per person was derived from Mitchell and Deane (1962, pp. 8, 252). According to the data on beer charged with duty, consumption steadily declined in the first 30 years of the nineteenth century. In 1800, beer consumption per person had been 27 gallons.

52.   For a useful bibliography on the history of childhood, see Sommerville (1972). More recent works of interest include Laslett (1972), DeMause (1974), Shorter (1975), and Stone (1977).

53.   Many children left home at an early age to become servants. See Kussmaul (1981).

54.   The argument that children stayed at home longer as income rose is based on Shorter (1975, pp. 26–28). According to Shorter, in the seventeenth and eighteenth centuries children left home earlier in the poor areas of France than in England or the more prosperous parts of France. I would argue that the age of leaving home had increased in England as income had increased.

55.   One important change that came about in the nineteenth century was that work outside the home no longer meant living away from home. Apprentices and farm servants in the eighteenth and earlier centuries left home when they entered the labor market. The children employed in industry in the nineteenth century continued to live at home while working elsewhere.

56.   The relationship between child and infant mortality and investments in health and education has been explored extensively in the human capital literature. For two important recent contributions, see Becker (1981, pp. 93–112) and Schultz (1981, pp. 18–39).

57.   The ambiguous attitude of historians toward childhood in nineteenth-century Britain can be seen in Sommerville (1982, pp. 160–178).

REFERENCES

Anderson, Michael (1971), *Family Structure in Nineteenth Century Lancashire*. Cambridge: Cambridge University Press.

Ashton, T. S. (1948), *The Industrial Revolution, 1760–1830*. London: Oxford University Press.

Aydelotte, William O. (1948), "The England of Marx and Mill as Reflected in Fiction." *Journal of Economic History*, 8, Supplement 8: 42–58.

Becker, Gary S. (1981), *A Treatise on the Family*. Cambridge, MA: Harvard University Press.

Bellamy, Joyce M., and John Savilee (eds.) (1972–1984), *Dictionary of Labour Biography*, 7 vols. London: Macmillan.

Blaug, Mark (1961), "The Productivity of Capital in the Lancashire Cotton Industry During the Nineteenth Century." *Economic History Review*, 13 (April): 358–381.

Boyson, Rhodes (1970), *The Ashworth Cotton Enterprise*. Oxford: Clarendon.

Brown, John (1823; 1966), *A Memoir of Robert Blincoe*. Derbyshire: Archaeological Society.

Cazamian, Louis (1903; 1973), *The Social Novel in England 1830–1850*, (translated by Martin Fido). London: Routledge and Kegan Paul.

Cipolla, Carlo M. (1980), *Before the Industrial Revolution*, 2nd ed. New York: W. W. Norton.

Clapham, J. H. (1939), *An Economic History of Modern Britain*, 3 vols. Cambridge: Cambridge University Press.

Cobden, John C. (1860; 1971), *The White Slaves of England*. Shannon, Ireland: Irish University Press.

Collier, Frances (1964), *The Family Economy of Working Classes in the Cotton Industry, 1784-1833*. Manchester: Manchester University Press.

Crouzet, Francois (1982), *The Victorian Economy*, (translated by A. S. Forster). New York: Columbia University Press.

Deane, Phyllis, and W. A. Cole (1969), *British Economic Growth, 1688-1959*, 2nd ed. Cambridge: Cambridge University Press.

DeMause, Lloyd (ed.) (1974), *The History of Childhood*. New York: The Psychohistory Press.

Dickens, Charles (1854; 1961), *Hard Times*. New York: New American Library.

Dodd, William (1842; 1968), *The Factory System Illustrated*. London: Frank Cass.

Driver, Cecil (1946), *Tory Radical: The Life of Richard Oastler*. New York: Oxford University Press.

Ekelund, Robert B., and Robert F. Hebert (1983), *A History of Economic Theory and Method*, 2nd ed. New York: McGraw-Hill

Engels, Fredrich (1845; 1968), *The Condition of the Working Class in England* (translated by W. O. Henderson and W. H. Chaloner). Stanford: Stanford University Press.

Engerman, Stanley L., and Eugene D. Genovese (eds.) (1975), *Race and Slavery in the Western Hemisphere: Quantitative Studies*. Princeton: Princeton University Press.

Eveleth, Phyllis B., and J. M. Tanner (1976), *Worldwide Variation in Human Growth*. Cambridge: Cambridge University Press.

Fenoaltea, Stefano (1984), "Slavery and Supervision in Compartive Perspective: A Model." *Journal of Economic History*, 44 (September): 635-68.

Fielden, John (1836; 1969), *The Curse of the Factory System*. New York: A. M. Kelley.

Fitton, R. S. and A. P. Wadsworth (1958), *The Strutts and the Arkwrights, 1758-1830*. Manchester: Manchester University Press.

Floud, Roderick, and Kenneth M. Wachter (1982), "Poverty and Physical Stature: Evidence on the Standard of Living of London Boys." *Social Science History*, 6 (Fall): 422-452.

Fogel, Robert W., and Stanley L. Engerman (1974), *Time on the Cross*, 2 vols. Boston: Little, Brown.

Fogel, Robert W., Stanley L. Engerman, Roderick Floud, Gerald Friedman, Robert A. Margo, Kenneth Sokoloff, Richard H. Steckel, T. James Trussell, Georgia Villaflor, and Kenneth W. Wachter (1983), "Secular Changes in American and British Stature and Nutrition." *Journal of Interdisciplinary History*, 14 (Autumn): 445-81.

Fraser, Derak (1973), *The Evolution of the British Welfare State*. New York: Barnes and Noble.

Freudenberger, Herman, Frances J. Mather, and Clark Nardinelli (1984), "A New Look at the Early Factory Labor Force." *Journal of Economic History*, 44 (December): 1085-1090.

Gaskell, Peter (1833; 1972), *The Manufacturing Population of England*. New York: Arno.

Gatrell, V. A. C. (1977), "Labour, Power, and the Size of Firms in Lancashire Cotton in the Second Quarter of the Nineteenth Century." *Economic History Review*, 30 (February): 95-139.

Great Britain (1819), Parliamentary Papers (Lords), *Report on the State and Conditions of the Children Employed in the Cotton Manufactories of the United Kingdom*.

Great Britain (1831-1832), Parliamentary Papers (Commons), *Report of the Select Commitee on the Bill for the Regulation of Factories*.

Great Britain (1833a), Parliamentary Papers (Commons), *First Report of the Factories Inquiry Commission*.

Great Britain (1833b), Parliamentary Papers (Commons), *Second Report of the Factories Inquiry Commission*.

Great Britain (1834), Parliamentary Papers (Commons), *Supplementary Report of the Factories Inquiry Commission*.

Great Britain (1842), Parliamentary Papers (Commons), *Mines Report of the Children's Employment Commission*.

Great Britain (1843), Parliamentary Papers (Commons), *Report of the Royal Commission on the Employment of Children in Trades and Manufactures*.

Great Britain (1851), Parliamentary Papers (Commons), *Report and Abstract of the Census of Great Britain*.

Great Britain (1834–1878), Parliamentary Papers (Commons), *Reports of the Inspectors of Factories*.

Hammond, J. L., and Barbara Hammond (1917; 1932), *The Town Labourer, 1760–1832*. London: Longmans.

Hammond, J. L., and Barbara Hammond (1923), *Lord Shaftesbury*. London: Constable.

Hartwell, R. M. (1971), *The Industrial Revolution and Economic Growth*. London: Methuen.

Hartwell, R. M., *et al* (1972), *The Long Debate on Poverty*. London: Institute of Economic Affairs.

Hobsbawm, E. J. (1964), *Labouring Men*. London: Weidenfeld and Nicolson.

Hunt, E. H. (1973), *Regional Wage Variations in Britain, 1850–1914*. Oxford: Clarendon.

Inglis, Brian (1971), *Men of Conscience*. New York: Macmillan.

Jefferson, Michael (1972), "Industrialization and Poverty: In Fact and Fiction." In Hartwell *et al*, pp. 188–238.

Kay-Shuttleworth, James Phillips (1832; 1970), *The Moral and Physical Condition of the Working Classes*. London: Frank Kass.

Kussmaul, Ann (1981), *Servants in Husbandry in Early Modern England*. Cambridge: Cambridge University Press.

Kydd, Samuel ["'Alfred''] (1857; 1965), *History of the Factory Movement*. New York: Burt Franklin.

Laslett, Peter (1965), *The World We Have Lost*. New York: Scribner's.

Lee, C. H. (1972) *A Cotton Enterprise*. Manchester: Manchester University Press.

Lindert, Peter H., and Jeffrey G. Williamson (1983), "English Workers' Living Standards during the Industrial Revolution: A New Look." *Economic History Review*, 36 (February): 1–25.

Lloyd-Jones, Roger, and A. A. Le Roux (1980), "The Size of Firms in the Cotton Industry: Manchester, 1815-41." *Economic History Review*, 33 (February): 72–82.

MacKinnon, Mary, and Paul Johnson (1984), "The Case Against Productive Whipping." *Explorations in Economic History*, 21 (April): 218–223.

Mantoux, Paul (1961; 1983), *The Industrial Revolution in the Eighteenth Century*. Chicago: University of Chicago Press.

Marcus, Steven (1974), *Engels, Manchester, and The Working Class*. New York: Random House.

Marx, Karl (1867; 1967), *Capital* Vol. 1 (translated by Samuel Moore and Edward Aveling). New York: International Publishers.

Matthews, R. C. O. (1954), *A Study in Trade-Cycle History*. Cambridge: Cambridge University Press.

Melanda, Ivan (1970), *The Captain of Industry in English Fiction, 1821–1871*. Alburquerque: University of New Mexico Press.

Mitch, David (1984), "Underinvestment in Literacy? The Potential Contribution of Government Involvement in Elementary Education to Economic Growth in Nineteenth-Century England." *Journal of Economic History*, 44 (June): 557–66.

Mitchell, B. R., and Phyllis Deane (1962), *Abstract of British Historical Statistics*. Cambridge: Cambridge University Press.

Mokyr, Joel (1977), "Demand vs. Supply in the Industrial Revolution." *Journal of Economic History*, 37 (December): 981–1008.

Nardinelli, Clark (1982), "Corporal Punishment and Children's Wages in Nineteenth Century Britain." *Explorations in Economic History*, 19 (July): 283–295.

Nardinelli, Clark (1984), "The Productivity of Corporal Punishment: A Reply to MacKinnon and Johnson." *Exploration in Economic History*, 21 (April): 224–228.

Plumb, J. H. (1982), "The New World of Children in Eighteenth-Century England." In Neil McKendrick, John Brewer, and J. H. Plumb, *The Birth of a Consumer Society*. Bloomington, Indiana: Indiana University Press, pp. 286–313.

Pollard, Sidney (1978), "Labour in Great Britain." In Peter Mathias and M. M. Postan (eds.), *The Cambridge Economic History of Europe*, Vol. 7: Pt.1 Cambridge: Cambridge University Press. pp. 97–179.

Redford, Arthur (1964), *Labour Migration in England, 1800–1850*. 2nd ed. Manchester: Manchester University Press.

Robinson, Joan (1969), *The Economics of Imperfect Competition*, 2nd ed. London: Macmillan.

Sanderson, Michael (1972), "Literacy and Social Mobility in the Industrial Revolution in England." *Past and Present*, 56 (August): 75–104.

Shaw, Charles (1903; 1977), *When I Was A Child*. Firle, Sussex: Caliban.

Shorter, Edward (1975), *The Making of the Modern Family*. New York: Basic Books.

Sommerville, C. John (1972), "Toward A History of Childhood and Youth." *Journal of Interdisciplinary History*, 3 (Autumn): 439–447.

Sommerville, C. John (1982), *The Rise and Fall of Childhood*. Beverly Hills,, CA: Sage Publications.

Steckel, Richard H. (1983), "Height and Per Capita Income." *Historical Methods*, 16 (Winter): 1–7.

Stone, Lawrence (1969), "Literacy and Education in England, 1640–1900." *Past and Present*, 42 (February): 61–139

Stone, Lawrence (1977), *The Family, Sex and Marriage in England 1500–1800*. London: Weidenfeld and Nicolson.

Tanner, J. M. (1981), *A History of the Study of Human Growth*. Cambridge: Cambridge University Press.

Thomis, Malcolm I. (1974), *The Town Labourer and the Industrial Revolution*. London: B. T. Batsford.

Thompson, E. P. (1966), *The Making of the English Working Class*. New York: Vintage.

Vincent, David (ed.) (1977), *Testaments of Radicalism: Memoirs of Working Class Politicians 1790–1885*. London: Europa.

Vincent, David (1981), *Bread, Knowledge and Freedom*. London: Europa.

West, E. G. (1975), "Educational Slowdown and Public Intervention in 19th Century England: A Study in the Economics of Bureaucracy." *Explorations in Economic History*, 12 (January): 61–87.

West, E. G. (1978), "Literacy and the Industrial Revolution." *Economic History Review*, 31 (August): 369–383.

Williamson, Jeffrey G.(1981), "Urban Disamenities, Dark Satanic Mills and the British Standard of Living Debate." *Journal of Economic History*, 41 (March): 75–83.

Williamson, Jeffrey G. (1982), "Was the Industrial Revolution Worth It? Disamenities and Death in 19th Century Britain." *Exploration in Economic History*, 19 (July): 221–245.

Williamson, Jeffrey G. (1984). "Why Was British Growth So Slow During The Industrial Revolution?" *Journal of Economic History*, 44 (September): 687–712.

Wrigley, E. A. and R. S. Schofield (1981). *The Population History of England 1541–1871*. Cambridge, MA: Harvard University Press.

FOUR EPISODES OF CORPORATE LAW REFORM IN THE RUSSIAN EMPIRE, 1836–1914

Thomas C. Owen

ABSTRACT

The history of tsarist corporate law illustrates the tension between two contradictory principles in the Russian economy: the idea of capitalist rationality, exemplified by an impartially administered body of enlightened laws, and the determination of the tsarist bureaucracy to govern arbitrarily, even in defiance of its own statutes. Although the government promoted industrial development, it maintained an arbitrary system if incorporation by concession and extended to corporations its various restrictions on foreigners, Jews, and Poles. The repeated failure of the imperial bureaucracy to modernize its corporate law clarifies the essentially anti-capitalist nature of tsarist economic policy.

Research in Economic History, Volume 11, pages 277–299.
Copyright © 1988 by JAI Press Inc.
All rights of reproduction in any form reserved.
ISBN: 0-89232-677-8

The development of capitalist institutions in the Russian Empire assumes great importance in light of the current discussion of the degree to which the tsarist regime adapted to the imperatives of economic modernization. By studying the history of Russian corporate law, we can discover both the evolution of tsarist policy toward modern capitalist institutions and the changing attitudes of Russian businessmen, whose interests were directly affected by the law, but whose opinions have not been well elucidated by historians. Fortunately, some useful empirical work on the state's policies has been done on this question, both by Russian jurists and by Soviet historians, notably Leonid E. Shepelev in Leningrad.

The present discussion focuses on four episodes in the history of Russian corporate law: the drafting of the statute of 1836, which remained in force until 1917; the attempts at reform in the early 1870s and at the end of the century, both of which ended in the failure to create a new law appropriate to the needs of the time; and the final debate over corporate law on the eve of World War I. In each of these episodes, the bureaucrats discerned serious defects in the existing corporate law and pursued (in the first three periods at least) a fairly well-defined goal of reform. At the end of their labors, however, they faced new and no less daunting dilemmas. From beginning to end, the tsarist regime failed to elaborate a system of corporate law that could satisfy both the imperatives of autocratic control and the needs of rational economic development. None of the solutions attempted by the regime—tutelage in 1836, imitation of European models in the early 1870s and in 1897–1901, or regimentation in 1910–1914—provided a satisfactory solution.

At each juncture, three issues inherent in the nature of corporate enterprise demanded resolution: how new corporations were to be licensed by the regime; how swindling by stock-exchange manipulation or "stock-jabbing" (*azhiotazh*, from the French *agiotage*) was to be minimized; and how restrictions on land-ownership were to be maintained in sensitive regions where corporations might be partly owned by stockholders who, as individuals, were barred because of their ethnic background from owning land in such areas. These three aspects of corporate activity—incorporation, the stock market, and ethnic restrictions on property ownership—proved especially crucial because a laissez-faire resolution of each issue would have posed direct challenges to the traditional social and economic institutions of the empire: the autocratic tsar, the centralized bureaucracy, the hierarchal system of social estates (*sosloviia*), and the preferential policies toward the Orthodox Christian gentry and peasantry. Unrestricted incorporation would have implied free enterprise for individuals of all social estates and ethnic groups; speculation would have grown more intense in an unregulated free market in corporate securities; and the unfettered transfer of landed property would have hastened the demise of the Great Russian and Orthodox Christian gentry and peasantry, whose fortunes were rapidly declining in any case, despite the regime's measures of financial support. The approaches of the tsarist regime to these three issues in the several periods under review reveal much about the changing attitudes of the government toward the corporation and, by extension, to modern capitalism in general. The historian thereby gains a valuable glimpse into the failure of the tsarist regime to accommodate itself to the social and economic consequences of its own policy of rapid industrial development.

Although a series of laws ensuring limited liability for investors in joint-stock companies had been published in the eighteenth and early nineteenth centuries, the total amount of capital invested in corporations grew slowly. In 1830, the government reduced the interest rate on savings accounts from 5 to 4 percent, so that investment in new corporations appeared more attractive than before (Shepelev, 1973, p. 25). Two problems faced the tsarist government as the pace of incorporation began to quicken. First, in the absence of a comprehensive corporate law (the decree on partnerships, *PSZ* 1-22418, dated January 1, 1807, barely mentioned the joint-stock company), the government faced the problem of passing an ever-increasing number of new laws, one for each company to be chartered by the state. In 1835 alone, for example, four new companies were created, with a total capitalization of over 3.9 million rubles, to be followed in 1836 by six corporations with over 7.5 million rubles of basic capital (Shepelev, 1967, pp. 173–174). Second, some of the companies formed in the early 1830s served merely as speculative ventures, in which the founders held a large block of shares, sold them to the public after the price rose, and then abandoned the enterprise with a quick profit. Alarmed by a flurry of bankruptcies, which not only hurt investors but also depressed the market for new corporate stocks and threatened the economic stability of the empire, Finance Minister Egor F. Kankrin and Minister of Internal Affairs Dmitrii N. Bludov set to work in late 1835 drafting a comprehensive statute on corporations. Signed into law by Nicholas I on December 6, 1836, it was to remain in force, with minor amendments, until the end of the tsarist regime (Shepelev, 1967, pp. 169, 176).[1]

Because the main problem perceived by Kankrin and Bludov in 1836 was that of speculation, the law specifically attacked stock-jobbing (*birzhevaia igra* or *azhiotazh*) by declaring null and void "any condition regarding delivery of shares at a future date and at a set price" (*vsiakoe uslovie o postavke na srok po opredelennoi tsene aktsii*). To this end, it also required that shares be issued by name to each stockholder, not "to the bearer." Curiously enough, it was Bludov, the highly cultured interior minister, who had resisted the prohibition on future deals, seeing it as detrimental to entrepreneurial freedom, while Kankrin, an extremely cautious bureaucrat, successfully defended restrictions on economic activity. Payment in cash was made mandatory, although partial payment was permitted. Founders were allowed to buy a certain percentage of the shares, but were forbidden to resell them within a specified period. The government claimed to strike a balance between the conflicting needs of entrepreneurs and investors, so that, as the tsar declared in his *ukaz* to the Senate (drafted by M. M. Speranskii), the law would grant to "all branches of industry . . . as much freedom as possible to progress and develop, while at the same time protecting [the empire] as much as possible from the [deleterious] consequences of thoughtlessness and careless enterprise'' (Shepelev, 1967, pp. 178, 180–85, 188, 192–93; Speranskii quoted on p. 194).[2] The law clearly devoted more attention to the latter than to the former.

The spirit of tutelage that permeated the law of 1836 is most apparent in the tight controls on the internal structure and activity of each new company: all resolutions of the general assembly of stockholders required a three-fourths majority, and the permission of the ministry of finance was needed for such changes as an increase or decrease in the size of basic capital, the issuing of new stocks or bonds, and all other matters of more than petty importance (Shepelev, 1967, pp. 192, 187). The urge to maintain supervision also underlay the procedure by which new companies were founded after 1836. As did European corporate law at that time, the Russian law specified a "concessionary system" (*razreshitel'naia* or *kontsessionnaia sistema*) of incorporation, under which every new company received a charter from the state, in the form of a separate law signed by the tsar. Apparently no thought was given at that time to the creation of a less restrictive procedure of registration of companies without prior approval, known in the juridical literature as a "registration system" (*iavochnaia sistema* or *iavochnyi poriadok*). As Kankrin stated: "It is better to refuse ten less than perfect companies than to allow one to harm the public and the business itself" (Shepelev, 1967, p. 196; Kankrin quoted on p. 181). (As for the issue of property ownership, so few companies existed and so eager was the state to encourage solid new enterprises that the law specified no restrictions on the amount of land that a publicly owned corporation could own.)

The system of incorporation established in 1836 immediately led to a strange anomaly. Entrepreneurs seeking to escape the detailed and restrictive provisions of the law of 1836 found that their most important avenue of evasion led through the government itself. Under the law, all new charters required the approval of the Committee of Ministers, and any seeking special privileges or subsidies required endorsement by the State Council as well. However, the rule that every new corporate charter must be approved by these governmental bodies in the form of a new law meant that each charter need adhere to the law of 1836 only to the extent that the tsarist bureaucrats themselves felt constrained to obey it. In other words, corporate law between 1836 and 1917 became whatever the tsar and his ministers considered useful at any given moment. Each charter established not only the rules for the representation of shares in the general assembly, but also the number of directors, their terms of office, and other essential features of the company's structure. This concessionary policy could be justified in the cases of large and expensive undertakings, in which the state itself participated through the granting of privileges, monopoly rights, and subsidies and often through the appointment of bureaucrats as members of the board of directors. Indeed, "most companies" founded in the 1830s received such special considerations. However, Shepelev detected a second goal behind the retention of the concessionary system: "The possibility of evading the provisions of the general law on corporations and, beyond that, of commercial-industrial legislation in general.'' Whether this arbitrariness constituted, as Shepelev wrote in an strangely pro-autocratic passage, "a relatively progressive" feature of the law (1967, p. 191; quotation from p. 196), in the sense that it allowed great flexibility to future policymakers, depends on one's view of the role of law in a modern society.

Shepelev correctly noted that the law of 1836, despite its many restrictions on corporate enterprise, failed to eradicate the evil of stock-jobbing. Various subsequent restrictions also had little effect, including one implemented in 1853, which required public disclosure of stock subscription records in the delicate period before the first general assembly of stockholders (Shepelev, 1967, p. 196; *PSZ* 2-27810, dated December 28, 1853). A burst of corporate entrepreneurship in the late 1850s and early 1860s, again spurred by a drop in the interest rate paid by the state savings bank (from 4 to 3 percent in July 1857), was marred by a speculative "stock-exchange fever" (*birzhevaia goriachka*), in which shrewd swindlers set up flimsy companies, drove up the price of shares, and then sold out, bilking gullible investors out of millions of rubles (Shepelev, 1973, pp. 70–75).

The tsarist policy makers attempted at the beginning of the 1870s a thorough reform of the law of 1836, long criticized as completely outmoded by legal experts (see Pakhman, 1861). The government itself stressed that the present system was plagued by "inconsistency caused by the variety of rules regarding joint-stock companies [and by] inevitable delays, which are inconvenient and costly for industry" (quoted by Kaminka, 1901, p. 391).[3] By 1872, only 28 of the 59 articles in the law of 1836 were being heeded, and many of these had been amended. One article (2160) in the 1863 Code of Laws (*Svod zakonov*) contained an absurd notation to the effect that individual charters issued since 1836 overruled it! (Shepelev, 1973, p. 108).

As might be expected, the fundamental tsarist attitude of tutelage remained strong even during this period, but the spirit of the "Great Reforms" could also be discerned. The commission headed by A. A. Butovskii sought to implement the latest principles of European corporate law, especially the registration system. Among the 14 members of the commission, which began meeting in November 1871, figured five economic experts from the ministry of finance, including Fedor G. Terner (Thörner), the author of a book on European corporate law. Other notables were Anatolii N. Kulomzin of the chancery of the Committee of Ministers and the president of the Petersburg Exchange, Aleksandr G. Zolotarev (Shepelev, 1973, p. 111; Butovskii commission, 1. 38).

The centerpiece of the new bill was the proposed abandonment of the concessionary system for new corporations in favor of a system of registration of charters without prior permission (*iavochnaia* or *registratsionnaia sistema*), adopted in England in 1862, in France in 1867, and in Prussia in 1870. This reform had several major advantages: it would simplify the incorporation procedure and remove any implication that the Russian state, by chartering a company, endorsed it or implicitly guaranteed its financial strength. Only certain companies must henceforth obtain prior approval from various ministries: those that received subsidies or privileges from the state, and insurance companies, brokerage firms, and credit institutions (Shepelev, 1973, pp. 112–13).

Paradoxically, however, the relaxation of controls embodied in the transition to registration led the Butovskii commission to set down a large number of rules for all new companies, so that its draft ran to 194 paragraphs, more than double the length of a half-hearted corporate law reform abandoned in 1867. Among the guidelines were strict minima for the price of shares (100 rubles); for the number of shareholders (7); and for the down payment in the initial subscription process (10 percent of the share price). Stocks issued "to the bearer," outlawed in 1836 but commonly permitted in subsequent charters, became legal, except that named shares were required in companies operating where restrictions existed for individuals (e.g., no foreigners were permitted to own shares in Caspian Sea shipping companies and in those engaged in coastal shipping—*kabotazh*—on the Black Sea) (Shepelev, 1973, pp. 111, 113-14). All capital stocks must be fully subscribed (*razobrany*) before a company could be considered created; at least 10 percent of the capital must be collected in cash; and all stocks must be sold within three years. If a company lost over half of its basic capital, it must be liquidated. Besides imposing complicated rules to protect the voting rights of small stockholders at the general assembly meetings, the bill also required the establishment of an elected audit commission (*revizionnaia komissiia*), which was to carry out yearly examinations of the company's books (Kaminka, 1901, pp. 392–93).

In the legislative process, which occupied 36 sessions to March 1874, still more restrictions appeared: a minimum size for companies (100,000 rubles of basic capital); a maximum on the portion of shares that the founders could own (50 percent); and a new paragraph making managers liable not only for violations of corporate law, but also for any harm done to the interests of the firm (Shepelev, 1973, p. 115).

Although the experts could not resist the temptation to impose ever more stringent regulations on new companies, they did show themselves willing to admit one feature of public life during the "Great Reforms," namely the principle of public discussion (*glasnost'*), completely repressed under Nicholas I. The Butovskii commission printed 600 copies of its bill in June 1872 and sent them to exchange committees, other business organizations, major corporations, and dozens of individuals. After the finance ministry received over 30 responses, ranging from letters in newspapers to statements from exchange committees, it published these in two booklets (of 400 copies each), to facilitate the flow of opinions. In addition, the Moscow and Petersburg exchange committees published their own commentaries on the bill (Shepelev, 1973, pp. 112–14). Shepelev did not specify the recommendations made by the various business groups in these brochures, but the Petersburg Exchange Committee made its position clear in its own publication. Although it welcomed the government's decision "to remove from [corporate] law every principle of tutelage [*vsiakoe nachalo opeki*] over the public," it perceived in the bill several remnants of that principle. For example, the bill sought to protect the public by allowing any person who had subscribed to shares in a new company to refuse to pay for them if, at a general assembly meeting, he disagreed with a decision of the majority. Rather than permitting a minority to cripple a company in this way, the corporate law should allow each investor to weigh "all the chances for the success of the enterprise" and to invest his money prudently. "The best safeguard against hollow and groundless enterprises is the discretion and caution of the public itself. . . ." (Birzhevoi komitet, 1873, pp. 2–5; quotations from pp. 2, 5). In other words, let the buyer beware and let the state refrain from interference in the operation of the free market. The Petersburg merchants also found the law too rigid and theoretical, in that all companies, whether large or small, fell under its provisions. For example, companies whose founders did not intend to sell shares to the public (many enterprises adopted the form of a corporation but remained relatively small, family-owned enterprises) should not be forced to conform to the many restrictions that the bill imposed on publicly owned ones for the alleged protection of investors. Instead of laying down absolute requirements, such as the minimum number of founders, the law should recognize the great variation among companies as to size and function, and leave questions of this sort to the founders themselves. In all, some 16 major revisions were needed, ranging from the establishment of clearer rules regarding the founders' contract to measures against what the merchants called "excessive arbitrariness on the part of subscribers" (1873, pp. 9–11; quotation from p. 10).

These candid comments demonstrated that the merchants of Petersburg, the most advanced in the empire in terms of their familiarity with modern European business practices, clearly resented the "protective" measures put forth by the Butovskii commission. The pamphlet's derogatory comments about "tutelage" also indicated the authors' exasperation with the outmoded law of 1836. The failure of the tsarist government even to implement its own reform must, therefore, have caused the most enterprising and capable merchants in the empire a good deal of concern, since the "inevitable delays, which are inconvenient and costly for industry," described by the commission itself, continued to exist for decades thereafter.

The work of the Butovskii commission came to a sudden, even comical, end in 1874. Although the ministries and business groups recognized the need for a coherent corporate law, and although the Butovskii commission had created in just over two years a bill to which no governmental agency raised serious objections, the grand effort failed to produce a new law. By early 1874, the finance minister, Mikhail Kh. Reutern, had come to doubt the wisdom of the basic principle on which the bill rested: the registration system of incorporation. As he explained eight years later, he withdrew the bill from the State Council "in view of the difficult financial position of the state and the fear that a less restrictive system of forming joint-stock companies would entail the undesirable development of small companies" (quoted in Shepelev, 1973, p. 115). The comedy, as Shepelev noted, took 15 years to play itself out. A corporate law drafted by tsarist bureaucrats between 1857 and 1867 and based on the concessionary principle was rejected because most European countries had adopted the more streamlined registration system by the late 1860s; but in 1874 Reutern abandoned his own reform, modeled on the latest European legislation. The European stock market crash of 1873 caused him to worry that the registration system might allow the proliferation of a multitude of small companies unable to survive future downturns in the business cycle. As one historian noted caustically, the crash of 1873 led several European countries to adopt "a stricter and more detailed normative system" of incorporation by registration under a set of clearly defined rules. In Russia, in contrast, the effect of the crash was to block the slightest move toward that system (Kaminka, 1897, p. 128).

This same spirit of bureaucratic caution underlay Reutern's regulations for joint-stock banks, signed into law by Emperor Alexander II on May 31, 1872. No new joint-stock banks were to be allowed in cities where one or more banks already existed; all banks must observe the financial restrictions previously contained only in the charters of individual banks, for example, the prohibition on direct participation in the establishment of new companies; and all new banks must have at least 500,000 rubles in basic capital and sell shares costing at least 250 rubles, to lessen the likelihood of speculation. The finance minister could henceforth approve the creation of new banks with basic capitalization below five million rubles (larger banks still required the tsar's confirmation), but numerous provisions were imposed to reduce the risk of bank failure: a minimum number of founders (five), a time limit on the sale of all shares (six months), minimum cash reserves (10 percent of the bank's liabilities), a maximum value of liabilities (five times the bank's combined share and reserve capital), and a prohibition on property ownership by banks except for their premises and the warehouses where collateral was stored (Shepelev, 1973, pp. 86, 117–19; PSZ 2-50913). The brief experiment with theoretical corporate laws based on European practice had passed, and the old pattern of tutelage asserted itself once more, even in the person of the most enlightened ministers of the 1860s, such as Reutern.

A quarter-century later, the impulse of enlightened reform reappeared, if briefly. The work of the commission on corporate law reform headed by Professor P. P. Tsitovich (1896–1900) strikes the historian as a repetition of that of the Butovskii commission in the early seventies. When Finance Minister Sergei Iu. Witte announced to the first session of the Tsitovich commission that Russian corporate law, "one might say, does not exist at all" (sovsem ne sushchestvuet; quoted in Spiridovich, 1897, p. 34), he appeared to be calling for a comprehensive modernization of the entire ramshackle system based on the law of 1836. Again, however, the attempt at reform ended in failure.

As under Butovskii, the new bill was intended to implement a simplified system of incorporation by registration for all but a few kinds of enterprises, namely railroads, insurance companies, banks, and firms with less that the suggested minima of basic capital (150,000 rubles) or of share price (150 rubles) (Shepelev, 1973, pp. 168–171). As before, the "simplified" law would have been far more complex than that of 1836 because of the need to regulate all new companies, whatever their size and function, and because many of the details of internal structure would be defined by the law instead of by the company's charter. Besides being open to criticism for some dubious and arbitrary provisions, such as the granting to the executive director more power than to the board, the bill contained so many complex regulations that one spokesman for merchant interests doubted whether all its provisions could be rationally assessed, even by an expert (Spiridovich, 1897, pp. 59–60, 62).

The main difference from the 1870s was that the most articulate representatives of existing companies now feared the standardization of the law that the registration system would have entailed. On this point they disagreed with the bureaucrats and economic experts on the Tsitovich commission. Managers of large corporations, especially those headquartered in St. Petersburg, pointed out that their charters, approved under the old concessionary system, contained special favors from the state that a normative system, based on simple registration, would wipe out (Spiridovich, 1897, p. 36). A different objection was expressed by Nikolai A. Naidenov, president of the Moscow Exchange Committee, who warned Witte in 1899 that the creation of "small companies with inexpensive shares" would increase the danger of economic instability, principally because large banks would be drawn into the establishment of such companies (Letter to Witte dated December 11, 1899, quoted by Petrov, 1982, p. 124). This warning reflected, of course, the conservative Moscow bankers' distrust of the big banks in St. Petersburg, which were prone to engage heavily in the launching of new corporations—*griunderstvo* (from the German *Gründertum*: "speculative mania," especially in 1871–74).

The ultimate failure of the Tsitovich commission's work owed less to the manufacturers' objections than to misgivings within the finance ministry itself over the issue of abolishing exceptions to the law. Moreover, the key problem of such "deviations" (*otstupleniia*) from the law of 1836 involved more than mere financial privileges, subsidies, and the like. A report to Witte written by V. I. Kovalevskii, director of the Department of Trade and Manufacturing, during the deliberations of the Tsitovich commission raised a new and fundamental objection to the registration system. Kovalevskii noted that approximately 70 out of a hundred new corporations chartered in the empire operated in areas affected by "a multitude of restrictive decrees regarding the rights of separate categories of people to engage in agriculture, various trades, etc." (quoted in Shepelev, 1973, p. 177). He had in mind a series of laws implemented since 1864 denying to Jews, Poles, and foreigners the right to own rural property in the western provinces, the Pale of Settlement, Turkestan, and other sensitive areas of the empire, as well as the prohibition against Jews and foreigners in mining.[4] He stressed that because many companies operating in these regions were allowed by their charters to issue shares "to the bearer" (i.e., unnamed shares), these firms had as stockholders and even managers numerous individuals "who were forbidden by these decrees from owning any property" and from carrying out as individuals the commercial and industrial functions in which their companies engaged. Under a registration system, exceptions would not be allowed for foreigners, Jews, and other persons to which these restrictive decrees applied. Moreover, corporations in the borderlands would be forced to issue named shares, ownership of which would be denied to foreigners and Jews. Besides causing economic chaos in these areas, the registration system, by abolishing the granting of exceptions to the law of 1836, would "deprive the government of any possibility of supervising the course of corporate development," Kovalevskii warned (quoted in Shepelev, 1973, p. 177).

A strange dilemna now presented itself to Witte and his advisors: to rationalize the corporate law meant to restrict the activity of some of the most capable corporate managers in the empire. As the ministry of finance candidly expressed the problem in 1901, "The introduction of the registration system would require the precise and firm observation of restrictions and would not only not facilitate the creation of joint-stock enterprises but would, on the contrary, make it more difficult" (Shepelev, 1973, p. 196). Having become conscious of this dilemma, Witte decided to abandon the Tsitovich commission's bill, but not before arranging for the publication in the Russian and European press, one week later, of a vague statement by the tsar reaffirming the need for corporate law reform. This misleading ploy seems to have been designed to attract foreign capital investments at a time when Witte realized clearly that, in Shepelev's words, the Tsitovich commission's bill "could not be applied to Russian conditions without causing direct harm to the establishment of corporations" (1973, p. 178).

Whether Witte would have preferred to abolish all the autocracy's ethnic and citizenship restrictions on property ownership and participation in corporations remains unclear. In any case, he seems to have realized the impossibility of a thorough reform of the corporate law in Russia in the foreseeable future, since the prevailing mood in the State Council and the ministries of internal affairs, justice, agriculture, and war tended toward a total ban on Jews and foreigners in companies operating in sensitive regions and economic sectors.

The main point of the Tsitovich episode for the student of Russian economic history is that Witte's tenure as minister of finance represented no great change, as far as corporate law was concerned, from the traditional pattern of government by autocratic fiat. He certainly hired capable administrators, whether Russian, Polish, or Jewish, and showed impatience with the obdurate, anti-capitalist courtiers and ministers who distrusted his policy of rapid industrialization. However, even as he proved too weak to override them, he showed a preference for the existing outmoded system of incorporation.[5]

Russian corporate law continued, therefore, to languish in "a sad state indeed" (*w smutnym zaiste stanie*), as a Polish legal expert wrote, because the tsarist ministers proved unable to implement their own reforms. "It is the characteristic feature of the Russian bureaucracy," he noted, "that in every realm of the law it prepares bills that subsequently pass into the archive" instead of being implemented (Kaczkowski, 1908, pp. 103–104). By 1896, only Russia, Austria (excluding Hungary), Holland, Serbia, Greece, and Turkey retained the concessionary system. Proof of the inadequacy of the law was the fact that many Russians went abroad to form companies and then applied (successfully) to operate them as "foreign" firms in their native land, simply to avoid the greater delays and restrictions that domestic incorporation entailed, compared to the permission granted by the finance ministry to foreign companies (Spiridovich, 1897, p. 39). The only major law on corporations to appear under Witte's stewardship, dated December 21, 1901, laid down yet more elaborate rules for general assemblies and audit commissions, in an effort to ensure democratic voting procedures within companies whose stocks were quoted on the exchanges. Even it bore the label "temporary" (*PSZ* 3-20874),[6] pending a general reform of Russian corporate law that never came. We see here a striking parallel between Reutern and Witte, two energetic and capable finance ministers who abandoned their own plans for reform and retreated to the familiar ground of government by arbitrary fiat.

The vigor with which several ministries defended ethnic restrictions on corporate enterprise justifies the label "repression" for the final major phase of tsarist policy regarding corporate law. Just as Witte failed to achieve a reform of the corporate law in his term as finance minister, so the partisans of reform in the last few years before World War I had no success in their campaign against the repressive policies of the late tsarist period. Although the desire for reform ran high in the State Duma, business organizations, and even the ministries of finance and of trade and industry, the tsar, supported by his ministers of internal affairs, war, justice, and agriculture, blocked all proposed reforms and even added an important new restriction.

The impetus for the final campaign in favor of corporate law reform came from the State Duma. In July 1910, 33 members introduced a bill designed to attract medium- and small-sized investments into corporations. The major innovation of the bill, as expected, consisted in the abolition of the concessionary system and its replacement by registration (*iavochnyi poriadok*) (Shepelev, 1973, p. 261).

Various business groups had proposed such a change in previous years. In December 1906, *Neftianoe delo* (The Petroleum Industry), the organ of the Baku Petroleum Association (BPA—*Sovet s"ezdov bakinskikh neftepromyshlennikov*), had called the rationalization of corporate law a "vitally necessary" reform, and had endorsed the registration system (December 31, 1906, col. 1054). The

Moscow Bureau of the newly formed Association of Industry and Trade (AIT—
Sovet s"ezdov predstavitelei promyshlennosti i torgovli) took an identical position that same year (Owen, 1981, p. 204). Even the minister of trade and industry
in early 1906, M. M. Fedorov, had proclaimed that the civil liberties promised by
the tsar in October 1905 should include a freer system of incorporation, namely
registration: "The state's tutelage [*opeka*] and supervision over the development
of industry are incompatible with the concept of a state based on the rule of law
[*pravovogo gosudarstva*] . . . ." (Memorandum to the tsar, quoted in Shepelev,
1973, p. 251).[7] Likewise, before the turn of the century the renowned legal expert
Lev I. Petrazhitskii had seen in the arbitrary concessionary system a violation of
"that most precious principle of every cultured state, namely the principle of a
state based on the rule of law . . . [and] administered on the precise [*tochnom*]
foundation of the law" (1898, p. 3).[8] Three business organizations in St. Petersburg—
the Exchange Committee, the Securities Exchange (*Sovet fondovogo otdela
Peterburgskoi birzhi*), and the Petersburg Society of Manufacturers (PSM—
Peterburgskoe obshchestvo zavodchikov i fabrikantov)—"categorically" endorsed
the registration system in 1911 after a two-year study of the issue. Even the
provincial merchants who were represented by the national organization of commodity exchanges, the Association of Trade and Agriculture (ATA—*Sovet s"ezdov
predstavitelei birzhevoi torvogli i sel'skogo khoziaistva*), had made the same
recommendation in late 1910 (Shepelev, 1973, p. 265–66).[9]

One of the most forceful arguments came from the Moscow business leader
Aleksandr I. Konovalov in the State Duma in June 1913. Under the outmoded
concessionary system, he asserted, every new corporate charter passed through
from two to six governmental agencies, any one of which could reject it, and the
entire process lasted three or four months on the average. Corporations in Russia
"above all need emancipation [*raskreposhcheniia*] from these fetters, which
shackle the formation and growth of joint-stock enterprises. . . . The arbitrariness of the administrative authorities" must give way to "the creation of firm
norms of law [*tverdykh norm zakona*], equal for all; this means the elimination of
red tape and tutelage [*opeku*]," as well as the abolition of all restrictions on
business imposed on "specific categories of the population. . . ." (quoted in
Shepelev, 1973, p. 286).[10] Konovalov belonged to the so-called "Progressist"
group of young Moscow industrialists, led by Pavel P. Riabushinskii, perhaps the
most liberal faction within the Russian business world (West, 1983). In view of
the fact that such strong criticisms of tsarist economic policy by Russian merchants were almost unheard of before 1905, in Moscow or elsewhere (Owen,
1981), Konovalov's remarks take on special significance as a symptom of the
growing rift between the autocratic state and modern capitalist businessmen.

From 1910 to the outbreak of the war in mid-1914, various agencies of the
tsarist government proposed ways to implement the registration system without,
however, dismantling the web of restrictions on Jews, Poles, and foreigners. It
proved to be an impossible task. In December 1911 a conference attended by

some 80 experts from the various ministries and all the major business organizations set to work, precisely as had the Tsitovich commission 14 years before. Minister of Trade and Industry S. I. Timashev offered for discussion a set of guidelines which, upon enactment into law, would have provided for registration of most new companies.[11] In the course of the debate, the ministry of trade and industry pressed strongly for the registration system, arguing that all European countries except Austria had adopted it (Timashev conference, 1. 124). However, the ministries of justice, internal affairs, and agriculture showed themselves less concerned with economic development than with the maintenance of the restrictions against Jews, Poles, and foreigners. Although the justice ministry offered no objection to registration in principle (Timashev conference, 1. 135), it preferred a "mixed" system of incorporation, under which registration would be allowed for most companies, but the concessionary system would be partially retained to ensure that new corporations operating in the western provinces observed ethnic restrictions. The ministry of agriculture also defended this position (Shepelev, 1973, p. 271). For its part, the ministry of internal affairs opposed all registration, arguing that it would "create grounds for evasion of a whole series of decrees that limit the acquisition of rural land by certain categories of individuals, which circumstance would be very undesirable." In vain, Timashev asserted that registration need not entail "the abolition or weakening of existing restrictions on joint-stock companies. . . ." (Timashev conference, 1. 130).

It might be expected that Timashev's attempt to find a middle ground (between the two extremes of registration without restrictions and the existing concessionary system) would have gained the support of the business representatives who served on the commission. In fact, they displayed great hostility toward the minister's position. One banker, Ia. I. Utin of the Discount and Loan Bank in Petersburg, even spoke in favor of the old system, but only because it allowed evasion of the ethnic restrictions (Timashev conference, 1. 124). The Warsaw Exchange Society, although it had first petitioned for a registration system in 1886, now favored the retention of the concessionary system for the same reason that Utin did: the Jewish business interests in that city saw the existing procedure, with all its irrational complexities and delays, as preferable to the enforcement of ethnic restrictions under a streamlined registration system (Shepelev, 1973, p. 266; Pelka, 1967, p. 164, n. 18). Representatives of the iron, gold, and platinum interests were willing to accept the mixed system, but only as long as large companies would continue to receive special permission to own huge tracts of land without complying with the restrictive laws (Timashev conference, 1. 125). Most business representatives agreed with Vladislav V. Zhukovskii, a State Duma member and leader of the AIT, who advocated the most liberal position expressed at the conference: all companies should be exempt from ethnic restrictions imposed on individuals who owned their stock or served on their boards. Without a dual reform—introduction of registration plus the abolition of restrictions on land ownership and industrial activity by corporations—the adoption of registration alone "might well destroy all of its benefits" by restricting productive activity in the affected areas (Timashev conference, 1. 127).

Another AIT member, S. S. Novoselov, stated this position even more clearly: the AIT could not endorse the registration principle as proposed in the bill because no one had specified precisely

> what bundle [*komplekt*] of civil rights joint-stock companies would enjoy regarding ownership of real estate and business activity. If it were firmly stated in the law that the extent of such [civil] rights is not determined by the scope of rights enjoyed by separate individuals in such matters who are participants [as stockholders or managers] in these companies, then one could only welcome a registration system that makes incorporation easier than it is now.

However, if a company could not enjoy more rights in agriculture and business than its most severely restricted stockholders, then the matter would be "completely different." Registration under existing laws would prevent all but two kinds of companies: those owning rural land, with named stocks issued only to Russian Christians not of Polish extraction, and without foreigners or Jews on the board; and companies with shares issued "to the bearer," limited to the ownership of urban real estate in the Jewish Pale and, if engaged in mining in these provinces, with no Jews on the board. Such a system of incorporation would only hinder trade and industry in the empire, not help it (Timashev conference, 11. 127–29).

By July 1912, it had become clear that the tsarist government would not abandon its ethnic restrictions. The AIT then delivered a strongly worded condemnation of the mixed system to the minister of trade and industry and the Council of Ministers (Shepelev, 1973, pp. 276–77). At its annual meeting in March 1913, the PSM likewise denounced the government's bill, explaining that "in Russia the introduction of a registration system entails new constraints and restrictions, precisely the opposite of the case in other countries" (Petersburg Society of Manufacturers, 1913, 1. 85 verso).

After several years of inconclusive debate, the tsarist government finally made two bold moves in the field of corporate law, both guaranteed to anger the proponents of rational reform. The new measures accorded perfectly with the general direction toward repression of the Jews from 1911 onward, at the time of the famous Beilis murder case (1911–1913), promoted by the minister of justice from 1906 to 1915, I. G. Shcheglovitov. The Senate banned the leasing of land in the Jewish Pale by first-guild Jewish merchants; all Jews were barred from the major fairs in Siberia and Nizhnii Novgorod; the police raided the exchange in Samara; and the economic activities of Jews in Kiev were restricted. Although not distinguished for their ethnic toleration, Russian merchants protested vigorously through numerous exchange committees and other business organizations, arguing, as did the Kursk Exchange Committee, that without Jews no grain could be sold. When Petr L. Bark became minister of finance in 1914, the problem grew even worse. In a rescript to the tsar, Bark condemned the policy of forced industrialization and criticized the large banks and international financiers. The reactionary and anti-Semitic *Novoe vremia* (New Times) exulted in the coming of "a new era" and the end to what it called the "liberal-cosmopolitan chancery domination" of the economy and the alleged power of Jewish bankers (Löwe, 1978, pp. 139–41).

It was in this malevolent spirit that the government directed two major blows against corporations. On June 28, 1913, the Council of Ministers ruled that no corporation operating where land ownership was denied to Jews could own more than 200 *desiatinas*, or 540 acres, of rural land (this limit had been imposed on new corporations in the Polish and western provinces since December 1884), and that any company owning land in these areas must have a majority of Christians as directors and no Jew as the manager of its real estate.[12] The very idea of corporate landholding in any area of the empire worried Rittikh, the vice-director of the Main Administration of Land Tenure and Agriculture (*Glavnoe upravlenie zemleustroistva i zemledeliia*). He had told the Council of Ministers in April 1913 that "large-scale ownership of land by corporations represents a serious danger [to the gentry and peasantry] and in the final analysis is more harmful than beneficial to the state" (quoted by Laverychev, 1982, p. 87).

Accordingly, in early 1914 the Council of Ministers adopted an even more stringent regulation proposed by the minister of agriculture, A.V. Krivoshein, which limited companies throughout the empire to a maximum of 200 *desiatinas* of land. To waive this limit required special permission from the ministry of trade and industry and the concurrence of the ministries of internal affairs, the land tenure and agriculture administration, and, in sensitive border areas such as Transcaucasia, the ministry of war. Corporations exploiting natural resources on their own land must have no Jews on the board or as managers of real estate, and companies that owned land exclusively as business premises must have a majority of non-Jews on the board. The ministry of internal affairs and the main administration of land tenure and agriculture supported this measure because a study in 1912 had found that 61 companies in the southern coal basin together owned 150,000 *desiatinas* of land. In many cases, corporations had bought land for speculation, and often the corporate form of ownership had allowed Jews to buy land in violation of existing laws. On April 18, 1914, the tsar signed this measure into law (Haumann, 1980, p. 45; Shepelev, 1973, pp. 279–80).

The mood of the business leaders now turned to open anger. It was to be expected that the liberal group of Moscow manufacturers, led by Pavel P. Riabushinskii, would criticize this arbitrary infringement on the use of private property ("unacceptable to Russian industry and to the Russian people," he called it with characteristic hyperbole). However, several business organizations that had carefully avoided political clashes with the tsarist regime in the past now protested vigorously. Jules Goujon (Iulii P. Guzhon in Russian), president of the Moscow Society of Manufacturers (MSM—*Obshchestvo zavodchikov i fabrikantov moskovskogo promyshlennogo raiona*), denounced what he called the dictatorship of the ministry of internal affairs over the other ministries. The eighth congress of the AIT, meeting in early May, evinced a strongly "oppositional character." Even the leaders of the mining and metallurgical companies of the Ukraine, many of whom depended directly on state aid and considered themselves full partners with the regime in the campaign to develop the empire's transportation infrastructure and military machine, lost their tempers. Through their organization, the South Russian Coal and Iron Association (SRCIA—*Sovet s"ezdov gornopromyshlennikov iuga Rossii*), they called on the French ambassador to intervene on behalf of an industry in which French investors had placed many million of francs (Haumann, 1980, pp. 45–46; Löwe, 1978, p. 142).

The wave of protest mounted during the summer. On July 4, the AIT bluntly pointed out the contradiction between the repressive new law and the most basic principles of modern capitalism. "The fundamental idea of the corporate form [of economic activity] consists in the ease with which shares in the enterprise circulate, making it possible for the firm to attract capital from the public at large. Named shares are an aberration" (quoted by Shepelev, 1973, p. 277).

So vociferous became these complaints that the government finally abandoned the law of April 18 (but not that of June 28, 1913). The president of the Council of Ministers told the tsar on July 15 that the recently enacted law had already begun to constrain corporate activity, and that the solution to the controversy lay in a return to the concessionary system as practiced in previous decades, under which individual companies could receive exemptions from the limits on land ownership mandated by law. The tsar signed this change into law the very next day (Laverychev, 1982, p. 88). No further talk of corporate law reform was heard in the short period before the outbreak of World War I.

Strange it was that after decades of debate over the reform of the corporate law, Russian business leaders would regard it as a victory of sorts to force the state to revert to the concessionary system in 1914. Universally regarded as hopelessly outmoded and arbitrary in the 1870s, this system continued in force to the very end, causing delays and exposing corporations to the familiar torments of bureaucratic tutelage. Swamped by an ever-increasing flood of petitions of incorporation, the ministry of internal affairs accumulated a backlog of almost 300 charters in 1914, while almost 50 proposals for new railroad lines lay unexamined in the ministry of finance (Oseroff, 1916, pp. 129, 134).

Despite dozens of petitions urging the abolition of both the concessionary system and the restrictions against Jews, Poles, and foreigners, the tsarist regime continually resisted the reform of its corporate law. Heinz-Dietrich Löwe may have exaggerated the degree to which the anti-capitalist policies of the state stemmed directly from the anti-Semitism of the tsar and his ministers (1978, p. 142), but it seems clear that the policymakers stood ready to sacrifice the campaign for industrial development whenever it threatened the interests of the gentry and peasantry and the principle of autocratic control, as perceived by the ministers in St. Petersburg.

We have examined the issue of corporate law reform in imperial Russia in four periods and, within each period, in terms of the problems that policymakers faced, the measures they took to improve the law, and the stubborn dilemmas that remained at the end of each period. The first period, from the mid-1830s to 1870, was characterized by the tutelage of the regime over a small number of corporations. The law of December 6, 1836, imposed a series of regulations that stifled free enterprise in an effort to protect investors from the vagaries of the stock market and from fraud by corporate manipulators. However, the regime also retained the concessionary system, under which each new corporation's charter had the effect of a separate law, so that many articles of individual charters conflicted with the provisions of the law of 1836. The results was the kind of confusion that only an untidy autocracy could tolerate for long.

The attempt to move from tutelage and confusion to an enlightened laissez-faire policy occupied the Butovskii commission in the early 1870s and the Tsitovich commission in 1897–1900. Again the efforts ended in failure. Eager to imitate European legal norms, the commissions drew up an overly theoretical plan of incorporation by registration. After the European stock market crash of 1873 showed the dangers inherent in the policy of laissez-faire, Finance Minister Reutern, often considered a man of enlightened views, abandoned the reform and reverted to the old concessionary policy and the much-amended law of 1836, now decades out of date. Faced with the problem of a major conflict between the property rights of corporations and the restrictions that the regime had placed on their Jewish, Polish, and foreign stockholders and managers, Witte in 1901 likewise abandoned his campaign to implement the principle of incorporation by registration.

In the final period, from the call for a new law in the State Duma in 1910 to the enactment of the reactionary decrees of June 28, 1913, and April 18, 1914, and the repeal of the latter the following July, the ministers and the tsar sought to regiment the now powerful economic forces represented by modern corporate capitalism. Although the ministers of finance and (from October 1905 onward) of trade and industry pressed for the abandonment of the concessionary system in favor of incorporation by registration together with some relaxation of the ethnic restrictions, the ministries of agriculture, internal affairs, and justice resisted such reforms. They succeeded in applying to corporations not owned and managed exclusively by Christian Russian subjects numerous restrictions that prevented Jews, foreigners, and Poles from owning land in sensitive areas and from engaging in such strategically important industries as mining.

This brief overview of the evolution of Russian corporate law has stressed the contrast between the economic policy of the tsarist state and the demands of modern capitalist rationality, as expressed by business organizations and legal experts in the empire. Accustomed as we are to regard many economic policies of the West-European state as somehow reflecting the interplay of group interests within the society that it rules, we are impressed with the tendency of the imperial Russian state to stand above society at each crucial juncture in the history of its corporate law. The patronizing tutor of 1836 became in 1871–1874 the expert legislator and guardian of economic stability, only to stand in 1897–1900 and 1910–1914 as an enemy of any reform that threatened to dilute its control over the economic activities of foreigners and ethnic minorities whose unfettered entrepreneurship it considered dangerous. Although the voice of business groups grew in importance over the decades, it remained relatively weak, to be disregarded in turn by Reutern, Witte, and Krivoshein. (Kankrin had not even bothered to seek the opinions of business leaders during the drafting of the law of 1836.) Indeed, the strengthening of anti-Semitic regulations between 1911 and 1914 seems to have been carried out by bureaucrats on their own initiative, rather than in response to whatever pleas were heard in St. Petersburg from landlords threatened by corporate speculators in land and from the anti-Semitic fringe parties. This point deserves special emphasis both because of the familiar Marxist notion of the state as the tool of the so-called "ruling class" and because of the concept, strongly rooted in the American intellectual tradition, of the state as a mechanism at least somewhat responsive to group interests.[13] Max Weber's musings on the tendency of the state to have interests and priorities of its own[14] serve well as a theoretical principle in this case, especially since the Russian autocracy manifested this tendency with particular virulence.[15]

These several episodes also bring into focus another point heretofore noticed by scholars such as Kaczkowski (1908), Kahan (1967), and McKay (1984) but insufficiently emphasized in the historical literature, namely the role of the tsarist state as an obstacle to capitalist development. As Richard Wortman noted in his discussion of the legal reform of 1864: "For the Russian autocracy to accept an independent judiciary required that it betray its essence and cease to be the Russian autocracy" (1976, p. 285). It was for similar reasons in the economic realm that the tsarist regime could not bring itself to implement a corporate law modeled on European practices. Neither tutelage nor abstract regulation nor the tightening of ethnically based restrictions on corporate activity could be considered consistent with the principles of modern capitalism, which, as Weber pointed out, demand "that the official business of the administration be discharged precisely, unambiguously, continuously, and with as much speed as possible" (1958, p. 215).[16] From the time of Peter the Great if not before, the tsarist state, impelled primarily by the necessities of war, stimulated the development of the largest industrial complexes in the realm in such key sectors as iron, coal, shipbuilding, transportation, and weaponry. The state's leading role has been a major theme of the historiography of Russian economic development. This pattern is not in dispute. However, it is essential to recognize that in the nineteenth and twentieth centuries, as in Peter's time, the tsarist state pursued its goals by autocratic means: arbitrary rule from the capital, favoritism toward amiable courtiers, excessive theoretical planning in ignorance of local conditions—in short, means ultimately incompatible with the principles of modern capitalist rationality.

The issue of corporate law is instructive in this regard precisely because it best represents the mode of modern capitalist behavior, based on economic rationalism, strict legality, and free scope for the exercise of financial and technical expertise regardless of ethnicity or citizenship. For better or worse, all these aspects of modern European culture were lacking in imperial Russian society, where the bureaucrat, the landlord, the *intelligent*, the patriarchal merchant, and the peasant remained the classic social types almost to the very end. The notion that the tsarist government gradually grew accustomed to the imperatives of modern capitalism, especially after 1890,[17] is directly contradicted by the history of Russian corporate law. Particularly important is the fact that the regime came very close to implementing a thorough reform on the European model in 1870–1874, but in 1910–1914 held to a strongly anti-capitalist position on this issue.

The fact that the tsarist regime refused to accommodate the principles of modern capitalism, especially in the final decades, also raises some important questions about the alleged political alliance between the tsarist state and Russian business interests. Certainly the Soviet historians are correct to note that most Russian business leaders refrained from political opposition to the autocracy, but their explanation—the dependence of Russian industry on the financial favors bestowed by the state and the need for the tsar's armed force to repress the unruly workers—admits only the crudest form of human motivation: greed and fear. It must be remembered that every statement on the question of corporate law issued by major business organizations from 1870 onward showed an intense frustration with the irrational tsarist legislation, no matter how tactfully they expressed their demands for reform. The hypothesis of a fundamental antagonism between Russian commercial and industrial interests and the tsarist state[18] opens up a series of new empirical questions, the foremost of which is why such a retrograde institution as the tsarist bureaucracy should have appeared to Russian business leaders, in spite of everything, as their most attractive political ally in the period from 1890 to 1914. Presumably other possible alliances—with the liberal intelligentsia, the reactionary landlords, the peasants, the workers—seemed unlikely or downright ludicrous. Whatever the reasons, they will become clear only from a careful examination of the views of the political actors themselves, not from the teleological cliches of Soviet historians about the rise of ''monopoly capitalism.'' At this point, the failure of the elements of a Russian middle class to unite against the autocracy and to triumph over it in the early twentieth century remains a complex and fascinating puzzle. The effects of the state's economic policies on the political attitudes of Russian business leaders will doubtlessly constitute a major component of the eventual explanation.

ACKNOWLEDGMENTS

Financial support for research on this topic was generously provided by the International Research and Exchanges Board, the Russian Institute (now Harriman Institute) of Columbia University, and the Kennan Institute for Advanced Russian Studies.

NOTES

1. Sodoffsky (1903, p. 61) mistakenly specified the date of the law of 1836 as June 20, not December 6.

2. On Bludov, see Wortman (1976, p. 6); on Kankrin, see Pintner (1967), esp. Part 1. In a brief reference to the law of 1836, Pintner (p. 103), called it "highly restrictive"; Wortman (p. 285) noted that "the government remained averse to the reforms in credit and commercial law necessitated by the new industrial economy."

3. Terner (1871, p. 133), noted that the Russian law of 1836 was the oldest such statute in Europe. See the cogent argument for the registration system by Pakhman (1861).

4. *PSZ* 2-41039, dated July 10, 1864, denied Jews the right to obtain rural land from landlords and peasants in the provinces subordinate to the governors-general of Vilna and Kiev. *PSZ* 2-42759, dated December 10, 1865, barred Polish individuals from acquiring rural land in the nine western provinces (*zapadnyi krai*) except by legal inheritance. *PSZ* 3-2633, dated December 27, 1884, forbade Poles to acquire rural property in the form of mortgage security (*otdacha v zalog*) in the nine western provinces (Kiev, Podolia, Volynia, Vilna, Kovno, Grodno, Vitebsk, Mogilev, and Minsk); and corporations could acquire no more than 200 *desiatinas* of land in these provinces. *PSZ* 3-4286, dated March 14, 1887, stipulated that in the 10 provinces of the Kingdom of Poland and in Bessarabia, Grodno, Kiev, Kovno, Courland, Livland, Minsk, and Podolia provinces foreigners were henceforth barred from acquiring land outside ports and other cities; in Poland, moreover, foreigners must not manage real estate for others; and foreign companies must also comply with these restrictions (Art. 6). *PSZ* 3-5664, dated December 24, 1888, extended the restrictions of 3-4286 to foreigners in mining and metallurgy. Typical of other statutes affecting various strategically vital borderlands of the empire was *PSZ* 3-10102, dated November 29, 1893; it required all corporations operating in Turkestan to have as stockholders persons who were either Christian Russian subjects or non-Christian natives of the region or of Central Asian states bordering Turkestan; all corporate acquisitions of real estate must in any case be approved by the governor-general of Turkestan and the ministry of war, with the concurrence of the ministry of finance.

5. Witte did support Kovalevskii's proposal in 1900–1902 for a normative system, under which the finance ministry would approve charters of new companies, based on a "model charter" (*normal'nyi ustav*), as long as they included no special privileges or exceptions to existing laws. The Kovalevskii bill also allowed the finance minister to exempt certain companies with shares to the bearer from these restrictions, for example, giving them the right to own up to 200 *desiatinas* of rural land and to have a minority of the board made up of foreigners and/or Jews. This fact indicates that Witte preferred registration as long as he could avoid making an open challenge to the existing property restrictions based on ethnicity and citizenship. On the 1900–1902 bill, which failed, however, to receive the endorsement of other interested ministries, see Shepelev (1973, pp. 188–201; on the exemptions, pp. 195–199).

6. See Shepelev's useful description of this law (1973, pp. 201–16); a longer treatment is Sodoffsky (1903).

7. Fedorov saw the registration system as the logical concomitant of the abolition of restrictions on the economic activity of Jews, a measure then being prepared by the ministry of internal affairs (Shepelev, 1973, pp. 256–57).

8. Fedorov and Petrazhitskii used the term *pravovoe gosudarstvo*, a direct translation of the

German *Rechtsstaat*: a state that obeys its own laws.

9. In a published statement issued apparently at about this time, these three organizations called for a very permissive system, including several features advantageous to corporate entrepreneurs: no minimum for basic capital; a very low minimum price of 25 rubles per share; stockholder suits against the management to be void unless supported by owners of at least one-fifth of the total stock and only in cases of conscious fraud; no prohibition against managers' participation in several companies at once, in view of the shortage of executive talent in Russia; and liquidation to be mandatory only when demanded by owners of one-fifth of the stock, not one-twentieth, as recommended by the ministry of trade and industry (*Proekt*, n.d., pp. 8, 16, 21–22, 24). Several of these recommendations are mentioned by Shepelev (1973, p. 26), who apparently cites a response to a reform bill put forth by the government in June 1911.

10. See also, the attack on the concessionary system by the economist A. S. Zalshupin in September 1912, cited by Laverychev (1974, p. 43).

11. The ministry of trade and industry suggested a minimum basic capital of 100,000 rubles and a minimum price of 100 rubles per share, with exceptions down to 50,000 and 50 rubles respectively for small projects of local significance; stocks, both common and preferred, to be issued by name before operations began and by name and to bearer thereafter; and the founders to purchase a certain percentage of the stock, for example, 10 percent (Timashev conference, 1. 51 verso = page 84).

12. On February 4, 1906, the tsar approved a regulation that required all companies with the right to own land in areas denied to Jews to have non-Jews as real estate managers; but Jews could serve as executive director, directors, and alternates. V. I. Timiriazev, the minister of trade and industry from October 1905 to February 1906, proposed that Jews be allowed to own stock in companies active in areas and industries denied to individual Jews (e.g., mining), but this idea was rejected by the Committee of Ministers on January 24, 1906 (Shepelev, 1973, pp. 252–53).

13. For a discussion of the Madisonian viewpoint (as in *The Federalist*, number 10) and others, see Beard (1922), which, curiously enough, lacks a chapter on Marxist theory.

14. "Of course, and above all, the sure instincts of the bureaucracy for the conditions of maintaining its power in its own state (and through it, in opposition to other states) are inseparably fused with the canonization of the abstract and 'objective' idea of 'reason of state'" (Weber, 1958, p. 220).

15. This impulse toward autocratic power insulated from the prerogatives of the citizenry was perfectly exemplified by Finance Minister Kankrin. In the words of Walter Pintner, "Kankrin's only consistent guiding standard or principle was the extent to which a given policy contributed to the strength of the state as an independent entity, separate not only from other states but from the welfare and happiness of the population itself" (1967, pp. 20–21). The case for the existence of a Russian "patrimonial" state standing above society is argued most strongly by Pipes (1974). With regard to another crucial economic policy question, that of import tariffs, Kahan noted that "overriding priorities of fiscal needs" led the Russian state to impose extremely high duties on imported goods in the 1880s and 1890s; this policy created "a conflict between [the state's] short-run fiscal interests and the objectives of industrialization" because the latter goal might have been better served by the imposition of low tariff duties on essential raw materials and equipment (Kahan, 1967, pp. 470–71). On the inability of Witte and other proponents of industrialization to appreciate the importance of market mechanisms in the Russian petroleum industry, see McKay (1984).

16. Elsewhere, Weber specifically defined "modern capitalism" as a complex of six institutional forms: rational accounting for business, separately from the family's finances; a free market, without formal restrictions on business activities according to an individual's social status; the application of new technology, specifically mechanization; a legal and administrative system operating without arbitrariness; a free labor force; and the public sale of shares in economic enterprises and property (1927, p. 276–78). On the other hand, "under the dominance of a patrimonial regime only certain kinds of capitalism are able to develop," specifically not the large corporation, which Weber defined as the "profit-making enterprise with heavy investments in fixed capital and a rational organization of free labor which is oriented to the market purchases of private consumers. This is altogether too

sensitive to all sorts of irrationalities in the administration of justice, in other forms of administrative practice, and in taxation'' (Weber, 1964, p. 357).

17. Gerschenkron, for example, wrote of Witte's policies that "the fear of industrialization, so much in evidence in the 1860's, was gone. Industrial development became an accepted and in fact the central goal'' (1962, p. 125).

18. The reluctance or inability of the tsarist state to embrace modern capitalist modes of action was noted by Kaczkowski, who stressed that the bureaucratic restrictions on corporations exerted "a negative influence on the economic progress of the country'' (1908, pp. 126–27). Although some American historians have also grasped this point, few Soviet researchers have paid sufficient attention to it. In this regard, Carstensen and Gregory Guroff recently made a useful distinction between "traditionalists" like Plehve; "industrializers" like Peter the Great, Witte in the 1890s, and Stalin; and "modernizers," who sought structural changes in the political realm in the interests of economic rationality. They concluded that "the debate over modernization was rarely heard and has always been settled in favor of the industrializers" (Carstensen and Guroff, 1983, pp. 353, 354).

REFERENCES

Beard, Charles A. (1922), *The Economic Basis of Politics*. New York: Knopf.

Birzhevoi komitet, St. Petersburg (1873), *Zamechaniia S.-Peterburgskogo birzhevogo komiteta i kommissii birzhevogo kupechestva, na proekt polozheniia ob aktsionernykh obshchestvakh.* St. Petersburg.

Butovskii commission (1871), Tsentral'nyi gosudarstvennyi istoricheskii arkhiv (TsGIA), Leningrad, f. 20, op. 3, ed. khr. 1916-a.

Carstensen, Fred C., and Gregory Guroff (1983), "Economic Innovation in Imperial Russia and the Soviet Union: Observations." In Guroff and Carstensen (eds.), *Entrepreneurship in Imperial Russia and the Soviet Union*. Princeton: Princeton Universiy Press.

Gerschenkron, Alexander (1962), "Russia: Patterns and Problems of Economic Development." In his *Economic Backwardness in Historical Perspective*. Cambridge: Harvard University Press.

Haumann, Heiko (1980), *Kapitalismus im zaristischen Staat, 1906–1917*. Königstein: Verlag Anton Hain.

Kaczkowski, Josef (1908), "Towarzystwa akcyjne w panstwie rosyjskiem: studyum prawno-ekonomiczne." *Ekonomista*, 8 (January) pp. 81–128.

Kahan, Arcadius (1967), "Government Policies and the Industrialization of Russia." *Journal of Economic History*, 27 (December) pp. 460–77.

Kaminka, Avgust I. (1897), "Proekt polozheniia ob aktsionernykh predpriiatiiakh." *Zhurnal ministerstva iustitsii*, 3 (January) pp. 127–56.

Kaminka, Avgust I. (1902), *Aktsionernaia kompaniia: iuridicheskoe issledovanie*. Vol. 1 [no more published], St. Petersburg: Landau.

Laverychev, Vladimir Ia. (1974), *Krupnaia burzhuaziia v poreformennoi Rossii*. Moscow: Mysl'.

Laverychev, Vladimir Ia. (1982), "K voprosu o vmeshatel'stve tsarizma v ekonomicheskuiu zhizn' Rossii v nachale XX v." In I. M. Pushkareva, A. P. Korelin, and S. V. Tiutiukin (eds.), *Samoderzhavie i krupnyi kapital v Rossii v kontse XIX--nachale XX v.: Sbornik statei*. Moscow: Institut istorii SSSR.

Löwe, Heinz-Dietrich (1978), *Antisemitismus und reaktionäre Utopie: Russischer Konservatismus gegen den Wandel von Staat und Gesellschaft, 1890–1917*. Hamburg: Hoffmann und Campe.

McKay, John P. (1984), "Baku Oil and Transcaucasian Pipelines: A Study in Tsarist Economic Policy." *Slavic Review*, 43 (Winter) pp. 603–20.

Neftianoe delo, Baku.

Oseroff [Ozerov], Ivan (1916), *Problèmes économiques et financiers de la Russie moderne*. Paris: Payot.

Owen, Thomas C. (1981), *Capitalism and Politics in Russia: A Social History of the Moscow Merchants, 1855-1905.* Cambridge: Cambridge University Press.

Pakhman [Pachmann], Semen V. (1861), *O zadachakh predstoiashchei reformy aktsionernogo akonodatel'stva.* Kharkov.

Pelka, Boleslaw (1967), "Organizacja i historia Lodzkiej gieldy pienieznej i jej akta." *Archeion,* 46, pp. 158–69.

Petersburg Society of Manufacturers (1913), minutes of annual meeting, March 1913. Tsentral'nyi gosudarstvennyi istoricheskii arkhiv (TsGIA), Leningrad, f. 150, op. 1, ed. khr. 58.

Petrazhitskii, Lev I. (1898), *Aktsionernaia kompaniia, aktsionernye zloupotrebleniia i rol'aktsionernykh kompanii v narodnom khoziaistve.* St. Petersburg: Ministerstvo finansov.

Petrov, Iu. A. (1982), "Moskovskie banki i promyshlennost' k nachalu XX veka." In I. M. Pushkareva, A. P. Korelin, and S. V. Tiutiukin (eds.), *Samoderzhavie i krupnyi kapital v Rossii v kontse XIX—nachale XX v.: Sbornik statei.* Moscow: Institut istorii SSSR.

Pintner, Walter M. (1967), *Russian Economic Policy under Nicholas I.* Ithaca: Cornell University Press.

Pipes, Richard (1974), *Russia under the Old Regime.* New York: Scribner.

Polnoe sobranie zakonov Rossiiskoi imperii (PSZ).

Proekt izmenenii v deistvuiushchem zakonodatel'stve o torgovo-promyshlennykh aktsionernykh kompaniiakh. (n.d.), St. Petersburg.

Shepelev, Leonid E. (1967), "Iz istorii russkogo aktsionernogo zakonodatel'stva (zakon 1836 g.)." In *Vnutrenniaia politika tsarizma (seredina XVI—nachalo XX veka).* Leningrad: Leningradskoe otdelenie instituta istorii SSSR.

Shepelev, Leonid E. (1973), *Aktsionernye kompanii v Rossii.* Leningrad: Nauka.

Sodoffsky, Gustav (1903), "Die Entwicklung der Aktiengesellschaften in Russland und die Bestimmungen vom 21. Dezember (a. St.) 1901." *Jahrbücher für Nationalökonomie und Statistik,* 3rd series, 26 (81).

Spiridovich, L. [pseud.] (1897), *Dela nashikh aktsionernykh kompanii.* Moscow: Universitetskaia tipografiia.

Terner [Thörner], Fedor G. (1871), *Sravnitel'noe obozrenie aktsionernogo zakonodatel'stva glavneishikh evropeiskikh stran.* St. Petersburg: Maikov.

Timashev conference (1911), Tsentral'nyi gosudarstvennyi istoricheskii arkhiv (TsGIA), Leningrad, f. 23, op. 14, delo 205.

Weber, Max (1927), *General Economic History,* trans. Frank H. Knight. New York: Greenberg.

Weber, Max (1958), "Bureaucracy." In Hans H. Gerth and C. Wright Mills (eds.), *From Max Weber: Essays in Sociology.* New York: Oxford University Press.

Weber, Max (1964), *The Theory of Social and Economic Organization,* trans. A. M. Henderson and Talcot Parsons. New York: Free Press.

West, James L. (1984), "The Rjabušinskij Circle: Russian Industrialists in Search of a Bourgeoisie, 1909–1914." *Jahrbücher für Geschichte Osteuropas,* N.S. 32 (September) pp. 358–77.

Wortman, Richard S. (1976), *The Development of a Russian Legal Consciousness.* Chicago: University of Chicago Press.

THE BIRTH-BAPTISM INTERVAL AND THE ESTIMATE OF ENGLISH POPULATION IN THE EIGHTEENTH CENTURY

John Komlos

ABSTRACT

The increase in the time elapsed between the vital event of birth and the ecclesiastical one of baptism poses a problem for demographers insofar as its variation leads to an undercount of births. In an epidemiological environment in which infant mortality was high and baptisms were restricted to live babies, even small variations in the birth/baptism interval could have a significant influence on the shortfall in baptisms—the difference between the unknown number of births and a measure used as its proxy, the known number of baptisms. This article explores changes in the birth/baptism interval by analyzing seasonal variation in baptisms. Average elapsed time was estimated to have increased from eight days in 1670 to 54 in 1810.

Research in Economic History, Volume 11, pages 301–316.
ISBN: 0-89232-677-8

Although this method is quite different from the one Wrigley and Schofield used, the results are quite similar to theirs.

The recent monumental work by the Cambridge Group for the History of Population (Wrigley and Schofield, 1981, p. 162) estimating England's population on an annual, indeed monthly, basis, promises to be a veritable mine of information for demographers, economists, and other social scientists. The book has been unconditionally acclaimed as a "masterpiece," by some (see Trussell's 1983 review); others while praising it have pointed out that its many assumptions leave room for further consideration (Flynn, 1982).

Wrigley and Schofield undertake three major corrections of raw data gleaned from Anglican parish registers to account for the shortfall in baptism registrations attributable to: (1) the existence of nonconformists; (2) delays in baptisms; and (3) residual nonregistration. They were criticized recently for their third adjustment (Lindert, 1983). My intention is to consider the robustness of Wrigley and Schofield's second adjustment procedure (1981, pp. 96–103, 561), the estimate of the shortfall in birth registration brought about by the lengthening of the birth/baptism interval during the eighteenth century. This parameter is important because by the early nineteenth century as much as a nine percent undercount of births was estimated on this account. Although the work covers three centuries of varied demographic experience, this paper is concerned with only the "long" eighteenth century, when this adjustment becomes important.

The elapsed time between the vital event of birth and the ecclesiastical one of baptism is an important determinant of the undercounting of births at any one time. Mortality among newborn infants leads to an undercount of baptisms, hence of births. Had the unbaptized child's death been registered, one could still estimate the actual number of births. By counting unbaptized burials, Wrigley and Schofield do estimate a shortfall in baptisms. By the eighteenth century, however, death registers were also incomplete; hence one cannot estimate unbaptized births from unbaptized deaths alone.

To the extent that the birth/baptism interval varied over time, the undercount, too, varied proportionately, This is crucial, since 50–60 percent of infant mortality occurred during the first month of life. Hence, the longer birth/baptism interval became, the higher was the probability that the number of unrecorded births rose because of the child's death.

This need not be the case if sickly children were consistently selected for early baptism. Then delayed baptisms would not precipitate a shortfall in the birth count. Having insufficient evidence substantiating this possibility, Wrigley and Schofield chose to disregard it. To the extent that this study also disregards this possible selection bias, my estimate of the population is an upper-bound one.

Another important variable in determining the birth/baptism shortfall is the level of infant mortality, particularly in the first month of life, which in turn is primarily a function of endogenous mortality. Although the data indicate a decline in infant mortality, especially during the first month of life (Table 1), this apparent decline is to some extent misleading. There was some decline in infant mortality during the first month of life in the course of the eighteenth century (Wrigley, 1977, pp. 305, 308; Wrigley and Schofield, 1981, p. 99), which is also reflected in rising life expectancy at birth (Wrigley and Schofield, 1981, p. 231), but the true decline has not been fully ascertained. The decline evident in Table 1, however, is no doubt an exaggeration, for it is also influenced by the birth/baptism shortfall. Since an upper bound for the population is to be estimated in any event, the assumption is made that the mortality decline evinced in Table 1 is entirely due to a shortfall in registered births.

The argument for the increase in the length of the birth/baptism interval is based on evidence from parishes where both births and baptisms were recorded. These entries indicate that in the early eighteenth century the interval between birth and baptism was on the order of eight days, but by the 1770s this interval had increased to 26 days, and by 1800 to more than a month[1] (Table 2). This information is derived from a small number of parishes, which might not be representative. Yet the consistency of this pattern in other studies (Ambler, 1974; Collins, 1977; Jackson and Laxton, 1977; Mills, 1973) leads one to have confidence in the results.

There is, however, an indirect way to estimate the increases in the elapsed time between births and baptisms. This method entails examining the cyclical nature of baptisms between 1670 and 1819,[2] after proper adjustment for changes in the

Table 1. Infant Mortality per 1000 Baptisms in England

		Elapsed time between baptism & death					
	Days			*Weeks*			
Decade	*5*	*1*	*2*	*3*	*4*	*8*	
1680s	34.9	39.5	54.4	67.0	75.0	90.0	
1730s	26.5	30.0	42.5	47.0	51.5	66.0	
1780s	18.0	18.3	23.7	28.3	33.7	42.0	

Source: Wrigley (1977, p. 29).

Table 2. Interval between Births and Baptisms

Decade	*N*	*Mean*	*Variance*	*S.D.*
1690/1700	14	8	22	4.7
1770/1780	21	26	115	10.7
1790/1800	32	35	582	24.0

N   = Number of parishes in samples.
Mean = Number of days elapsed between birth and baptism calculated as a simple mean of the medians of
      the various parishes found in Berry and Schofield (1971).

calendar in September of 1752.[3] At first, cycle relatives (CR) were calculated,[4] which were averaged in decade intervals (Table 3 and Figure 1). These measure the frequency of baptisms in a month relative to its expected value of 100, which would be obtained if the births were distributed evenly throughout the year. (The measure was standardized for the varying lengths of the months.)

Baptisms took place most often in March or April and least often in August, at least until the nineteenth century (Figure 1). Another feature of the cycles is their continuous attenuation after the 1730s (Figure 2). It is also apparent that the shape of the cycles themselves changed abruptly in the 1730s: the March peak decreased by six points, while the relatively low values for May, June, and July increased by 3 or 4 points (Table 3).

The birth/baptism interval can be estimated by assuming that neither the lengthening of the interval nor its variance was a function of the month in which the baptism took place. That is, the hypothesis is that the interval changed

Table 3. The Cycle Relatives of Births in England (Decadal Averages)
1670–1810

Year	Jan	Feb	Mar	Apr	May	Jun	Jul	Aug	Sep	Oct	Nov	Dec
1670s	103.2	111.9	122.2	121.1	104.3	89.3	81.3	82.5	91.1	98.6	99.3	96.4
1680s	104.0	114.1	117.6	116.1	105.9	90.6	82.6	81.6	93.1	99.2	98.0	98.5
1690s	105.4	115.7	120.5	118.9	104.4	90.8	85.0	83.6	87.4	96.0	96.4	97.1
1700s	104.7	115.6	121.2	114.5	102.4	91.6	84.6	86.2	90.3	96.7	96.6	96.7
1710s	99.3	110.9	119.5	116.7	105.0	91.1	87.8	87.7	93.0	96.0	96.4	97.7
1720s	105.4	115.3	118.9	113.9	103.5	91.5	84.3	83.7	91.6	98.1	97.8	97.2
1730s	104.8	111.4	112.3	114.6	106.3	94.1	88.0	84.1	91.4	98.7	97.1	98.0
1740s	104.3	110.6	114.8	115.0	109.5	100.4	91.3	85.5	89.1	92.8	93.5	94.1
1750s	103.6	108.8	112.6	118.5	104.9	98.7	92.7	84.4	93.2	97.0	89.7	96.5
1760s	105.7	108.1	110.2	113.0	105.6	100.8	94.8	88.4	90.2	95.9	93.0	94.8
1770s	99.8	107.2	109.9	118.9	104.5	103.6	94.3	87.1	91.7	94.6	89.9	99.2
1780s	102.0	108.4	107.1	114.4	104.0	102.2	96.7	85.2	94.7	96.5	89.8	99.8
1790s	103.0	103.0	108.0	114.0	107.0	101.0	96.5	87.0	94.3	93.2	90.4	99.8
1800s	97.9	99.2	103.4	116.5	108.5	108.5	99.3	91.1	95.4	96.8	89.9	93.7
1810s	97.1	97.4	105.0	110.0	106.9	106.3	98.7	96.7	98.5	95.0	91.0	97.2
1670–1729 (average without 1710s)												
	103.7	113.9	120.0	116.9	104.2	90.8	84.3	84.2	91.1	97.4	97.4	97.3

Source: Wrigley and Schofield (1981, Table A2.4, pp. 507–10).

Figure 1.   The cycle relatives of births in England (decadal averages),
1670–1810

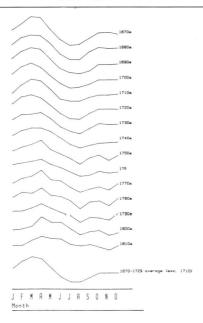

Source: Wrigley and Schofield, (1981, Table A2.4., pp. 507–10).

uniformly throughout the year. (The variance of the interval may have increased
over time, but within a decade, the assumption is that it remained constant.) If
this interval increased by a week, say, then approximately one-fourth of the
births registered in a particular month would be registered thereafter in the
subsequent month. In addition, though the underlying true seasonal pattern of
births may have changed, the assumption is made that if it did, such a change did
not correlate with the changes in the birth/baptism interval. Therefore it would
not influence the regression coefficients. After calculating the cycle relatives
averaged over a decade (Table 3), one can test the hypothesis that the CR of one
decade was a function of those of the previous decade by regressing one on the
other. Formally:

$$CR(1710) = a\ CR(1700) + b\ [CR(1700)_{-1}] + \varepsilon \qquad (1)$$

where a and b are coefficients and CR(1700) is the average cycle relative for the
12 months in the first decade of the eighteenth century and where $CR(1700)_{-1}$
indicates lagged values of the cycle relatives by 1 (or 2, etc.) month(s). The
regressions have been forced through the origin because the expected value of the
constant is zero. (The expected value of both the dependent variable and the sum
of the independent variables is 100.) Results of these regressions (Table 4) show

Figure 2.   Area under the curves in Figure 1.

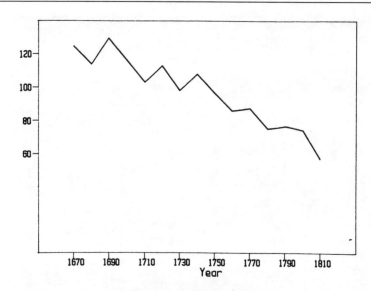

no evidence of any shift in the birth/baptism interval during the late seventeenth and early eighteenth centuries, with the exception of the period 1710–1719, since the value of *a* is close to 1 and the value of *b* is not consistently or significantly different from zero until the 1730s.

Table 4.   Testing Equation (1) 1670–1730 Independent Variable: CR(1670–1720)[a]

Dependent Variables	a	b	R^2	D.W.
CR(1680)	.935	.06	.96	1.72
	(11.3)	(.8)		
CR(1690)	.92	.08	.96	1.2
	(10.9)	(.9)		
CR(1700)	.989	.00	.93	1.2
	(9.4)	(.08)		
CR(1710)	.837	.159	.90	.97
	(7.7)	(1.5)		
CR(1720)	.97	.03	.93	1.2
	(9.5)	(.2)		
CR(1730)	.734	.262	.85	1.0
	(5.1)	(2.0)		

[a]t-statistics in parentheses.

We can, therefore, average the cycle relatives of 1670–1700 and 1720 as though they represented a homogeneous pattern of births throughout the year. (From now on we refer to this average as 1670–1720.) This average will then be assumed to be the standard cycle relative pattern prior to the beginning of a significant shift in the birth/baptism interval, and against which the cycle relatives in the other decades will be judged. The results (Table 5) indicate that there was a continual shift in this interval relative to the interval of about a week obtained for the period of 1670–1720. From now on, CR(1670–1720) will be used as the independent variable.

Notice that although the value of b increases over the century, the model is able to explain a smaller and smaller percentage of the variation in the cycle relatives, as the decreasing R^2 values indicate; by 1800, the model is inadequate. The a coefficient for 1800 is not significantly different from zero, and R^2 (adjusted for the degrees of freedom) actually becomes negative. The results for 1810 are similar to the ones for 1800 in both of these respects; they are not presented in Table 5.

The formulation for 1800 and 1810 found to yield reasonable results is:

Table 5. Testing Equation (1) for 1710–1810.
Independent Variable: CR(1670–1720)

Dependent Variables	a	b	R^2	D.W.
CR(1710)	.824	.174	.94	0.86
	(8.36)	(1.78)		
CR(1730)	.767	.230	.92	1.10
	(7.20)	(2.2)		
CR(1740)	.472	.525	.91	0.70
	(4.0)	(4.5)		
CR(1750)	.593	.403	.80	1.77
	(3.5)	(2.4)		
CR(1760)	.492	.502	.62	0.82
	(2.5)	(2.58)		
CR(1770)	.358	.637	.68	1.80
	(1.81)	(3.2)		
CR(1780)	.458	.536	.38	1.51
	(1.88)	(2.2)		
CR(1790)	.33	.663	.43	1.22
	(1.44)	(2.9)		
CR(1800)	.121	.869	−1.64	0.59
	(.344)	(2.47)		

$$CR(1800) = b\ CR(1670)_{-1} + c\ CR(1670)_{-2} + d\ CR(1670)_{-3} + \varepsilon \quad (2)$$

The estimates of the coefficients are found in Table 6.

How long a birth/baptism interval do these coefficients imply? For 1710, for example, $a = .824$, $b = .174$. This means that the cycle relative for any month consists of 82.4 percent of the value of the cycle relative for the same month for the average of 1670–1720, and 17.4 percent of the value of the cycle relative for the previous month. In other words, 17.4 percent of the baptisms of January (1670–1720) occurred in February in the period 1710–1719. If one assumes that the baptisms were distributed uniformly during the month, then 17.4 percent of 30 days, or five days' worth of January baptisms, occurred in February in the period 1710–1719. The estimated elapsed times between births and baptisms are shown in Table 7.

Table 6. Testing Equation (2) for 1800–1810.
Independent Variable: CR(1670–1720)

Dependent Variables	b	c	d	R^2	D.W.
CR(1800)	—	.597	.382	.745	1.98
		(12.0)	(8.0)		
CR(1810)	.173	.444	.366	.76	2.5
	(1.2)	(3.3)	(7.6)		

Table 7. Estimated Birth-Baptism Intervals in Days

Decade	A	B
1670s	0	8
1710s	5	13
1730s	7	15
1740s	13	21
1750s	12	20
1760s	14	22
1770s	19	27
1780s	16	24
1790s	20	28
1800s	41	49
1810s	46	54

Sources: Tables 3 and 4.

A = Change in birth-baptism intervals relative to 1670–1720.

B = Absolute value of birth-baptism interval (A + 8 days).

Note: The value for 1670 is from Wrigley and Schofield (1981) and is assumed here to be valid for 1670–1700 and the 1720s.

Two patterns emerge. One is the uncanny similarity between the intervals estimated here for the 1780s and the one Berry and Schofield enumerated (Table 2). The average birth/baptism interval of 25.5 days for 1770–1780 and 38.5 days for 1790–1800 is very close to the 26.5 days and 35 days, respectively, that they found in the register data. However, Wrigley and Schofield's assumption that the birth/baptism interval increased linearly with time during the intervening decades in which data are not available is not supported by the estimates in Table 7. Rather the estimates reveal sudden increases in the 1710s, the 1740s, the 1770s, and the 1800s. How much of an effect the discrepancy between Wrigley and Schofield's assumption and the present estimates has on the estimate of the aggregate population is worth investigating further.

To estimate the shortfall in births, suppose that all of the decrease in infant mortality between 1670 and 1780 (Table 7) is explained by a shortfall in registered births, because of the lapse of time between births and baptisms. That is, assume that the pattern found in parish registers for 1680 is the true rate, with only a week of elapsed time between birth and baptism. Assume furthermore that this rate would have prevailed throughout the eighteenth century were it not for the shortfall in registered births due to the lengthening of the birth/baptism interval.

With these assumptions, one can calculate an upper bound for the shortfall of registered births. In the period 1710–1719 the birth/baptism interval lengthened by five days relative to that of 1670–1720. The difference in infant mortality during the first five days of life (Table 8) is $34.9 - 26.5 = 8.4$, or 8.4/1000. The number of births has to be increased by .0084. Wrigley and Schofield, however, applied a correction factor of 1.041 for the 1670s, even when the birth/baptism interval was only eight days on average. I accept this figure for the 1670s, for I am primarily interested in the change in population between 1670 and 1819. The number of births estimated on the basis of the baptismal registers should be increased by 1.0494 (1.041 + .0084) for the 1710s. The ratios Wrigley and Schofield used and the revised ratios are shown in Table 9.

The English population can be re-estimated as follows: the difference was calculated between the extrapolated value of Wrigley and Schofield's adjustment ratio and the ratios listed in the first column of Table 9 for a particular decade. Baptisms in that year were multiplied by this difference times the Wrigley-Schofield final adjustment ratio (1981, pp. 138, 540). This estimate was accumulated, over the average life of an individual, about 38 years, taking the initial value of the population in 1669 as given.

The difference between the two estimates reaches an apex of 97,000 individuals, or less than 1 percent of the population, in 1769. Generally, however, it is much less than that, supporting thereby the robustness of the Wrigley and Schofield population estimates with respect to the birth/baptism interval. In fact, the revised estimate of the population (Table 10) suggests a growth rate only marginally

Table 8.   Shortfall in Births per 1000 Baptisms

	Days	Weeks				
Decade	5	1	2	3	4	8
1730s	8.4	9.5	11.9	20.0	23.5	24.0
1780s	16.9	21.2	30.7	38.7	41.3	48.0

Source: Table 1.

Table 9.   Upper-Bound Ratios Used to Estimate Births from Baptisms

Decade	Revised	Wrigley and Schofield
1670	1.0400	
1680	1.0410	1.041
1690	1.0410	
1700	1.0410	
1710	1.0494	
1720	1.0410	1.051
1730	1.0495	
1740	1.0526	
1750	1.0522	
1760	1.0529	
1770	1.0774	1.074
1780	1.0740	
1790	1.0786	
1800	1.0848	
1810	1.0846	
1819	1.0891	
1825		1.090

Sources: Tables 1 and 5; Wrigley and Schofield (1981, p. 97).
Note: For the intervening years Wrigley and Schofield (1981) calculated ratios by means of a linear interpolation.

slower than theirs between 1670 and 1769, and only marginally faster than theirs thereafter. Hence this adjustment to their estimates actually reinforces, albeit slightly, their thesis of an acceleration of population growth after 1770.

In conclusion, the above exercise confirms Wrigley and Schofield's estimates of the changes in the elapsed time between births and baptisms in eighteenth-

Table 10. Revised Estimates of the English Population 1670–1818

Year	Wrigley and Schofield	Revised	Difference
1670	5021781	5021913	−132
1671	4982687	4982912	−225
1672	4973342	4973636	−294
1673	4993190	4993518	−328
1674	5008493	5008821	−328
1675	5008659	5008956	−297
1676	5003488	5003715	−227
1677	5021160	5021282	−122
1678	5055751	5055738	13
1679	5023676	5023505	171
1680	4989069	4988702	367
1681	4930385	4929782	603
1682	4900118	4899244	874
1683	4886292	4885093	1199
1684	4888077	4886520	1557
1685	4870784	4868848	1936
1686	4864762	4862386	2376
1687	4879202	4876347	2855
1688	4896666	4893294	3372
1689	4916833	4912915	3918
1690	4916081	4911598	4483
1691	4930502	4925410	5092
1692	4935334	4929612	5722
1693	4963190	4956813	6377
1694	4950496	4943482	7014
1695	4950662	4942893	7769
1696	4961692	4953091	8601
1697	4978072	4968637	9435
1698	4997611	4987313	10298
1699	5015098	5003913	11185
1700	5026877	5014733	12144
1701	5057790	5044579	13211
1702	5091997	5077689	14308
1703	5134009	5118564	15445
1704	5156714	5140134	16580
1705	5167186	5149429	17757
1706	5182007	5163061	18946
1707	5198807	5178696	20111
1708	5214985	5193512	21473
1709	5224968	5202210	22758
1710	5238156	5215402	22754
1711	5230371	5207624	22747
1712	5217996	5195255	22741
1713	5224785	5202045	22740

continued

Table 10 (continued)

Year	Wrigley and Schofield	Revised	Difference
1714	5242213	5219476	22737
1715	5246260	5223523	22737
1716	5275978	5253223	22755
1717	5310048	5287264	22784
1718	5343506	5320686	22820
1719	5378136	5355270	22866
1720	5357759	5333430	24329
1721	5350465	5324647	25818
1722	5353441	5326004	27437
1723	5370904	5341733	29171
1724	5387727	5356883	30844
1725	5406168	5373670	32498
1726	5449957	5415657	34300
1727	5480307	5444133	36174
1728	5425467	5387745	37722
1729	5335527	5296255	39272
1730	5269100	5229727	39373
1731	5263374	5223717	39657
1732	5283764	5243739	40025
1733	5310276	5269860	40416
1734	5363165	5322349	40816
1735	5409030	5367699	41331
1736	5450392	5408520	41872
1737	5480925	5438462	42463
1738	5504321	5461229	43092
1739	5536582	5492821	43761
1740	5564656	5520657	43999
1741	5576197	5532018	44179
1742	5516469	5472063	44406
1743	5512230	5467416	44814
1744	5547818	5502498	45320
1745	5603475	5557516	45959
1746	5634781	5588181	46600
1747	5657650	5610305	47345
1748	5668980	5619480	49500
1749	5702768	5651089	51679
1750	5739364	5685223	54141
1751	5772415	5715769	56646
1752	5810512	5751293	59219
1753	5855895	5794038	61857
1754	5899694	5835149	64545
1755	5942912	5875554	67358
1756	5993415	5923217	70198
1757	6021018	5948099	72919

(continued)

Table 10. *(continued)*

Year	Wrigley and Schofield	Revised	Difference
1758	6038563	5964301	74262
1759	6062922	5987055	75867
1760	6101593	6024311	77282
1761	6146857	6068050	78807
1762	6173425	6093008	80417
1763	6162402	6080407	81995
1764	6194858	6111161	83697
1765	6245527	6160054	85473
1766	6277076	6189606	87470
1767	6294963	6205400	89563
1768	6314318	6221130	93188
1769	6357503	6260531	96972
1770	6405166	6310258	94908
1771	6447813	6354961	92852
1772	6498765	6407963	90802
1773	6552106	6463370	88736
1774	6601608	6514864	86744
1775	6674251	6589524	84727
1776	6740370	6727342	82685
1777	6807906	6727342	80564
1778	6881506	6802579	78927
1779	6949296	6871903	77393
1780	6989116	6912277	76839
1781	7042140	6965996	76144
1782	7068884	6993471	75413
1783	7126530	7051863	74667
1784	7144515	7070558	73957
1785	7217228	7143864	73364
1786	7289039	7216267	72772
1787	7370599	7298408	72191
1788	7461509	7390021	71488
1789	7542738	7471963	70775
1790	7648209	7579542	68667
1791	7739889	7673330	66559
1792	7842063	7777549	64514
1793	7936885	7874474	62411
1794	8024644	7964309	60335
1795	8100800	8042339	58461
1796	8198445	8141820	56625
1797	8285135	8230486	54649
1798	8398737	8345916	52821
1799	8500584	8449765	50819
1800	8606033	8559505	46528
1801	8664490	8622087	42403

(continued)

Table 10. (continued)

Year	Wrigley and Schofield	Revised	Difference
1802	8728212	8690178	38034
1803	8836648	8803042	33606
1804	8958695	8929289	29406
1805	9116801	9091593	25208
1806	9267570	9246518	21052
1807	9400058	9393380	16678
1808	9528047	9509811	18236
1809	9650602	9630821	19781
1810	9762413	9741506	20907
1811	9885690	9863588	22102
1812	10010037	9986713	23324
1813	10163058	10138368	24690
1814	10296594	10270431	26163
1815	10480975	10453101	27874
1816	10651629	10621983	29646
1817	10827421	10795887	31534
1818	10985092	10952531	32561

Figure 3. Differences between Wrigley-Schofield estimate of the
English population and the revised estimates, 1670–1819

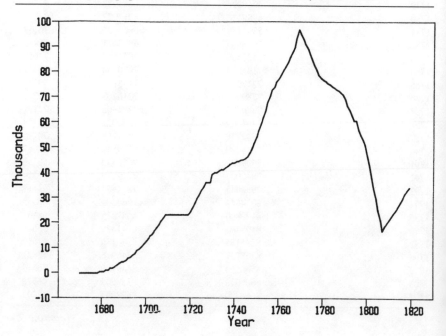

century England.[5] These estimates are subsequently used to derive an upper bound estimate of the shortfall in baptism registrations and in turn of the population of England. The assumptions made in the process of this derivation are themselves worth further research: (1) that the length of the birth/baptism interval was not a function of the parent's subjective evaluation of the probability of the child's dying within the first month of life; (2) that the length of the birth/baptism interval was not a function of the season of birth; and (3) most critically, that the decline in enumerated infant mortality was entirely due to the lengthening of the birth/baptism interval. Besides confirming the Wrigley-Schofield estimates, this paper also increases our understanding of the secular changes in the birth/baptism interval by showing that its increase was not linear over time: abrupt increases took place in the 1710s, 1730s, 1770s, and 1800. The reasons for the existence of these various stages in the lengthening of the birth/baptism interval are themselves worth further investigation.

ACKNOWLEDGMENTS

I am indebted to E. A. Wrigley and R. S. Schofield for comments on an earlier version of this study.

NOTES

1. There were high concentrations of baptisms on Sundays and Holy Days. However, regional variation abounds: In Colyton (Devon), for instance, there was a tendency for increased concentration on Sundays as the century progressed. In 1700 only 19 percent of baptisms took place on Sundays; by 1800 this share had risen to 76 percent (Duchesne, 1975).
2. A delay of baptisms would cause a rightward shift in the baptism curve. Such a shift over time is indeed evident (Wrigley and Schofield, 1981, p. 288).
3. For the years prior to September 1752, the data on births Wrigley and Schofield published were moved forward by 11 days, to adjust for the changeover from the Julian to the Gregorian calendar. The data are from Wrigley and Schofield, 1981, pp. 507–510.
4. Cycle relatives are calculated by dividing the number of births in a particular month by the average number of births per month for the year and multiplying this ratio by 100. The expected value for any month is 100 (Burns and Mitchell, 1946; Mills, 1924).
5. This finding is contrary to a recent assertion that "baptism delays did not lengthen enough from the 1750s to the 1810s to suggest the rate of deterioration found in the large Wrigley and Schofield residual adjustment" (Lindert, 1983, p. 138).

REFERENCES

Ambler, R. W. (1974), "Baptism and Christening. Custom and Practice in Nineteenth Century Lincolnshire." *Local Population Studies*, no. 12 (Spring): 25–27.
Berry, B. Midi, and Roger S. Schofield (1971), "Age at Baptism in Pre-Industrial England." *Population Studies* 25 (November): 453–63.

Burns, Arthur F., and Wesley C. Mitchell (1946), *Measuring Business Cycles*. Studies in Business Cycles, no. 2. New York: National Bureau of Economic Research.

Collins, Harry (1977), "Age at Baptism in Pre-Industrial England." *Local Population Studies*, no. 19 (Autumn): 50–51.

Duchesne, Louis (1975), "Weekly Patterns in Demographic Events (with examples from Canada and England)." *Local Population Studies*, no. 14 (Spring): 53–56.

Flinn, Michael W. (1982), "The Population History of England, 1541–1871." *Economic History Review*, ser. 2, 35: 443–57.

Jackson, S., and P. Laxton (1977), "Of Such as Are of Riper Years? A Note on Age of Baptism." *Local Population Studies*, 18 (Spring): 30–36.

Lindert, Peter H. (1983), "English Living Standards, Population Growth, and Wrigley-Schofield." *Explorations in Economic History*, 20: 131–155.

Mills, Dennis R. (1973), "The Christening Custom at Melbourn, Cambs." *Local Population Studies*, 11 (Autumn): 11–22.

Mills, Frederick C. (1924) *Statistical Methods Applied to Economics and Business*. American Business Series. New York: Holt.

Trussell, James (1983), "Population under low Pressure: Reviews of the Population History of England." *Journal of Economic History*, 43 (March): 307–10.

Wrigley, Edward Anthony (1977), "Births and Baptisms: The Use of Anglican Baptism Registers as a Source of Information about the Numbers of Births in England before the Beginning of Civil Registration." *Population Studies*, 31.

Wrigley, Edward Anthony, and Roger S. Schofield (1981), *The Population History of England, 1541–1871: A Reconstruction*. Studies in Social and Demographic History. Cambridge, MA: Harvard University Press.

Research in Economic History

Edited by **Paul Uselding**
School of Business, University of Northern Iowa

Volume 1, 1979, 371 pp.   Institutions: $58.50
ISBN 0-89232-001-X   Individuals: $29.25

CONTENTS: Foreword, *Paul Uselding.* **Manufacturing in the Antebellum South,** *Fred Bateman, Indiana University and Thomas Weiss, University of Kansas.* **Transference and Development of Institutional Constraints Upon Economic Activity,** *J.R.T. Hughes, Northwestern University.* **Three Centuries of American Inequality,** *Peter H. Lindert and Jeffrey G. Williamson, University of Wisconsin.* **English Open Fields as Behavior Towards Risk,** *Donald N. McCloskey, University of Chicago.* **The Business Advisory Council of the Department of Commerce, 1933-1961: A Study in Corporate/Government Relations,** *Kim McQuaid, Northwestern University.* **Stagflation in Historical Perspective: The Napoleonic Wars Revisited,** *Joel Mokyr, Northwestern University and N. Eugene Savin, University of British Columbia and Cambridge University.* **Cross-Spectral Analysis of Long Swings in Atlantic Migration,** *Larry Neal, University of Illinois.* **Socio-Economic Patterns of Migration from the**

JAI PRESS

Netherlands in the Nineteenth Century, *Robert P. Swierengo, Kent State University and Harry S. Stout, University of Connecticut.* **In Dispraise of the Muckrakers: United States Occupational Mortality, 1890-1910,** *Paul Uselding.*

Volume 2, 1977, 389 pp.   Institutions: $58.50
ISBN 0-89232-036-2   Individuals: $29.25

REVIEWS: "This volume contains an unusual variety of papers, several of which are refreshingly different from the usual run of journal articles ... Most of the papers ... diverge in length or approach ..."
—*Journal of Economic History*

" ... The various authors ... exemplify the sophistication and competence, as well as the occasional over-commitment to particular techniques, which British historians cannot yet match. They also exemplify the sort of 'revelance' at which the best economic historian has always aimed."
—*The Economist*

Supplement 1 - Recent Developments in the Study of Economic and Business History Essays in Memory of Herman E. Kroos
Edited by **Robert E. Gallman,** *University of North Carolina*

1977, 315 pp.   Institutions: $58.50
ISBN 0-89232-035-4   Individuals: $29.25

REVIEW: "... Given the quality of essays, with their general success in meeting the initial assignment of surveying and extending recent research and providing bibliographic aid, the volume makes an excellent reference work for scholars as well as for graduate students."
                    — Journal of Economic History

Volume 3, 1978, 378 pp.   Institutions: $58.50
ISBN 0-89232-056-7   Individuals: $29.25

REVIEWS: " ... consistently excellent selection of articles. There is none of the uneven quality that often characterizes eclectic collections."
                    — Business History Review

Volume 4, 1979, 356 pp.   Institutions: $58.50
ISBN 0-89232-080-X   Individuals: $29.25

REVIEWS: " ... a stimulating collection which is justifiably held by its editor to be 'a representative sampling of the most interesting new work'... The papers all relate to major topics in mainstream British or American economic history."

— *Economic History Review*

"Paul Uselding has performed yet another valuable service to the profession in editing this fine volume."

— *Agricultural History*

Great Britian and the United States: The Kondratieff
Cycle Revisited, *Raymond S. Hartman and David R.
Wheller, Boston University and Massachusetts Institute
of Technology.* The Profitability of Northern Agriculture
in 1860, *Fred Bateman, Indiana University and Jeremy
Atack, University of Illinois.* The Farm Enterprise: The
Northern United States, 1820-1860s, *Clarence H.
Danhof, Sangamon State University.* Urban Improve-
ment and the English Economy in the Seventeenth and
Eighteenth Centuries, *E.L. Jones, LaTrobe University
and M.E. Falkus, London School of Economics and
LaTrobe University.* Occupational Structure, Dissent
and Educational Commitment: Lancashire, 1841,
Alexander James Field, Stanford University. Industrial
Work and the Family Life Cycle, 1889-1890, *Michael R.
Haines, Cornell University.*

Volume 5, 1980, 301 pp.   Institutions: $58.50
ISBN 0-89232-117-2   Individuals: $29.25

REVIEW: "Volume 5 of this annual compilation of
research attest to the continuing vitality and diversity of
the field. This fine collection of extended essays virtually
encompasses the world and exhibits a variety of
approaches. No common thread ties these contributions
together, yet they suggest direction of research in the
postcliometric era."

— *Technology & Culture*

J A I P R E S S

Volume 6, 1981, 254 pp.   Institutions: $58.50
ISBN 0-89232-119-9   Individuals: $29.25

CONTENTS: Foreword, *Paul Uselding*. **Climate Change in European Economic History,** *John L. Anderson, LaTrobe University.* **The Tonnage of Ships Engaged in British Colonial Trade during the Eighteenth Century,** *John J. McCusker, University of Maryland.* **The U.K. Money Supply, 1870-1914,** *Michael David Bordo, Carleton University.* **The Development of Steamboats on the Volga River and its Tributaries, 1817-1865,** *Richard Mowbray Haywood, Purdue University.* **Entrepreneurship and Technical Progress in the Northwest Coast Pig Iron Industry: 1850-1913,** *Robert C. Allen, University of British Columbia.* **Rent Movements and the English Tenant Farmer, 1700-1839,** *J.R. Wordie, University of Reading.* **Bank Deposit Currency Before 1700 A.D.,** *Morris A. Copeland, Cornell University (emeritus).*

Volume 7, 1982, 361 pp.   Institutions: $58.50
ISBN 0-89232-198-9   Individuals: $29.25

CONTENTS: Foreword, *Paul Uselding.* **The Structure of Pay in Britian, 1710-1911,** *Jeffrey G. Williamson, University of Wisconsin.* **Legally Induced Technical Regress in the Washington Salmon Fishery,** *Robert Higgs, University of Washington.* **Fiscal Incidence and Resource Transfer Between Jews and Arabs in Mandatory Palestine,** *Jacob Metzer, Maurice Falk Institute for Economic Research in Israel.* **Regional Exports to Foreign Countries: United States, 1870-1914,** *William K. Hutchinson, Miami University.* **The Fertility of American Slaves,** *Richard H. Steckel, Ohio State University.* **A General Equilibrium Model of the Eighteenth Century Atlantic Slave Trade: A Least-Likely Test for the Caribbean School,** *William A. Darity, Jr., University of Maryland.* **Melanesian Labor and the Development of the Queensland Sugar Industry, 1863-1906,** *Ralph Shlomowitz, Flinders University of South Australia.*

Supplement 2 - Variations in Business and Economic History: Essays in Honor of Donald L. Kemmerer
Edited by **Bruce R. Dalgaard,** *Director, Center for Economic Education, University of Minnesota*

1982, 217 pp.
ISBN 0-89232-262-4

Institutions: $58.50
Individuals: $29.25

CONTENTS: Preface, *Bruce R. Dalgaard.* **Foreword,** *Albro Martin, Harvard University.* **The Canadian Newsprint Industry, 1900-1940,** *Robert Ankli, Department of Economics, University of Guelph.* **E.W. Kemmerer: The Origins and Impact of the "Money Doctor's" Monetary Economics,** *Bruce R. Dalgaard, Center of Economic Education, University of Minnesota.* **Government and Business in Early Eighteenth Century England: Anticombination Acts and the Stability of the Newcastle Coal Cartel, 1700-1750,** *William J. Hausman, Department of Economics, University of North Carolina, Greensboro.* **Regulations Without Historical Justification: The Case of Household Moving,** *Dana Hewins, Department of Economics, Ohio University.* **Labor Absorption: Conventional Wisdom and Additional Data for Latin America,** *John M. Hunter, Latin American Studies Center, Michigan State University.* **African Entrepreneurs: A Case Study of Nigerian Industrialists, 1964-1965,** *E. Wayne Nafziger, Department of Economics, Kansas State University.* **The Civilian Conservation Corps: A Work Fare Solution,** *Robert F. Severson, Jr., Department of Economics, Central Michigan University.* **U.S. Teacher Organizations and the Salary Issue, 1900-1960,** *Robert J. Thornton, Department of Economics, Lehigh University.* **A New Look at the Gold Standard: Is Donald Kemmerer Right?,** *Richard K. Vedder, Department of Economics, Ohio University.* **Some Monetary Standard of Value Concepts of the Latter Nineteenth Century,** *Richard Winkleman, Department of Economics, Arizona State University.* **The New Economic History and Capitalist Growth: The Moral Perspective,** *Stephen T. Worland, Departmentof Economics, University of Notre Dame.*

Volume 8, 1983, 298 pp.
ISBN 0-89232-216-6

Institutions: $58.50
Individuals: $29.25

CONTENTS: **Foreword,** *Paul Uselding.* **U.S. Economic Growth, 1783-1960,** *Stanley L. Engerman, University of*

Rochester and Robert E. Gallman, *University of North Carolina-Chapel Hill.* **The Development of the Russian Petroleum Industry, 1872-1900,** *John P. McKay, University of Illinois.* **Casual Theories About The Origins of Agriculture,** *Frederic L. Pryor, Swarthmore College.* **Railroad Cartels Before 1887: The Effectiveness of Private Enforcement of Collusion,** *Thomas S. Ulen, University of Illinois.* **Asset Markets and Investment Fluctuations in Late Victorian Britain,** *Barry J. Eichengreen, Harvard University.* **Creating Coordination in the Modern Petroleum Industry: The American Petroleum Institute and the Emergence of Secondary Organizations in Oil,** *Joseph A. Pratt, Texas A&M University.* **Regional Preferences and Migrant Settlement: On the Avoidance of the South by Nineteenth Century Immigrants,** *James A. Dunlevy, Miami University.* **The Telegraph and the Structure of Markets in the United States, 1845-1890,** *Richard B. DuBoff, Bryn Mawr College.* **British Rearmament and Industrial Growth, 1935-1939,** *A.J. Robertson, University of Manchester.*

Supplement 3 - Technique, Spirit and Form in the Making of the Modern Economics: Essays in Honor of William N. Parker
Edited by **Gary Saxonhouse,** *University of Michigan* and **Gavin Wright,** *Stanford University*

1984, 300 pp.   Institutions: $58.50
ISBN 0-89232-414-7   Individuals: $29.25

CONTENTS: List of Contributors. Preface, *Gary Saxonhouse and Gavin Wright.* Acknowledgements, *Gary Saxonhouse, University of Michigan and Gavin Wright, Stanford University.* PART I. ORGANIZATIONAL FORMS IN ECONOMIC HISTORY. **Two Forms of Cheap Labor in Textile History,** *Gary Saxonhouse, University of Michigan and Gavin Wright, Stanford University.* **Family and Enterprise in the Silk Shops of Lyon: The Place of Labor in the Domestic Weaving Economy, 1840-1870,** *George J. Sheridan, Jr., University of Oregon, Eugene.* **Are Cartels Unstable? The German Steel Works Association Before World War I,** *Lon L. Peters, Portland, Oregon.* **Currency and Credit in the Gilded Age,** *Barry Eichengreen, Harvard University.* **Peasants, Potatoes and Poverty: Transactions Cost in Prefamine Ireland,** *Elizabeth Hoffman,*

Purdue University and Joel Mokyr, Northwestern University. **PART II. SCIENCE, TECHNOLOGY, AND PRODUCTIVITY. The Decline and Rise of the Dutch Economy, 1675-1900,** J. de Vries, University of California, Berkeley. **The Shifting Locus of Agriculture Innovation in Nineteenth-Century Europe: The Case of the Agricultural Experiment Stations,** George Grantham, McGill University. **Mid-Nineteenth Century Crop Yields and Labor Productivity Growth in American Agriculture: A New Look at Parker and Klien,** Jeremy Atack, University of Illinois, Urbana, and Fred Bateman, Indiana University. **The Eco-Technic Process and the Development of the Sewing Machine,** Ross Thomson, New School of Social Research, New York. **Rings and Mules Around the World: A Comparative Study in Technological Choice,** Gary Saxonhouse, University of Michigan, and Gavin Wright, Stanford University.

Volume 9, 1984, 253 pp.   Institutions: $58.50
ISBN 0-89232-415-5   Individuals: $29.25

CONTENTS: List of Contributors. **The Performance of the British Cotton Industry, 1870-1913,** William Lazonick, Harvard University and William Mass, University of Massachusets, Boston. **Agricultural Output and Efficiency in Lower Canada, 1985,** Frank D. Lewis and Marvin McInnis, Queen's University, Canada. **A Cross-Sectional Study of Legitimate Fertility in England and Wales, 1911,** N.F.R. Crafts, University College, Oxford. **Notes on Economic Efficiency in Historical Perspective: The Case of Britain, 1870-1914,** William P. Kennedy, London School of Economics. **The Economic Policy of the Mandatory Government in Palestine,** Nachum T. Gross, The Hebrew University of Jerusalem. **Bank Deposits and the Quantity of Money in the United Kingdom, 1870-1912,** Forrest Capie and Alan Webber, The City University, London. **Energy Sources for the Dutch Golden Age: Peat, Wind and Coal,** Richard W. Unger, University of British Columbia.

Supplement 4 - Emergence of the Modern Political Economy
Edited by **Robert Higgs,** Department of Economics and Business, Lafayette College

1985, 224 pp.   Institutions: $58.50
ISBN 0-89232-619-0   Individuals: $29.25

Volume 10, 1986, 308 pp.   Institutions: $58.50
ISBN 0-89232-676-X   Individuals: $29.25

JAI PRESS INC.
55 Old Post Road - No. 2
P.O. Box 1678
Greenwich, Connecticut 06836-1678
Tel: 203-661-7602